Planting the American Flag

Planting the American Flag

Twelve Men Who Expanded the United States Overseas

Peter C. Stuart

McFarland & Company, Inc., Publishers
Jefferson, North Carolina, and London

LIBRARY OF CONGRESS CATALOGUING-IN-PUBLICATION DATA

Stuart, Peter C.
      Planting the American flag : twelve men who expanded the
United States overseas / Peter C. Stuart.
         p.   cm.
      Includes bibliographical references and index.

      ISBN-13: 978-0-7864-2983-7
      (softcover : 50# alkaline paper) ∞

      1. United States — Insular possessions — Biography.
   2. Statesmen — United States — Biography.   3. Politicians —
   United States — Biography.   4. United States — Biography.
   5. United States — Armed Forces — Biography.   6. United
   States — Insular possessions — History.   7. United States —
   Territorial expansion.   I. Title.
   F970.S78   2007
   920.073 — dc22   2006102415

British Library cataloguing data are available

©2007 Peter C. Stuart. All rights reserved

*No part of this book may be reproduced or transmitted in any form
or by any means, electronic or mechanical, including photocopying
or recording, or by any information storage and retrieval system,
without permission in writing from the publisher.*

Cover image ©2007 Comstock

Manufactured in the United States of America

*McFarland & Company, Inc., Publishers
   Box 611, Jefferson, North Carolina 28640
      www.mcfarlandpub.com*

Acknowledgments

Bringing to life the sires of America's little empire has entailed, in most cases, resuscitating them from vaults of historical records all but forgotten. The endeavor relied on the resources and cooperation of a range of libraries, archives, repositories, and their staffs.

These ever-knowledgeable research partners include the Library of Congress, particularly its manuscript division; the U.S. Army Center of Military History; the U.S. Navy Historical Center; the library of the National Geographic Society; Lauinger Library at Georgetown University; the District of Columbia public library, all in Washington. Farther afield are the Friends Historical Library at Swarthmore College in Swarthmore, Pennsylvania; the U.S. Army Heritage and Education Center in Carlisle, Pennsylvania; the John F. Kennedy Library in Boston; the Wellesley (Massachusetts) Free Library; the Westminister (Massachusetts) Historical Society; the Richmond County Museum in Warsaw, Virginia.

The staffs of all these facilities have earned my collective thanks. Special tributes are due Christopher Densmore, curator of the Friends library; Mark Landry of the Westminister historical society; Stephen Plotkin, research archivist at the Kennedy library.

Gratitude also is extended to Lonnie J. Hovey, director of preservation, architecture, and construction, Executive Office of the President.

Beyond the musty realm of manuscripts and yellowing letters, several people whose ties to the subjects of this book are more personal provided gracious assistance. The late Barbara Pearson Lange Godfrey, daughter of Governor Pearson, and her own daughter, Julie Lange Hall, made available a copy of Mrs. Godfrey's privately-published biography of her father — the only such work. Anthony M. Solomon, the last surviving territorial "founding father," generously granted an interview greater in scope and candor than I had any right to expect. Each of them is accorded warmest thanks.

The helpfulness of all of the aforementioned carries no responsibility, of course, for the use made of their input in these pages. That remains solely my own.

In getting the book into print, fellow author Fairlie Maginnes graciously recommended a publisher.

Loving thanks, finally, are owed my wife, Vicky, for enduring so amiably the long presence in our household of a dozen unseen, but nonetheless demanding, callers from the territorial past.

Contents

Acknowledgments	v
Preface	1
Introduction	3
1. Captain Charles Wilkes • *Opened Relations with Samoa, 1839*	7
2. Commander Richard W. Meade III • *Negotiated Samoa Treaty, 1872*	27
3. Albert B. Steinberger • *Premier of Samoa, 1875–1876*	38
4. Captain Henry Glass • *Captured Guam, 1898*	50
5. General Nelson A. Miles • *Conquered Puerto Rico, 1898*	60
6. Commander B.F. Tilley • *First Governor of American Samoa, 1900–1901*	88
7. Senator Joseph B. Foraker • *First Congressional Overseer, 1899–1909*	99
8. Representative William A. Jones • *First Congressional Reformer, 1899–1918*	118
9. General Frank McIntyre • *Military Administrator, 1905–1929*	134
10. Theodore Roosevelt, Jr. • *Governor of Puerto Rico, 1929–1932*	146
11. Paul M. Pearson • *First Civilian Governor of U.S. Virgin Islands, 1931–1935*	167
12. Anthony M. Solomon • *Inaugurated Acquiring Northern Mariana Islands, 1963*	186
Chapter Notes	205
Bibliography	243
Index	249

Preface

This book profiles the makers of America's overseas possessions — twelve people who did most to build the country's present collection of appendages in the world beyond.

Their exploits have planted the American flag permanently in the Caribbean and Pacific, but remain uncelebrated and practically unknown.

In examining the evolution of the country's territories for my book *Isles of Empire: The United States and Its Overseas Possessions*, a dozen figures stood out as seminal. Yet so unrecognized were they that most had escaped the notice of biographers, outside the secluded little realm of scholars and family historians. Those receive here their first published biographies.

The lives of the fathers of external America have been reconstructed through exhaustive research — in sepulchral archives, in the torrid tropics, and in the snug den of the last surviving founder. All of the island dependencies have been visited. While the book chronicles the entire lives of these men, it necessarily concentrates on their contribution to territorial history.

It is hoped that these pages enhance awareness of persons too long underappreciated.

Introduction

Americans rule the largest overseas empire on earth.

"Empire," however, may be a rather grandiose term for it. The country's collection of possessions qualifies as the biggest — encompassing the most people — by default. Most empires have been dismantled. Imperialism is out of date and out of favor. The proprietors of the largest remaining such regnancy shrink from calling it an empire. It swells with pride few American breasts, puts a spring into few steps along Main Street. It has inspired no patriotic ballads, no Kiplings, no Empire Days. Most Americans are only dimly aware, if at all, that their country even possesses territories elsewhere in the world.

Yet none of this diminishes the fact that the United States' clutch of five island dependencies in the Caribbean Sea and Pacific Ocean dwarfs all others. The more than four million outsiders under American reign exceed the sway of the present day's other two leading empires, those of France and Britain, combined.

If, to most Americans, their overseas possessions are but distant acquaintances, their founding fathers are total strangers. That's a shame. As persons to get to know, they have much to commend them. In a historical perspective, they probably have done more than any other individuals to make the United States the world territorial suzerain that it is today. On a personal level, they're an engaging bunch.

At first encounter, these people united in pursuits imperial appear bewilderingly disparate. They include briny sea captains and erudite college professors ... a battle-hardened general and a desk-bound army bureaucrat ... congressional lawmakers poles apart in just about everything ... the son and namesake of a president, and an adventurer who never quite shed the reputation of a knave.

While many were contemporaries, there is no evidence that they ever met one another outside the line of formal duties in scattered cases. The two legislators served together, at arm's length, in Congress. And several of the men in uniform were cast together briefly by military assignments. The begetters of the American empire gathered around no convivial dinner table before a crackling fire to compare notes and swap tales of tropic isles. There flowered no fraternal friendships, no Adams-Jefferson lingering colloquy on what they had wrought.

Have these men anything in common — clues to the makings of an imperial trailblazer? It goes without saying, perhaps, that those who push a nation's boundaries beyond its shorelines share a viewpoint that peers outward. Most were, indeed, for their era, cosmopolites. Yet others remained essentially American burghers. Befitting an interest in the wider world, most were scholarly, or at least well read. Nearly half had taught at colleges or military academies. Even more wrote books of their own.

The trait that recurs most may be an inner restiveness. There was a discontent with comfortable old ways — in the military, the halls of learning, politics, in governing racial minorities at home or indigenes abroad. And there was a determination to do things in one's own, presumably better, way. This streak of independence enabled the possessors to follow their own dictates, but it also landed many of them in trouble. Three of the military officers were court-martialed, one twice. Others in the group were deported, demoted, reprimanded, ostracized.

A touch of rebelliousness may seem an unlikely attribute of those engaged in anything as authoritarian as building an empire. These builders, however, entertained a concept of overseas lordship that veered from the traditional. Men of action, on the whole, they weren't given to idealism. But they expected the United States to transcend the mode of imperialism of its Old World predecessors. The Yanks would be more enlightened. A new style of rule sprang in part from a new perception of the ruled people. The islanders so often scorned as little more than savages were accorded by most of our protagonists an appreciation in advance of their day.

The vision of America as a model sovereign, alas, was to flicker and fade all too quickly in practice. For all their worldly wisdom, the founders may have been a trifle naïve.

Singling out the principal sires of the U.S. overseas empire isn't easy. Unlike the founding fathers of the republic, they were no small band working closely together for a short period. The offshore possessions are the product of scores of people, or even hundreds, spread over nearly a century and a half. The individuals chosen for this book are those deemed most instrumental in incorporating into the nation its current outlying territories. Some led their military conquest. Others initiated bilateral ties of one sort or another. Others served as crucial early governors, or shaped the imperial endeavor from Washington.

Included among them, strange to note, are two professed anti-imperialists. But one (General Miles) adopted the posture only after doing much to further the nation's outward expansion. The other (Congressman Jones) showed himself in actuality to be less a foe of U.S. presence overseas than a reformer of it.

The book leaves aside places once under American jurisdiction but now gone their ways, such as the Philippines and the Panama Canal Zone. It confines itself to the five inhabited entities that the country possesses today: Puerto Rico, the U.S. Virgin Islands, Guam, the Northern Mariana Islands, and American Samoa. Each is represented by at least one founder. Within these parameters and those of space, the choice of individuals is necessarily somewhat subjective.

A couple of caveats may be in order. Spotlighting the Americans who imposed foreign rule, and not the native people upon whom it fell, may smack of literary imperialism. It can only be hoped that the reader will find these Americans and their unheralded contribution to the nation's history to warrant exploration in their own right. Inhabitants of the territories, in any event, are hardly absent from these pages. And their part in the imperial saga has been examined by the author more fully elsewhere.

One regret about the subjects profiled is that all are male. It may be a reflection of the epoch during which the American possessions evolved that there could be discovered no "founding mother." But every effort has been made here to give the participation of women in other capacities due recognition.

This is a book about people and also about places, both remarkably little known. The pages that follow may offer a dual introduction — to the establishers of America's empire, and, through them, to the empire itself.

1
Captain Charles Wilkes
Opened Relations with Samoa, 1839

America's dawning interest in acquiring territories beyond her shores was mobilized and put under sail by a young seaman with an old salt's cantankerousness, to whom troubles flocked like gulls to the foaming wake of a schooner.

Opinionated. Imperious. Combative. Twice court-martialed. He was all of these. But, at the same time, somehow lovable — at least at the forgiving distance of more than a century.

So hazardous a concoction of personal qualities, oddly, seemed the very ones needed to lead the enterprise to success — when, that is, not threatening to sink it altogether.

For years, the endeavor had been an idea drifting in desperate search of the right person to take it in charge.

The idea was the nineteenth century's equivalent of the next century's exploration of outer space. Instead of Mercury and Apollo rockets, a covey of American sailing ships would be launched into the trackless seas to probe their farthest reaches. The oceans were then scarcely better known than the heavens. The Western world knew that beyond the southern watery horizon were to be found other lands and peoples, but had only a vague notion where and who.[1]

The expedition would expand the frontiers of knowledge and scout out commercial possibilities, while incidentally showing the rest of the world the youthful nation's seafaring and scientific mettle.[2]

The scheme wasn't original, but it was precocious for a newly-independent small country. Several of the founding fathers with a scientific turn of mind or an expansive worldview had been intrigued by the voyages in the late eighteenth century of British explorer James Cook. George Washington, John Adams, Thomas Jefferson, and Benjamin Franklin all followed them closely. Accounts of subsequent cruises by other European powers also attracted an avid readership in the United States.[3]

It fell to the last and, alas, least politically adept of the founder-presidents, James Madison, to elevate the idea of an American expedition to a formal plan.[4] After persuasive advocacy in 1810 by a Pacific sea captain, Madison ruminated two years and then commissioned "an Exploring and Discovery Expedition to the South Seas, and around the world."[5] His timing was improvident. Three months later erupted the War of 1812, and the project was drydocked for more than a decade.[6]

Sails were hoisted once again on the concept two presidential administrations later by John Quincy Adams. He seized the occasion of his first annual message to Congress in 1825 to pay tribute to the voyages of discovery by other nations, which "have not only redounded to their glory, but to the improvement of human knowledge." The United States, he suggested, should consider "imitating their example."[7]

Adams was a dabbling scientist and backyard naturalist, given to roaming the grounds of the White House with the gardener to learn the names of plantings. Such interests may have attracted him to an exploring expedition.[8]

Prospecting for territorial possessions for the country elsewhere in the world formed no explicit motive in the expedition concept. After all, the United States had only recently cast off its own yoke of colonization. But an exploration voyage was envisioned as extending America's influence and enlarging its commerce — well-trod precursors of annexation. And such enterprises by British and French explorers generated for their budding empires a string of colonies.[9]

Adams himself was alive to opportunities to expand the country's boundaries. As the secretary of state of his predecessor, James Monroe, he had negotiated Spain's cession of Florida. He wanted American explorations of the Pacific to begin with a proprietary look at the Pacific Northwest region of the home continent.[10]

The president put forward two plans: a scaled-down voyage sailing only to the Northwest, and a cruise into the far seas. Both were scuttled by a Congress that stymied most of the initiatives of his frustrated presidency.[11]

Amid the expedition's fitful course through Washington's political shoals began the affiliation of the man who ultimately would lead it to fulfillment. Chosen to purchase the nautical instruments for the aborted 1820s undertaking was a young naval officer named Charles Wilkes.[12]

Wilkes's background had providentially prepared him for the endeavor that awaited him — and shaped the temperament that alternately aided and undermined its accomplishment.

He grew up in a household so steeped in maritime affairs as to make the briny sea an almost palpable presence.[13] Born in the twilight of the eighteenth century in 1798, he was the son of English immigrant John de Pointhieu

Wilkes, who had settled in New York City as an agent of trading firms in London and Le Havre.[14] His mother came from the same world of shipping. Mary Seton Wilkes was the daughter of her husband's Scottish business partner. But she passed away when Charles, the youngest of three children, was three years old.[15]

As a toddler, his favorite toys were tiny ships.[16] As a boy, he sat entranced at his father's dinner table hearing tales of hair-raising voyages and intrepid mariners.[17] He enjoyed stealing away from his home in Greenwich Village and ambling to the harbor to watch the parade of sailing ships.[18]

Captain Charles Wilkes, as a midshipman, circa 1826, in an oil portrait by Thomas Sully (Naval Historical Foundation).

Along with the scent of the sea, there was in the Wilkes family a strain of contentiousness. When the winds of revolution swept the American colonies, Charles's father clung to his Tory loyalties and decamped to England during the ensuing war for independence.[19] Charles's great-uncle had been a hot-headed agitator on the other side of the struggle. Englishman John Wilkes published a newspaper that made bold to reproach King George III, landing him in jail in 1763 for libel and making him a hero in the American colonies. A town in Pennsylvania renamed itself Wilkes-Barre in honor of Wilkes and his friend Isaac Barre, a member of Parliament who championed the colonies.[20]

Despite his upbringing in so nautical a family, young Charles had to battle to be allowed to go to sea. His father envisioned for his son a land-based career in the commercial side of seafaring. Upon finishing secondary school, he took a job in a shipping company's business office, but chafed at the monotonous routine. He switched to his father's less regimented establishment. But his real desire remained to sail the open seas.[21]

"The hankering after a naval life & roving life," he was to write later, "still grew stronger & stronger."[22]

He began taking lessons in navigation and nautical science.[23] Then, at age seventeen, he learned that his acquaintance Matt Perry had been commissioned a midshipman in the navy (later to become the commodore who compelled Japan to open its ports to American ships). Charles begged his father to get him a similar commission, but was rebuffed.[24] His father, he found, was "greatly adverse to my going to sea."[25]

As a counterproposal, an uncle offered him a well-paid position in his bank.[26] The young man archly refused to become what he called a "money changer."[27]

Finally consenting, Charles's father petitioned the navy for a midshipman's commission.[28] Informed that a commission could be expedited by a spell of service in the merchant marine, he was sent to sea aboard a commercial vessel. An unwelcome surprise awaited him. His father and uncle, unreconciled to a shipboard career for Charles, secretly had conspired with the ship's owners to, as he later put it, "sicken me of sea life." He was dished out an extra portion of seagoing hardships.[29]

Not only did he brave the harsh treatment, but also came to the rescue of the captain who so tormented him. During the transatlantic voyage, the captain discovered that he had left behind a crucial chart of the English Channel. Rather sheepishly, one supposes, he asked the help of Wilkes. From his nautical training, the teenager drew a map of the Channel that guided the ship safely to port.[30]

Far from souring him of life at sea, the experience whetted his appetite for more. Two subsequent trips aboard merchant ships — to Wilmington, North Carolina, and Le Havre — qualified Wilkes, now twenty years old, for a commission in the navy.[31] In those early years of the republic, such matters went to the desk of the president, and Wilkes's commission was approved in 1818 by President Monroe.[32]

Accepting at last his son's chosen future, Charles's father bought him a dashing, new naval uniform complete with cocked hat and sheath for his dirk. On the young officer, the braided epaulets and high collar undergirded a long face in which a proportionally long-bridged nose looked right at home. Round eyes seemed to take in all. A lock of thick, wavy hair drooped over the brow. The full lips of a small mouth formed an inward smile of one living his boyhood dream.[33] Upon first seeing his son in uniform, Charles noticed his father's eyes welling with tears.[34]

His father accompanied him to a stagecoach for a clattering trip to Washington for his introduction to the navy. In the capital city, the mere midshipman was feted like top brass. Hosted by the French minister, a family friend, Wilkes was introduced to persons helpful to his career, including President Monroe. The elation of the visit, however, was soon shattered. En route home at an overnight stop in New Jersey, he was told that his father had fallen seriously ill. He reached the bedside only an hour before his father's passing.[35]

He was lifted out of mourning by his first naval orders, assigning him to the training ship *Independence* in Boston.[36] Distinguishing himself there, he was selected for overseas cruises to the Mediterranean and the Pacific coast of South America.[37] On these early voyages began to emerge propensities that came to characterize Wilkes as a naval commander. He admired superiors who were disciplinarians, demanding strict obedience to orders and proper attire. But he imposed rigid moral discipline on himself, too, shunning the legendary vices of sailors.[38]

While in love with life at sea, Wilkes also fell in love on shore. Between the two voyages, he met a young woman about twenty years old, of Scottish extraction like his mother.[39] Jane Renwick's own mother had the distinction of having had her beauty celebrated poetically by Robert Burns ("She talk'd, she smil'd, my heart she wiled").[40] Wilkes was drawn to Jane's intellect and compassion. In a description likely to have evoked from her a mixed response, he wrote many years later:

> Though not handsome, she had more in the expression and gracefulness of her bearing. Her features, though irregular, showed great intelligence, and she was a perfect lady in all her thoughts and expressions, liberal in thought and deed, and ever open to administer to the wants of others.[41]

Wilkes may have been unduly deprecating of Jane's appearance. Others have said that she inherited her mother's comeliness, and a painted portrait shows a pretty woman with dark curly hair.[42]

The couple was married, and two days after the wedding in 1826 the bridegroom was promoted to lieutenant.[43]

While wooing a wife, between his naval excursions to the Mediterranean and South America Wilkes found time for another pleasurable activity: delving into science. He had long shown scientific proclivities. He excelled in nautical science and, inspired perhaps by mariners' reliance on the stars for navigation, loved astronomy.[44] During the respite at home in New York, he studied mathematics and engineering, and attended lectures on chemistry. In nonscientific fields, he applied himself to French, Spanish, and drawing.[45]

The spate of academics, he wrote, "put me well up in many subjects belonging to my profession."[46]

Marriage drew Wilkes closer to the world of science. His brother-in-law, James Renwick, a teacher of his at Columbia College, was a scholar who became one of the new nation's most eminent scientists.[47]

The conjunction of Wilkes and an American exploring expedition was somehow natural — even, it might seem, foreordained. The enterprise was an idea that he had heard favorably aired since boyhood. It had been a pet crusade of his father's. The elder Wilkes repeatedly had espoused such a voyage to a skeptical government.[48] For its part, the government had come to recognize young Wilkes's scientific talents. Secretary of the Navy Samuel L.

Southard and even President Adams himself quietly nurtured the lieutenant's growing reputation as the navy's man of science.[49]

When nautical instruments were to be bought for the Adams administration's proposed voyage of discovery, Wilkes was the obvious choice for the assignment.[50] Although that expedition never set sail, his involvement left him eager to participate in a future such endeavor. He had "studied with this in view," he declared, "ever since the first Expedition was talked of."[51]

Interest in the idea was kept alive — both for Wilkes and the American public as a whole — meantime, by a well-publicized private expedition in 1829–31 to the south polar regions.[52] It was immediately followed by another scientific voyage scarcely noticed at the time. The HMS *Beagle* began a five-year journey bearing young British naturalist Charles Darwin, whose findings would revolutionize man's concept of his origins.[53]

With the arrival of a new president and a growing consensus for a government-sponsored expedition, Congress at last was ready to authorize the project. No longer was it enmeshed in the perpetual feuds with Adams, defeated for reelection by Andrew Jackson. And the proposition had been skillfully lobbied in Congress by an array of respected nautical figures. Lawmakers approved an expedition in 1836, and Jackson promptly signed the bill into law.[54]

Preparations at first proceeded smoothly. Jackson awarded command of the expedition to a seaman who had helped Old Hickory's troops defeat the British at the Battle of New Orleans in 1815, Captain Thomas ap Catesby Jones. The captain had since sailed the Pacific and become a proponent of an exploration voyage. He drew up plans for a flotilla of five ships and nearly six hundred men.[55]

Wilkes followed it all with interest, while deepening his scientific pursuits. Using his own money and telescope, he erected on Capitol Hill what is believed to be the nation's first astronomical observatory.[56] In an official capacity, he took over the navy's new Depot of Charts and Instruments.[57]

For the revived expedition, as for its short-lived predecessor eight years before, Wilkes once again was dispatched to Europe to buy instruments, charts, and other necessary paraphernalia.[58]

But when the secretary of the navy proposed putting the budding naval scientist in charge of the expedition's nautical sciences and giving him command of one of the smaller vessels, there erupted the first of the clashes between Wilkes and his superiors that were to punctuate his career. Captain Jones was willing to let the lieutenant supervise some scientific activities, but wanted him stationed aboard the flagship "under my immediate command and direction." Such subordination was an affront to Wilkes. He withdrew his name.[59]

Assuaging any disappointment by hard work, he left Washington for a series of naval surveying assignments: the fishing grounds off Cape Cod known as Georges Bank, and the harbors of Beaufort and Wilmington, North Carolina.[60]

In the capital, preparations for the expedition became mired in disputes and dithering. A year and a half after authorized, it showed no signs of going anywhere.[61] Jackson and Congress grew impatient. "All I wanted to hear about the exploring expedition," quipped former president Adams, now a congressman, "was that it had sailed."[62] Jones was relieved of command, perhaps nudged gently out by his old friend Jackson. So unappealing had the job become, however, that no replacement could be found. Three ranking captains turned it down.[63]

Fulfilling the expedition idea had now eluded three presidents. The latest heir, Jackson's successor, Martin Van Buren, saw a need for bold action. He switched control of the project from a dawdling secretary of the navy to a secretary of war uniquely qualified for such an enterprise.[64] Besides showing organizational abilities, the new overseer was himself a bona fide scientist. Joel R. Poinsett was the discoverer of the scarlet-leafed plant destined to immortalize his name—the poinsettia. He envisioned the exploring expedition as a vehicle for collecting exotic flora and fauna to stock a proposed national museum in Washington.[65]

But he, too, had trouble finding a commander. After two more senior officers refused, Poinsett gave up searching the high ranks. He offered the command to the militarily junior but scientifically advanced Wilkes.[66] It was a weighty responsibility for a lieutenant who had just turned the age of forty. Wilkes himself was undaunted. "I felt myself fully Master of the subject in all its details," he wrote, "as I had Made it a kind of hobby for the few years before."[67]

To critics of bestowing command on a lowly lieutenant—and there were loud grumbles—Poinsett had a ready reply. Britain and France, in choosing leaders for their voyages of discovery, he pointed out, disregarded rank. "But in every case [they] have selected junior officers, of sufficient scientific attainments and fitting qualifications. Captain Cook was not even a commissioned officer."[68]

Wilkes's second in command was a fellow lieutenant, a man of prominent forehead and bushy muttonchop whiskers, named William L. Hudson. Despite being four years older than his commander and two years longer a lieutenant, he consented to serve under him, but seemed never fully reconciled to the relationship.[69]

Poinsett and Wilkes set to work making the half-prepared expedition ship-shape. The ineptness of its previous organizers left the new commander aghast. "I was shocked at the ignorance of some and disgusted with others," he said with typical outspokenness.[70] Rapidly the project was pulled together.

Its mission was spelled out. The United States Exploring Expedition, as it was to be called, would circumnavigate the globe, investigating Antarctica, charting portions of Polynesia, visiting the East Indies and Japan, and surveying the coast of the American Northwest.[71]

Six ships were outfitted: the frigate *Vincennes*, which already had sailed twice to Oceania and became Wilkes's flagship; the sloop of war *Peacock*, built for the expedition scrapped a decade earlier; the gun brig *Porpoise*, previously used by Wilkes in coastal surveys; two schooners and a storeship. A force of four hundred was chosen to man them.[72]

A team of nine civilian scientists was recruited — specialists in plant life, geology, minerals, corals and shells, primitive cultures and languages. Two artists were signed on to depict the wonders which the voyagers were expected to encounter. (One unsuccessful civilian applicant was the novelist Nathaniel Hawthorne, who had hoped to become the voyage historian until Wilkes decided to write the annals himself.)[73]

Dignitaries trooped down from Washington to visit the squadron moored at Hampton Roads, Virginia, a few weeks before the scheduled sailing — clearly relieved that it was finally going to depart. President Van Buren clambered aboard the flagship, together with the secretaries of war and the navy.[74]

When the expedition was all but ready to weigh anchor, Wilkes found himself again in conflict with those above him. In an effort to enhance his authority on board ship and his respect among other mariners and foreign officials whom he would meet, the lieutenant asked that he and his second in command be temporarily promoted to captain for the duration of the voyage. The request was denied.

Without divulging the denial, just before sailing Wilkes and Hudson assumed the higher rank anyway. They donned the captain's uniforms purchased in misguided anticipation of promotion. Wilkes justified the action as a way of gaining "the advantage which was necessary for the true discipline and Means of carrying out the end sought to be obtained."[75]

Setting out from home in August 1838 for a voyage of several years into uncharted quarters of the earth, Wilkes suffered twinges of sadness and apprehension that belied his external confidence. Ahead might lay mutiny, shipwreck, failure. At his house on Washington's Capitol Hill, he bid farewell to his wife and four children, ranging in age from eleven-year-old Jack to baby Eliza, born just a few weeks earlier.

"On that day," he confided, "I left my home to encounter all the anxieties, troubles & dangers of a lengthened absence into far distant Seas & to undergo the privations and trials incident to the Command."[76]

Even the exhilaration of raising sails into a welcoming Atlantic breeze failed to dispel a sense of foreboding. Retiring to his cabin to begin the journal of the expedition, he penned in scrawly script: "It required all the hope I could muster to outweigh the intense feeling of responsibility that hung over me. I may compare it to that of one doomed to destruction."[77]

As the flotilla bore along the coast of South America en route to Antarctica, the gloom soon gave way to his old feistiness. At Rio de Janeiro, Wilkes asked the commodore of a visiting American warship for a supply of fresh bread to replace the squadron's stock infested by vermin. Stung by his refusal, Wilkes bought bread from another ship and then vengefully sent the spoiled batch aboard the commodore's vessel "that it might not be wasted."[78]

The ships plunged into the frigid waters of the south polar zone. Pushing southward where few had ever ventured, wintry clouds descended and icebergs floated eerily from the gloom. The sights he was witnessing evoked from Wilkes's pen eloquent descriptions destined to be read eagerly by a public hungering to learn about the little-known region. He poetically pictured the towering icebergs dwarfing his vessels as "an immense city of ruined alabaster palaces"— imagery commended by no lesser literary figure than James Fenimore Cooper.[79]

Racing against the onset of winter, rough weather suddenly struck.[80] "The brig's deck was covered with ice and snow.... Ice formed rapidly on the deck, and covered the rigging," wrote the anxious commander.[81] The expedition turned back, just seventy miles, or one degree of latitude, short of man's southernmost penetration by Captain Cook sixty-five years earlier.[82] The Americans would return later in the voyage.

The expedition was plying prime habitat for whales, and one of its duties was to serve the country's whaling industry by drafting the first worldwide chart of whaling grounds. Wilkes did as he was charged, but without enthusiasm. He was repelled by the bloody, greasy, and smelly whaling ships, groaning with fleshly cargoes of lamp oil. He also held little respect for their skippers and owners. Talking in various ports with seamen who had deserted from whalers convinced him that conditions on board often were so barbaric as to provoke desertion.[83]

Wilkes was interested in whales not as a huntsman but a naturalist. While the ships picked their way through the icebergs, he pursued his hobby of observing the majestic creatures with a scientist's eye and recording detailed notes.[84]

The men of the squadron were becoming acquainted with two of the commander's traits unpopular belowdecks: a paternalistic probity and a stern discipline. Wilkes hoped that the enterprise would be remembered for the exemplary way it conducted itself. "I trust," he wrote, "that the Expedition will compare advantageously with any other that has preceded it, in its moral and correct deportment."[85]

In ports where the ships called, he strove to divert his men — and, as he saw it, protect the expedition — from the temptation of waterfront drinking joints and pier-side prostitutes. He frowned on the risqué dances sometimes performed for the visitors. Of a sensual *cueca* danced for them in Chile, upon returning from Antarctica, Wilkes remarked: "I can not say much for its moral tendency." The devout Episcopalian did admire, however, the *Oración* or sunset prayer that, at the tolling of church bells, halted all Chilean life for a moment of devotion.[86]

While some captains sought to mold their crews into smooth-running teams through mutual affection, Wilkes — no fraternizer — relied on discipline. He deemed it necessary to keep the long expedition on course toward its objectives.[87] "The curb of discipline became more and more tightened," he reported, "and had the effect to produce harmony, though it at times seemed to annoy."[88] His discipline could be severe. Before departing Valparaiso, he ordered two sailors who had tried to jump ship to be administered, instead of the prescribed twelve lashes with the cat-o'-nine-tails, thirty-six and forty-one. He defended the punishment as more lenient than would have been imposed by a court-martial.[89]

At sea now nearly a year, the squadron at last pointed its prows toward the destination to which it was to devote the largest share of its time: Polynesia.[90] After the frozen wastes of the polar region, the green tropic isles seemed an idyll. Something of the allure is captured in Wilkes's description of the first island sighted — a word picture befitting much of Oceania:

> Its trees, seen at a distance, seemed like the masts of a fleet of vessels that rose and sank with the movement of the ocean. The white beach consisted of a narrow belt of land, with the surf breaking over it. Inside the coral reef was a blue-tinted lagoon.[91]

The inhabitants sometimes proved less hospitable, however, than the setting. Approaching an island in the Tuamotu archipelago to begin surveying, the visitors were greeted by a volley of coral hurled by warriors armed with clubs and spears. Efforts to show the expedition's peaceful intentions failed. Shooting several rounds of blank cartridges produced no effect. Then Wilkes ordered muskets loaded with mustard seed and fired at the islanders' legs. The defenders retreated and the Americans splashed ashore.[92]

"I felt no disposition to do them harm," as the commander later explained what had come to be known as the "Mustard Seed Battle," "and yet I had no idea of letting them see and feel that they had driven us off without landing."[93]

The ships charted fifteen islands there, two of them newly discovered. The methods were crude yet surprisingly accurate. Among other devices, distances were measured by the time elapsed to hear a cannon fired from a distant ship. To protect the necessary exactitude of the work, Wilkes imposed a displeasing ban on alcoholic drink during surveying missions. Two lieutenants who defied it found themselves shipped home.[94]

At Tahiti, the commander sought to leaven the carnal attractions that made the island a seafarers' favorite port of call by injecting a measure of piety and refinement. He arranged a performance of Friedrich von Schiller's drama *Robbers* for a bemused audience of South Seas Europeans and native Tahitians.[95] On Sunday, he ordered his ships' crews to attend a church service "under their officers." Sulkily, even the most godless went forth to worship.[96]

It was the next surveying stop — Samoa — where the Wilkes expedition was to leave its mark most tangibly on the American nation.

There the squadron undertook the police work expected of naval vessels of that era. The Americans arrested a Samoan who confessed to killing a crewman from a New Bedford whaler, sparing the islander's life but banishing him from Samoa.[97] They had less success tracking down a renegade chief accused of murdering three Nantucket whalemen. The "most savage & unprincipled native," as Wilkes called him, eluded all efforts to capture him.[98]

That outlaw aside, the Samoan chiefs and the leader of the American expedition got on well. The chiefs, arcadians in bare feet and naked torsos, and the captain, a sophisticate in cocked hat and gold braid — from worlds so different — somehow struck up a mutual fondness. Perhaps the cultural divide was bridged by a fellowship of those vested with ruling authority.[99] "The intercourse I had with the Native Chiefs," Wilkes stated, "greatly enhanced my opinion and respect for their Sense and determination to do what they believed to be right...."[100]

With the cases of the slain New England whalemen fresh in their minds, they began discussing, through interpreters, ways of protecting whaling ships visiting Samoa. They agreed upon a set of rules and regulations. This 1839 document was to achieve a significance beyond the narrow scope of its contents. It was the first agreement reached between a representative of the United States and the chiefs of Samoa. And it inaugurated official relations between the two entities that culminated sixty-one years later in political union.[101]

The expedition provided the home country with a wealth of information about its future possession. With the thoroughness of a trained scientist, Wilkes compiled forty pages of data and observations on every conceivable aspect of Samoan life — from tides and wildlife to courtship and warfare. The squadron's artists sketched people, everyday scenes, and flora.[102] The geography of the islands was reliably mapped for the first time.[103] The natural feature that has proven to be the archipelago's most coveted asset — the harbor at Pago Pago — was rated "one of the most singular in all the Polynesian isles."[104]

The Americans conducted perhaps the first census of Samoa. The population was estimated at 56,600, or about a quarter of today's inhabitants. Wilkes, a defender of religious missionaries against their critics, took pains to reckon the number of Christian converts (14,850, served by 11 missionaries).[105]

His opinion of Samoans was mixed. On the favorable side, he pronounced them "kind, good-humoured, intelligent, fond of amusements, desirous of pleasing, and very hospitable." Yet he also uncharitably ascribed a damning assortment of less endearing qualities. "As a shade on this picture, they are indolent, covetous, fickle, deceitful, and little reliance can be placed upon them."[106]

As an emissary from across the seas, Wilkes tried to better acquaint the isolated islanders with their place in the wider world. A terrestrial globe was fetched from one of the ships, and the location of their islands pointed out. The demonstration "excited great surprise," the commander reported, because most local people believed Samoa to be the only country on earth.[107]

After ship repairs in Australia, the expedition headed back toward the south pole for fuller explorations.[108] The goal was to determine whether Antarctica was not just an expanse of ice but an actual land mass. The rewards that beckoned were the selfless expansion of human knowledge as well as personal honors for the discoverer. The prize had escaped Cook, and Wilkes yearned to claim it.[109]

Probing the ice fields for weeks, one day in January 1840 the ebullient searchers sighted on the icy horizon peaks that could only be mountains — "conical summits," in their commander's words, "that seemed to be unmistakably of the earth."[110]

They had found Antarctica to be a continental land formation. But the achievement soon was enveloped in controversy. A French mariner, Dumont d'Urville, had made a similar discovery almost simultaneously elsewhere in Antarctica, and a dispute arose over who had been first.[111] Then errors were alleged in Wilkes's reported position.[112]

No one, however, questioned that the American expedition, whether first or not, went on to show most convincingly that Antarctica was a place of rock and soil. A captain less resolute (or obstinate), and less demanding of scientific proof, might have been content with his sighting. But Wilkes drove his flotilla to confirm it conclusively by following the ice barrier westward for one thousand five hundred miles, spotting land frequently and collecting soundings of mud and stones.[113]

"We had made it evident to all," Wilkes said of his accomplishment, "that the Antarctic Continent existed...."[114]

Cruising the perimeter of the continent after the discovery provided the commander one of the expedition's happiest interludes. Chancing upon a rock-ribbed bay, the ships dropped anchor and the men poured out onto an island of ice for a "picnic" in the bright polar sun. Wilkes took a pencil and pad of paper, and sketched the occasion — sailors relaxing, collecting icy drinking water, digging shellfish, while their three-masted frigate reposed below cliffs of ice.[115]

From the frozen polar zone, the expedition's zig-zag itinerary took it back to the tropical latitudes for more surveying. On the way, the vessels picked up the corps of scientists left behind in Australia during the Antarctic trip. Regarded as curiosities by much of the crew — landlubbers with butterfly nets, fish drags, and thick books — Wilkes welcomed their companionship. He referred to them affectionately as "Gentlemen of science."[116]

The charting of Fiji brought painful personal tragedy. A melee between a surveying party and villagers on the island of Malolo took the lives of two officers, one of them Wilkes's own nephew. The commander had been a seagoing father to his namesake, Wilkes Henry, the only child of his sister. He had taken the young man to sea as his captain's clerk when surveying the Georges Bank years earlier, and watched over him ever since. For the two deaths, the Americans inflicted heavy retaliation, killing forty Fijian warriors and destroying two villages.[117]

From the hitherto uncharted atolls of the South Seas, Wilkes's ships turned in 1841 to the only little better known northwest coast of the home continent. The expedition surveyed Puget Sound, eight hundred miles of coastline, and explored the forested interior. Its men prepared the first accurate map of the Oregon Territory, a tract encompassing three present American states and parts of two others, whose possession was still disputed with Britain.[118] Although "infested with hostile bands of Indians," Wilkes saw in the wild land great promise.[119]

The explorations cost the squadron a second ship. One of its schooners had disappeared during the first year of the voyage in a storm off Cape Horn. Now the vessel of the second in command, the *Peacock*, was lost trying to negotiate the roily mouth of the Columbia River.[120]

The expedition, already three years long, was to conclude with a final sweep across the Pacific to the shores of Asia. Short of ships and of time, one destination — Japan — reluctantly was dropped.[121] The Americans confined themselves to visiting the Philippines, the pirate-ridden Sulu Sea, and Singapore.[122] Almost at the journey's end and quite by accident, they discovered in the empty openness of the central Pacific tiny, uninhabited Wake Island. Claimed by the United States half a century later, it remains an American military outpost to this day.[123]

The Wilkes expedition had spent nearly four years and logged almost 90,000 miles probing the boundaries of the seas.[124] It had been one of the longest and most ambitious ever undertaken. And it was destined to be the last of its kind under sail.[125]

The bounty was considerable. The enterprise had surveyed 280 islands, produced 180 charts, collected 10,000 species of plants, 1,000 varieties of birds, and hundreds of other specimens of natural life, many unknown to Westerners. It had scouted out the nation's Pacific Northwest, identified Antarctica as a continental land mass, and introduced to Americans a Polynesian people who one day would join the national family.[126] The price, too, had been considerable. The expedition had lost 2 of its 6 ships, and 121 of its 342 crewmen through desertion, death, or discharge.[127]

On a June day in 1842 long awaited on ship and shore alike, the travel-weary vessels began arriving at Staten Island. Wilkes's flagship was first to dock. The erratic sea-mail system of the day had left the commander without word of his family for fourteen months. He was hastily assured by relatives in Manhattan that his wife and children were well.[128]

But if the returning voyagers had expected to be welcomed with testimonials and accolades from a grateful nation, they were to be sorely disappointed. Much of the American public hailed them as valiant discoverers, but others found the scientific pursuits arcane. Few national newspapers had followed the expedition's progress.[129]

The official reception was as icy as the Antarctic. The political climate in Washington had changed. The Democratic administration of Van Buren that had launched the project had given way to a Whig regime intent on degrading the deeds of its predecessor.[130]

Back home once again in the capital, Wilkes waited several days with mounting impatience for an acknowledgment from the president that the exploring expedition had returned. None came. He strode to the White House to call on John Tyler, recently elevated from vice president by the passing of William Henry Harrison.

He found the president seated before a fire at the middle of a semicircle of a dozen cronies who struck the visitor as "ruffian looking fellows." Fusillades of tobacco juice flickered the fire and streaked the white marble hearth. The men joshed and joked as they chawed.

"It was," he thought, "just like a Virginia or North Carolina bar room."

The naval commander, stiffly erect with a proud set to his jaw, stood for a few awkward moments as no one stirred to venture a welcome. Finally Tyler, an obligatory Virginian cordiality seeming slowly asserting itself within him, arose, extended his hand, and motioned for a chair.

"Be seated, sir!"

Wilkes joined the group, but the exploring expedition merited no mention. He soon excused himself, his departure occasioning not so much as a pause in the private banter. "I have great doubts if the President knew who I was...," he reflected afterward.[131]

Similar aversion was shown by Tyler's secretary of the navy. He withheld a promotion.[132] He peremptorily dismissed the expedition's scientists upon their stepping ashore.[133] The administration resisted even authorizing the commander to write an account of the voyage.[134]

Vexed, Wilkes related the rebuffs to one of the enterprise's originators and staunchest supporters: John Quincy Adams. The president-turned-congressman was incensed at the government's "cold and insulting silence."[135] He and other influential Washington figures convinced of the importance of the expedition encouraged the commander to publicize the results of the voyage in a speech.[136]

The venue chosen was the imposing Patent Office Building, where the expedition's collections were being housed. Crates of specimens had begun trickling into Washington early in the voyage. They first were gathered at the home of Poinsett, the scientifically-minded secretary of war instrumental in getting the endeavor afloat. There they became the nucleus of a "National Institution for the Promotion of Science," a humble, home-based forerunner of today's thirteen-museum Smithsonian Institution. Outgrowing the Poinsett house, the cruise's trophies were moved to the patent building.[137]

In the building's great hall, before an audience of Washington luminaries, Wilkes expounded the expedition's accomplishments. When he had finished, Adams and an important senator arose to commend the project. The ringing words of support from leading legislators goaded the navy secretary, Abel P. Upshur, to his feet. Even he was compelled, dutifully, to join in the compliments.[138]

Any amity between Wilkes and the navy, however, was to be temporary. No sooner had the achievements of the expedition begun to be evaluated than the process was overshadowed by a bitter exchange of court-martial charges. The commander, never content to leave a perceived wrong unpunished, levied allegations against four of his officers for misdeeds during the voyage.[139] For their part, two disgruntled officers (including one accused by Wilkes) initiated charges which the navy was only too willing to pursue against the commander.[140]

The verdicts largely vindicated Wilkes. Three of the four officers whom he had accused were judged guilty and imposed assorted sentences.[141] Of the eleven charges against the commander, for variously exceeding his authority, he was acquitted of all but one: undue punishment of enlisted men. He received the relatively mild sentence of a public reprimand, subsequently read aloud at the New York Navy Yard.[142]

Wilkes, unrepentant, deemed his court-martial as part of a political vendetta—"to throw discredit upon our well-earned & successful explorations."[143]

The court-martial proceedings behind him, he finally was able to devote himself, after four tumultuous years on the open seas, to resuming life with his family in the quiet streets of the capital. His eldest son, Jack, had followed him into the navy. The fifteen-year-old had been commissioned a midshipman during the last year of the exploring expedition, and was away on duty in Brazil when his father returned. The youngest child, Eliza, newly born when her father last had seen her, was about to turn four.[144]

The family attended gilt-steepled St. John's Church across Lafayette Square from the White House, and vacationed in the Blue Ridge Mountains in Virginia. The commander honed his nautical skills by sailing on the Potomac River and Chesapeake Bay. His wife summered at Newport, Rhode Island. In winter, the family sought warm refuge at the plantation of Wilkes's brother near Charleston, South Carolina.[145]

Wilkes was eager that the exploits of the exploring expedition gain greater dissemination through publication. Despite lack of enthusiasm from the Tyler administration, the idea won much support in Congress and the scientific community, including the naturalist John James Audubon. It was a moment of satisfaction for the commander when Congress voted to underwrite publishing a full record of the voyage.[146]

The quarterdeck captain became a closeted writer. He shut himself in his home on Capitol Hill with his ship's journals and notebooks, and began penning the story. He incorporated extracts from fellow officers and the civilian scientists, and illustrated the text with drawings by the expedition's artists and himself.[147] The project, he wrote, "afforded me an interval of rest which I greatly enjoyed."[148]

His son Jack helped edit the work and accompanied him to Philadelphia to oversee the printing. From the presses emerged in 1845 *A Narrative of the United States Exploring Expedition* in five volumes and an atlas. Wilkes and his son feted publication of the first volume by buying a new invention they had discovered in Philadelphia—an ice cream freezer—to bring home for a family celebration.[149]

The *Narrative* was recognized at the time as an American graphics masterwork.[150] It became a national best-seller, one of the period's most widely read travel books.[151] The tale of the voyage was followed in succeeding years by a series of nineteen scientific volumes, including the commander's own on meteorology. The publishing endeavor wound up extending thirty years.[152]

Soon after the books began appearing, the Mexican War erupted. Wilkes asked to be given a command, but, short on normal military experience, received none. His son Jack, however, served commendably in the Gulf of Mexico.[153]

The happy family life that Wilkes led in Washington was regrettably brief. Only six years after being reunited with her seagoing husband, Jane injured a leg during a summer rail journey to Newport, and complications took her life. Wilkes was devastated. He drew inward, burying himself in naval and publishing matters. Three children remained in the sorrowful home. Daughter Janie became, at age nineteen, a surrogate mother to her younger brother and sister. Jack returned to the household after the Mexican War, assigned by the navy to help his father complete the exploring expedition's charts and other nautical records.[154]

After five years as a widower, Wilkes remarried. He wed Mary H. Bolton, widow of a commodore, both of whom had long been friends of the Wilkeses. But the arrival of a step-mother—together with her mother and invalid sister—precipitated the departure of the children. Janie moved to her uncle's plantation in South Carolina. Edmund, an engineer, soon married and migrated westward to Utah. Eliza boarded at an academy for young women in Philadelphia.[155]

The long years of ostracism began to give way to an appreciation of Wilkes at the highest levels of government. Zachary Taylor, a hero of the Mexican War whose popularity swept him into the presidency, took a liking to his fellow military commander. Wilkes found himself invited to the rustic White House levees held by "Old Rough and Ready."[156] Not long afterward, he finally received the captain's rank that he had all too prematurely assumed at the outset of the exploring expedition seventeen years earlier.[157]

Similar recognition came, amid the gathering storm clouds of the Civil War, with the accession of Abraham Lincoln. The new president knew of Wilkes's explorations. As a progeny of the country's westward settlement, he valued the mariner's contributions to national expansion by bearing the flag into the South Seas and surveying the Pacific Northwest.[158]

Wilkes and his wife had moved near the White House. First they lived in a home on Lafayette Square once occupied by Dolley Madison—fittingly, in light of her husband's paternity of the exploring expedition—and then another house around the corner. A relationship with Lincoln developed when two neighbors joined the president's cabinet: William H. Seward, as secretary of state, and Gideon Welles, as secretary of the navy. Mrs. Wilkes, for her part, helped the utterly unprepared Mary Todd Lincoln host Saturday social receptions.[159]

The captain, a member of the new Republican party of which Lincoln was its first president, admired the Illinoisan's earnestness, an attribute they shared, as well as another rarely associated with Wilkes: kindliness. Lincoln, watching with alarm the country's uniformed ranks decimated by departing Southern sympathizers, regarded the loyal Wilkes as a national military asset.[160]

When the captain proposed, through Seward, a plan to tighten the naval blockade of Southern ports, the president readily assented. He was given command. After forty-three years in the navy, it was Wilkes's first combat assignment — and he executed it with the poise of a hardened veteran. He and his men captured two forts at the entrance of Pamlico Sound off Cape Hatteras. The victory in August 1861, on the heels of a Union defeat at Bull Run, helped lift spirits in the North.[161]

His next wartime mission offered more of the arbitrariness and controversy that Wilkes seemed almost to court. While cruising the Caribbean later in that year in search of Southern prey, the captain learned that the Confederate commissioners to Britain and France had evaded the federal blockade at Charleston and sped to Havana. From there they were to proceed to England on the British mail steamer *Trent*. Wilkes's sloop of war, the *San Jacinto*, intercepted the *Trent* en route to Europe, sent marines aboard, and seized the two commissioners.[162]

Upon his return, Wilkes received the hero's welcome never accorded the exploring expedition. He was paraded in Boston, given the ceremonial keys to the city in New York, and serenaded by bands in Washington. Congress applauded his "brave, adroit, and patriotic conduct."[163]

But international political pressure undid the high-seas abduction. Britain threatened retaliation unless the commissioners were released, and the Lincoln administration backed down. The Confederates were taken to a seaport in Maine and put aboard a British vessel.[164] Wilkes was left livid with "a glow of shame for my country."[165]

Now a popular figure in the nation, he was accorded an active part in the naval war against the South. He was elevated to commodore, consulted on strategy, and entrusted with command of squadrons on the rivers of the two wartime capitals — Richmond's James River and Washington's Potomac.[166]

The unaccustomed halo of favor soon passed. Promoted provisionally to rear admiral, Wilkes was put in charge of hunting down Confederate ships plundering Northern commerce in the West Indies. He was singularly unsuccessful. Not only did his men-of-war fail to bag any prize privateers, whose elusiveness had become the stuff of legend in the South, but the flotilla's use of foreign ports in its Caribbean search had irritated European powers.[167] Wilkes was relieved of command and, for the second time in his career, hauled before a court-martial.

To anyone knowing Wilkes, the charges carried a familiar ring: disobedience, insubordination, disrespect to a superior officer, conduct unbecoming an officer. Navy Secretary Welles, who ordered the court-martial, had formed a harsh judgment of the admiral. "He is very exacting towards others, but is not himself as obedient as he should be," he confided in his diary. "He has ability but not good judgment in all respects."

The court seemed to concur. It found Wilkes guilty on all counts and suspended him from duty. His admirer in the White House, however, took a more compassionate view. Feeling that a naval life of so much accomplishment shouldn't bear such a stain, Lincoln nullified — "remitted" is the word he chose — the entire proceeding after a year's suspension.[168] Wilkes was sullen but grateful.[169]

Realizing ruefully that his days of sea command were over, the beached mariner sought solace as he had in previous spells of dejection. He returned to the musty records of the exploring expedition a quarter of a century ago, and mined them for further findings to publish.[170] The seemingly endless publishing venture, however, was testing the patience of Congress. Lawmakers capped the stream of books in 1872 with the completion of three volumes then in the works. Wilkes, retired from the navy as a rear admiral a year after the Civil War ended, holed himself up in his house on H Street to finish the expedition's volumes on physics and hydrography.[171]

He also undertook a more monumental writing project: his autobiography. First putting pen to it in 1871 at the age of seventy-three, Wilkes ground out more than two thousand eight hundred pages of manuscript, completing it four years later. The work was as idiosyncratic as the life it chronicled. It rambled. It digressed. It left blank spaces that never got filled. It gave vent to vintage Wilkesian diatribes. The near-illegibility of the handwriting probably is responsible, as much as any other factor, for deterring transcription and publication for a century.[172]

The retired admiral also dabbled in business. Shortly before mustered out of the navy, he had bought fourteen thousand acres of land at High Shoals in southwestern North Carolina, hoping to rejuvenate an old iron works there. His nautical savvy proved a poor investment guide. The necessary funds couldn't be raised. The placed closed in 1870, and four years later Wilkes's land was sold at auction.[173]

Unlike most others packing away their uniforms after nearly half a century in the navy, Wilkes could enjoy the satisfactions of home life with a second family. Although his four elder children had grown up and gone their ways, daughter Mary, by his second wife, was a girl of just seven years when he retired.[174]

After completing his autobiography, however, the admiral sank into invalidism. He passed away at home in 1877 at the age of seventy-eight.[175]

Never one to doubt his destiny, Wilkes was confident that his contributions to country and humanity would be remembered. He had roamed the seas as widely as any maritime explorer, testing their bounds. In his long wake, he left two Pacific landfalls — the American Northwest and Samoa — associated more closely with the United States. And he left Antarctica confirmed as a continent whose eastern coastal region would be known to posterity as Wilkes Land.[176]

In no endeavor did he take greater professional pride than his prodigious surveying of the world's sea lanes. A century afterward, a descendant followed him into the Pacific aboard a latter-day navy ship. World War II was raging. The eyes of Commander C. Denby Wilkes fell on the name on the nautical charts he was using. He discovered that, in the epic struggle for control of the Pacific, the American fleet was relying on charts drawn by his forebear.[177]

The lordly old admiral would have been pleased. But not surprised.

2

Commander Richard W. Meade III

Negotiated Samoa Treaty, 1872

Like many twelve-year-olds, the boy had formed an idea of what he wanted to do when he grew up. He was going to become a naval officer.

His father, whose name he shared, Richard Worsam Meade, had led a life of seagoing adventure worthy of a son's emulation. He had captained swashbuckling men-of-war across the oceans to locales of dreamy enchantment.[1] Fatherly narratives were embellished by boyish reading of the day. The popular *Robinson Crusoe* novels filled young heads with visions of tropic islands populated by companionable "man Fridays."[2]

The aspiring seafarer had been packed off to school in an environment that could hardly have been more remote from the bounding main he craved. Mount St. Mary's College was the adjunct of an austere Roman Catholic seminary tucked away monastically in Maryland's Catoctin Mountains, a sixty-mile carriage journey from the family home in Washington, D.C.[3]

Young Richard — the ancestral line appended to his name, "III," as a heritage to live up to — was fortunate in having a father who could help him fulfill his ambition. Despite a reputation in the service for troublesomeness, an officer often at odds with his fellows, Captain Meade still commanded the attention of important ears in Washington.[4]

On a winter's day in 1849, he picked up his pen and in elegant, Spencerian strokes wrote a letter to the secretary of the navy recommending his son for appointment to the United States Naval Academy.

> Richard will be 13 years old in nine days.... The lad's pleasure and prospects of success, are not to be controlled, which feeling led him to return to College to await orders for the naval school.[5]

Commander Richard W. Meade III, as a lietuenant, circa 1861 (Naval Historical Foundation).

2 — Commander Richard W. Meade III

Not content to let the matter rest there, the elder Meade petitioned a higher authority. Then in a follow-up letter a month later, he reported with a note of triumph:

> "President Polk promised it to my son ... in the presence of Mr. Vice President Dallas."[6]

Clinched by an interview by an irrepressible father with James K. Polk and George M. Dallas in the closing days of their administration, young Meade won admission to the naval academy's next class. He gave his sponsors no cause for regret. Six years later, he graduated fifth in his class.[7]

Setting off to sea, the new naval officer finally gained the life of action and discovery for which he had yearned. He sailed the West Indies, the Mediterranean, and the coasts of Africa in the final years of such dispersion before the Civil War drew the navy closer to home.[8] He early established a pattern that was to mark his career: choice assignments and regular promotions, with a streak of rebelliousness.[9] Barely four years after receiving his commission, a violent dispute with a marine lieutenant led to a court-martial.[10]

The Civil War plunged the militarily untested officer into three years of rigorous combat. Entrusted at age twenty-four with his first command, Meade guided the ironclad *Louisville* through the hostile waters of the Mississippi River, narrowly escaping disaster in a fierce battle with Confederate guerrillas off Helena, Arkansas. At the helm of subsequent warships, he showed himself particularly adept at catching blockade runners — boarding, seizing, or destroying thirty-four of them.

Even a presumed respite from the war, an assignment far from the war zone in his native New York City, afforded no relief. Riots broke out against the military draft, in which one thousand ultimately perished. Meade was put in charge of a naval battalion helping to restore order in lower Manhattan.

Back at the front, he was participating in the siege of Charleston on Christmas Day 1863 when his gunboat came under withering attack. Three of his men killed, himself wounded, and the vessel's hull riddled, Meade nonetheless mounted a defense later officially commended as "gallant conduct."[11]

For the professional warriors in the Meade family, the wartime experience proved painfully contrasting. Richard collected honors, along with his higher ranking and more prominent uncle, General George G. Meade, a hero of the Battle of Gettysburg.[12] But Captain Meade, Richard's father and the general's brother, languished most of the war without a command. He finally was given in 1864 a steam frigate operating in the eastern Gulf of Mexico, only to have it lost in a gale in the Bahamas. The incident cost his suspension from duty and three trials by the navy.[13]

The end of the war enabled the younger Meade to cultivate a quieter life centered on home and academe. A month after the guns stilled, he married. The bride, Rebecca Paulding, sprang from another notable naval family. Her father was a rear admiral. The household eventually grew to be filled with five children.[14] The bridegroom returned to the Annapolis he had left nine years earlier, supervising instruction at the naval academy in seamanship and tactics. He also became an author, publishing a textbook on naval architecture whose advocacy of technological reform rankled much of the service's conservative top brass.[15]

Meade secured a niche in maritime racing history in the first challenge for the America's Cup world yachting championship trophy in 1870. He commanded, although not from on board, the yacht *America* in outracing a British rival.[16]

The realm of naval exploration — famed by circumnavigators from Cook to Wilkes — had been opened to Meade prior to the racing competition. Newly commissioned as a commander, he had led one of the first surveys of the coast of Alaska, just purchased in 1867 by the United States from Russia. It was the precursor of a more momentous voyage of investigation that lay ahead.[17]

Meade was now a sturdy, thick-necked man in his mid-thirties. But the sympathetic, hooded eyes, sunken cheekbones, and refined nose gave more the appearance of a neighborhood shopkeeper than someone who had served fifteen years before the mast.[18]

A long string of successful commands, and perhaps especially the reconnoitering of Alaska, commended Meade to his superiors as the right choice to head an expedition to the South Pacific. Since Wilkes's visit thirty years earlier, Oceania had evolved from a site of exotic curiosity to an object of imperial and commercial interest. The American government reckoned it was time to pay a return call on Samoa.

The honor of so important a responsibility was diminished, however, by the resources allocated to fulfill it. Meade was assigned a weary old sloop, the *Narragansett*, which resisted the onrushing era of steam by still relying on sails, keeping its steam engine in reserve.[19] And the vessel came with a complement of tars notoriously unruly.[20]

Nursing his ship and molding his crew, Meade in 1871 sailed for the southern latitudes.[21] Both the craft and its men were soon put to the test. Rounding the tip of South America on a tempestuous night, they were lashed by one of the Strait of Magellan's legendary storms.

"The wind veered constantly from point to point," he wrote later, "and the squalls came with blinding and terrific force." But his years on the waters had convinced Meade that those who go to sea enjoy divine dispensation. And so it proved.

Everything held well, and the Providence which watches over "poor Jack" sent us a slant of wind which enabled us to make an offing during that dark, dismal, and anxious night.[22]

Traversing the strait brought melancholy family memories. The *Narragansett* dropped anchor in a little bay where passing ships often paused in their journeys. It had become a custom for each vessel to leave a record of its stop, and boards nailed to the trees served as an informal log of half a century of callers.[23] The visiting Americans idly surveyed the boards.

"A very conspicuous one drew our attention," Meade reported. "It read: 'U.S. sloop of war *Decatur,* Dec'r 11th, 1854. All well.'" He instantly remembered the circumstances. The unfortunate ship had been stranded eighty days in the strait before towed to safety by the USS *Massachusetts* under the command of Meade's father. The relic was a poignant reminiscence of the father whom he had lost the preceding spring.[24]

"Before leaving," Meade wrote afterward, "the *Narragansett*'s board, '5 days in the straits; all well,' was nailed above the *Decatur*'s."[25]

Heaving into the Pacific, the expedition set a course for San Francisco, Hawaii, and thence Samoa.[26]

In a repertoire of roles not unusual at the time for navy skippers, Meade, on his mission to Polynesia, was to perform multifariously as diplomat, policeman, and business agent.

As an advance man for American business interests, the commander had been lobbied relentlessly on behalf of a New York steamship line that just had opened service between California and Australia. The company was eager to route its ships through Samoa. A fellow sea captain, Edgar Wakeman of the Webb shipping line, sent Meade a series of letters—one filling seventeen pages—urging him to stabilize the government in the islands to make the place more attractive for investment.

The naval officer seemed less than enthusiastic about promoting private commerce, but dutifully promised to try arranging a coal depot where steamers could refuel.[27]

The diplomatic assignment was more straightforward. The high-profile visit by an American warship was to counter growing influence in Samoa by a Germany embarked by its new chancellor Otto von Bismarck on a campaign of territorial expansion. The islands were becoming an outpost of German settlers and trading firms.[28]

"Important American interests are at stake," Meade wrote to the secretary of the navy a few days before departing Honolulu. Then he offered an observation that was to prove prophetic. "I think some kind of treaty with the native chiefs will be necessary to frustrate foreign influence...."[29]

On top of these responsibilities, the commander was charged with the handcuffs-and-nightstick chores of maritime constabulary work — tracking down deserters, punishing offenses committed against seamen, pursuing pirates.

Although surveyed by Wilkes and visited by ships of the world's imperial powers, Samoa in the 1870s remained a distinctly alien destination. It held as much mystery for most contemporary seafarers as did the Africa of Bushmen or the Amazonia of headhunters.

Eighteen days out of Honolulu — days lengthened by inactivity and awaiting what might lie ahead — on a radiant Wednesday morning the crew of the *Narrangansett* beheld the rugged coast of Tutuila rise from the watery horizon. The vision, for Meade's clerk, as doubtless for many others on board, was never to be forgotten.

> To the mariner's eye is presented one of those Eden like scenes rarely to be found on our globe. Resting upon the tops of mountains are seen clouds peculiar to these regions. The most perpendicular ridges from the mountain tops to the sea, intersected with beautiful valleys covered with foliage of all kinds, with the rain pouring down in torrents in one, in the next the sun shining brightly, in a third the fog hurrying from the mountain tops to the beach, a fourth is scarcely visible with the many tinted rainbow forming an arch across the whole, the ocean expending its force upon the white coral reef. The long line of Cocoanut trees along the beach with the native villages here and there, these mountains and ridges, slopes and valleys, of varied form and sizes covered with the luxuriant vegetation which a moist tropical atmosphere produces, furnish a scene of extreme romantic beauty.[30]

Gliding into Pago Pago's meandering harbor, the ship attracted a flotilla of canoes of curious Samoans.[31] The next morning brought a more impressive reception. In some alarm, the Americans saw themselves being borne down upon by a colossal canoe, propelled at breakneck speed by perhaps four dozen warriors, their naked bodies painted ferociously.

> The naked savage on the bow dancing his war-dance, and as his club moved from side to side, the fifty paddlers struck the water amidst the chanting and yelling of the paddlers and the beating of some kind of drum.[32]

It was the state canoe, bringing the local ruling chief, the Mauga — despite the aggressive appearances — on an altogether peaceable official visit to the newcomers.

The Samoa which received the Meade expedition was a long-isolated South Seas archipelago emerging with some awkwardness from cultural innocency. Islanders still stenciled their bodies with tattoos and decorated their hair with lush blossoms of scarlet and white, adornments from time immemorial.[33] But the loincloth rapidly was giving way, under missionary influence, to a more decorous, rustic sarong.[34]

Caucasians had visited often enough to have acquired a term in the

Samoan language — *papalagi,* meaning cloud-bursters or those who break through the heavens — although early notions of their supernatural origins had long since been discarded.[35] Their all too earthy accouterments — liquor, firearms, and beachcombers — were beginning to infest island society.[36]

The graceful coconut palm, a casual village resource for millennia, was being transformed by entrepreneurial Germans into an export crop encompassing large plantations.[37]

Getting a feel for the place before undertaking the major objectives of his visit, Meade attended first to more prosaic business. Completing the work of Wilkes thirty years earlier, he finished charting Pago Pago Bay. To the salvation of countless ships ever since, his surveyors mapped a route to the harbor averting the treacherous offshore submerged bank.[38]

The Americans also targeted human perils to shipping. When the brigantine *Leonora,* slim as a rapier and black as gunpowder, the craft of the infamous pirate Captain William Henry "Bully" Hayes, was spotted at anchor at Apia on the western Samoan island of Upolu, Meade hasted there. Marines were dispatched to the outlaw ship, and returned with Hayes a prisoner.

In captivity, the buccaneer whose name struck fear in the hearts of mariners throughout the South Pacific looked surprisingly harmless. Tall and stout, he was described by a member of the crew as "gentlemanly-looking..., with white hair and beard, frank and open countenance, ... the opposite of what one expects to see in a sea-rover." But he lived up to his reputation for elusiveness. A three-day court-martial aboard the *Narragansett* failed to turn up sufficient evidence, and Hayes was freed.[39]

Meade was more successful on shore. The commander was well seasoned at guiding shiploads of disparate men, in conditions of both war and peace, in settings both familiar and foreign, to desired ends. He drew on this experience to quickly forge a working relationship with Samoan chiefs. Within a fortnight of his arrival, he and the chiefs promulgated commercial regulations for the port of Pago Pago. (The American steamship interests so desirous of such help would be gratified.)[40]

A proclivity in Meade to go his own way — beyond the usual discretion of any skipper on a distant voyage — also showed itself.[41] Without diplomatic credentials or prompting from Washington, he undertook to unite the warring chiefs of Tutuila into a confederation.[42] He even designed for them what is believed to have been Samoa's first flag — two crescents of the moon forming an S superimposed on blue and white stars and stripes.[43]

Interjecting himself into the political circumstances of the little archipelago, Meade assumed a position that was part civics instructor and part fatherly adviser. Addressing a gathering of chiefs, he exhorted Samoans to maintain their national independence. It was, of course, a thinly veiled appeal to resist German expansionism.[44] He suggested that the islands might enhance their political viability by reforming their chronically unstable government. The recommended model, not surprisingly, was the American system.[45]

The commander, resplendent in his uniform of high collar and brass buttons, volunteered the services of his country in helping the Samoans achieve both objectives. The United States, he told them, would

> from time to time send ships of war (and they have many) to your islands and also no doubt wise persons to assist you in framing good laws for yourselves and the foreigners who may settle among you and will aid you by its influence and protection to establish a sound and stable form of Government under which the Samoan people can grow prosperous and happy.[46]

He hastened to assure the islanders that his nation's intentions were solely altruistic, not territorial. "The Government and people of the United States seek your friendship and welfare and will aid you to establish yourselves as a nation by peacefully exerting its great influence to prevent your independence from being taken away from you by any foreign power," he said. Americans, he declared, do "not seek an inch" of Samoans' territory nor "the control" of their affairs.[47]

A groundswell of goodwill for the visiting Americans enabled Meade to negotiate an agreement that, while stopping short of violating the islands' territorial integrity, awarded the United States a privileged standing. At a place called Gagamoe, where a stream of the same name dribbles down from the mountains into a flat field and trickles into the butt end of the harbor, the commander met with the Mauga and fellow chiefs from the eastern side of Tutuila. The Samoans ceded to the United States the exclusive right to build and operate a naval station at Pago Pago. In return, they would receive "the friendship and protection of the great government of the United States."[48]

Sent to Samoa merely to explore the feasibility of establishing such a naval installation, Meade had procured its official authorization.[49]

After a busy one-month stay in the islands, the *Narragansett* weighed anchor and departed.[50] In its wake, amity toward Americans continued and even intensified. There was less talk of protecting the islands' independence, and open discussion of the United States enfolding them in a protectorate. The Meade expedition had been gone less than a month when chiefs at Apia, on the other side of Samoa, sent a petition to the president in Washington asking Americans to annex the entire chain of islands.[51]

Meade and his crew, meanwhile, sailed northward, turning their attention to other matters. They surveyed. They collected political, economic, and shipping information. They visited the Gilbert Islands in Micronesia, and took formal possession of Christmas Island.[52]

Upon returning home in 1873, the *Narragansett* in two years had journeyed sixty thousand miles — a distance greater than encircling the globe at its equator twice. It won the praise of the navy's top admiral, David D. Porter, for conducting "more professional work than any other ship that has been afloat for the past two years in the Navy."[53]

The accomplishment deemed the prize of the expedition — the agreement giving the United States a strategic foothold in Samoa — got a less rapturous reception. Meade had forwarded the document to Washington while completing his mission, and found upon arrival that President Ulysses S. Grant had transmitted it to the Senate as a treaty for ratification. But Grant's recommendation was so heavily qualified as to repel support. The president told senators that Meade "was without special instructions or authority to enter into such agreement." He also faulted "the protection on the part of the United States which it seems to imply." He suggested tepidly that the treaty be approved "with some modification."[54] To no one's surprise, it wasn't.[55]

Although offering no solace for Meade's sense of disappointment, history has come to judge his unratified treaty a bilateral landmark, accelerating Samoa's gravitation toward the United States. It inaugurated close relations between the two unlikely partners — a fast-industrializing continental power and a cluster of languid South Seas isles. Succeeding years were to bring a stream of petitions, like the one sent soon after the expedition's departure, requesting American protection or even absorption.[56] From a diplomatic perspective, Meade's initiative precipitated a series of events destined to draw Samoa geopolitically steadily nearer the United States.[57]

After his long circuit of some of the earth's remotest waters, Meade received a shore assignment in the city of his birth. But his years at sea had bred a restless mind and impatience with convention. Such iconoclasm assured that the tour of duty would be anything but quiescent.

While helping oversee the New York Navy Yard, he began to establish a reputation — not always flatteringly — as an advocate for overhauling a navy drifting into barnacle-encrusted neglect. In his spare time, he wrote articles urging modern management techniques and an up-to-date fleet of steel and steam. He also wrote two pieces of congressional legislation that attempted — unsuccessfully — to reform the navy. An early naval theorist, he preached the importance of sea power in world affairs.[58]

At the navy yard itself, Meade bridled at the cumbersomeness and corruption he found. He spoke out unsparingly at congressional investigation hearings in 1876. In a probable tacit reprimand, the navy gave him no posting for two years.[59]

Chastening completed, Meade was delegated another mission of seaborne quasi-diplomacy. He took the *Vandalia* from one extremity of the continent to the other, gathering intelligence in the Isthmus of Panama and patching up battered Canadian-American relations in Newfoundland. Promotion to captain signaled a return into the navy's favor.[60]

The tireless exponent of navy modernization welcomed opportunities in the 1880s to put his ideas into practice. He recommended a version of the newly-invented torpedo, and saw it become a standard weapon in the navy's arsenal. He tested one of the country's first steel warships, the dispatch boat *Dolphin*. Putting it through its paces at sea, he rendered a judgment that sent shipbuilders back to their drafting tables.[61]

Between these two technological assignments, Meade took a sabbatical far afield from the navy. The naval careerist was dogged by financial concerns. He had long fretted that his navy salary, even for a ranking officer, might fall short of assuring financial security for him and his large family. He sampled the unfamiliar world of private business — and the equally unfamiliar world of land travel — working for the Missouri Pacific Railroad. But after a year-and-a-half leave of absence, he again pulled on his uniform and returned to the navy.[62]

After enduring for years Meade's chiding about its hidebound administrative practices, the navy offered him a chance to do something about them. The service tapped him to head a special board to investigate and make recommendations. The Board of Inventory in 1886–87 found the systems of purchasing, accounting, and storage to be careless and inefficient, and proposed procedures more "business-like." The resulting reforms helped to shape the organization into a world naval power.[63]

Put in charge of another navy yard — the one at Washington — Meade built it into a leading developer and producer of weapons, ammunition, and other naval ordnance.[64]

But Meade the technocrat and bureaucratic gadfly also had a common touch. As the navy's emissary to the World's Columbian Exposition at Chicago in 1893 — a showcase of the Gilded Age — he hatched the idea of building a replica battleship for visitors to tour. The "Brick Ship" became one of the fair's top draws and helped to popularize the navy among the American public.[65]

Now a rear admiral at the pinnacle of his career, Meade in 1894 was awarded command of the North Atlantic fleet.[66] During more than forty years in the navy, he had served aboard twenty-four vessels, commanding half of them.[67] But the flagship *New York* was to be his last. The admiral's headstrong ways and outspokenness finally undid him. He disputed the navy's positioning of some of his ships in the Caribbean, a region growing tense in the approach of the Spanish-American War. He was incensed to then find his flagship shunted into strategic backwaters where he might provoke no trouble. An apostle of greater military interventionism, Meade also took issue with the cautious policy of President Grover Cleveland.[68]

In high dudgeon, he relinquished command.[69] His indignation, however, didn't end there. Back on shore, he vented his criticism of the Cleveland administration in an interview in the *New York Tribune*. There were dark threats of court-martial.[70] Soon afterward, and four years before mandatory retirement, Meade in 1895 piped himself out of the navy.[71]

In retirement, the admiral pursued the interest in exploration and the oceanic orb that had first drawn him to the sea as a youth. He became an active member of the National Geographic Society, giving lectures at its headquarters in downtown Washington and writing an article for its magazine.[72]

Two years after departing the service to which he had devoted his life, he passed away in Washington.[73]

Meade is remembered most as the ocean-spanning sea captain of his boyhood ambition — as leader of an expedition since rated "one of the most remarkable cruises on record."[74] On that voyage, as throughout his naval career, he felt a responsibility to perform his duty as he saw it, not necessarily as the navy expected. The autocracy he showed in parleying with the Samoans was unwelcome among his superiors at the time, as much as the similar determination he later displayed in seeking naval reform. But he had the satisfaction of living to see his conduct vindicated. The navy became more professionalized.[75] And his resourcefulness in the South Seas set Samoa on a course visibly leading toward a special relationship with the United States.

3

Albert B. Steinberger
Premier of Samoa, 1875–1876

The isles of the South Seas always have attracted from less hospitable northern climes more than their share of arresting originals.

An other-worldly vision of sparkling lagoons and swaying palms, and a remoteness found practically nowhere else on earth, have lured adventurers testing society's limits. So incendiary a cargo of outsiders turned these tranquil archipelagos in the eighteenth and nineteenth centuries into an unlikely setting for daring, devilment, debauchery.

Rebellious painter Paul Gauguin coaxed from a primitive Polynesian life in Tahiti and the Marquesas sensual Post-Impressionist masterpieces.[1] Other interactions were less salutary. Fletcher Christian and fellow mutineers from HMS *Bounty* implanted on Pitcairn Island their notion of a South Seas Eden, which all but self-destructed in barbarous blood-letting.[2] Wayward missionaries such as the Reverend Shirley Baker in Tonga perverted piety into despotism.[3] Mercenaries of the likes of Paddy Connell in Fiji introduced firearms as well as weapons of moral destructiveness. Connell claimed to have a hundred wives.[4]

In ports of call throughout the South Pacific, "the Beach"—a term designating not just a place but a subculture—was repository of a human driftwood of shipwrecked seamen, deserters, castaways, freed convicts from penal colonies, and assorted other fugitives from unmentionable pasts.[5] It was a place where the daughter of any respectable European or American resident islander was strictly forbidden to set prim foot.[6]

No venturesome westerner alighted upon the South Seas with more panache, nor rose to greater heights, than did Albert B. Steinberger. In the 1870s, his escapades captivated American newspaper readers and occupied Washington officialdom, up to the president himself. Yet today he is forgotten—his renown swept away like a moldering frangipani blossom scattered by the trade winds of his adopted Samoa.

Steinberger's origins were about as far removed imaginable, geographically and culturally, from the balmy South Seas. He grew up in the gritty

Appalachian coal mining country of eastern Pennsylvania. Born on Christmas Day in 1840 — the year after the Wilkes scientific expedition had charted Samoa — he was the sixth of nine children of a Schuylkill County physician and his French-American Huguenot wife.

But if the setting offered no hint of future Pacific adventurism, young Steinberger's upbringing betrayed elements of striving and wanderlust later evident in him. His father, escaping the confines of a rural medical practice, dabbled in the coal and iron industry, only to be ruined in a national economic crash three years before Albert's birth. When fifteen years old, the family began a westward migration first to Council Bluffs, Iowa, and then to Bellevue, Nebraska.[7]

Albert B. Steinberger, 1875, in a wood engraving from the *New York Daily Graphic* (Library of Congress).

Steinberger struck off on his own into the world as he neared nineteen, drawn farther west by the glittering discovery of gold at Cherry Creek, Colorado. There he showed an early flair for two lasting inclinations: politics and drama. He became a youthful founding father of the future metropolis of Denver, one of two residents chosen soon after his arrival in 1858 to obtain from the territorial legislature a charter for the proposed town. He also became Colorado's first playwright, penning a four-act melodrama celebrating the then-new mountain territory.[8]

The restless young man two years later was on the move again. He headed back eastward, basing himself in New York during the decade of the 1860s.[9] Like so many Americans, he was embroiled in war activities — but, in his case, not the civil war then convulsing his country. Although of prime age for military service, Steinberger evidently (so far as records reveal) took no part in the conflict.[10]

His elder brother Justus had pursued a career in the army on the western frontier, becoming in the 1850s the chum of a rough-edged junior officer named Ulysses S. Grant. When Grant went east to eventual military glory in the Civil War, Steinberger took wartime command of a regiment in the Pacific

Northwest territory of Washington. The two Steinberger brothers frequently found themselves confused by the press and others — confusion that Albert only abetted by adopting as a title lending a certain prestige his brother's rank of "Colonel."[11]

The younger Steinberger's military involvement was farther afield and purely pecuniary. With few qualifications except his own aplomb, he sailed to France and secured an interview with Napoleon III. Under the French emperor's apparent sanction, he then negotiated a lucrative contract for a syndicate to supply munitions to the French in the Franco-Prussian War of 1870–71. The deal, alas for Steinberger, went awry. Financial snags emerged. A congressional committee noisily investigated possible incursions on American neutrality. And Steinberger suffered heavy losses which he sought to recover by litigation that dragged on through the rest of his days.[12]

Joy also turned to ashes, meantime, in his personal life. Steinberger in 1867 took a wife, Caroline L. Ely, daughter of a recently-retired congressman in Rochester, New York. But Carrie never recovered from the difficult birth of the couple's only child, and in 1871 left her husband a widower.[13]

Not long after, the exotic isles of Samoa made their fateful way into his life.

Steinberger's assignation with Samoa seems to have sprung from no prior association with the place. He evidently did know some investors in a Samoa land speculation firm, based in California, of which another brother, John, was a director. But Albert Steinberger's casting for a role in these far-off islands would appear to be based mostly on personal attributes. Here was a man, people sensed, with ability to deftly size up a situation and win others' confidence.[14]

Contemporary portraits show a man more self-possessed than one just in his middle thirties. Dark eyes brim with assurance. A strong chin juts from beneath a flowing military moustache. Hair is swept purposefully back from a sloping brow.[15] He is described as a figure of ingratiating charm — fluid conversationalist, entertaining storyteller, avid listener. In such suavity, however, less charitable observers detected signs of affectation and manipulation.[16]

On the New York business circuit, Steinberger evidently became acquainted with steamship tycoon William H. Webb, who operated a South Pacific shipping service for which he was seeking a federal subsidy. Samoa lay along international trade routes and inspired in the 1870s imperialistic designs by leading maritime powers, including the United States. Greater American influence in Samoa apparently was seen by Webb as advantageous for his shipping line. Six months after Commander Meade in 1872 had negotiated an agreement granting the United States privileged access to eastern Samoa, Webb recommended to his friend President Grant that he send Steinberger to the islands to investigate conditions. The suggestion meshed with the president's own desire for naval moorings there and his resolute expansionism.[17]

Steinberger was keen. He met with Grant, exuberantly going so far as to offer to serve without pay. "I ... can only pledge my earnestness and good faith," he confessed with disarming candor in a follow-up letter to the president the next day.[18] His candidacy may benefited from Grant having known his elder brother (as the old general fondly remembered) "intimately for more than fourteen years."[19] Steinberger was duly credentialed by Secretary of State Hamilton Fish in the spring of 1873 as an "intelligent special agent." He was promised compensation of twelve dollars a day, provided a letter of introduction signed by the president, and packed off to the South Seas.[20]

When the American sailed into Pago Pago harbor, he entered a Polynesian outpost feeling the first touches of western commercial discovery. The winding cove, so favored by Pacific sea captains, beckoned toward a gaggle of white clapboard buildings nestled beneath spindly coconut palms and spreading breadfruit trees. The little settlement was dwarfed by mountains swathed in tropical greenery to their knife-edged ridges, enclosing Pago Pago in a hulking volcanic collar.[21]

Tall-masted sailing ships, like Meade's *Narragansett*, not long ago the only inter-ocean visitors to the port, now shared its waters with their chugging and puffing steam successors. Native canoes still darted about. But the titanic canoes of chiefs, rowed by a crew of naked, painted warriors, such as the craft that had greeted Meade, had given way to less ferocious "missionary boats" of decorously clad Samoans reverently paddling their pastor on his rounds.[22]

It was Steinberger's good fortune that conditions for his visit were propitious. One of Samoans' periodic wars between rival chiefly factions had just drawn to an exhausting end. Weary of combat, they were open to outside advice and ready to work together. Resident foreigners, too — merchants, missionaries, and consuls of countries vying for control of the archipelago — yearned for stable government.[23]

Steinberger began circulating among the islanders. They were eminently approachable. Loping along the sandy lanes or lounging beneath the thatched domes of their open-sided *fale* houses, Samoans were quick to flash a smile or call a greeting.[24] The contrasting attire must have absorbed the interest of each. The American, known as a sharp dresser, probably draped in one of the copious, waistcoated suits of the period, interviewed Samoans wearing only long, wraparound skirts called *lava lava*s, made of *tapa* cloth pounded from tree bark.[25] Unacquainted with the Samoan language, he took along as interpreter a resident Englishman.[26]

The sympathetic interest in their affairs shown by someone cloaked in the authority of a major nation, enhanced by manners so engaging, quickly made him a favorite.[27] Soon he was moving beyond merely gathering information, to issuing advice.[28] He told a gathering of chiefs on the island of Tutuila that he had "come over many miles of land and water from the Great Chief of the United States of America to offer 'a friendly hand.'"[29]

He waded into one of the most turbulent issues of the day. Speculators had been gobbling up Samoans' land — a scarce commodity in the tiny clutch of islands, and one wreathed with mystical significance in the cultures of Oceania.[30] An American company, by the time of Steinberger's appointment, had bought up claims to more than a third of all the archipelago's land.[31] The firm (the Central Polynesian Land and Commercial Company, of San Francisco) boasted powerful political connections back home. Its investors were said to include members of the president's family.[32] Another stockholder, a U.S. senator from California, persuaded the secretary of state to replace the country's commercial agent in Samoa with one of the company's own employees.[33] Serving on its board was Steinberger's brother John.[34] But heavy political clout was matched by heavy debt. Money had been lavished on land that few showed interest in buying.[35]

To Samoans, the firm was something of an ogre. With the support of his government, Steinberger sided with the islanders against the land speculators. He advised the Samoans to stop selling land to foreigners, thereby endearing himself throughout the kingdom.[36] As an act of political courage, however, his stance in bucking potent business interests was diminished by the company having gone bankrupt shortly before his arrival.[37]

His popularity presented Steinberger an opportunity to leave a more lasting mark on Samoa. Islanders were then drafting their first constitution and code of laws. The legislative assembly (known as the Fono) welcomed the American as an adviser, according him the status of a "talking chief" (as one who represents a high chief, in his case presumably the American president). He became a guiding force in the constitution and law code subsequently enacted.[38]

Steinberger's visit sometimes has been embellished with a romantic angle. He is reputed to have conducted an affair with the half–Samoan daughter of the recently-replaced U.S. commercial agent. Whether such a liaison was fact or fancy, the young woman, Emma Cole, then in her twenties, later became a fabled figure in the Pacific. "Queen Emma"— regal in bearing as well as ancestry, as a member of Samoa's royal family — operated from New Guinea a commercial empire of plantations, shipping, trading, and stores, and her offspring were the first colonizers of what became German New Guinea and today is Papua New Guinea.[39]

After two busy months in Samoa, Steinberger prepared to return home.[40] He departed in an effusion of mutual admiration. Leaders of the reorganized

Samoan government gave him a letter to President Grant extolling the "peacefulness and the amiability" of his agent, urging his return, and inviting a union of the two countries.[41] He may have had a hand in writing the letter to Grant, one suspects, but other commendations seem spontaneous. Missionaries, stern critics of many temporal authorities, chorused their praise.[42] The American, for his part, pronounced his Samoan hosts "brave, earnest, and honest people."[43]

On the long voyage back to San Francisco — a trip taking as much time as had his stay in Samoa — Steinberger wrote a detailed report of his findings. It painted a glowing portrait of a bustling South Seas center flowering under American tutelage:

> Under guidance and protection, [Samoa] would develop and concentrate a great trade. To the touch of industry its harbors would be busy marts, its timber utilized, and its valleys and mountain slopes teeming with native products.[44]

The rosy prospectus met unenthusiastic eyes in Washington. The report gathered dust on the secretary of state's desk, unacknowledged, until Steinberger pried from him a reply. "Replete with novel and valuable information," Fish finally responded, with no indication that the report had altered official thinking on Samoa.[45] Grant forwarded the document to the Senate. It was deemed newsworthy enough to be reprinted in Horace Greeley's *New York Daily Tribune*.[46] But strengthening ties with Samoa stirred little interest, in the public or the Senate, and the report was shelved.[47]

The tepid reception failed to temper Steinberger's conviction that a greater destiny awaited Samoa. And he was determined to be a part of it. He lobbied tirelessly among the influential in Washington to be sent back to the islands. He peppered the secretary of state with letters.[48] He importuned the chief of the navy, Admiral David D. Porter — who may have harbored a familial interest in Polynesia from his father's having in 1813 led the country's first military visit there — to have a word with the president.[49] He cultivated Grant's private secretary, Orville E. Babcock, himself, like Steinberger, a former U.S. agent overseas.[50]

Steinberger's hopes were buoyed by an invitation to the gala White House wedding of Grant's adored daughter Ellen, known as Nellie. While awaiting the outcome of his representations on Samoa, he undertook a brief trip to Germany.[51]

His persistence paid off. As Babcock had confided to him in a note jotted on presidential stationery: "Had a talk with the old man and it all looks well ... O. E. B."[52] Grant interviewed the applicant at the presidential summer cottage in the village of Long Branch on the New Jersey shore, then advised the secretary of state that he wished Steinberger returned to Samoa.[53]

The expedition, Grant later wrote to him expansively, held "great interest to the people of those productive and balmy Islands," promising "a closer union of interest between us and them."[54] After a sixteen-month interregnum, the reappointed "special agent" again was on his way to the South Seas.

On his first trip two and a half years earlier, Steinberger had been just another voyager, booking his own passage on a commercial steamship.[55] This time, he traveled as a dignitary. On the first leg of the journey, from San Francisco to Honolulu, evidently at the president's behest, he luxuriated aboard the USS *Pensacola* as a royal escort for Hawaiian King Kalakaua, a sybaritic monarch returning from an American visit.[56] Steinberger completed the trip on a navy gunship, the USS *Tuscarora*, a pugnacious wooden steamer bristling with masts and a stovepipe funnel.[57]

He was received in Samoa as a returning savior. Arriving on a warship elevated his stature, creating the impression, however misleading, that he commanded the full authority and might of the United States. The perception was reinforced by the *Tuscarora* lingering for some time in the harbor at Apia as if standing by to support the agent whom it had deposited.[58]

Jubilant islanders feted Steinberger with a festival and a mass meeting.[59] He presented them the odd assortment of gifts he had brought: guns, ammunition, band instruments, American flags, and a redesigned version of the Samoan flag which Meade had given them three years before.[60]

One reason for the American's joyful welcome was that political conditions had deteriorated in his absence. Deadlocked on the choice of a king, chiefs had settled for the predictably unworkable compromise of electing two coequal kings from rival families. The kingdom veered toward another war.[61] Steinberger assumed the role of peacemaker and political mentor. Sailing from island to island aboard a small schooner bought in California, the *Peerless*, he discussed with chiefs the outlines of a revised constitution.[62]

The new constitution that Steinberger devised finessed the competing claims for the kingship by providing for the two contending families to take turns filling the office for four-year terms.[63] The constitution democratically enlarged the membership of both houses of the legislature.[64] But its most significant innovation was to create a position of premier vested with powers that would be the envy of his contemporaries Gladstone and Disraeli. Not only was the premier deemed the king's equal in conducting the affairs of the kingdom, but his powers in important respects eclipsed the monarch's. The king was required to notify the premier before taking any official action.[65]

The premiership seemed framed for the framer himself. And he soon occupied it. The constitution was quickly adopted and a king selected. The sovereign, a mild, missionary-educated young man named Malietoa Laupepa more at home in the ecclesiastical realm than the political, offered the post to the American.[66] He accepted it on the Fourth of July in 1875.[67]

The patriotic flourish in his choice of timing proved ironic, for Steinberger's appointment stirred a storm of controversy back in his homeland. He was an American citizen and a special agent of his country in the ambiguous position of serving as an official of a foreign government.[68] Newspapers from New York to San Francisco raucously questioned American involvement in Samoa and faulted the Grant administration's conduct.[69] The State Department which had dispatched Steinberger to the islands found itself on the defensive.[70]

Heedless of the furor on the other side of the Pacific, Steinberger proceeded to take firm control of the island government he had designed. He installed as his top aide a fellow American whom he had brought with him, John H. B. Latrobe, Jr., evidently an outcast of his prominent Baltimore family. The many-hatted Latrobe served as the kingdom's secretary of war, military commander, treasurer, chief justice, and private secretary to the premier.[71]

At the helm of government, Steinberger showed himself to be something of a reformer and champion of the Samoans.[72] He supported investigating foreign land claims.[73] He worked with the missionaries to improve working conditions at coconut plantations and crack down on the seamiest activities on the waterfront.[74] His rule was virtually absolute.[75] But it gave the islands their first stable and functional government since the influx of sizable numbers of foreigners.[76]

Power so autocratic and policies so disturbing to some, however, were bound to draw enemies. Resident foreigners were made uneasy by a zeal for the interests of native Samoans.[77] Some settlers feared losing their landholdings.[78] The British and German communities took affront at growing American influence.[79] Even the missionaries, once so laudatory, became disaffected.[80]

Meanwhile, Steinberger's ties with the American government, on such ostentatious display when he arrived, were fast tattering. As the press discredited their man in Samoa, the president and secretary of state discreetly distanced themselves from him. His correspondence to Grant went unanswered. Loss of official support in Washington left the premier vulnerable to his foes in the islands.[81]

The chief conspirator against Steinberger was one of his own countrymen. Samuel S. Foster, whose shady reputation elsewhere in Polynesia had followed him to Samoa, had been manager of the big California land speculation company in Pago Pago when political manipulation engineered his appointment as the archipelago's first U.S. consul. He is suspected to have resented the premier's opposition to foreign land sales and his outranking of the consul in the local American hierarchy.[82]

When a British warship, the sleek sailing barque HMS *Barracouta*, glided into Apia harbor in December 1875 after Steinberger had ruled five months, Foster and his allies had their chance.[83] The American consul plotted with his British counterpart, a leader of the missionaries, and the commander of Her Majesty's vessel.[84] Then Foster and several escorts from the *Barracouta* boarded Steinberger's yacht, the *Peerless*, removing a cache of arms and personal papers.[85]

Lurking in the papers seized was a secret more damaging to the premier's credibility than any of his public deeds. A set of documents revealed that Steinberger may have returned to Samoa not solely to help the islanders but also to enrich himself. On the trip to Germany before his reappointment, he had bargained a deal in Hamburg with J. C. Godeffroy & Son, the largest trading company in the South Pacific. The American would promote a favorable business climate by establishing an orderly government, and then award the German firm a virtual trade monopoly. In return, he would collect a 10 percent commission on government purchases from the company and on Samoan commodities sold to the firm.[86]

A clandestine commercial relationship with his political right-hand man also came to light. In an agreement signed shortly before setting off for Samoa, Steinberger was to help Latrobe make enough money there to repay a $13,500 debt which the Baltimorean owed him, and then give Latrobe a 25 percent cut of the proceeds of his business dealings.[87]

These discoveries were as much of a revelation to Steinberger's superiors in Washington as to his constituents in Samoa. While he had informed the secretary of state at the time that he had traveled to Germany and "conferred with Messrs. Godeffory," he had given no inkling (as far as can be learned from surviving correspondence) of his arrangements with the German firm or Latrobe.[88]

The little South Seas kingdom was plunged into a two-month-long wrangle over the legitimacy of its premier. Leaders of the foreign community and the British naval commander charged that Steinberger was a charlatan, and implored Samoans to disown him. The consuls—including the acting German consul, ironically an agent of the trading company with which Steinberger also was affiliated—threatened to remove foreign residents from Samoan jurisdiction. Samoan leaders defended their premier with equal ardor. King Malietoa Laupepa declared him "a gentleman," and joined the legislature in vowing "to stand by and support Steinberger at all hazards."[89]

The king's backing proved disastrously fickle. Enticed aboard the *Barracouta*, he was bullied into signing a letter blaming Steinberger for the political crisis. Ashore, he told the legislature he was dismissing the American as premier. Steinberger was hastily arrested by the warship's commander and incarcerated on his vessel.[90]

The betrayal of their popular premier incensed Samoans. Later the same day, angry legislators deposed the king and exiled him to the adjoining island of Savai'i.[91] When the *Barracouta* retrieved the ousted king six days later and the consuls sought to reinstall him in an outdoor ceremony, a gunfight broke out between Samoans and British marines. Four bluejackets and three islanders perished, and many others were wounded.[92]

Leaving Samoa behind, sullen and bloodied, the *Barracouta* sailed off toward New Zealand.[93] Steinberger, its prize prisoner, was confined like a dangerous felon. He was kept on deck in a room eight feet square without window or ventilation in the tropical heat.[94] Repelled by treatment so harsh, sympathetic officers, whenever possible, invited the prisoner to dine at their mess.[95]

A fellow prisoner was the U.S. commercial agent supplanted by Consul Foster. Jonas M. Cole, among the first Americans to settle in Samoa thirty years earlier, was the father of the young woman sometimes linked romantically with the man with whom, by an odd turn of events, he now found himself in custody. An ally of Steinberger, he was accused of fomenting disorder.[96]

The ex-premier's associate, Latrobe, meanwhile, had been hustled aboard another ship and sent home to Baltimore.[97]

The triumph of military intervention, however, was brief. When the *Barracouta* paused in its journey at Fiji, it was greeted not with honors but rebukes. The governor of the British colony, Sir Arthur H. Gordon, vexed previously by the bellicose ways of the ship's commander, Captain Charles E. Stevens, was aghast at what had transpired in Samoa. He ordered Steinberger and Cole immediately released.[98]

Evicted from both his premiership and his preferred homeland by dubious means, Steinberger, once freed, launched a campaign to clear his name.

The image of an American as the chosen ruler of "a confiding, half clad, dusky population" of South Sea islanders, in the words of one newspaper,[99] had captured the imagination of many of his nineteenth century compatriots. The obscure cluster of Polynesian islands suddenly occupied the nation's news columns — attention probably unmatched, either before or since.

When news of his demise trickled across the Pacific, it touched off in the press a vigorous debate over Steinberger. Some newspapers rushed valiantly to his defense. James Gordon Bennett's *New York Herald* called upon the country to "protect her own dignity."[100] Charles A. Dana's *New York Sun*, normally a stout critic of the Grant administration, went so far as to advocate war against the European nations whose consuls had conspired against the premier.¹⁰¹ Others, however, denounced Steinberger as an "adventurer" (*New York World*)¹⁰² engaged in "ridiculous intrigues" (*New York Times*).¹⁰³

Upon gaining his freedom in Fiji, Steinberger hasted to Auckland, New Zealand, where Captain Stevens was expected to face a court-martial. Instead, the whole troublesome business was forwarded to higher authorities in London.¹⁰⁴ Steinberger requested compensation from the British government for his seizure, without success.¹⁰⁵ Yet there was retribution. Bringing down the Samoan premier also brought down the perpetrators. Captain Stevens was drummed out of the navy.¹⁰⁶ And both the American and British consuls were removed from office.¹⁰⁷

From New Zealand, Steinberger repaired to neighboring Australia, where he wrote a succession of stinging newspaper articles attacking his enemies and defending himself.¹⁰⁸ He also claimed, in a letter to the secretary of state, that his contract with the German trading company had been arranged legitimately while he was a private citizen and "abrogated by mutual agreement" at the outset of his second assignment to Samoa.¹⁰⁹ He then is said to have proceeded to Britain to press his case for remuneration.¹¹⁰

Back in the United States, calls arose for a full investigation, either by the president or Congress. None took place.¹¹¹ The government limited itself, in succeeding months, to publication by Congress of hundreds of pages of documents from the president on the Steinberger affair. Their release left Congress strangely mute—no debate nor even so much as a word of comment on an episode that lawmakers may have found perplexing or politically perilous.¹¹² Washington was still wrestling with the matter more than a decade later. President Grover Cleveland, whose antipathy toward overseas expansion was as great as Grant's fondness, prepared for Congress in 1888 an exhaustive, 311-page postmortem.¹¹³

Unmoved by the sharp differences of opinion that Steinberger aroused in his home country, Samoans remained touchingly attached to him.¹¹⁴ Weeks after his abrupt departure, the island legislature petitioned Grant for his return. "We wish still to have Colonel Steinberger as our premier," the chiefs wrote, "because he has done right and with a true love and great patience."¹¹⁵

Steinberger never returned to Samoa.¹¹⁶ After seeking redress of his grievances in the antipodes and Britain, he is believed to have resettled in 1877 in New York City.¹¹⁷ There, the following year, he apparently remarried. The bride is identified as the daughter of a wealthy judge. A photograph handed down through the family depicts a woman of rather haughty expression, small dark eyes, thin lips curling downward, dark hair gathered atop her head. She is wearing a low-cut formal dress. A ribbon choker clasps her slim neck, below dangling earrings.¹¹⁸

Ever the chaser of grand schemes, Steinberger is said to have involved himself in several major development projects of the day, including the Cape Cod Canal.[119]

He slipped out of the public eye as quickly as he had burst upon it several years earlier. When he was casting so dashing an image on the international scene — his name mentioned in the same breath as those of world leaders — the *New York World* in 1876 gushed that Steinberger was "destined always to remain a tremendous historical figure."[120] He was destined, instead, for obscurity. His passing, in 1894 in Dorchester, Massachusetts, received little notice.[121] Even tiny Samoa, where he once loomed so monumental, today has no known statue, memorial, nor other commemoration — and scarcely any recollection of him.

Steinberger's enduring legacy may be less tangible: fostering among the islanders a receptivity to subsequent American acquisition of the eastern part of their archipelago.

In historical perspective, his exploits in Samoa are viewed with increasing favor.[122] To be sure, Steinberger remains tainted by undercurrents of corruption — his own and the Grant administration's.[123] And as a U.S. agent, he probably exceeded his authority.[124] But he devised and operated a strong government that advanced the interests of Samoans.[125] In an age of hated imperial masters, he was a rarity: an outside ruler loved by the people.[126] A year after leaving, the former premier was reckoned by the U.S. consul to be "more popular today in Samoa than ... any other man, native or foreign."[127]

Steinberger assiduously promoted political merger between the United States and Samoa, an objective repeatedly endorsed by island leaders.[128] If he had remained in power and managed to bring the islands under Washington's protection, some have suggested, Samoa might have escaped the quarter of a century of internal turmoil and belligerent competition among Britain, Germany, and the United States which preceded the eventual emergence of American Samoa.[129]

4
Captain Henry Glass
Captured Guam, 1898

Hot on the electrifying news of the American destruction of the Spanish fleet in Manila Bay, the cruiser *Charleston* chugged at full steam in June 1898 from harbor in Honolulu, bound for the Philippines war zone.[1]

The warship was escorting three troop transports laden with two thousand five hundred soldiers who had flocked into army enlistment offices on the West Coast as war fever swept the country.

The captain stood on the bridge, feet planted combatively apart in a kind of personal war posture.[2] His broad face, high cheekbones, wide-set eyes, and heavy dark moustache were the visage of a bulldog spoiling for a fight.[3] His trim figure was uniformed in cannonball blue. On his head squatted a hat with flat top and visor — a hat not for the parade ground, but for the line of battle.

Henry Glass watched Diamond Head begin to recede into the choppy Pacific, and then retired to his cabin.[4] There he unsealed a confidential order from the secretary of the navy:

> On your way [to Manila], your are hereby directed to stop at the Spanish Island of Guam. You will use such force as may be necessary to capture the port of Guam, making prisoners of the governor and other officials and any armed force that may be there. You will also destroy any fortifications on said island and any Spanish naval vessels that may be there, or in the immediate vicinity.[5]

He quickly commanded his little convoy to change course for a diversion as obscure as it was unexpected.[6]

The order from Washington doubtlessly set Glass and his navigators scouring their nautical charts. The captain and most others in the navy knew next to nothing about the island he was to seize. Few had ever heard of it.[7] Guam happened to have caught the eye of a knot of the service's long-range thinkers — the U.S. Naval War Board — as well positioned for a coaling station for ships traversing the Pacific in the Philippine campaign. The board recommended its capture.[8]

The officer delegated the assignment had little inkling that he was about to make constitutional history for his country. Yet, in the odd way that men and events sometimes conjoin, much of Glass's life seems to have been readying him, unawares, for just such a mission.

Hardly so, however, at first. The future mariner sprang from a family that had forsaken the seaside and gravitated through the generations deep into the country's interior. His forebears had settled in the colonial Virginia nautical center of Norfolk.[9] But Glasses had since emigrated inland as far as western Kentucky. There, in the little county seat of Hopkinsville, Henry was born in 1844.[10] Like another Kentucky family — the youthful Abraham Lincoln's — the household then moved farther westward to Illinois.[11]

Captain Henry Glass, 1898 (Naval Historical Foundation).

In a setting so utterly landlocked, Henry Glass somehow acquired a fancy for the navy. At age sixteen, in the year that Lincoln went off to the White House, Glass left for the U.S. Naval Academy.[12]

Barely had his studies at Annapolis begun before the Civil War erupted. He was commissioned an ensign at the height of the conflict in 1863, and then the nineteen-year-old was rushed to the war front.[13] He took part in bombarding Confederate forts and batteries along the South Carolina coast.[14] The experience instilled a fondness for combat that was to last throughout his career.[15]

When the war ended, the young officer made his first acquaintance with the Pacific — an ocean of which he would develop some intimacy. He steamed the Asian-Pacific region almost continuously during the eight years immediately following the war.[16] The only interruption was a tour of duty in the Caribbean aboard the *Tuscarora*, the vessel that six years later transported Steinberger to Samoa.[17]

After a respite back in the United States, Glass got first-hand exposure to the nation's territorial expansionism, a movement to which he later was to contribute importantly. He served in 1880 as the naval officer in charge of what was then classified as "Indian affairs" in the newly acquired territory of Alaska.[18]

There followed several years of further cruises to Asia and the Pacific, now on ships under his own command.[19]

Wanderings in the unruled oceans had stirred an interest in the laws that prevail on the high seas. Between voyages, the commander compiled the relevant laws into a book. He intended it, as he stated in the preface, as a shipboard handbook for "the naval officer on service." The work long served as a text at the naval academy.[20]

His skills as a skipper attracted sufficient esteem to win Glass successive commands of two newly-launched warships. He took on their maiden voyages the cruiser *Cincinnati* in 1894 and, the following year, the stubby, heavy-plated battleship *Texas*.[21]

The outbreak of war with Spain gave the United States an opportunity to make strategic use of Glass's experience as a battle-tested rover of the Pacific. Who better, the navy's admirals seem to have reasoned, to snatch the Spanish island of Guam?

He was handed command of the *Charleston*, hurriedly being reconditioned in San Francisco, not far from the camp where, with equal frenzy, thousands of recruits were being readied for combat.[22] They would be the first American servicemen in history sent to war beyond the country's borders.[23]

Glass and his lumbering, three-hundred-foot-long cruiser joined the three chartered troop ships which had preceded him to Honolulu — christened with the fittingly Eastern names of *City of Pekin*, *City of Sydney*, and *Australia*.[24] The squadron then set off for enemy waters.

Its new and not a little nebulous destination was an island chanced upon by the Spanish circumnavigator Ferdinand Magellan in 1521.[25] Guam, once its surrounding seas were more fully explored in succeeding centuries, turned out to be the largest island in the north Pacific between Hawaii and Asia.[26] And the island blessed with the best harbor.

"Largest," in the context of the sparsely-isled north Pacific, of course, remains by most any other reckoning rather small. Guam is an outcropping of volcanic rock and coral limestone, shaped like a human footprint, thirty miles long and four to eight miles wide. It's roughly the size of the Mediterranean island of Corfu, or a quarter of the size of the smallest American state of Rhode Island.[27]

Despite its strategic assets, Guam long had languished almost forgotten by its Spanish rulers. Never a busy port of call for Iberian vessels, the steady contraction of Spain's empire had reduced traffic to a trickle. Contact with the mother country in recent years had been limited largely to visits by a steamer subsidized by the Madrid government every two months.[28]

The archipelago which Guam anchors was named by its discoverer, disparagingly, the Ladrone Islands — "robber islands" — after islanders rifled Magellan's ships.[29] Although formally renamed a century later as the more respectful Mariana Islands,[30] the old designation persisted on maps and nautical charts into Glass's day.[31] Now the name was to be given new appropriateness by American plans to steal Guam.

Seeking intelligence about the island in preparation for an assault, Glass was pleased to discover during the two-week voyage thither a valuable resource fortuitously on board his convoy. The third officer of the troop carrier *Australia*, while captaining a whaling ship years earlier, happened to have visited Guam. He promptly was drafted as pilot to guide the invaders once the island was reached.[32]

The twentieth of June dawned murkily, amid a threat of rain. The dim daylight revealed a phalanx of vertical cliffs rising beyond a gnarled reef. It was Guam's northern tip.[33]

Picking its way warily along the western coast of scrubby green hills, the squadron hove into the bay that sheltered, behind a ring of coconut palms, the capital city of Agana. Not a vessel was to be seen.[34] The Americans proceeded southward to the island's principal harbor, San Luis de Apra, a spacious anchorage for Pacific mariners since the era of Spanish galleons.[35]

"It was expected that a Spanish gunboat and a military force would be found," Glass reported later, "a rumor to that effect having reached me while at Honolulu."[36]

He found, instead, quite the opposite. Fort Santiago, high on a rocky promontory commanding the entrance to the harbor, lay an empty ruins.[37]

The puzzling dilapidation of insular defenses emboldened Glass to advance into the harbor. Taking no risk with the teeming troop transports, however, he instructed them to wait behind at a safe distance.[38] Now eight thirty in the morning, the weather — in the absence of any other opposition — was mounting a resistance of its own. Thick tropical rain squalls pelted the flotilla.[39]

Through the cloudbursts churned the *Charleston* into the port. Sighting atop an interior reef another bulwark, Fort Santa Cruz, the cruiser fired at it a few shots. None was returned. This fort, too, was unoccupied. Glass positioned his ship where it could control the harbor and ordered the anchor dropped.[40]

The only other vessel in port was a square-rigged trading brigantine from Yokohama. Watching the action with what must have been some apprehension, the Japanese seamen spotted the *Charleston*'s American flag and timorously hoisted their colors.[41]

A skiff splashed into the water from the deck of the warship to carry an emissary to the Japanese craft to learn whatever he might about conditions on shore. No sooner had the boat shoved off, however, than there approached a launch flying the Spanish flag.[42]

With the two nations locked in all-out war, the arrival alongside his hulking gunship of the little unarmed enemy boat likely struck the battle-hardened American captain as either recklessly valorous or supremely foolhardy. Guardedly, he welcomed the occupants aboard. They comprised a strangely unwarlike delegation: a Spanish navy lieutenant commander who was captain of the port, a Spanish army surgeon serving as port health officer, and a local American resident as translator.[43]

As they talked, it began to dawn on Glass that his visitors had no idea of the state of affairs between their countries. He queried them.

"In answer to my questions," he recounted later, they "told me they did not know that war had been declared between the United States and Spain."[44]

They had received no news of the outside world since the last mail steamer from Manila stopped at Guam two months earlier.[45] The volley which they had heard fired from the *Charleston* was taken to be a friendly salute. They had come to apologize for failing to return the tribute with their own cannon. Regrettably, they had run completely out of ammunition.[46]

Glass wasted no time in acquainting his guests with the hard truth. Their nations were at war, it was his duty to inform them, and the Spaniards were now prisoners of war. Reckoning Spanish forces incapable of defending the island, he released the officers temporarily to return to shore and fetch the colony's governor.[47]

Once the callers departed, the Americans inspected the emerald water of the harbor, marking navigational hazards with buoys. The transports filed in to join their flagship.[48]

The governor, a lieutenant colonel in the Spanish army named Juan Marina, proved a bit balky. The discomfiture of his military disadvantage was accentuated, perhaps, by a touch of Castilian pride. He dispatched his secretary, an army captain, to Glass with a letter politely refusing to come to the *Charleston*. He proposed, instead, a meeting on shore.[49]

The governor's evasiveness irked the American commander. Glass was not a man to be trifled with. The resistance of a foe tightened the set of his jaw, lifted the pugnacious nose, and darkened the slits of eyes flashing beneath heavy brows.[50] Had sundown not been approaching and the tide low, Glass was ready to send a contingent of marines storming ashore at once.[51] Rather, he organized a landing force primed for action the following morning.[52]

In the meantime, he wrote an ultimatum to be delivered in the morning to the governor. The letter called for the island's immediate surrender.

Sir:

In reply to your communication of this date [20 June], I have now, in accordance with the orders of my government, to demand the immediate surrender of the defense of the island of Guam, with arms of all kinds, all officials and persons in the military service of Spain now in this island.

This communication will be handed you to-morrow morning by an officer who is ordered to wait not over one-half hour for your reply.

Very respectfully,
Henry Glass
Captain, U.S. Navy,
Commanding[53]

The day of a showdown arrived. At eight thirty in the morning, platoons of American troops in battle gear — thirty marines from the *Charleston*, others from one of the transports, and two companies of Oregon infantrymen — landed near the harbor.[54] Once they had taken up positions, Glass's navigator, Lieutenant William Braunersreuther, also sailed ashore. Under a flag of truce, he marched to the grey stone palace in the Plaza de España with the captain's letter.[55]

Governor Marina opened the letter, then excused himself to consider his plight. Twenty-nine minutes later — one minute before the deadline — he emerged with a letter to the American commander. Braunersreuther broke the seal and read it.[56]

The "sad necessity of being unable to resist such superior forces," the Spaniard wrote, left no choice but to accede "regretfully" to the demand for surrender. He concluded, gallantly: "God be with you."[57]

Braunersreuther hustled together the deposed governor, his staff, and three fellow Spanish military officers, and escorted them to the *Charleston*. There they were confined in the relative comfort of staterooms, and allowed to write letters of farewell to family and friends who would be left behind on the island.[58]

The representatives of Queen María Cristina in custody, all that remained was to formally proclaim Guam as American. The victorious commander climbed into a shallop and plowed his way to Fort Santa Cruz, its perch in the harbor affording maximum conspicuousness. As a band on the deck of one of the transports struck up the national anthem, at two forty-five in the afternoon Glass raised an American flag. A twenty-one gun salute from the *Charleston* rang out across the water, sending startled gulls fluttering into the sky.[59]

The colony's garrison of fifty-four Spanish soldiers and two lieutenants was mustered at harborside, disarmed, and herded aboard the *City of Sydney* as prisoners.[60]

The island still had, however, another armed force: a militia of local

Guamanians. How best to neutralize it gave the conquerors pause. "The natives," Glass mused, "are quiet and inoffensive and thoroughly well disposed."[61] It was decided, after taking their weapons, to release the sixty militiamen. The freed soldiers broke into joyful smiles, and in appreciation pinned their military buttons and badges on their surprised American guards.[62]

The captain conducted his country's first inspection of its brand new possession. Militarily, the findings were hardly auspicious. The four forts standing protection over the island were useless wrecks. The only guns found were four obsolete pieces, reserved for saluting but no longer safe even for ceremonial purposes. There was no coal for fueling steamships.[63]

As an ominous sign of Guam's isolation, Glass discovered that no Spanish warship had called there in a year and a half.[64]

The exhilaration of capture ended on a note of tentativeness. Unsure whether the United States intended to keep the island, and perhaps sobered by his grim inspection, Glass ordered the flag that he had run up so proudly a few hours earlier at Fort Santa Cruz to be quietly removed at day's end and packed away on the ship.[65]

The commander was in a hurry. This was conquest on the run. His orders had specified, with confidence bordering on audacity, that the job at Guam "should be very brief, and should not occupy more than one or two days."[66] His gunship, his shiploads of troops, and his ammunition were awaited by Admiral Dewey in the Philippines.[67]

The convoy must depart the next day, even if it meant leaving affairs on the island, under its sudden change of sovereignty, in some disarray. Spanish rule of nearly four centuries' duration was to be plucked away and nothing substituted.[68]

The island numbered, among its inhabitants, one known citizen of the country that had just acquired ownership. He was the translator who had accompanied two Spanish military officers to the *Charleston* upon its arrival. Francisco Portusach, like most residents of the little island washed by waves of foreigners, was an ethnic amalgam.[69] He was a Chamorro mestizo, an islander of mixed Guamanian and European blood. He evidently had taken American citizenship while residing for a time in San Francisco, working at the offices of the *Chronicle* newspaper as an elevator operator. He also is reported to have had an American wife.

On his native island, Portusach was a one-man business conglomerate. He owned a store in Agana and boats at the harbor. He is attributed, in addition, with a financial interest in coconut plantations elsewhere in the Marianas.[70]

As the American convoy prepared to steam away, it occurred to Glass, almost as an afterthought, that perhaps he ought to leave someone in charge of matters in the new possession. The lone fellow countryman whom he had met — to all appearances, a responsible sort — loomed a natural choice. The captain apparently summoned Portusach and vested him verbally with authority to tend to American interests, as a kind of unofficial governor, until U.S. rule could be formalized.[71]

His makeshift arrangements for Guam's first American administration having been completed, Glass and his flotilla upped anchor and resumed their passage to Manila. They had spent at the island three days.[72]

In the exigencies of capturing a prize of unknown peril and then rushing to the Philippine battle zone, neither the commander nor anyone else in the squadron seems to have indulged in much reflection on the significance of what had transpired at the island astern of them. Guam, after all, had been regarded from the outset as nothing more than a quick detour.

The speed and peaceableness of Guam's seizure — bloodless and almost powderless — rank it as perhaps the most efficient military victory that the United States ever has achieved in the Pacific.[73] It came to be celebrated in the years thereafter, however, less for the attackers' prowess than for the defenders' ineptitude. The Spanish garrison's blithe unawareness of the war, its misconstruing of the American shelling, its empty ammunition magazines ... all became sources of public mirth.[74] "A bit of opéra bouffe warfare," snickered the *San Francisco Chronicle* a decade later.[75] The chortling was to prove tragically smug. During World War II, Guam was left little better defended by the Americans, and fell to the Japanese in 1941 as swiftly as it had in 1898.[76]

But Glass and his men had done more than pull off a fast military triumph. They had bestowed the United States its first conquest of populated territory beyond its shores.[77] It would be followed in rapid succession by others: Puerto Rico two months later, and the Philippines at year's end — both grander trophies.[78] Little Guam, however, holds the distinction of having anointed the United States an imperial power.

Glass's acquisition, its place in national ambitions incidental and even its retention uncertain, nonetheless was to become the outlying possession most enduring. Guam has remained part of the American constitutional family since the captain of the *Charleston* unfurled the Stars and Stripes over Apra harbor.

As they sped from Guam to Manila, most of the men in the expedition probably entertained no thought of ever returning to the island or having any further association with it — and, indeed, never did. But aboard the convoy were two junior officers destined for important future roles in the new dependency. A young lieutenant, Robert E. Coontz, came back fourteen years later as naval governor.[79] A shipmate, Josiah S. McKean, who eventually rose to the top echelons of the navy, did his best as nations drifted toward World War

I to remedy the island's vulnerability that he had witnessed so graphically in 1898.[80]

Eight days at sea brought the captors of Guam to Dewey's waiting fleet, struggling to complete American conquest of the Philippines. They arrived in time to help follow up the sinking of the Spanish armada by blockading Manila Bay.[81] The blockade strangled the besieged capital. The Spanish were reduced to slaughtering their horses for food, and the Filipinos their household pets.[82] The guns of the *Charleston* in August joined in a bombardment echoed polyphonically by the thunderclaps of violent morning rainstorms.[83] American troops sloshed in, and Spanish defenders waved white banners of surrender.[84]

Glass remained in the Philippines for the rest of the war with Spain. He served as captain of Manila's newly liberated port. His cruiser prowled the coast, supporting American army operations on shore.[85]

When the war against the Spanish metamorphosed into a war against insurgent Filipino nationalists,[86] the *Charleston* continued in the thick of the action, but evidently with Glass no longer at its helm. The ship participated in September 1899 in capturing Subic Bay, an important harbor west of Manila later to become a huge American naval base.[87]

But after so many military laurels, the cruiser was headed toward an inglorious fate. Rounding the northern tip of the main Philippine island of Luzon a few weeks after its latest triumph, the *Charleston* struck an uncharted reef. Hull slashed open and sea gushing in, it had to be vacated. The crew fled to a nearby islet, then bivouacked on larger Camiguin Island while the ship's sailing launch went for help. The marooned men finally were rescued by a navy gunboat ten days later. No such deliverance awaited the *Charleston*. Deemed wrecked beyond salvaging, it was abandoned.[88]

News from Guam may have trickled to Glass during lulls in the fighting in the Philippines. He had left his conquest a precariously undefended American outpost surrounded by the islands of European colonial powers craving for new possessions.[89] Germany, the most avaricious, snatched a swath of the Caroline Islands south of Guam through a secret pact with Spain just two weeks after guns fell silent in the Spanish-American War.[90]

The immediate threat to Guam's welfare, however, came not from without but from within. Soon after the triumphal Americans had departed, a renegade local politician named José Sisto had tried to seize control of the island. Glass would have been gratified to learn that his delegated overseer, Portusach, armed with nothing more than a revolver and vague moral authority, had managed to quell the rebellion.[91]

Portusach kept watch over the new U.S. protectorate for six months. The navy sent a gunboat in December to confirm American acquisition and replace him as provisional governor with a respected Guamanian elder, Joaquin Perez.[92] The first of what would become a long blue line of naval governors arrived the following August.[93]

Completing his long tour of duty in the war-tossed Pacific, Glass received a dry-land assignment back home. He took command of the Mare Island Navy Yard in San Francisco Bay.[94] Despite his zest for battle at sea, the warrior, now fifty-six years old, may have welcomed an opportunity to enjoy family life for longer than brief spells of shore leave. His family made its home in nearby Berkeley. Glass and his wife, Ella, were parents of a daughter, Katherine, and a son, Frank.[95]

The captain advanced to the select company of flag officers, and as rear admiral held a succession of other commands on the California coast. He retired in 1906.[96]

The fierce combatant on the high seas was discovered to be a sociable companion ashore. Trading shipboard existence for the life of a leading citizen of the Bay area seemed to temper Glass's military demeanor. His views became less doctrinaire naval. He cultivated a wide circle of friends. He found that he liked the congeniality of city clubs, and joined no less than four of them on both sides of the Bay — the Olympic, Union, and University clubs in San Francisco, and the Faculty Club in Berkeley.[97]

The admiral made a sanative visit to the southern California town of Paso Robles, hoping to improve his health at its hot springs. There in 1908 he passed away.[98]

For nearly a century, the consummate seaman-at-arms who had won for the United States its first peopled territory overseas remained uncommemorated in Guam. Perhaps the capture had been all too swift, all too easy. There had been no epic struggle nor heroism under fire to inspire a towering monument or sculpted memorial. Eventually, Glass received just the sort of pragmatic nautical remembrance that the unsentimental skipper probably would most have appreciated.

A long breakwater was built after World War II at the entry of Apra harbor to better shield from the open ocean the bay where the *Charleston* had made its conquest. In 1991, with due ceremony, it was named Glass Breakwater.[99]

5
General Nelson A. Miles
Conquered Puerto Rico, 1898

The American flag was first raised over Puerto Rico on a July morning in 1898 atop a makeshift heap of ammunition crates.[1] The clatter of the impromptu little ceremony rattled down the sole street of the south coast hamlet of Guánica, interrupting a Caribbean reverie of pastel-hued houses and scarlet poinciana trees.[2]

Peaceably propping up Old Glory turned out to be perhaps the highest service rendered by cartridge boxes in the ensuing military contest for the island. Their lethal contents remained largely unopened, undrawn from leather ammunition belts slung across the shoulders of American soldiers, unfired from their Springfield rifles and Krag-Jorgensen carbines.[3]

The campaign that has left the Stars and Stripes flying above Puerto Rico to this day was a conquest of cakewalk dexterity.

Teased Mr. Dooley, droll satirist of the Gilded Age:

> I'd give five dollars ... if I was out of this [place] tonight, an' down with Gin'ral Miles's gran' picnic and moonlight excursion to Porther Ricky. 'Tis no comfort in bein' a cow'rd whin ye think iv thim br-rave la-ads facin' death be suffication in bokays an' dyin' iv waltzin' with th' pretty girls iv Porther Ricky.[4]

The "gran' picnic" was hosted, so to speak, by one of the country's greatest combat generals. And it's somehow fitting that the largest of today's overseas possessions was won for the United States by a conqueror who was himself a figure of dimensions so outsized. Formidable in physical vigor. Formidable in military prowess. Formidable in ego.

Nelson A. Miles fairly embodied forcefulness — driving and unrelenting, on the battlefield and off. It was both a gift and a curse. Miles the field commander was admired. Miles the colleague, even among his advocates, was suffered. Miles the public persona was lampooned.

So dominant a character began to assert itself early, as if unrestrainable by mere boyhood. The environment in which he grew up was a superb incubator for a future aggressive general. Nelson was the youngest of four children in the rural Massachusetts family into which he was born in 1839, and evidently the favorite.[5] Comely curls of brown hair concealed an uncomely willful disposition that sometimes set a steeliness in his blue-grey eyes.[6]

His father, Daniel, whose glowering brows and pursed mouth gave him a look of severity, was a successful farmer, lumberyard operator, and local officeholder. He also zealously practiced the flinty New England tenet of speaking his mind. His son Nelson would ever after esteem worldly success and volubly let his views be known.[7]

From his mother, Mary, plumpish, affectionate, and piously Baptist, the son acquired a quiet religious faith and private devotion to family at odds with the hardened image he projected.[8]

General Nelson A. Miles, 1902 (Library of Congress).

The rolling hills surrounding the white Cape Cod style family home near Westminster, west of Boston, bred within the sturdy, rambunctious boy a love of outdoor life that he was never to lose. These were golden years of discovering the natural world, summertime swimming, wintertime skating and sledding, hunting and trapping.[9]

The game of which he was most fond was unknowingly prophetic. "One of the favorite pastimes for our boyhood days was playing at war," he recalled later. "'Playing Indian,' was, perhaps our greatest sport."[10]

A masterful horseman was sired. The toddler first rode horseback balanced in front of his father, and then at age six was given a pony of his own. "I cannot remember," he wrote, "when I was not at home on the back of a horse."[11]

For a headstrong child of nature, the upbringing was idyllic:

> No more ideal setting for innocent and happy childhood could be found than my home ... and my happiest memories are of that period of my life.[12]

The ambition for military life was ignited at the family hearth. On winter evenings in the glow of burning embers, his imagination was fired by his father's tales of the military deeds of his forebears. One of the first of his family in the New World, a Welsh clergyman, had taken up arms against Native Americans in 1675 in what was known as King Philip's War. Nelson's grandfather and great-grandfather had fought the redcoats at Lexington, wintered with George Washington at Valley Forge, and witnessed the British surrender at Yorktown.[13]

"My own heart became enthused," he remembered, "with a longing for the military profession."[14]

The allure of manly adventure extinguished interest in formal education, already scant.[15] It also disaffected him with prospects in his tiny hometown, comprised of three general stores, a handful of tradesmen's shops, and two churches.[16] The family homestead would never be his, he knew, but would be inherited by his brother Daniel, twelve years his senior.[17]

At age sixteen, Nelson left home for Boston.[18] For the aspiring rural, the nation's fifth largest city was a magnet of commercial vitality and intellectual ferment.[19] It offered Nelson the added attraction of containing three maternal uncles prepared to help the new arrival. He worked at an uncle's fruit stand, then clerked at a crockery store in which an uncle had a financial interest.[20]

Seeking to rectify his deficient education, he put aside his prejudice against academic training to push himself through night classes at a commercial college, skimping on sleep to study and on meals to buy textbooks.[21] He also attended fiery abolitionist meetings at Faneuil Hall and Tremont Temple, emerging a convinced foe of slavery.[22]

The learning that he enjoyed most, however, was military. His reading tastes weren't the usual young man's light entertainment. "Books on military history, manuals of army regulations, and treatises on strategy and military tactics," he recounted, "became my favorite reading."[23]

The Westminster farm boy was an awkward, ill-at-ease teenager in his adopted city. His six feet of height was stretched on a gangly frame of less than one hundred fifty pounds.[24] Uprooted from family and old friends, he mixed poorly socially. He came across as stiff, prone to argue, and easily offended.[25]

While these traits regrettably were never to be shed, the young Bostonian soon found congenial comradeship among those sharing his military interests. He and fellow enthusiasts formed a martial training club drilled by a former French army colonel.[26] The timing was fortuitous. It was 1860, and the country was hurtling toward civil war.

Once the war erupted, the shock of the defeat of Union forces at the first battle of Bull Run elevated the recreational drilling into real soldiering. Roused to action, Miles raised the substantial sum of three thousand dollars (from his father and an uncle), and organized and outfitted a company of army volunteers in Roxbury.[27]

The men quite naturally elected their young organizer as company captain. But worldly ways intervened. Miles's youthfulness — he was twenty-two years old — and political favoritism led the Massachusetts governor to refuse him the commission. The captain's bars went to another with political connections, and Miles grudgingly settled for first lieutenant. It was a rebuff that he never forgot. Never again would he naïvely assume that ability and hard work were sufficient to assure advancement. Thereafter he would assiduously court his superiors and cultivate influential friends.[28]

The Twenty-second Massachusetts Infantry Regiment went off to war.[29] It swelled the stream of troops choking the muddy streets of wartime Washington. Soldiers bivouacked around the one-hundred-fifty-foot stub of the unfinished Washington Monument. Cavalrymen trampled past the construction site of the Capitol building. Miles's regiment marched in review before the somber figure of President Lincoln on the steps of the White House.[30]

As a rite of passage from civilian society, Miles's brother had come to Washington to bid farewell. Daniel's responsibilities as a father of four young children kept him out of uniform. He accompanied Nelson to a bridge arching over the Potomac River to the Confederate state of Virginia, beyond which noncombatants were forbidden. The brothers parted, and the younger strode across the river into a military world that would absorb his life.[31]

No longer was he the scraggy teen of his Boston days. Military drilling, perhaps, had fleshed him out into a young man of swaggering robustness.[32] Marching in blue uniform and shiny new sword to join the Army of the Potomac, the raw lieutenant imbibed the thumping of regimental boots, the roll of drums, the cry of bugles, and sensed that he had found his calling.[33]

Encampment near the Virginia country town of Falls Church was barely under way before the stirring of a restless ambition that came to pervade Miles's career. Brief assignment to a general's staff had implanted a yearning for duties more lofty than those of a foot soldier. He struck up an acquaintance with the commander of a Pennsylvania brigade, Brigadier General Oliver O. Howard. The ardently abolitionist general with the flowing beard of a Biblical holy man took the lieutenant as an aide-de-camp, becoming the first in a long line of army cohorts to help Miles — and eventually feud with him.[34]

But his baptism in combat showed the young officer to possess battlefield gifts matching his ambition. When casualties left his regiment short of field officers at the Battle of Fair Oaks in May 1862 east of Richmond, Miles was rushed into service. Shaking off a foot wound, he rallied the retreating men and regrouped them to repulse further Confederate attacks. His leadership stood out prominently in the bloody standoff.[35]

The few short hours of combat revealed much to Miles about himself and successful warfare. He found (as superiors, too, were quick to notice) that he was blessed with an instinctive comprehension of terrain and positioning of troops. And his native aggressiveness impelled him to press the offensive — to tenaciously advance.[36]

The battle also left a sobering impression of war's carnage. The fighting had raged back and forth across a field where eleven thousand men perished. "A more gruesome scene cannot be imagined," he shuddered. Later he had the equally repellant experience of watching the amputation of Howard's injured right arm.[37] The resulting empathy evoked a career-long concern for the welfare of the troops whom he drove so strenuously.[38]

The divided nation's continuing internecine struggle afforded Miles ample opportunity to demonstrate his abilities as a field leader.[39] Battle after battle found him shoulder-to-shoulder with his troops in the whistle of bullets and roar of cannon, often as not out in front heedlessly exhorting the powder-smudged ranks forward. As senior officers fell, he won greater responsibility and rapid promotion.[40]

At the tender age of twenty-three, when most civilian contemporaries were just beginning careers as farmers, mechanics, or clerks, Miles was commanding a regiment at the Battle of Antietam. (Characteristically, he wrote: "My first order was to advance.")[41] He led a full brigade at Spotsylvania,[42] earning the star of a brigadier general from Lincoln.[43] He headed an entire division at Reams's Station,[44] and a corps of twenty-six thousand men in the war's closing battles at Sutherland's Station and Sayler's Creek as a twenty-five-year-old brevet major general.[45]

The war's grievous casualties, which so accelerated military advancement, didn't altogether spare Miles. He was wounded four times. Two of the bullet injuries — at Fredericksburg and Chancellorsville — necessitated convalescent leaves back home in Massachusetts. The valorous circumstances of the latter wound, sustained while spearheading his troops on horseback, brought him the nation's highest award for military bravery, the Medal of Honor.[46]

Recuperative leave, for the ambitious young officer, became an occasion not merely to heal his body but to forward his career. Determined to heed the political dynamics that had cost him his first commission, upon recovering from his Fredericksburg wound Miles traveled to Albany and New York City to lobby for promotion to general in his New York regiment. ("I don't believe there is a Col. in the Army who has better recommendations than mine but I am not a politician," he wrote to his brother.)[47]

Six months later, discarding his crutches after the second wound and heading back to the war front, Miles stopped en route at Washington to solicit support for higher command. He called at the White House, hoping to petition his commander-in-chief, but found Lincoln out.[48]

The fiery cauldron of the Civil War matured Miles as a man and molded immutably his philosophy as a soldier. The fresh-faced lieutenant who looked so unsure of himself when posing in a photographer's studio with his new sword at the opening of the war scarcely resembled the trimly-bearded brevet major general who sat for a similar portrait near the war's end. The arms folded resolutely across the chest and the gaze fixed sternly on the camera oozed self-confidence.[49]

Miles's tenacity and personal courage in battle brought inspiration to his men, victories to his army, and accolades to himself. "In the great drama, I had been exceedingly successful," he reckoned.[50] But his style of leadership was attended by heavy loss of life. At both Fredericksburg and Spotsylvania, for example, his units had lost a quarter of their strength.[51] There were occasional demurs that Miles unnecessarily put his troops at risk.[52]

The commander, of course, viewed the issue differently. Miles prided himself on pushing his men to their limits, but paternalistically looking after them.[53] He was far from oblivious to the war's terrible toll. In a letter to an aunt from the decimated Confederate town of Warrenton, Virginia, he wrote of the "sadness" of seeing that "almost every lady is dressed in mourning."[54] But he accepted the human cost as an unavoidable consequence of war and bore it as a badge of honor.[55] He broadcast almost boastfully that his Second Corps's "aggregate wounded and killed in battle exceeded in number that of any other corps."[56]

Miles's attitude toward warfare — doggedly storming ahead, inured to the cost — paralleled that of his commander, General Ulysses S. Grant. The two men shared a mutual professional respect. "Miles ... deserves the highest praise," Grant wrote after the fighting at Sutherland's Station, "for the pertinacity with which he stuck to the enemy until he wrung from them the victory."[57]

The years of war, so wrenching for the nation, also tore asunder the family home life that Miles remembered so glowingly. Midway through the conflict, he learned that his parents had separated. Although his father later visited him in Virginia, bringing a hometown gift of a sword to replace one lost at Chancellorsville, the two drifted apart. The elder Miles moved to Brattleboro, Vermont, and the son began turning to an uncle as a family confidant.[58]

The end of hostilities recast Miles, and the army as a whole, in the unfamiliar roles of promoting peace and healing divisions in the South which they had so recently ravaged.[59] An ambitious federal program of reconstruction had long been urged by Miles.[60] He tackled the new assignment with vigor untempered by caution. He was put in charge of Fort Monroe, a stone citadel guarding the entrance of Hampton Roads, Virginia, and soon found himself presiding over one of the Reconstruction era's most emotionally charged episodes.[61]

The president of the defeated Confederacy, Jefferson Davis, was apprehended in the pine barrens of Georgia, along with another former Confederate official, and brought to Fort Monroe for incarceration.[62] Warned that Davis might escape or be rescued, Miles responded with the instinctive thrust of a field commander who needn't trouble himself with political considerations.[63] Authorized by the Department of War to do so "whenever he may think it advisable," he ordered his famous prisoner's ankles placed in manacles. The leg irons—Miles called them "light anklets"—were removed five days later when heavy, grated doors were installed outside the Confederates' cells.[64]

But a political storm had been set off. Fettering the former president aroused resentment among Southerners and sympathy among Northerners. Davis came to personify "the suffering South," and his jailor, the oppressing North.[65] The beleaguered Miles pleaded "no desire or purpose to cause him any unnecessary humiliation."[66] The experience was a painful lesson that a military man capable of routing the most fearsome foe in battle may be bushwhacked by evanescent political subtleties.

Subsequent Reconstruction duties brought additional professional frustration—offset by personal happiness. Miles was sent farther southward to North Carolina with a regiment of troops to assure law and order, protect freed slaves, and oversee formation of provisional governments.[67] The work was vexing, and he welcomed opportunities to slip away to Washington to hobnob with those potentially helpful to his career.[68]

Visiting the home of one such Washington personage, Senator John Sherman of Ohio, Miles found his interest captured by the senator's niece. Mary Hoyt Sherman exuded a lively, auburn-haired radiancy. The visitor may also have perceived her to be blessed with social graces he lacked, such as tact and drawing-room poise. Her appeal could only have been enhanced for Miles by belonging to so prominent a family as the Shermans. Her father, Charles T. Sherman, was a federal judge in Cleveland and a commissioner of the transcontinental Union Pacific Railroad. Another uncle, besides the senator, was Miles's army superior, General William Tecumseh Sherman.[69]

The trim Ohio lass and the strapping colonel fell in love, and Miles was soon writing to her father for his consent to marriage. "I have felt less trepidation in meeting our enemy," he confessed, "than I do in addressing you on the subject."[70] The couple was wed in 1868 at a ceremony in Cleveland glittering with pomp. There was the august presence of a Supreme Court justice, and the medal-bedecked flourish of General Grant and Civil War cavalry hero Philip H. Sheridan in full-dress uniforms. (Uncle William came in civvies.)[71]

A cooler reception awaited the newlyweds in the Reconstruction South. Miles's peacemaking efforts won him few friends, and the niece of a general still bitterly remembered there as a scourge was hardly a popular figure.[72]

Miles's abolitionist ideals also were sorely tested. Demobilizing most of the army after the Civil War — over one million men, mostly volunteers and draftees, diminished to just fifty-four thousand regulars — had forced him, like other careerists, to scramble for openings.[73] The brevet major general had stepped downward in grade to become colonel of a regiment of newly-recruited African-American enlisted men and white officers.[74]

Leading a contingent of blacks to help rebuild the postwar South manifested Miles's anti-slavery sympathies, as well as his friendship with General Howard who headed the federal Freedmen's Bureau.[75] But racial tensions undermined the regiment's effectiveness. Miles transferred out — out of the unit (to one all white) and out of the quixotic Reconstruction venture.[76]

Leaving behind, with palpable relief, the devastated and distraught South, Miles and his wife set off for a new assignment in a new part of the country. His new regiment was stationed in the young state of Kansas on what was then the nation's western frontier.[77] It was to be the region with which the colonel, approaching his thirtieth year, would be most memorably associated.

Clattering westward from St. Louis aboard a train, the proud New Englander and veteran of the epic battles of the Civil War might be forgiven for regarding his new post with some condescension. The land was far from the corridors of power so important to him, uncivilized, in his view, and the military adversaries were mere bands of unruly native peoples. But the raw topography emerging through tufts of locomotive smoke began to interest him. At windswept frontier stations where the hissing train paused — the platforms bearing increasingly the impassive forms of Native Americans in blankets — he became the first passenger to hop off the train and the last back on.[78]

Settling into the command of his regiment at Fort Leavenworth, Miles soon found the camaraderie, independence, and limit-testing outdoor habitat of frontier soldiering much to his liking. He became a confirmed westerner.[79]

> Every day's duty was a pleasure, and no company more agreeable than the company of brave men.... Marching, scouting, hunting, exploring, with an occasional campaign and encounters with hostile Indians, was the best schooling for the military profession. When an officer marched over the Divide with a command, great or small, he was immediately thrown upon his own resources. He had to think, plan, and act for the welfare and safety of his command.[80]

The army had been sent west, of course, on a mission of serious national intent. The bluecoats were the mailed fist of American expansionism. The end of the Civil War had opened the floodgates of westward migration. By wagon train and rail, settlers streamed into newly-organized extremities of the United States already occupied by indigenous inhabitants. As their ancestral lands were gobbled up, treaties disregarded, and financial aid neglected, some Native Americans mounted an armed resistance. The army was summoned to make the West safe for settlement.[81]

For the next twenty years, Miles rode at the forefront of what came to be known as the country's "Indian wars." He led a succession of campaigns against an array of tribes, from upper plains grasslands to Rocky Mountain passes to Southwestern deserts. Capture of the storied Geronimo and Chief Joseph, as well as his part in the surrender of chiefs Crazy Horse and Sitting Bull, earned Miles recognition as one of the army's ablest Indian fighters.[82]

Native American warriors were far different foes than Confederates, as many transplanted Union officers less perceptive than Miles were all too slow to learn. Miles adapted more successfully. He evolved a style of warfare that combined the headlong assaults which had served him so well in the Civil War with a tough endurance admirably suited to engaging an elusive adversary on a spacious, debilitating frontier — and to the colonel's own innate perseverance.[83]

Miles borrowed the painted warriors' great weapon of mobility and turned it against them. He pursued them tirelessly. For him, stalking wasn't just a prelude to catching the prey. It was the contest itself, even if the quarry never were cornered. The relentless chase eventually wore down the hunted and they gave up. Keeping the native people on the run, the colonel figured, would make their lives unbearable.[84] "My opinion," he wrote, "was that the only way to make the country tenable for us was to render it untenable for the Indians."[85]

In his first major campaign, the so-called Red River War in 1874–75 in the Texas panhandle, months of pursuit by a column of troops headed by Miles and his setter, Jack, finally exhausted and depleted the tribesmen. Two thousand Kiowa, Cheyenne, and Comanche surrendered.[86]

Two years later, Miles refused to let a campaign in Montana against a coalition of Cheyenne and Sioux, led by Sitting Bull, be deterred by anything as trifling as the northern plains winter. "They expected us to hive up," he explained, "but we were not of the hiving kind." His men tramped over five hundred miles through numbing cold and blinding blizzards bundled up like Eskimos in wool masks and boots wrapped in grain sacks. More than two thousand harried Indians capitulated, and Sitting Bull fled to Canada.[87]

The constant pursuits imposed strenuous physical demands on both sides. During the Red River War, a weary Miles wrote to his wife:

I have just dismounted after a long and most fatiguing ride. I have been in the saddle for about 22 hours, making about fifty four miles. The Indians are still before us.[88]

The colonel, ever at the side of his men, asked no more of them than of himself. But he was endowed with an iron constitution, and couldn't sympathize easily when others flagged.[89]

Besides hell-bent determination, the prolonged chases required the meticulous work of careful planning. And Miles proved a master at it. Sound preparation, to him, meant "never, by day or night, to permit my command to be surprised ... and always ready to act on the offensive."[90] Far from army posts and continually on the move, his troops could count on good scouts, sound pack animals, and ample supplies.[91] Miles pestered his superiors, and even Congress itself, with requests for his men — from extra clothing to promotions and medals.[92]

The tactic that complemented fierce pursuit was the very different one of patient negotiation. The hard-charging field commander, anything but diplomatic in most of his relationships, showed a surprising affinity for bargaining peace agreements with Native Americans. Miles succeeded in gaining the confidence of the chiefs by listening empathetically and acceding to many of their demands. In hammering out peace terms with Chief Joseph, he agreed for the Nez Percé to return to their Northwest homeland. In parleying with Geronimo, Miles consented to reunite the Apache with their families in Florida.[93]

Other officers' failure to show proper sensitivity in conflicts with tribespeople drew his ire. Miles was appalled by the tragic Battle of Wounded Knee, which public revulsion helped to make in 1890 the last major armed clash of the Indian wars. He censured the cavalry commander who had disregarded his cautions for "incompetence."[94]

Miles's personal views on the West's native peoples, whom he was so resolutely removing under a national policy now universally condemned, are a little complex.

Like most of his contemporaries, he regarded what were then called Indians as obstacles to the country's inexorable westward expansion. "The wave of civilization was moving over the western horizon," he philosophized. "Its onward march was irresistible."[95] The indigenous inhabitants who had the misfortune to stand in the way were seen as nothing more than barbarians. The southern plains "should be swept of these miserable savages and opened to settlements," he urged General Sherman.[96] A letter to his wife denigrated tribesmen as "wily savages ... governed by all the savage instincts of their nature."[97] No apostle of extermination, Miles advocated disarming and dismounting Native Americans and assimilating them into a Caucasian America.[98]

Yet he sympathized with their plight. The hardened Indian fighter was moved by the sight of the bedraggled hordes who surrendered to his troops, angered by the injustice of treaties violated by his government, and irked by the ineptness of the federal Bureau of Indian Affairs. At his encampment in Montana, Miles set up a camp for displaced Indians, instructing them in farming and sharing with them the outpost's own scanty stock of food.[99]

The shabby treatment of the Nez Percé, after a surrender he had negotiated, aroused Miles's unremitting opposition. He protested the government reneging on allowing them to go home to the Northwest, until the depleted tribe finally was resettled in the territory of Washington eight years later. He continued to lobby unsuccessfully for a return to their beloved Wallowa River valley elsewhere in the territory for two decades until the passing of Chief Joseph in 1904.[100]

The fate of the Apache also distressed Miles. He deplored removal of the tribe to Florida, where they wasted away. "Very bad policy and unjust," he complained in a letter to his wife. More humane, he felt, would have been a reservation of the Apache's choice in their native Southwest.[101]

While harboring no appreciation for Native American culture, Miles did esteem individual chiefs. The Sioux leader Sitting Bull, sinewy and silent, elicited from the colonel the tribute: "No other Indian possessed such power to draw and mold the hearts of his people."[102] Chief Joseph, a dignified presence from the feathers in his braided black hair to his beaded leggings and moccasins, was eulogized as "the highest type of the Indian I have ever known."[103] Even Geronimo, whose perpetual scowl exuded antipathy, impressed the soldier with his intelligence and purposefulness. His "sharp, dark eyes" reminded Miles of those of the sagacious General Sherman.[104]

Such respect — one warrior for another — often was reciprocated. Chiefs with whom he negotiated found him trustworthy. "You never say anything false," the Sioux chief Short Bull complimented him. "You keep every one of the promises you make."[105]

His years among the Western tribespeople, in war and more peaceable encounters, had earned Miles a reputation as something of an Indian authority. Despite a lifelong aversion to scholarship, he supplemented his first-hand knowledge by reading voraciously about the native peoples. He kept up a lively correspondence on Indian issues with politicians and reformers, gave newspaper interviews, delivered speeches, testified to Congress — even wrote an essay for the prestigious *North American Review*.[106]

He was considered in his day an Indian reformer. He was part of the growing movement opposing many discredited policies of the Indian Bureau, including herding the tribes onto large and isolated reservations.[107] He envisioned peaceful cohabitation under strict supervision:

The white man and the Indian should be taught to live side by side, each respecting the rights of the other, and both living under wholesome laws, enforced by ample authority and with exact justice.[108]

Miles's imperious manner — browbeating others with his views and courting publicity — regrettably undercut his influence. But he did gain the ears of important senators and a reformist secretary of the interior, Carl Schurz. His espousal of breaking up reservations into homesteads for Native American families was embodied in the Dawes Act of 1887.[109]

In respites between hostilities, life at the various frontier posts that he commanded was comfortable for Miles and his wife. Their household at Fort Leavenworth, for example, included a housekeeper, nurse, and soldier-servant or "striker."[110] But Mary, city bred, was slow to adjust to the untamed hinterland and her husband's long absences giving chase to his foes.[111] She returned east to Cleveland a few months after arriving in Kansas for the birth of their first child, a daughter named Cecilia (after Senator Sherman's wife).[112]

When reassigned to a new camp in the even less hospitable Yellowstone area of Montana, Mary exiled herself for a year in Cleveland and Washington.[113] Her subsequent trip back west with her sister in 1877 to rejoin Miles was trailblazing — "the first white women to visit that remote region and call a soldiers' camp their home," in the colonel's proud words.[114]

For a man for whom allegiance to others often seemed less than that to the army and his career, Miles's relationship with his wife was remarkably close and enduring. "The companion of my life," he called her with evident attachment.[115] Mary appears to have been the one person to whom Miles, who found candor difficult, could bare his soul.[116] He signed his letters to her with the tender phrases "Ever thine own, Nelson" and "Thine ever loving, Nelson." Another letter, after twenty-one years of marriage, ended: "With lots of kisses I am entirely and devotedly thine own."[117]

The colonel lost both his parents, nine months apart, in 1875.[118] But he and Mary added to their little frontier family in 1882 a son, christened Sherman for his prominent maternal kin.[119]

The hearty fellowship of life at western army posts appealed to Miles. Hosting younger officers or visiting dignitaries in the relaxed setting of his parlor, the commander, hair now flecked with grey and puffing the big cigars popularized by Grant, became a raconteur. His glittering war record provided the aura, and his combat experiences the material, for evenings of engrossing storytelling.[120]

The boyhood hunter also relished the sport offered by western game — sometimes on a grand scale. One six-day hunt in Montana with nineteen army colleagues and five Native Americans felled prey that filled ten six-mule wagons: sixty deer, three antelopes, a mountain sheep, five elk, seventeen buffalo, seventy prairie chickens, and six ducks.[121] Buffalo hunter that he was, Miles nonetheless rued the wholesale slaughter of the bison that once had roamed the West by the millions.[122]

He also undertook a quieter kind of hunting: for financial opportunities. Practically since first donning his army uniform, Miles had tried to supplement his military salary with a civilian nest egg. During the Civil War, he sent much of his pay home to his father to be invested.[123] In his Reconstruction posting, he and his brother speculated in southern timber.[124] Within a year of coming west, he sounded out two generals on acquiring land in Kansas and the territory of Colorado. He then teamed up with his uncle-in-law, Senator Sherman, to invest in real estate in the northern plains — with profitable results.[125] The colonel also helped a nephew who had followed him west to obtain government work and buy prime acreage that eventually earned him a considerable fortune.[126] Miles himself dabbled in real estate in Washington, D.C., becoming a landlord of lucrative properties.[127]

Besides increasing his net worth, Miles also worked assiduously at advancing his career. He jumped at chances to publicize his exploits, hiring a newspaper reporter as a scout in the Red River War and inviting artist Frederic Remington to join his investigatory expedition to Wounded Knee.[128] He feuded with army rivals perceived as impeding his path to promotion.[129] A quarrel over apportioning the credit for the surrender of Chief Joseph ruptured irreparably Miles's long friendship with General Howard.[130] He wearied his superiors with constant complaints that his talents were insufficiently appreciated.[131] One of the most heavily lobbied (by both him and Mary), General Sherman, once proffered a piece of pointed advice: "In due time you will rise to the top of the pile, unless by inordinate ambition you spoil your own chances."[132]

Such self-centeredness was fast marking Miles as an officer who was gifted but difficult.[133] So unflattering a repute reached even his commander-in-chief. Under consideration for promotion in 1890 by President Benjamin Harrison, Miles was told candidly by Senator Sherman: "The President recognized the merits of your service, but thought you were if not disobedient, at least a troublesome man to get along with."[134]

A garrisoned life in the military didn't shelter Miles — never one to shrink from controversy, anyway — from being drawn into the social issues confronting the nation. Amid his Indian campaigns, the colonel in 1880 drew the thankless assignment of presiding over a court-martial case that brought uncomfortably to the fore Americans' inner torment over race. An African-American cadet at the U.S. Military Academy, long the target of racial innuendos, had been found bound and beaten in his room. West Point authorities strained credulity by accusing him of staging the incident. Miles, his once-ardent abolitionism perhaps tempered by a desire to ingratiate himself with the army's top brass, procured a verdict convicting the cadet of deception and lying.[135]

Strife between employers and employees in the fast-industrializing nation also caught up Miles. When a strike in Chicago by Pullman railway car workers and their union allies paralyzed rail traffic throughout the North in 1894, the veteran campaigner against Southern rebels and Indians was conscripted for urban peacekeeping. He was ordered in with a regiment of troops to protect mail service.[136] He felt himself to be at "the very storm-center of an industrial convulsion."[137] The confrontation between laborers, many of them foreign born, and management brought forth the latent nativist and capitalist in Miles. As the unrest grew violent, he asked permission to open fire on strikers.[138] "Revolutionists," he branded them in a letter to his wife.[139] Cooler heads prevailed. President Grover Cleveland and army leaders refused his request—and averted a bloodbath in the streets of Chicago.

Miles's service in the West was at an end. The Native Americans had been hounded into submission. His army rivals for promotion had been outmaneuvered or outlived. His superiors were retiring.[140] Having reached the service's top echelon and held all important commands in the West, the postings open for Miles lay in his native East.[141]

He was now a general,[142] and looked every inch as one. He carried his two hundred pounds with military bearing. The cocked jaw, the piercing eyes, the smoke-grey hair and mustache seemed forged in the fire of battle.[143]

Miles in 1894 took command of most of the eastern seaboard, succeeding his one-time friend General Howard upon the latter's retirement. His New York headquarters placed him gratifyingly near the center of the country's social and political life. His home on Governor's Island became a trophy hall of the general's career—adorned with battle flags, a mounted buffalo head, and Indian artifacts, including a warbonnet bearing the hole of the bullet that felled the brave who had worn it. He swapped reminiscences of the West with the likes of Frederic Remington and Theodore Roosevelt. He commissioned a life-size oil portrait of himself in full-dress uniform. Ever the devotee of the vigorous life, he took up the un-armylike recreation of sailing, as well as two others just bursting upon the public scene: football and bicycling.[144]

The general also composed an autobiography. *Personal Recollections and Observations of General Nelson A. Miles* was a tome of 591 pages, copiously illustrated by engravings and 15 original drawings by Remington. But the book skirted anything remotely controversial in the author's career, apparently for the sake of nascent political ambitions. It confided no new insights into the often momentous events in which he had participated. And it was larded with extraneous tracts. Sales, not surprisingly, were slow.[145]

When the army's crowning position — commanding general — fell vacant the following year, Miles's seniority and stellar record left him the only real candidate. The self-made country lieutenant had reached the pinnacle, treading the footprints of his admired predecessors Winfield Scott, Sherman, and Sheridan. His refined sense of status savored an office in the sumptuous State, War, and Navy Building next to the White House, and a succession of residences nearby in the capital's fashionable West End.[146]

The Miles family cut a prominent figure in Washington society. Mary developed interests in advance of her time, supporting women's rights and (in an ironic foil to her husband's avid hunting) animal protection. Daughter Cecilia led the life of a belle, often in the company of an up-and-coming aide of her father's named John J. Pershing, destined for future military renown.[147]

The general's contributions to the improvement of the army over which he presided, however, proved less luminary. Although he foresaw the outmoding of the cavalry and the potential of gasoline-powered vehicles, Miles recommended nothing bolder than introducing bicycles and motor wagons. He showed little vision for preparing the service for the demands of the twentieth century. While the navy ambitiously built a fleet of modern warships, under the inspiration of Admiral Alfred Thayer Mahan, Miles tinkered at minor upgrading and bureaucratic adjustments.[148]

One innovation attracted hardly the kind of attention the general desired. He redesigned the commanding general's dress uniform, embellishing it with gold embroidery on the sleeves and collar, a striped sash, and a belt of Russian leather piped with gold bullion. The fancywork stamped Miles in the public mind as a strutting coxcomb. Chided Mr. Dooley: "Seize Gin'ral Miles' uniform. We must strengthen th' gold resarve."[149]

Events just beyond the nation's shoreline were about to test the army's readiness. Cuban insurgents were fighting for independence from the disintegrating Spanish empire, and Americans instinctively sympathized. Relations with Spain grew increasingly hostile. But the army that the United States could field against a seasoned European power was basically the same one used to counter bands of ill-equipped indigenous warriors. It had fewer men in uniform — less than thirty thousand — than Spain had garrisoned in its Caribbean colonies alone.[150]

When the blowing up of the U.S. battleship *Maine* in February 1898 in Havana harbor propelled the two countries inexorably toward war, the United States raced to remedy its military deficiency. The size of the army was doubled practically overnight, just four days before the nation declared war in April. Recruiting offices were thrown open, and training camps hastily set up.[151]

Strains in military leadership were papered over. Miles, so aggressive in the field against Confederates and Indians, found himself in the unusual position of counseling restraint. He deplored the jingoistic war fervor stirred up by the yellow journalism of the day, and felt bilateral differences could be settled by arbitration. But his caution cost him the confidence of President William McKinley. Frustrated with both Miles and Secretary of War Russell A. Alger, the president turned to other military advisers and took charge personally in a White House war room outfitted with maps and twenty telegraph wires.[152]

Cuba was chosen as the first target for invasion, after much internal dispute. Puerto Rico had been the preference of Miles and much of the navy's top brass, as offering an easier conquest while buying time for fuller preparation and drier weather in Cuba.[153]

Miles suffered another rebuff in the choice of commander for the Cuban expedition. He was passed over for the ostensibly less qualified Major General William R. Shafter. The latter's immobilizing three-hundred-pound ponderousness and assorted physical infirmities made him an odd selection for the exigencies of tropical combat. The McKinley administration, some speculated, sought to deprive Miles of the glory of a victory in Spain's largest Caribbean colony that might make him a formidable political force.[154]

The near-chaos prevailing at some of the training camps, as the army struggled to absorb a flood of raw recruits, confirmed the commanding general's ill-received cautions about a precipitate rush into war. In the sweltering summer heat of southern camps, men were issued wool uniforms. At Tampa, the camp railhead was choked with three hundred freight cars with no bills of lading. Miles stormed in, ordered the cars opened and their contents unloaded, much of it rotting food.[155]

The ensuing military campaign in Cuba was fraught with similar difficulties. Supplies ran short and transportation scarce. Malaria and yellow fever exacted the toll of which Miles had warned, laying up nearly a fifth of American soldiers. The invaders' attacks were uncoordinated, and resistance stouter than expected. But victories began to be won. Lieutenant Colonel Theodore Roosevelt and his so-called Rough Riders, a colorful amalgam of eastern swells and western Indian fighters, captured San Juan Hill. An American squadron destroyed the Spanish fleet at the mouth of Santiago harbor.[156]

When the U.S. assault began to falter, McKinley dispatched Miles to the war front. His presence seemed to prod Shafter out of lethargy, and a truce was soon negotiated. The three-week contest ended with the surrender of twenty thousand Spanish troops.[157]

Once Cuba fell, the next American military objective became Puerto Rico. Although ranking as Spain's second largest possession in North

America, with a population greater than half of the states of the union (just under one million people), Puerto Rico had been ignored in Washington's war plans.[158]

One reason was the island's relative tranquility. Unlike their Cuban neighbors, Puerto Ricans had raised no armed revolt against Spanish control. They had just been granted, less than a year earlier, home rule. So had Cubans, but the concession somehow meant more to Puerto Ricans. It proved more generous than they had expected, and had been negotiated in large measure by their own local political leader, Luis Muñoz Rivera.[159]

When war broke out with the United States, Spain appealed to islanders to resist the invaders in the spirit of Hispanic brotherhood. Exhorted Governor and Captain General Manuel Macías y Casado:

> Providence will not permit that these countries which were discovered by the Spanish nation the echo of our language should ever cease to be heard nor that our flag should disappear from before our eye.... *Viva Puerto Rico,* always Spanish, *Viva España!*[160]

The island government lined up loyally behind the home country. "We are Spaniards," grandiloquently declared Muñoz Rivera, "and wrapped in the Spanish flag we will die."[161]

An afterthought it may have been, but Puerto Rico began to assume for Americans a certain urgency.[162] Politically, its conquest would help to persuade Spain to abandon the Caribbean. Militarily, the operation must be undertaken quickly before the war ended.[163]

Invading Puerto Rico had been authorized as soon as American troops had established themselves in Cuba, four days after wading ashore. And Miles, who had been pressing for such action for a month, was given command. An expeditionary force was assembled from fresh Stateside regiments mustered at southern seaports and veterans of the Cuban campaign already in the Caribbean.[164]

The twelve thousand American invaders would be pitted against about eight thousand Spanish regulars and a similar number of Puerto Rican militiamen. But the island's defense capabilities were highly suspect. The local volunteers' competence was as uncertain as their loyalty. Aside from a few guns at the capital city of San Juan, the Spanish had no artillery. The two other largest cities, Ponce and Mayagüez, had no defenses at all.[165]

The U.S. convoy set off from Charleston and Tampa for Cuba, and then, four days after the surrender there, steamed from Guantánamo. After the bumbles that nearly had turned the Cuban campaign into a debacle, Miles was determined to mount a smoother operation. The improvements began manifesting themselves at once aboard the troop transports. Instead of pens of suffocation, they were uncrowded, well ventilated, and furnished with hammocks. To avert the confusion that had reigned at dockside in Cuba, care was taken to match men with their gear upon arrival.[166]

Leaving behind him the vexing world of bureaucrats and politicians, and once again leading men into battle, Miles was buoyant. He found his ship, the converted liner *Yale,* "magnificent." He enjoyed the company of his servant's lively English terrier, Jubilee. He basked in four days of glassy seas and clear skies.[167]

As the nine transports and their man-of-war escorts, led by a battleship fittingly bearing the name of Miles's native state, the *Massachusetts,* converged on Puerto Rico, the general hatched a tactical surprise. He was beginning to question the plan to land at Point Fajardo on the island's eastern tip. That was the invasion site anticipated by most people — presumably including the Spanish. But Miles was pondering the findings of an army undercover intelligence agent, a lieutenant who had reconnoitered the island the previous month disguised as a British merchant seaman. The infiltrator had found the south side of Puerto Rico a hive of colonial discontent. On the south coast lay the island's largest city, Ponce, and nearby, at Guánica, a deep-water harbor suitable for a military landing.[168]

Miles proposed to the commander of the naval convoy a change of destination. He suggested that the ships make only a diversionary feint at Point Fajardo, then under cover of darkness proceed to Guánica for a swoop on Ponce. "It is always advisable not to do what your enemy expects you to do," he explained. His navy cohort put aside misgivings and agreed.[169] To safeguard the element of surprise, the change was communicated neither to a second flotilla of transports following two days astern nor to the War Department in Washington.[170]

First morning light the next day revealed to the arriving covey of American warships a picturesque little port flanked by high cliffs. Spyglasses disclosed no defense fortifications. An armed yacht, the *Gloucester,* was sent into Guánica harbor to investigate. Sighting a government blockhouse, the vessel fired at the yellow and red folds of a Spanish ensign flying atop it and steamed into the quiet cove. A landing party rowed ashore. The sailors barricaded the town's single street with stone and barbed wire, and set up a Colt machine gun. A troop of Spanish cavalry appeared on a hill, black belts glistening against their pale uniforms. The machine gun peppered them, killing four. The remaining Spaniards fled, joined by most civilians.[171]

Finding themselves in possession of a deserted town, the sailors on shore unfurled semaphore flags and wigwagged an "all clear" to the waiting ships. The transports throbbed into the harbor, and landed a brigade of infantrymen and a battery of artillery. Doughboys pitched tents along the street. Civilian inhabitants were emboldened to return. Laughing and shouting, they extended the visitors a warm welcome. Soldiers were soon coddling naked brown babies in their laps. Guánicans also showed a shrewd grasp of the commercial opportunities, selling horses to the officers for extortionate sums.[172]

The invasion had been a model of military precision — uncontested and, for the Americans, without loss of life. Moving quickly to capitalize on the surprise landing, troops began clearing the approach to Ponce the next day. They advanced eastward from Guánica to Yauco, where they met their first resistance. Spanish defenders were put to heel, ceding control of the rail line to Ponce.[173]

Ships carrying the rest of the American force chugged the following day into the port of Ponce. The barrels of their cannons glared menacingly at a cowering row of buildings strung along the beach, two miles seaward from Puerto Rico's metropolis. The executive officer of the cruiser *Dixie* went ashore and strode into the harbormaster's office. He demanded of the port captain an unconditional surrender. The Spanish officer gave a resigned shrug, replying that the invaders already held the port anyway. Shortly a delegation from Ponce — the British and German consuls, accompanied by local businessmen, representing the Spanish commander — boarded the cruiser and agreed to surrender the city. Five hundred Spanish troops in Ponce hastily evacuated. The island's largest city had fallen without a shot.[174]

The newly arrived transports unloaded troops that nearly quadrupled the strength of Miles's 3,415-man vanguard. Among the uniformed throngs was a young Signal Corps company commander whose relationship with the general was destined to become more than just professional. Samuel Reber a year and a half later married Miles's daughter.[175]

Columns of American soldiers marched into Ponce the next day in an atmosphere of celebration. Smiling residents peered down from the tall windows and iron balconies of two-story Spanish colonial buildings at a street crammed with bobbing ranks of doughboys in blue shirts, red bandannas, leggings, and wide-brimmed hats with pinched crowns. Bayonets, canteens, and metal drinking cups dangled from ammunition belts angled across their chests. Rifles reclined on their shoulders. American flags fluttered from hand-carried staffs.[176]

A lank Puerto Rican elder searched out Miles and presented him a letter, sewn inside his shirt to conceal it from Spanish authorities. It pledged the Americans the support of "the great masses."[177]

Feted like conquering heroes, Miles and a fellow field commander, Major General James H. Wilson, attired themselves in full dress and took up positions on the balcony of the mayoral palace to preside over an event of great pomp to mark the occasion: a parade of the municipal fire brigade.[178]

The first evidences appeared in what was to become over the years a relentless process of Americanization. Shops in Ponce promptly began to sport signs announcing, "English Spoken Here." Within a day, newsstands were selling a bilingual newspaper called, appropriately, *La Nueva Era* (*The New Era*). Music issuing from the bandstand in the central plaza switched from patriotic Spanish fare such as the "March of Isabella" to American tunes like "Rosy O'Grady" belted out by Yankee servicemen.[179]

Miles issued a proclamation calculated to rally islanders' support by casting the U.S. invasion not as conquest but liberation. The Americans, he asserted, "come not to make war upon the people of a country that for centuries has been oppressed."

> They come bearing the banner of Freedom.... They bring you the fostering arm of a nation of free people, whose greatest power is in its justice and humanity to all those living within its fold.... This is not a war of devastation, but one to give to all ... the advantages and blessings of enlightened civilization.[180]

Such high-flown benevolence did not extend to the Spanish, of course, and against them the general devised a fast-paced, corralling military campaign. His strategy sought to dislodge Spanish troops from their lairs in the island's interior villages and rugged mountain spine, and drive them northward into San Juan. There in the capital on the Atlantic coast, they would find themselves trapped by American naval and ground forces, and compelled to surrender.[181]

To carry out the plan, Miles sent his troops across the island in four columns. Three set forth from the Ponce area and one from Arroyo, forty miles to the east. On the left flank, the smallest column and the only one composed entirely of regulars (1,464 men under Brigadier General Theodore Schwan) headed to Mayagüez, the island's third largest city, and then inward. Another column (3,060 men under Brigadier General George A. Garretson) advanced northward through Adjuntas and Utuado to join the left-flank column at Arecibo. A third column (3,417 men under General Wilson) made its way northeastward through Coamo to Aibonito, high in the mountains. On the right flank, the largest column (4,790 men under Major General John R. Brooke) moved from Arroyo inland through Guayama to Cayay toward Aibonito.[182]

Instead of frontal confrontations, the troops were instructed to rely on flanking maneuvers and skirmishes. The reasons were two-fold: speed and safety. Although sometimes hidebound, Miles was alert to advances in warfare since his Civil War and Indian campaigns — notably the withering power of modern defensive weaponry.[183]

As the regiments of Americans from northeastern mill towns, southern crossroads, and midwestern farms tramped off into the interior of Puerto Rico, the apprehensions of heading to battle in a strange land quickly faded.

They found conditions surprisingly hospitable. The climate was mild. The hills were verdant and the valleys lush with sugar cane. Tropical fruit and rice abounded. People lined the roadsides to greet them. Their commanders inspired confidence.[184]

The cordial reception accorded the invaders by islanders demoralized their Spanish rulers. "The majority of this country [does not] wish to call itself Spanish, preferring American domination," Governor Macías cabled his minister of war in Madrid. "This the enemy knows, and it is proved to him today by greetings and adhesions in towns that are going to be occupied."[185]

Much to the disappointment of Miles, ardent wooer of publicity, press coverage of the Puerto Rican offensive was sparse. While the war in Cuba — with its pitched battles, romantic Rough Riders, and glaring bungles — provided a journalistic bonanza, the quietly efficient operation on the smaller island seemed a dull sideshow. Cuba had attracted a hundred correspondents. Puerto Rico drew only two newsmen at the outset of the campaign, and never more than eighteen.[186]

Outside the gaze of a disinterested press, the military conquest of Puerto Rico proceeded expeditiously. Spanish forces were defeated at Guayama and near Cayey in the southeast. Two ranking Spanish officers were killed and 167 of their men taken prisoner at Coamo. Defenders were driven from their trenches below Aibonito. The Mayagüez garrison was routed, and doughboys marched into the city to the brassy cadences of a military band.[187]

"The army in Porto Rico," marveled Richard Harding Davis, one of the few journalists there, "advanced with the precision of a set of chessmen."[188]

It also advanced unhampered by the tropical fevers that had ravaged American forces in Cuba. Miles had taken the precautions of upgrading health services and imposing a strict quarantine.[189]

An ambush of Spanish troops fleeing Mayagüez across the Rio Prieta — a one-sided encounter that well typified the entire contest between the two nations — took on an historical significance which none of the combatants realized on that warm August day. It turned out to be the last engagement of the Spanish-American War. Word was filtering out to units in the field that President McKinley the previous day had signed an armistice with the Spanish ambassador in Washington. Spain had surrendered sovereignty of Cuba, Puerto Rico, and Guam, and agreed to negotiate future control of the Philippines at peace talks in the autumn.[190]

Across the island guns fell silent and jubilant doughboys flung their hats into the air.[191] An exultant Miles couldn't resist pointing out to the secretary of war the commanding position that his forces had achieved. "Please notice on a map," he cabled Alger, "our troops occupy best part of Porto Rico. They are moving in such strong column[s] that nothing could check their progress."

He reckoned they could have subdued the rest of the island in four more days.[192]

Indeed, it had been for the Americans a textbook campaign. Resistance admittedly had been light, from an unready Spanish army unsupported by adequate defense fortifications or a navy. But Miles had taken maximum advantage of these vulnerabilities, while correcting the lapses on his own side revealed so painfully in Cuba.[193]

The war in Puerto Rico had occupied just nineteen days. It had produced only six engagements. Casualties among the attackers had been mercifully few. Of the 6,343 Americans who took part in combat, 7 were killed and 36 wounded. The Spanish toll ran roughly ten times greater. As Miles later wrote: "Not a single reverse or disaster occurred. Not a single soldier, gun, color, nor an inch of ground was captured by the enemy."[194]

The victorious invaders became an army of occupation. As de facto military governor, the general took steps to secure the allegiance of the United States' new subjects. He pressed Spain to release Puerto Rican political prisoners held there. He enforced proper behavior by soldiers toward civilians. When an Illinois militiaman was found to have cheated a local restaurateur with Confederate money, he was made an example—court-martialed and sentenced to thirteen months of solitary confinement in a federal penitentiary.[195]

Miles waded into the brewing national debate over the future of the war's territorial spoils by advocating that Puerto Rico be absorbed as a permanent possession. U.S. control, he believed, would bestow on islanders the benefits of American government and culture, and give the ruling country domination of the Caribbean.[196]

However lasting was to be American sovereignty in Puerto Rico, calls arose soon after the end of hostilities to bring the troops home. The volunteers agitated to return to hearth and workplace, and home front pressures became a political imperative. The war had been over less than two weeks when Miles felt obliged to propose sending back to the United States a third of his manpower. The War Department decided to demobilize entire regiments, and authorized the general to immediately ship home cavalry units from New York and Pennsylvania.[197]

Miles also ordered himself home. It was to be a return of majestic triumph. His wife and children had come to the island to accompany him back to the mother country to which the conqueror had so deftly delivered Puerto Rico. The general and his family trooped aboard a transport with one of his repatriating regiments, the Second Wisconsin Volunteers. For the homecoming, the ship's bow and stern had been adorned with Puerto Rican palm fronds as garlands of victory.[198]

As the bulky transport plowed through the fog of an early September morning into New York harbor, the ship's railings lined with Wisconsinites straining for their first glimpse of Manhattan, other vessels let off a welcoming chorus of hoots and whistles. Sailors cheered. Crowds at the docks waved handkerchiefs. A shipboard band struck up "Hail to the Chief."[199]

A crewman on a tugboat called out: "Miles, old man, you took care of your boys, and you don't have to square yourself with the widows and orphans."[200]

The tribute doubtlessly pleased the general, but distressingly little more was to follow. After a health inspection, the transport was shunted to Weehawken, New Jersey, where the Wisconsin volunteers were whisked aboard trains for home. Many muttered their disappointment. They had expected to revel in the big city's adulation. Miles himself bade farewell to the officers, and slipped away with his family. They were ferried to Manhattan and driven to the Waldorf-Astoria Hotel. The general ambled in wearing his fatigue uniform, stirring few glimmers of recognition.[201]

A gala dinner at the hotel, celebrating the army's return, turned out to be for Miles an experience less honorific than chagrining. His wooden rhetoric was outclassed by the bombastic oratory of another war hero, Theodore Roosevelt.[202]

There was to be no grand parade up Broadway, their commander at the forefront, for victorious troops from Puerto Rico.

Nor did an elaborate welcome await in Washington. Miles passed through crowds of well-wishers at Union Station, in a jaunty blue serge suit and broad-brimmed white hat, back to sedentary duties at the War Department.[203]

The glories of triumph over Spain enjoyed a luminous afterglow in civic auditoriums and meeting halls across the country. The lecture circuit kept the war's celebrities busily booked. Among those most in demand were Miles and Roosevelt. On the platform, they were fulsome in mutual compliments. "It was not his taste to remain at a desk," the general said of the former Rough Rider, "but he drew his sword among the bravest of the brave on the field of battle."[204]

Other public pronouncements of Miles, regrettably, sat less comfortably.

Testifying before a presidential commission a few months after the war, he issued a stunning charge: meat supplied to U.S. troops in the Caribbean had been tainted. The canned beef had been unfit to eat. The refrigerated beef, worse still, had been processed in unhealthy chemical preservatives — producing "what you might call embalmed beef."[205]

The allegation created a sensation. "Tons of Bad Meat Sent to Troops in Porto Rico," cried a headline in William Randolph Hearst's *New York Journal*.[206] The War Department was incensed at a defaming of its commissary service. The McKinley administration was affronted at an aspersion on its conduct of the war. There were efforts to remove him. Roosevelt rallied to Miles's defense. Other veterans of army chow lines agreed that the beef was unpalatable, but few were prepared to declare it unhealthy.[207]

The controversy, ironically, sullied an important advance in military provisioning. The American soldiers had been among the first in history to be served refrigerated meat.[208] Miles's charges eventually fizzled. Two government investigations found them unsupported, and both he and the army's commissary general were censured.[209] But the accusations, for all their recklessness, proved prescient. They foreshadowed an explosive exposé of the meat packing industry seven years later by muckraking novelist Upton Sinclair.[210]

Miles's unbridled tongue and unbending obstinacy were about to earn him powerful enemies. He unnecessarily alienated the new secretary of war, Elihu Root, with petty complaints and requests to procure his son's entry to the West Point military academy. He feuded with him over control of the army, then broke completely by opposing Root's plan to reform the military using modern management techniques.[211]

Theodore Roosevelt was transformed from ally to antagonist. The process evidently began when Miles rashly suggested in a speech in 1901 that Roosevelt, who by then had become vice president, hadn't led the storied charge up San Juan Hill. "What a scoundrelly hypocrite the man is!" fumed Roosevelt. The enmity deepened when Roosevelt became president upon McKinley's assassination and clashed with Miles repeatedly over matters of policy.[212]

Their division epitomized a split in the nation as a whole on one contentious issue: territorial expansion. The ardent expansionism of Roosevelt encountered an unlikely opponent in Miles. The general had actively aided the country's enlargement — clearing the western frontier of indigenous peoples for American settlers, sending expeditions to Alaska, conquering Puerto Rico and urging its retention. But the bevy of acquisitions won overseas in the Spanish-American War prompted him to rethink. He concluded that expansionism betrayed the nation's founding principles. Thereafter he tried to curtail the U.S. role in Cuba. He opposed American occupation of the Philippines and advocated its independence. Puerto Rico, however, remained an awkward anomaly in his anti-imperialism, likely because he had been too close to its acquisition to countenance letting it go.[213]

Disengagement in the Philippines became for Miles a personal crusade. It endeared him to the anti-imperialism movement, stirring talk of a presidential candidacy. But the stance infuriated Roosevelt. The general had long asked to be sent to the Philippines to examine conditions. Perhaps simply to be rid of him for a while, the administration finally consented. It was a trip that trod sensitive ground. He investigated allegations of atrocities by

American troops against Filipinos resisting U.S. colonization. In Guam, he interviewed the imprisoned Philippine nationalist leader Apolinario Mabini. The general's findings led to the conviction of several servicemen for mistreating prisoners.[214]

The episode of vintage Miles acrimony, occurring in 1902 just months before mandatory retirement at age sixty-four, was his recessional. The reforms of Root and Roosevelt, so repellent to him, were to abolish the office of commanding general and substitute a general staff. Miles would be the nation's last commanding general.[215]

But before mustering out, the defiant old general had up his sleeve one more escapade. As part of a drive to shape up what he perceived as a flabby army, Roosevelt had ordered all officers to prove their fitness by riding horseback ninety miles in three days or else face possible retirement. The challenge was too tempting for the proudly robust commanding general to resist. Less than a month before retiring, he headed west to the open horse country of Oklahoma. Saddling up at Fort Sill, he galloped the ninety miles to Fort Reno in nine hours and ten minutes flat, exhausting a succession of horses but arriving himself exhilarated.[216]

But the last in the exchange of derogatory gestures was to come from Miles's nemesis in the White House. On his final day in the army, the Roosevelt administration, with studied calculation, treated the event as perfunctorily as the routine discharge of a buck sergeant. The official announcement was brutal in its brevity:

> The retirement from active service by the President, Aug. 8, 1903, of Lieut. Gen. Nelson A. Miles, United States Army, by operation of law, under the provision of Congress approved June 30, 1882, is announced. Lieut. Gen. Miles will proceed to his home. The travel enjoined is necessary for the public service.[217]

No tribute. No words of appreciation. No mention of forty-two years of service in warfare against three diverse foes as one of the nation's most valorous and successful field commanders. "Nothing," grumped Roosevelt, "will hire me to praise him."[218]

Muted as his departure was, Miles had no intention of quietly retiring to a rocking chair at the Old Soldiers' Home.

Wily investing had bestowed the financial security for him and Mary to retain their prominence in Washington society.[219] Their grand home, tended by a staff of four African-American servants, opened its gilded doors to the influential and well-connected.[220] The absence of their married daughter and West Point cadet son, however, made the place sometimes seem a little empty. Miles missed "the children."[221]

A deeper loss occurred a year after retiring. While spending the summer at West Point to be near Sherman, Mary passed away. Miles had leaned on her emotionally more heavily than his magisterial demeanor ever revealed, and was left with an abiding loneliness.[222]

Becoming a widower put no brake on his vigorous pace of life — calling on government chums, tooling around in a flashy automobile, frequenting clubs in Washington and New York, wintering at a hotel in Boston.[223] His son, building a promising career in the army, married in 1909 the daughter of his father's long-time personal secretary.[224] Both of Miles's children named sons in his honor.[225]

Links with the past were renewed. Miles made frequent pilgrimages back to his Massachusetts hometown, to welcomes almost reverential for its famous progeny.[226] He addressed Civil War veterans' groups, and lent his presence to patriotic functions.[227]

The Indian wars evoked special nostalgia. Long after tomahawk and army carbine had ceased to be raised in anger, the general returned to the Southwest. Reunited with another Indian fighter and former scouts under a large tent, he sat down with his old Native American foes — those from a different tribe every night for two weeks — to relive old campaigns. Over the years, Miles assembled a collection of Indian artifacts eyed enviously by museums and galleries.[228]

The general collaborated on a quasi-documentary film project of the American West with William F. "Buffalo Bill" Cody, an Indian scout-turned-showman whom Miles had known since frontier days. But insistence on scrupulous authenticity eventually provoked his departure. The film fared no better with critics.[229]

Puerto Rico occupied a smaller niche in Miles's retirement interests. Plans for a series of historical markers commemorating the triumphal military offensive against the Spanish pleased him. But he couldn't restrain a typically quarrelsome response, challenging the reported surrender date.[230]

Never modest about propagating his life's accomplishments, the general cranked out in 1911 a second autobiography. While less verbose and blandly circumspect than his first one fifteen years earlier, *Serving the Republic* cast little new light on the man or his exploits.[231]

Shedding his army uniform freed Miles to venture into the arena of partisan politics that long had tempted him. The general had drawn sporadic mention as a candidate for president since the glories of his Indian campaigns in the late 1880s. While publicly downplaying or ignoring such speculation, he clearly relished the attention and regarded it as eminently befitting a man of his qualifications.[232]

First to evince presidential interest in the newly retired general was the Prohibition party. Temperance had been for Miles a lifelong canon. From his father he inherited a zealous conviction of the evils of alcohol, and put it into practice in his various military commands. In the Reconstruction South, he organized Lincoln Temperance Societies among freedmen. At frontier forts, he periodically banned the sale of liquor. "Probably as many men [in the western army] lost their lives by the use of alcoholic liquors," he contended, "as were killed by Indians." His personal lobbying helped persuade President Rutherford B. Hayes to issue an executive order forbidding liquor sales on military posts. Such ardor made Miles a natural favorite of prohibitionists for their party's banner in 1904.[233]

The nomination of a minor party, however, fell short of the general's ambitions. Hitherto a rock-ribbed Republican, Miles recognized that the enmity of presidential nominee Roosevelt currently deprived him an elective future there. He became a Democrat. Impelled by support from a few factions of the party and a satisfying sense of revenge against Roosevelt, the general pursued the Democratic nomination. He made the rounds of the party faithful touting his war record, anti-imperialism, aversion to labor unions, and constitutional conservatism. At the nominating convention in St. Louis, Miles attracted just two votes, both from his old Indian-fighting bailiwick of Kansas.[234]

Rallying gamely behind the winning nominee, New York lawyer Alton B. Parker, Miles campaigned hard against the incumbent Republican, attacking his "extravagant ideas of expansion." Roosevelt, elected by a landslide, commented derisively that the general's political efforts left him "amused."[235]

Although disappointing, the foray into the presidential wars earned Miles a political payoff from his adopted party. The Democratic governor of his home state gave the general a position in the militia where he had begun his military career four decades earlier. He served for a year as adjutant general.[236]

Suggestions arose of a candidacy for governor of Massachusetts or New York, but generated no groundswell.[237] Miles made one more try for elective office. He rejoined the Republican party in 1913 to seek nomination for a congressional seat that had fallen vacant in his home district. He failed, and glumly forsook politics.[238]

As Miles watched the nation drift, for a third time, toward war, he followed events closely. On the eve of what was to become World War I, he traveled in 1913 to the Balkan tinderbox that soon would ignite it.[239] He visited his son, serving as military attaché in Sofia, Bulgaria, and cast his professional eye on war preparations. "I am afraid," he warned prophetically the following year, "that one of the most terrible wars in the history of the world is at hand."[240] He recommended plowing money into two new weapons destined to reshape modern warfare: submarines and airplanes.[241]

But the general was prepared to offer more than advice. Eighteen days after the United States entered the war in 1917, Miles, an active seventy-eight years old, volunteered to organize and lead an expeditionary force into Russia. The War Department politely declined. He drew some solace from the choice of his former aide Pershing to lead the country's fighting men in Europe.[242]

The only command left the silver-haired general was the gentler assignment of leading a troop of his grandchildren about Washington. No battlefield honors brought more enjoyment. His vivid remembrances made granite statues and pedestaled effigies come alive before their young eyes. The bronze general on horseback was their grandpa's tough, grizzled uncle-in-law William Tecumseh Sherman. The austere figure seated in marble was the kindly president who had scratched "A. Lincoln" on his commission as a brigadier general.[243]

A favorite outing — as much for Miles as the grandchildren — was the circus. The daredevilry, the wild beasts, the pageantry of color and music seemed to appeal to his own sense of showmanship. The Barnum and Bailey Circus's visit to town one day in May 1925 was an event eagerly awaited. Miles paraded the youngsters and his son's mother-in-law to the circus ground. Before entering the big top, the general accosted owner John Ringling. "You know I never miss the circus," he bellowed to the pleased impresario. The group filed into seats in the grandstand, and the ringmaster beckoned in the first act. During the performance, Miles suddenly expired. He was eighty-five years old.[244]

At graveside, old animosities were interred with him. The ceremony at Arlington National Cemetery summoned even the president, Calvin Coolidge, a tribute that would have gratified the general so heedful of rank. The self-advancement, the vanity, the prickliness were forgotten. Miles was remembered only for his enduring contribution under arms, as one of the nation's greatest fighting soldiers.[245]

6

Commander B.F. Tilley

First Governor of American Samoa, 1900–1901

The gently rolling swells of the South Pacific were parted by a slender surf boat, oars flashing rhythmically in the grasp of ten burly Polynesians done up smartly in white shirts, blue sarongs, and red waistbands. To the chants of a coxswain, the craft sculled with the smooth power of a piston.[1]

Slipping through an opening in the reef, it coasted across a glassy lagoon to an arc of sparkling sand. Palms and breadfruit trees shaded a cluster of unwalled, round houses with thatched domes, like beehives on posts.

From the beached boat arose a spare figure whose dark beard set off the white duck uniform of a United States naval commander. He straightened himself and stepped ashore. The first governor of American Samoa was paying a call on one of the villages in his domain.

The United States' delve into empire probably came closer in Oceania than anywhere else to the exotic Victorian adventuring of a Lord Curzon or a Cecil Rhodes. There was a culture, so utterly alien to Americans, to be discovered. There were trappings of imperialism, suitably impressive, to be devised. There were dictates, on matters beyond the ken of superiors back home, to be improvised.

But any suggestion of a South Seas idyll, an imperial playground, is deceptive. Along with the rewards came also the malaise of empire.

In the cabin of the station ship, baking in the tropic sun at its mooring in Pago Pago harbor, the heat could be suffocating and the sense of isolation intense.[2] A displaced westerner might fall prey to that scourge of the outposts of empire everywhere: the bottle.

And relations with one's own compatriots could prove more perilous than with the native islanders. Accompanying Commander B. F. Tilley on the surf boat visits to his constituents was a fellow officer who entertained a sharply conflicting view of proper gubernatorial decorum.[3] The brooding disapproval of the station's medical officer was a smoldering ember ready to burst into flame.

His torrid South Seas realm lay a world apart from the chill waters of New England where Tilley had originated. He was born in 1848 into an America learning of far-off Samoa through the explorations of Captain Wilkes. His parents, Benjamin Rogers Tilley and Susan Easterbrookes Tilley, named their son in honor of two fathers: his own and one of the nation's.[4]

Benjamin Franklin Tilley grew up in the nautical setting of Bristol, Rhode Island, thrust on a finger of land into the midst of Narragansett Bay.[5] Surrounded by water, a career at sea seemed a natural progression. After public schooling in Bristol,[6] he enrolled at the U.S. Naval Academy. While the country was locked in civil war, he studied academic war-making in the more tranquil precincts of Annapolis. He found the life of a midshipman a perfect match, and graduated in 1867 first in his class.[7]

The promising young ensign first went to sea in the Atlantic upon which he had gazed longingly most of his life. He served aboard the flagships of two of the country's fleets, including his namesake, the USS *Franklin*.[8] Even amid the glacial pace of promotion in the post–Civil War navy, Ben Tilley (as he was known) advanced in grade swiftly to lieutenant.[9]

He was introduced to the South Pacific, later to become so well known to him, on a charting expedition aboard the *Pensacola*. The vessel was an early steamer that looked like a sailing ship, low and sleek with three masts for raising canvas if desired. It was soon to host another future American ruler of Samoa — transporting Albert Steinberger from San Francisco to Honolulu with Hawaiian king Kalakaua.[10]

Tilley returned to the Atlantic for a two-year tour of duty, but found his thoughts increasingly absorbed by a young woman. Back home, just after turning thirty years of age in 1878, he and Emily Edelin Williamson were married.[11] The family grew to two sons and a daughter as Tilley spent twenty years alternating between the classroom and the quarterdeck. He did four stints of teaching at the naval academy. Annapolis became, for the itinerant mariner and his family, a homey mooring between voyages. He also trained sailors in ordnance at the Washington Navy Yard.[12]

When the Spanish-American War broke out in 1898, Tilley, now a commander, had been captaining his own vessels for two years. In the war, he skippered the *Newport* as it helped blockade Havana and captured a trove of Spanish ships.[13]

After the war, he was placed in charge of the navy yard at Norfolk, Virginia.[14] It was there that he received an assignment that — both for him and the navy — constituted a plunge into the unknown.

In a classic case of big powers high-handedly carving up the globe, a

Commander B.F. Tilley, 1890s (Naval Historical Foundation).

commission representing the three nations with proprietary interests in Samoa had just partitioned the archipelago. The United States, already owning rights to a naval station at Tutuila under the agreement negotiated by Commander Meade in 1872, was awarded the eastern portion of the islands. (Germany took the western sector, and Britain swapped its claims for territories elsewhere in the Pacific and west Africa.)[15] The navy was deputed to administer the new acquisition. The place needed a governor (initially given the more customary naval title of commandant).[16]

For the fledgling imperial power, it was a position virtually without historical antecedent. The only forerunner, the naval governor of Guam, had been on the job just six months. Tilley, with three decades of experience in leading men under varied conditions, was chosen to introduce American rule to Samoa.[17]

The governor-designate was a man whom seafaring seemed to have leached and honed like a mollusk. His lank frame and lean face looked purged by the salt air.[18] As a young officer, his neatly trimmed beard and moustache were as black as the ocean's depths, but by the time he was named governor the whiskers were flecked with grey. The hairline was retreating from a high forehead.[19] The mild eyes, almost soft in their gaze, imparted a sense of serenity — what Alphonse Daudet has called "that placidity of expression given by the habitual presence of great expanse and far horizons."[20]

Tilley was to bring the outward manifestation of U.S. authority in Samoa — in the form of a naval station — along with him, quite literally. The navy had purchased a site for the installation on Pago Pago's inner harbor. It had hired a San Francisco contractor to build a modest little complex of a dock, a corrugated iron coal shed, and assorted outbuildings. The construction materials were to be hauled there by the incoming governor.[21]

To import American naval governance to Samoa, Tilley was assigned an unprepossessing scow neither American nor a man-of-war. The *Abarenda* lay low in the water as if weary with overwork. A small cabin crouched at the center of its main deck, in front of a tall funnel. Two small masts stood fore and aft. The vessel had been built seven years earlier in Newcastle, England, as a merchant ship. The U.S. navy, caught short of ships in the Spanish-American War, bought it and refitted it as a collier to ferry coal and ammunition to its fleet in Cuba. Now the versatile *Abarenda* was transmogrified for a new mission. After carting the governor and the makings of a naval station to Pago Pago, it was to double as his office and living quarters.[22]

Bidding farewell to his family, Tilley eased the ship out of Norfolk harbor on an April day in 1899. A voyage around Cape Horn, along coastal Chile, westward to the *Bounty* mutineers' Pitcairn Island, and Tahiti brought the little expedition three months later to Samoa.[23]

The serpentine harbor at Pago Pago drew him inward, an alluring Siren, as it had his predecessors Wilkes, Meade, and Steinberger, to the magnetic presence of Mount Pioa (The Rainmaker), a green volcanic fist thrust skyward, washed by mists at one moment and bathed in sunlight the next.[24] But unlike the Americans before him, he came as his country's designated overlord.

It was a realm centered on one island, Tutuila, a tangle of jungly basalt peaks about twice the size of Manhattan.[25] The new territory also encompassed six ancillary isles and atolls, one them just offshore and the others flung eastward across one hundred thirty miles of the Pacific.[26]

The newest tract of American soil hadn't yet been given a name, other than that of its unbuilt military facility. For expediency's sake, the entire possession was called simply "U.S. Naval Station, Tutuila."[27] It wasn't to acquire the name "American Samoa" for eleven years.

The commandant began to survey his dominion. The panorama of Polynesia parading before him — the *lava lava* sarongs of beaten tree bark, the elaborate body tattooing, the hair dyed white with lime, the chiefs with their staffs and fly switches — must have intrigued even so well-traveled a seaman as Tilley.[28]

This far corner of the South Seas had been dealt to the United States by its fellow western powers, but the Samoans themselves had yet to be consulted on the arrangement. Sixty years of relations with Americans, generally friendly and occasionally even eliciting unsolicited requests for annexation, had led to a presumption that islanders would readily consent.[29] And so it proved.

Tilley and the chiefs drew up, in the spring, a deed of cession. It granted all but the outer islands — still under negotiation — to the United States "to rule and to protect."[30] The document was a three-page, typewritten declaration, in English and Samoan, of quaintly-worded fealty.

> Let all the nations of the earth know and all people dwelling therein, that in order to set aside all possible doubts in the future concerning our true desire at this time on account of the Rule of the United States of America ... we do confirm all the things done by the Great Powers.... We depend on the [U.S.] Government and we hope that we indeed and the Government will be prosperous, that the Government will correctly guide and advise us.[31]

The bottom bore, in careful turn-of-the-century penmanship, the signatures of twenty chiefs.[32]

The signing was followed two weeks later in April by a showy ceremony. Hundreds of Samoans, American sailors, and Germans visiting from their country's side of the archipelago gathered on a little bluff above the construction site of the naval station-to-be. The excavated earth below them, sporting a newly-built coal shed and an unfinished dock, evidenced the ambitions of the new sovereign. The assembled pupils of the London Missionary Society school in Fagalele sang "America" in well-practiced English. The Stars and Stripes was briskly run up a flagpole.[33]

The flag-raising was repeated in June in the territory's eastern sector, the Manu'u islands, sixty miles away.[34]

As the diplomatic niceties were being tended, other matters crowded upon the governor. Nothing in his background had prepared Tilley for the responsibilities of presiding over an alien populace. Yet rulings awaited on a myriad of issues largely unfamiliar, from the trivial to the foundational. From the outset, his actions were marked by a sensibleness and sensitivity that few might have expected. Somehow this uninitiated outsider seemed to possess an instinctive touch for the right balance of firmness and deference to traditional ways.

Edicts began to issue from the swaying deck of the moored *Abarenda*. After disposing of a few items of internal housekeeping and public order (imposing customs duties and banning sale of liquor to Samoans),[35] Tilley turned quickly to the fundamentals setting the future course of the little American protectorate.

Foremost was an issue of anguished concern to Samoans: loss of their land to foreigners. So complete was the buyout that the claims of overseas landowners collectively exceeded the actual total acreage of Samoa, an international tribunal had found in 1894.[36] To halt further alienation, Tilley promulgated among his first ordinances a ban on sale of land to outsiders. It has come to be regarded as perhaps the navy's single most important action ever undertaken in Samoa.[37]

Meanwhile, land was wrested back to local control. The navy already had bought most foreign-owned acreage, and Tilley rushed to acquire the remainder. Virtually all of the territory's land was put into the hands of islanders or their government — where it has remained to this day.[38]

After living among the Samoans eight months, versing himself in their conventions, the governor felt ready to devise for them a form of government. As in protecting their land, Tilley strived to preserve islanders' traditional social organization. Any Samoan law or custom not conflicting with U.S. laws, he proclaimed, would continue.[39] He retained age-old internal political boundaries.[40] He kept the system of rule by chiefs or *matai*, and their assembly, the Fono.[41] As prefect in each of the island's three districts, he appointed the ranking chief.[42] Tilley did, however, cut the number of chiefs. "Too many chiefs," he complained to the navy secretary, and reduced them to one per village.[43]

His philosophy of government, unlike much of the domineering imperialism of the era, was one of respectful restraint:

> I considered that the best way to govern these people was to let them, as far as possible, govern themselves, by continuing their good and time-honored customs and gradually abolishing the bad ones.[44]

Their ostensibly new system of government introduced only two institutions unknown to Samoans.[45] One was western-style courts. Traditional enforcement of codes of social behavior by family settlements, under the aegis of chiefs, was replaced by written laws and neutral judges.[46] It was a change whose consequences would reach far — farther than foreseen, perhaps, as Tilley was to discover in one of the new judicial system's first tests.

A man named Fagiema had gone fishing and caught a skipjack, a fish reserved solely for high chiefs. He kept the forbidden fish. His family was grilling it for dinner when the high chief improvidently happened by and witnessed the offense. His response was swift and harsh. He ordered Fagiema's house burnt to the ground, his banana and taro patches uprooted, and the entire family evicted from the village.

When the governor learned of it, he did the hitherto unthinkable. He had the high chief arrested and hustled into court at the naval station. In a spartan courtroom of whitewashed concrete, a judge convicted him of violating U.S. law. He was sentenced to make restitution to Fagiema, and suspended as high chief for a year. The blow, however, fell not only on the chief. His public humiliation, as Tutuila's senior chief was to observe years later, undermined the traditional authority of chiefs throughout the territory.[47]

The other new institution of government, novel to Samoans, stirred no such ruckus. Tilley was concerned that the islands lacked protection against threats, external or internal, to their peaceful welfare. Security rested with a tiny police department and a handful of U.S. marines.[48] To fill the breach, the governor concocted the idea of a local constabulary, part police and part military. It won the navy's blessings. And so was born the Fita Fita (Guard), a small force of Samoan peacekeepers, trained and supervised by the navy. Barefoot and fitted out in white shirts, blue ankle-length *lava lavas*, and red waistbands — a garb later made even more dashing by turbans — they soon became a familiar local sight. So effectively was the Fita Fita to perform in ensuing years that no marines were deemed needed to be stationed in Samoa until World War II.[49]

The commandant reshaped not only the governance of Samoa, but also the face of Samoa itself. In true American send-the-dirt-flying style, Tilley undertook a series of ambitious public works projects. Finding that Tutuila had no thoroughfares beyond crude trails, he laid out its first highway. It rimmed the southern coast along flat shorelines and reef shelves.[50] To facilitate travel by sea, passages through reefs reckoned dangerously narrow were widened by the severe expedient of underwater blasting.[51]

Such cavalier destruction of reefs, and similar depredations on the natural world, took place with the sublime obliviousness of an age of environmental innocence.

The need also became apparent for a seat of government more permanent than the *Abarenda*, rocking at anchor in the harbor. Conditions aboard the station ship, for working and living, were atrocious. Under the relentless tropical sun, the temperature in the stuffy cabin never dipped below ninety degrees. The solution, as in colonial outposts the world over, was to build an official proconsular residence.

Tilley chose a site on a ridge between the inner and outer harbor, sufficiently elevated to catch cooling mountain air currents and to position the symbol of U.S. authority where few could miss seeing it. The favored hilltop turned out to be too small to accommodate the edifice planned, however, and builders suggested scaling back the design. The commandant would have none of it. Instead, he ordered the crest of the hill flattened. On this lopped-off promontory was built a white, two-story mansion. It has housed territorial governors ever since.[52]

The commander's move to quarters on land freed the *Abarenda* for more useful, if less exalted, service as an interisland transport. Its decks often crowded with as many as fifty Samoans, it ferried people and cargo between Pago Pago and Apia in the western part of the archipelago.[53]

The governor, meanwhile, barged into the hazardous waters of economic controls. The islands' major export — and virtually its only one — was the dried coconut meat known as copra, the source of coconut oil for household products ranging from candles to soap. Tilley felt that coconut growers (mostly Samoans) were being shortchanged by the traders (mostly outlanders) who bought their copra. Led by his sense of economic justice rather than any particular expertise in marketplace economics, he made the copra trade a government monopoly. Copra was sold to the territorial government instead of private traders. The government paid farmers a price reckoned to be fair, and earned itself a tidy revenue that promptly became the dependency's primary income. But the takeover of their business, not surprisingly, enraged traders.[54]

The remote cluster of islands that had come under U.S. stewardship also possessed, at the dawn of the twentieth century, pressing social needs. It was a place devoid of public services.[55]

Among the most evident wants was education. American Samoa didn't lack for schools—fifty-seven of them. But all were run by Christian missionaries, and provided only the most basic education. They had succeeded in rendering nearly all islanders literate in their own language, but schooled in little else.[56] Tilley was eager to raise the level of education and introduce English as a "world language." He proposed founding a public school system. The navy proved less enthusiastic, however, and denied his request for $5,000.[57] Tilley's plan didn't materialize during his tenure, but it had been set in motion. A subsequent governor two years later, using money from the copra fund, opened near Pago Pago the territory's first public school.[58]

Another of Samoa's needs was health care. Americans had inherited a land unserved by medical attention in the western sense, save for occasional doctors dropping by from the other side of the islands or from passing ships.[59] The first regular medical care arrived on its shores in the person of a member of Tilley's crew of territorial founders: the medical officer.

Dr. Edward M. Blackwell was cast into undoctored Samoa as a novice surgeon, a lieutenant junior grade just starting a naval career.[60] He found himself suddenly the family physician of five thousand South Seas islanders.[61] Inaugurating a medical practice as novel to him as to them, he began commuting from the anchored *Abarenda* to operate a clinic at the harborside town of Fagatoga. He made calls in his own distinctive boat, a flat-bottomed skiff painted white and adorned with a red cross.

To meet a growing demand for his services, Dr. Blackwell opened a dispensary in a vacant trader's store near the waterfront. The dilapidated shop was spruced up into a diminutive three-bed ward for naval patients. Next door was built a thatched Samoan *fale* house for islanders under his care. The mean little set of buildings went by the grandiose name of The Government Hospital.[62]

To reach more distant places under his medical responsibility, when the governor took his excursions by surf boat and Fita Fita oarsmen to (in the doctor's words) "get in touch with the natives," the young surgeon traveled with him.[63]

The brand of rule introduced by Tilley was popular among most of his new American subjects. Despite a predilection toward the United States, Samoans had harbored nagging apprehensions about how they might fare at the hands of their incoming sovereign. They worried that military administrators might trample callously upon the *fa'aSamoa* or Samoan way of life. Instead, they got a governor who, while exercising autocratic authority, protected their customs and championed their interests. They were reassured.[64]

After more than a year of his governorship, a collection of chiefs petitioned Tilley's reappointment with a ringing endorsement:

> Our great fear at first was, that we would be cast aside in our government; our customs, which we honor, would be changed or interfered with, we feared the rule of the soldier (military rule). But now our doubts are finished. We are satisfied because the good Governor you sent us has been faithful and kind to us and has kept his promises. He has made good laws, with wisdom.[65]

The chiefs' encomium extended even to the imported U.S. justice system, whose acceptance had been less than smooth. "In days gone by, such laws as we had were indiscriminately broken, but now the wrong-doer fears the law."

Missionaries, often severe judges of secular rulers, echoed their parishioners' high regard for Tilley. "He has made many friends, and he has won great respect," averred the local leader of the London Missionary Society, the largest such group in Samoa. "Indeed, I have heard natives expressing the hope that he might remain for a long time to come."[66]

An American visitor described islanders' admiration in the condescending tone of the period: "The natives ... looked upon him as their 'White Father.'"[67]

Reflecting on his year and a half in the islands, the governor could draw much satisfaction. His annual report to his superiors in Washington for 1901 painted a genuinely rosy picture of a territory launched forth on American affiliation with its populace contented.

> Summing up the results of all that has been done since Tutuila has been annexed by the United States, it will be found that there is now in this island an organized and successful government, under which the natives are quiet and happy and are advancing rapidly to a higher civilization.[68]

Not that Tilley had no detractors. The traders, who constituted the bulk of the business community, bitterly resented his government usurping the copra trade.[69] Other, more dangerous foes lurked even closer at hand.

Ben Tilley appears to have been a gregarious man, and one who enjoyed a nip of liquor. The languid pace of the tropics and the separation — not just from home and family (to which a navy skipper becomes inured) but from the fellowship of shipboard life among large numbers of men at sea — might have spawned a yearning for sociable diversion. Whatever the impulsion, rowdy drinking sessions among the governor and naval cohorts began to attract notice.

Dr. Blackwell, a confirmed teetotaler, viewed the bouts of drinking admonishingly. So did at least one other. A woman was impelled to pen a letter to the navy secretary in Washington accusing the governor of unbecoming conduct.[70]

The navy took the allegation seriously. Tilley, rounding out his second year as governor, was ordered home in April 1901 in preparation for a court-martial on charges of "drunkenness and immorality."[71]

A preliminary investigation was conducted in Washington, and six months later all Stateside participants in the pending trial — Tilley with his wife, the court-martial panelists due to hear the case, witnesses on both sides — were shipped off to Samoa under what must have been awkwardly close quarters aboard the battleship *Wisconsin*.[72]

One of the passengers was the governor's disaffected former colleague, Dr. Blackwell, who had completed his tour of duty in the islands several months before. Upon reaching Pago Pago, Tilley invited the doctor to the cottage where the governor and his wife were staying. They discussed the case. Blackwell told him "I would have to testify that he was drunk but could not testify that he was immoral."[73]

The presiding officer of the court-martial, Rear Admiral Robley D. Evans, a long-time acquaintance of Tilley's, sleuthed around Samoa. He detected "something peculiar about the way the charges had been prepared." His probing turned up "no evidence to sustain them," and he suggested they be dropped. The navy demurred, however, and the trial went forward.[74]

In a makeshift courtroom on the *Wisconsin*, for four days in November, the governor's deportment was scrutinized. Navy prosecutors called three witnesses. Two wound up testifying in Tilley's favor. Only Dr. Blackwell claimed to have seen the governor intoxicated, and under cross-examination conceded that Tilley might only have been suffering from the heat. In support of the governor, defense attorneys had lined up a hundred witnesses, some to be fetched from outlying islands by steamer. In the end, fifteen or twenty of them took the stand. The verdict: not guilty.[75]

The decision cleared Tilley, but failed to lay the matter to rest. The presiding officer excoriated the navy for ordering the trial. "In all my experience with courts-martial," declared Evans, "I have never known a case so weak as this one, nor one where there was so little ground for charges."[76] Dr. Blackwell, on the other hand, saw collusion. "All the other witnesses who caroused with him testified for him and, as the saying goes, 'Dog won't eat dog.'"[77]

The sailors of the *Wisconsin*, who had journeyed halfway around the world for the proceedings, offered their own juridical opinion. Out of earshot of their officers, they chorused a satirical verse to the tune of a popular song of the day called "Just Because She Made Those Goo-Goo Eyes":

> Just because they said he hit the booze,
> They sent us on a ten-thousand-mile cruise.
> The court it didn't think that he ever took a drink,
> And so they proved he never hit the booze.[78]

His navy record officially wiped clean, but his reputation unavoidably stained and his feelings bruised, Tilley resumed the territorial governorship from which he had been suspended for the court-martial.[79] But he remained in Samoa only a few weeks. He won promotion in December to captain—some solace—and was placed at the helm of the navy yard at Mare Island in San Francisco Bay. There, in a nice historical congruence, he succeeded another pioneering figure in the nation's expansion into the Pacific: Admiral Glass.[80]

After several years of shore assignments, Tilley must have welcomed a return in 1905 to the sea. He commanded the battleship *Iowa* in the north Atlantic.[81] He also had the opportunity to mete out military justice from the opposite side of the bar where he himself recently had stood, serving in 1906 on two courts-martial.[82]

Tilley joined the rarefied ranks of flag officers as a rear admiral in 1907 while overseeing the navy yard at League Island in Philadelphia.[83] It was an honor he wasn't long to savor. Three weeks later, at the navy yard, he suddenly passed away. He was eleven days short of his fifty-ninth birthday.[84]

Among the family whom the admiral left behind was a son who would carry onward his father's naval calling, as well as his name. Benjamin Franklin Tilley, Jr., when he lost his father, was a midshipman at the naval academy, embarked on a career in navy blue.[85]

The admiral was buried at Annapolis, where he had begun his life in the navy forty-four years earlier.[86]

In Samoa, Tilley's towering esteem long outlived him. Fifty years after the departure of the first governor, the compiler of a history of the territory found approbation any ruler would envy. "To this day," he wrote, "no Samoan has ever spoken an ill word of him."[87] Today Tilley is little remembered and his legacy less personal. It lies in a spirit of restraint and trust, between home country and scion, that he inaugurated a century ago.

7

Senator Joseph B. Foraker
First Congressional Overseer, 1899–1909

Neither his own times nor history has been kind to Joseph B. Foraker.

He was a man all too easy to scorn. A machine politician. A wrangler whose combativeness turned opponents into hostile enemies. An agent of the forces of reaction. A malfeasant driven from office by scandal.

But the popular reputation has obscured, beneath the forbidding exterior, a more tender underside. The man who appeared so hard and hidebound had pulsing within him an unlikely strain of compassion and sense of social justice. These urges put him, in certain respects, ahead of his era which so often seemed to have passed him by. And they equipped him to provide signal service to his country's overseas possessions.

Foraker's attraction to politics, as well as his more latent idealism, surfaced early.

He was the scion of aspiring Western European forebears, of mixed English, Scottish-Irish, and German extraction, who had emigrated to the Atlantic seaboard of the alluring, newfound continent.[1] In the early nineteenth century, both sets of future grandparents headed farther westward. The impetus wasn't so much economic as moralistic: repugnance toward slavery. They left Virginia and Delaware for regions opening up for settlement free of slaveholding beyond the hazy ridges of the Appalachians.[2]

The Fouracres—as the old Devonshire family name then continued to be rendered—and the Reeces transplanted themselves in the southern hills of the newly organized state of Ohio near the village of Rainsboro. Two of their offspring, Thomas A. Foraker and Margaret Reece, married. On the day after Independence Day in 1846, they became the parents of a son.[3] The devout Methodists named him for the author of a denominational commentary on the Bible: Joseph Benson.[4]

Ben, to which the name quickly was shortened, grew up in a frontier household that was entrepreneurial and religious. His father operated not only a farm, but also the flour mill and sawmills built by his maternal grandfather at a place that had come to be known as Reece's Mills. The family spent much of its Sundays at church. The Sabbaths were interludes of quiet in an otherwise strenuous boyhood. School homework for Ben competed with farm chores. In summertime, when work was finished he churned up the local swimming holes, gaining repute as an accomplished swimmer.[5]

From early years, he displayed a marked seriousness. While sharing the favorite rural pastime of fishing — an enjoyment he would retain throughout his life — the hours whiled away dangling lines at Rocky Fork of Paint Creek weren't idle. He relished the opportunity for long talks with the family's other keen angler: his mother.[6]

At the age of ten, when most boys idolized military heroes or Indian fighters, Ben was excited by a politician: the colorful John C. Frémont, then campaigning as the first presidential candidate of the new Republican party. The youngster rigged up a pole from a sapling, implanted it at the family farm, and hoisted atop it a homemade Republican banner.[7] When the next Republican standard-bearer, Abraham Lincoln, stumped through Ohio four years later, the teenager traveled to Cincinnati to hear him speak.[8]

Cooly at ease before others, Ben discovered what he later was to describe as "an aptitude for declamation."[9] At school he excelled at the then much-studied art of elocution — a skill later to serve him well in public life.[10]

The farm boy was a prodigious reader. "Ben," as it later was said of him, "read down all the dip candles in the house." He once won a prize for memorizing an astounding total of 1,396 verses of the Bible. He read aloud to his mother *Uncle Tom's Cabin,* a searing indictment of slavery by Harriet Beecher Stowe that instilled a lasting abhorrence of racial inequality.[11]

At age fifteen, gird with nothing more than a backwoods country-school education, the teenager made his start in the wider world. His first job also was his inauguration into what would become almost a lifetime of government service. At the county seat of Hillsboro, he worked as a clerk for an uncle who was a local officeholder, the county auditor.[12]

But Ben's tenure at the county courthouse was brief — interrupted, as were the lives of millions of other young men his age, by the outbreak of civil war. Nine days after his sixteenth birthday in 1862, he enlisted in an Ohio infantry regiment. He fought as a foot soldier in the Chattanooga and Atlanta campaigns, marching to the sea with General Sherman. In the risky duty of messenger, during action at Savannah and Bentonville, Arkansas, he twice was singled out for bravery. His performance under arms advanced the buck private to first lieutenant and brevet captain.[13]

Among fellow combatants drawn to the field of battle by a diversity of motives, from misty romanticism to forcible conscription, for Foraker one impulsion loomed paramount: he was fighting the institution of slavery. The zealous young bluecoat had wanted the war to continue, he declared in a letter to his mother, "until slavery is abolished, and every colored man is made a citizen, and is given precisely the same civil and political rights that the white man has."[14]

He emerged from the war, which had decimated three-quarters of his regiment, as a nineteen-year-old mature beyond his years.[15] He brought with him new career ambitions and sharp awareness of his deficient schooling. The ex-soldier returned to his home state determined to improve his qualifications. He studied for a year at Salem Academy. He then enrolled at Ohio Wesleyan University, training to become a lawyer.[16]

While at the university, in the central Ohio community of Delaware, Foraker began courting a fellow student at its sister institution for women. Julia Bundy, not quite a year younger than he, shared his southern Ohio roots—her hometown of Wellston lay about fifty miles east of Rainsboro—and his zeal for politics. She was, if anything, more of a political devotee than he.[17]

Senator Joseph B. Foraker, circa 1902 (Library of Congress).

Politics had occupied as much a part of her upbringing as dolls and sewing needles. Her family home had been a throbbing political rotunda. "Every day," she recalled, "men of affairs stopped at our farmhouse for twelve-o'clock meal and to feed their horses." Ever since, "politics have set for me an absorbing pace." Those politics were dyed-in-the-wool Republican. "[I took] the Republican Party to my heart when I was ten."[18]

The patriarch of this consummately political household, Julia's father, was Hezekiah S. Bundy, a friend of Lincoln and periodic congressman. He pieced together a disjointed congressional career of three nonconsecutive terms spaced over thirty years. He was temporarily out of office when Foraker wooed his daughter.[19]

Foraker forsook Ohio Wesleyan — but not Julia Bundy — after attending two years. Tantalized by a new college being set up in Ithaca, New York, he joined the first class to enroll at Cornell University. He graduated a year later in 1869, top among its eight members. The young graduate was admitted to the bar, moved to the burgeoning Ohio River town of Cincinnati, and began practicing law.[20] His profession established, he and Julia wed.[21]

His abilities as a lawyer proved sufficient to earn Foraker, a decade later, a judgeship on the city's superior court.[22] But more compelling were his talents as a political organizer. He teamed with another shrewd political manager, millionaire businessman Marcus A. Hanna, to build the Ohio Republican party apparatus into one of the nation's most powerful electoral machines. But the two men had divergent geographical bases — Foraker in Ohio's south and Clevelander Hanna in the north — and personal ambitions of their own. They soon became less partners than rivals.[23]

Political boss Foraker decided to come out from behind the scenes and place himself before the voters. He ran in 1883 for Ohio governor. As a debut in elective politics, it was hardly auspicious. He lost.[24] Defeat in his big opportunity for high office, however, left Foraker remarkably undismayed. At thirty-seven years old, he was still politically young and endowed with an assurance that precluded brooding. "The first defeat," his wife said, "never touched my buoyant husband."[25] He promptly began preparing for a re-match. In the race two years later, he sharpened his debating thrusts and fattened his campaign chest with money from Hanna, and had the satisfaction of beating his former vanquisher.[26]

As governor, Foraker showed a touch of the humane as well as a flair for the dramatic. One of his proudest achievements was an overhaul of the state's archaic criminal justice system, softening the stiffest punishments, reforming Dickensian conditions of incarceration, and — true to his party's business tenets — making prison industries profitable.[27]

He attracted national attention for spurning a gesture by President Grover Cleveland intended to help heal sectional divisions lingering from the Civil War. The president, in a spirit of reconciliation, ordered in 1887 the return of captured battle flags. The unreconstructed Union veteran in the Ohio statehouse refused to comply. "No rebel flags will be surrendered," he vowed, "while I am governor."[28]

Foraker was gaining a reputation as a fierce partisan armed with withering verbal firepower. He was a tall young man with cropped hair and flowing moustache. The profile was combative and the eyes flashing.[29] His was not the oratory of smooth-tongued charm, but of the rousing exhortation and the biting censure. It was fired by an emotiveness that seemed churning just beneath the surface. It was set off at other times by a temper notoriously short fused. "Fire Alarm Foraker," he was coming to be called. His speeches were events to which Ohioans flocked in treks of many hours over rutted back roads. A boy who later became a prominent Washington newspaperman once traveled twenty-nine miles in a springless wagon to hear Foraker hold forth.[30]

He served as governor two terms, but in seeking a third term in 1889 again tasted defeat.[31] He went home to Cincinnati and resumed his law practice. He became the archetypal legal fixer for the business barons of the Gilded Age, representing a dozen major industrial and transportation corporations. The experience cemented unshakably an identification with concentrated wealth.[32]

A more tangible legacy of so moneyed a clientele was a financial recompense to all appearances munificent. The Forakers had exchanged a life of toil on the farm for a life of comfort in the metropolis. But Julia Foraker, perhaps out of dutiful modesty, disputed the perception that she and her husband had become people of means. She claimed to be "rich only in children."[33] The childly wealth numbered five: three daughters and two sons, two of them perpetuating the names of their parents.[34] All grew up in a home resounding in politics. "Political talk," Mrs. Foraker recounted, "was mother's milk to my children."[35]

The household's other politico found ample time, while minding his corporate clients, to moonlight in Ohio politics. When the governorship which he had lost came up for filling in 1891, Foraker and other Republican moguls turned to another party stalwart who also found himself unceremoniously out of office. William McKinley had served in Congress fourteen years, rising to one of the leaders of the House of Representatives, until ousted in 1890 by a partisan redrawing of his northern Ohio district.[36] Although allied more strongly to Hanna than Foraker, McKinley asked the Cincinnati lawyer, likely in tribute to his speaking prowess, to nominate him for governor at the state party convention. Foraker obliged with stirring adulation that brought McKinley the nomination by acclamation.[37]

The former governor, meanwhile, kept close watch on his own political fortunes. An interest in national office had been tweaked during his second term in the statehouse when mentioned in passing for a spot on the 1888 Republican presidential ticket.[38] The speculation evaporated, but other ambitions welled up when the elder statesman of Ohio politics, Senator John Sherman, that year did seek the party's presidential nomination. Foraker cast covetous eyes at the Senate seat that Sherman might vacate. Sherman's subsequent failure to land the nomination (won by Benjamin Harrison) cost Foraker not only a chance for advancement but also his friendship with Hanna. The party co-leaders fell out over Foraker's support of Sherman in a manner felt to have been half-hearted.[39]

When another Senate opportunity beckoned seven years later, Foraker marshaled all his organizational skills to grabbing it. Outmaneuvering Hanna, he seized control of the state party convention in 1895 and wrested from it an endorsement of himself for the Senate.[40]

In the ensuing campaign, however, his own candidacy wasn't the only one demanding Foraker's services. McKinley, completing a second term as governor, had emerged as a leading contender for the Republican nomination for president.[41] As party boss, Foraker owed his Ohio confrere staunch support. He gave it. With his usual bombast, he nominated McKinley at the GOP national convention in 1896 in St. Louis. He then stumped the country on behalf of the successful nominee, joining McKinley at campaign's end on the by-then famous gingerbread front porch of his house in Canton.[42]

The voters sent both candidates to Washington. While McKinley was packing for the White House, a new Republican majority in the Ohio state legislature (which at that time elected senators) rewarded Foraker with the Senate seat so long craved.[43]

His triumph was tarnished only slightly when, the very next day after taking office, he was joined in the Senate by Hanna. His rival had procured appointment to succeed Sherman, now secretary of state in the McKinley cabinet.[44]

In the Senate, Foraker was a formidable presence, physically and orally. His six-foot height and broad shoulders radiated authority. His blue eyes brimmed with certitude. His thinning white hair and droopy white moustache lent an aura of seniority. His attire bespoke a man of importance: frock coat, wing collar, Chesterfield overcoat, derby hat, and in summertime a white linen waistcoat. His voice rang as clear as a gong and voluminous enough to reach the back row of any assembly hall in the land.[45]

He had made a name for himself as an orator, on the campaign trail and at his party's national conventions. For his speeches in the Senate chamber, the galleries filled. Spectators were treated to histrionic spectacles, as the senator from Ohio turned the clever phrase and skewered the opposition.[46]

But the same volatility that made Foraker a riveting speaker also made him, for many, a ticklish customer. He was heeded as a constitutional lawyer and respected as a legislator. Less flatteringly, he was seen as impetuous, highly strung, and unsparing toward foes.[47]

It was a temperament practically the opposite of the new president's. McKinley was cautious almost to exasperation, deliberative, diffident, unflappable.[48] Yet the two colleagues, forged in the same crucibles of the rural frontier, the Civil War, and turbulent Ohio politics, in Washington worked together productively. "I knew him," Foraker wrote later, "rather intimately."[49] The relationship never approached that between McKinley and Hanna, rooted in manifest affection. Foraker and the president regarded themselves as friends, but friends united less by warmth than mutual self-interest. They shared professional esteem for each other and broad agreement on most public issues of the day.[50]

When restiveness in Spain's colonies in the Caribbean fired the United States with dreams of imperialistic glory, Foraker showed himself more expansionist than the president who is so often associated with the policy.[51] He was blithely unencumbered by the twinges of conscience felt by McKinley, or the reluctance of Hanna to becloud the business climate. Extending the nation's influence abroad — and its borders — had no more ardent advocate in Washington than the senior senator from Ohio.[52]

He early championed the insurgency in Cuba, and used his position on the Senate Foreign Relations Committee to urge American intervention. He chafed at the guardedness of McKinley, who in his inaugural address had cautioned: "We must avoid the temptation of territorial aggression." Foraker, to the discomfiture of his fellow Ohioan, in the spring of 1898 called for war against Spain. Not long after, the beleaguered president asked Congress to declare war.[53]

Once the war had been won and the territorial spoils collected, Foraker was outspoken for keeping them. He saw the acquisitions of the Spanish-American War as the foundation of a colonial empire which, as an emergent world power, the United States ought rightly to be assembling.[54] And the empire of his fertile vision was no mere scattering of refueling stops and isolated atolls:

> As a matter of simple business policy we owe it to ourselves to retain the whole…. Share no patience with those who preach of retention of a coaling station or a single island — England, Russia, Germany, or France will gobble them up.[55]

Foraker's driving expansionism over the years played no small part in establishing his country, just as he had sought, an overseas suzerain. Besides the prizes from Spain, while the war still raged in 1898 he helped to annex Hawaii.[56] He labored to finesse through a balky Senate in 1901 a treaty granting the nation exclusive right to construct and control an isthmian canal in Panama.[57] He worked to buy the Virgin Islands from Denmark in 1902, a deal aborted and eventually consummated fifteen years later.[58]

His most direct contribution to offshore America was still to come. Finding itself suddenly heir to a bounty of outlying possessions after the

Spanish-American War, the United States scrambled to assume the unaccustomed role of colonial overlord. It was a role that the country, itself a former rebellious colony, hitherto had spurned. But the apostate anti-imperialist plunged into its new responsibilities with zest.

To oversee the acquisitions, Congress in 1899 created three committees: one for Cuba, another for the Philippines, and a third for "Pacific Islands and Porto Rico." (The corrupted spelling of Puerto Rico's name prevailed on the mainland at the time.) This last panel was put under the chairmanship of Foraker.[59] As Cuba and the Philippines went their independent ways, it was to become the only one to endure (in varied forms) to the present day.

The stability prevailing in Foraker's domain of Puerto Rico, in contrast to the insurrection inflaming the Philippines and the prompt liberation promised Cuba, gave the Ohioan the opportunity to take the lead in writing constitutional history.[60] He tackled the assignment with the absorption of a constitutional scholar and the dexterity of a legislative tactician, mixed with flashes of a quality few might have expected: the crusading fairness of a Lincolnian Republican.

Newcomers to the business of governing overseas dependencies, Foraker and his colleagues had to start at the very beginning. The first task was the foundational one of deciding just how the possessions were to fit into the American system of government.

The treaty ceding the conquests from Spain — the Treaty of Paris of 1898 — had dodged the constitutional issue by handing it over to Congress.[61] After tortured deliberation, lawmakers came up with a solution that annexed the acquisitions to the nation without making them an integral part of it. The new appendages were cloaked with American sovereignty. "Porto Rico," as Foraker told the Senate, "belongs to the United States of America."[62] But the possessions were denied the full, automatic guarantees of the Constitution and, unlike their fellow territories on America's continental frontier, anticipation of eventual statehood.[63]

Their position in the body politic settled, however untidily, the dependencies next needed civil governments. Lacking a regnant pattern of their own to follow, the architects of American imperialism looked overseas. The model borrowed was that of the British Empire crown colonies.[64] In its protectiveness of London's central control, the prototype appealed to the executive department delegated to administer Washington's new charges. Its head, Secretary of War Elihu Root, espoused "tutoring" possessions deemed unready for self-rule. He proposed an accordingly restrictive version of the British system that conceded the new American subjects little voice in their government.[65]

Conspicuously missing from the War Department blueprint was a most basic democratic institution: an elected legislative assembly.[66] Foraker had been able to abide a broad, ill-defined second-class constitutional status for Puerto Ricans and other territorial people. But at denying them so prominent a feature of the American tradition of representative government, he rebelled. The omission, like much of the empire planners' imperiousness, was tinged with a tone of racial, or at least cultural, superiority.[67] The man who had been stirred as a boy by the plight of slaves, and later had taken up arms against the slaveholding South, could not countenance such slighting of Americans of darker skin. Although the machine politician was hardly a utopian democrat, he insisted that the United States show more openness.[68] "We had a general duty," he explained later, "to govern that people in accordance with the spirit of our institutions...."[69]

A local governing body, moreover, represented for Puerto Ricans an unfulfilled dream. In a belated attempt to shore up its tottering Caribbean empire, Spain in 1897 had agreed to give islanders an elective assembly. But just six weeks after the reform was to have taken effect, the Spanish-American War broke out. The promise never materialized.[70]

Foraker drew up his own sketch for a territorial government. Not surprisingly, it bore strong resemblance to the governmental structure of the federal entities most familiar to Americans: their states. There would be a governor (appointed by the president) and, most decidedly, a legislative assembly. The parliamentary body would comprise a lower house to be popularly elected and an upper chamber to be appointed.[71] He expected selection entirely by voters to follow. "Nobody will be happier than we when we can give over the whole matter to themselves," he declared with what was to prove lucid prescience. "I hope and believe that the day is not far distant...."[72]

While neither a model of pure democracy nor new in concept to Puerto Ricans, Foraker's legislative body would extend them greater self-rule than most of their Caribbean neighbors. British Virgin Islanders, for example, weren't to gain an elected assembly for fifty years.[73]

In framing a government for Puerto Rico, Foraker also sought to be generous financially. The war had left an already poor island destitute. "Poverty, bankruptcy, and ruin prevailed everywhere," he was distressed to learn.[74] The hard-pressed dependency consequently would be exempted from federal income tax.[75] And the principal monetary link — trade — would be freed up.

The senator, indeed, was prepared to abolish all duties. But opposition from mainland agricultural interests, notably sugar producers wary of island competition, rendered the proposition politically impracticable. So Foraker forged a compromise. He agreed to a nominal tariff on trade with the new motherland of 15 percent of prevailing rates, with revenue retained on the island to bolster the strapped territorial treasury. The levy would end as soon as the new insular government began raising money of its own, and the president was authorized to invoke free trade at any time.[76]

More accustomed to representing the moneyed and influential moguls of the corporate boardrooms, Foraker seemed to take a penitent's delight in helping a poor and powerless people. "The Porto Ricans have been favored in the matter of taxation," he boasted, "with the most liberal and generous provisions that have ever been made for anybody by our Government...."[77]

In this founding-father exercise, the issue perhaps most vexing to Foraker — and to Puerto Ricans — concerned citizenship. Although there had arisen from islanders no outcry to become citizens of the country that had just conquered them,[78] the flush of magnanimity accompanying the United States's sudden rise to imperial power generated within the new world power a movement to bestow the presumed honor of American nationality. The gesture was recommended by a commission McKinley had sent to study conditions in Puerto Rico, and the administration seemed receptive. Citizenship was urged by many Americans, out across the land and in the halls of Congress.[79]

One of its most staunch advocates was Foraker. His master plan for governing the new possession would anoint islanders with citizenship en masse and at once.[80] Anything less, he felt, would betray American egalitarian ideals:

> We concluded ... that the inhabitants of that island must be either citizens or subjects or aliens. We did not want to treat our own as aliens, and we do not propose to have any subjects. Therefore, we adopted the term "citizens."[81]

Scarcely had the ringing calls for citizenship been uttered, however, before sober reconsideration began to set in. Extending citizenship to Puerto Ricans, it dawned on some, might obligate Americans to do the same for Filipinos, whose larger numbers and greater "foreignness" made them less welcome candidates for such beneficence.[82] Citizenship for Puerto Ricans also suggested to many Americans a closer connection to the mother country than they were prepared to accept. It might imply eligibility to become a state of the union.[83]

Citizenship disappeared from the McKinley administration's agenda for Puerto Rico.[84] Support in Congress dwindled. Yielding to the hard political realities, Foraker backed away from full U.S. citizenship and settled for a status reckoned to be the best he could extract from resistant lawmakers. He proposed designating the islanders "citizens of Porto Rico, and as such entitled to the protection of the United States."[85] The ambiguous phrase was to define — and, just as often, muddle — Puerto Rican nationality for the ensuing seventeen years.

Despite disappointments along the way, the governing plan for Puerto

Rico which Foraker shepherded into law in the opening months of the twentieth century — to be known thereafter as the Foraker Act — constituted a legislative and constitutional landmark.

Mindful perhaps that he was writing law for posterity, for historians, for generations of outlying Americans, the senator had labored with special care. Being Foraker, he did roar. He bluffed. He cut deals. He sprang surprises. But, by dint of mighty effort, he also evened his temper and bridled his tongue, save for the occasional relapse.[86] An old friend back in Ohio, well acquainted with his comrade's legendary testiness, marveled: "Just exactly how the Foraker I knew years ago controlled his temper, through the many provocations he had to endure, I am somewhat at a loss to know."[87] Colleagues in Washington were surprised to observe unusual patience, tolerance of dissent, and readiness to compromise.[88]

The bill's successful journey into law in April 1900 earned its author the gratitude of his party and his president.[89] Foraker, remarked McKinley appreciatively, "did things."[90]

Affirmation of a more substantive sort soon followed. The constitutional ingenuity of the Foraker Act was upheld a year later by the Supreme Court. In a series of rulings that have come to be called the Insular Cases, the court agreed that constitutional protections needn't apply fully in annexed territories — the Constitution, in popular parlance, doesn't follow the flag — and that those places and their inhabitants occupy a constitutional frontier zone somewhere between foreign and domestic. Foraker the constitutional authority was corroborated.[91]

In the laboratory of day-to-day practice in the dependency for which it was written, Puerto Rico, Foraker's plan of government functioned well. The territory's first civilian governor, Charles H. Allen, concluded after a year's experience that Congress had legislated as best "as it possibly could."[92]

Higher commendation came a few years later. President Theodore Roosevelt in 1906 paid a visit to the island, incidentally making history as the first president to leave the country while in office.[93] On his return, he sent a note to Foraker impelled by something deeper than courtesy, for the two men then were barely on speaking terms. "All those competent to judge," Roosevelt wrote, "are as a unit in feeling that the law for the government of the Island is one of the best bits of legislation ever put upon our statute books." The tribute became for the senator a prized trophy.[94]

Among Puerto Ricans themselves — largely excluded from the process of framing a government for their own island — reception to the Foraker Act was mixed. Local leader Luis Muñoz Rivera, whose attitude toward American rule see-sawed, in a stinging letter to McKinley denounced the law as "unworthy of the United States which imposes it and of the Puerto Ricans who have to endure it."[95] After living under its provisions for some years, however, a delegation of prominent Puerto Ricans made their way to Cincinnati to thank the law's author. It was a gesture that he always would remember warmly.[96]

Some of the objectives that had eluded Foraker during his bill's arduous passage through Congress began, one by one, to be realized. Rapid economic recovery and an influx of local tax revenues in Puerto Rico hastened the demise of the tariff to which he had grudgingly acceded. Little more than a year after the law took effect, McKinley proclaimed the free trade that the senator had sought.[97]

The Puerto Rican legislative assembly became elected entirely by the people in 1917 — as Foraker had hoped, but regrettably too late for him to witness.[98]

The issue of granting American citizenship to Puerto Ricans continued over the years to wax and wane in public sentiment. But it was a goal from which Foraker never wavered. The midwesterner had grown fond of his new Caribbean compatriots and championed their fitness for citizenship. Perhaps in their Latin effervescence he felt a kinship of temperament. He could have been speaking of himself in describing them as "of quick and excitable temper." He added that "they are at the same time patient, docile, frugal, and most of them industrious."[99]

As an interim step toward citizenship for all, Foraker tried in two successive Congresses to relax the naturalization laws to allow Puerto Ricans who had immigrated to the mainland to become U.S. citizens.[100]

The endorsement of American citizenship for the islanders by President Theodore Roosevelt in 1905 injected new vigor into Foraker's crusade. The senator promptly reintroduced his legislation.[101] In a private letter, Roosevelt told Foraker: "I most earnestly hope that it will be put through as speedily as possible."[102] The hope was forlorn. Even presidential support couldn't secure enactment. Subsequent advocacy by Roosevelt and his successor, William Howard Taft, as well as inclusion twice in Republican party platforms, proved no more effective.[103] Foraker's dream of citizenship for Puerto Ricans would have to be deferred.

More than just a governmental framework for Puerto Rico, the Foraker Act became for the expansionist United States a model much copied.[104] Its author had anticipated so from the start, and deemed its wider use "a distinction and honor I have always appreciated."[105] The plan has served as a pattern, modified for local conditions and current political trends, for the government of every American overseas possession. Its imprint remains stamped plainly today on America's little empire in the Caribbean and Pacific.

Foraker volunteered more direct help in designing governments for two Pacific dependencies under his congressional jurisdiction. He drafted plans for replacing improvised military regimes in Guam and American Samoa with governments—on the Puerto Rican model—duly constituted by law. His proposals cleared the Senate, but languished in the House of Representatives. The legislative stalemate set up those islands for a long wait. It would be half a century before Guam would receive a government formally organized by Congress. Samoa still awaits one.[106]

The senior senator from Ohio, husky and restless like a monument in motion, had become in the nation's capital a figure of importance, both politically and socially. It was a standing enhanced by a chosen mode of life unusual in the Washington of his day. Most of his fellow senators left their wives and children back in their home states, visiting Washington only for congressional sessions and procuring temporary lodgings near the Capitol. Foraker had other ideas. From his very arrival, he had established himself in Washington full time. And his politically attuned wife had come with him.[107]

They desired in the capital a home that was large—commodious enough for entertaining the political elite, and, in the era before congressional office buildings, for the senator's legislative offices.[108] The Forakers had bought a corner lot on fashionable Sixteenth Street, eight blocks north of what was then known as the Executive Mansion, now the White House.[109] They hired the architect of the elegant Library of Congress, just completed to great acclaim, to design a suitable house.[110] Its price: the then-astronomical sum of one hundred fifty thousand dollars.[111]

There arose in 1897 a four-story mansion of yellow brick as imposing as the senator himself. A heavy, columned porch anchored the front, a balcony jutted above, and a massive parapet rimmed the roof like a castle. Visitors entered a palatial interior of Neoclassical mantels and mural-adorned ceilings. The second floor contained a ballroom in the style of the eighteenth-century French court.[112]

The place instantly became one of Washington's most prestigious addresses. Guests of honor at the first dinner party were President and Mrs. McKinley, attended by Vice President and Mrs. Garret A. Hobart, and cabinet members with their wives.[113] Formal dinners for dignitaries thereafter were routine, prepared by a large household staff. The affairs often were rushed together on the shortest of notices. Julia Foraker, dark hair heaped stylishly atop her head, might return from her afternoon round of social calls to be told that the senator had invited a dozen friends for dinner.[114]

The swirling social venue also was a lively home for the Foraker family. The eldest son, known by his middle name of Benson, served as secretary of a Senate committee on which his father sat, until embarking for the Spanish-American War.[115] The youngest daughter—named, like her mother, Julia—was married in the ballroom. In true Foraker magnificence, the occasion was embellished by the presence of President and Mrs. Theodore Roosevelt.[116]

The demands of a high-profile life in Washington, however, didn't permit Foraker to neglect his responsibilities in Ohio. The senator returned regularly to the state that he represented, keeping in touch with constituents, delivering speeches, tending his political machine. On such visits home, a great delight was to indulge his love of fishing. With relish, he would loosen his necktie, plop a wide-brimmed straw hat on his head, grab a fishing rod and tackle box, and escape to a lake. A stringer of fish at the end of the day brought as much satisfaction as many a Senate parliamentary victory.[117]

Back in the capital, people were glimpsing in Foraker, the power broker and man-about-town, a social conscience of which few had been aware. The burning sense of racial equity, which had influenced his legislative efforts in regard to Puerto Ricans, was glinting forth in other directions.

Toward Chinese immigrants, for one. An influx of thousands of coolies into California had unleashed a backlash of labor displacement fears and virulent racism that in 1882 had shut American portals to Chinese workers. When the exclusion law came up for renewal in 1902, Foraker fought it. He felt the measure would "discredit us" and "work prejudice." While succeeding in curtailing its scope, he was unable to prevent the law's reenactment.[118] Defending the dreaded hordes of the Yellow Peril was a thankless undertaking, but it won quiet respect in some quarters. Secretary of War Taft privately commended Foraker for "the fight you made in the Senate in behalf of decency in treatment of that nation."[119]

But the racial minority accorded Foraker's stoutest patronage were African-Americans. Theirs was a cause less than entirely respectable at the turn of the twentieth century, even in the party of the Great Emancipator. Detractors accused the senator of political posturing, of pandering to Ohio's black voters.[120] And it was a cause that would cost him dearly politically. It would earn him the enmity of his president and the day's most popular politician, Theodore Roosevelt.

The two men ostensibly were political soul-mates on the race question. They had become acquainted, indeed, at the first Republican presidential convention each had attended in 1884 in Chicago, by working together to install a black delegate as temporary chairman of the proceedings.[121] When Roosevelt as president in 1901 had entertained black leader Booker T. Washington, one of the first African-Americans hosted at the White House, Foraker was quick with praise.[122]

Later, however, the senator began to question the president's commitment to improving the condition of black people. Roosevelt's resort to gunboat diplomacy in 1906 to spare Cubans an outbreak of civil disorder underscored, for Foraker, an absence of comparable concern for a racial minority at home victimized by institutionalized segregation and vigilante violence. "It is important to protect Cubans in Cuba," he chided Roosevelt, "but it is even more important to protect Americans in America."[123]

Disenchantment flared into outrage when Roosevelt later that year took harsh punitive action against a battalion of African-Americans accused of a shooting rampage in the Texas town of Brownsville. On evidence that many deemed suspect, the president ordered all one hundred sixty-seven men discharged from the army dishonorably.[124]

The white-maned lawmaker took up their case with the ardor of a young defense attorney. With help from a biracial group of civil rights advocates,[125] he gathered every scrap of information he could turn up and dissected it with lawyerly precision. From the stacks of letters and newspaper clippings heaped around him in the office of his home arose mutters that foretold for his wife a brewing storm. Foraker concluded that the evidence against the soldiers was flimsy and based on a presumption of guilt.[126] They had been denied protections entitled any American. The soldiers, he said, asked for "no favors because they were Negroes, but only for justice because they are men."[127] He persuaded the Senate to investigate.[128]

The fury of the president at the impugning of his authority as commander-in-chief and his moral leadership on the race issue burst into the open at a banquet in 1907 before the assembled national press. Both Roosevelt and Foraker were guests of a group of Washington journalists known as the Gridiron Club. The president could remain in his seat no longer than the first course of oysters and green turtle soup before popping up to speak. Glowering at the senator, he passionately defended his Brownsville action. Foraker, ashen faced, rejoined with equal feeling. He implored humane fairness for "many men with splendid records as soldiers, absolutely innocent, yet branded as criminals, and dismissed without honor."[129]

Retribution was to follow. Visitors to the big yellow house dwindled. Many Washington dining rooms were closed to the Forakers. The senator's recommendations for federal appointments in Ohio were refused. Most chillingly, he noticed that his mail was being opened.[130]

The official verdict on the Brownsville controversy dealt Foraker another blow. After investigating for more than a year, a Senate committee in 1908 ratified Roosevelt's dismissals.[131] Solace might be found, however, in the far more dubious opinion rendered by the American public — and, in moments of private candor, by the president himself.[132]

Foraker long had harbored ambitions of his own for the presidency. He had envisioned himself perhaps succeeding McKinley. But any such dreams were dashed when the president was assassinated and replaced by the popular Roosevelt.[133] The senator settled for leading rearguard opposition to Roosevelt and his policies.[134]

When William Howard Taft won Roosevelt's blessing in 1908 as his successor, he inherited Foraker's hostility. The secretary of war was a kindred Cincinnatian and an early political protégé of Foraker, who as governor in 1887 had appointed the twenty-nine-year-old Taft to a vacant judgeship.[135] But friendly alliance had evolved over the years into grim competition. The two men kept in frequent contact, the affable Taft, eleven years Foraker's junior, maintaining a respectful courtesy. But the senator did his utmost to discredit Roosevelt's anointed in Washington and to deny him the party's support in Ohio.[136]

At the Republican convention in Chicago, Foraker put his own name forward. He finished an ignominious dead last, collecting just 16 votes of the 976 cast. Taft was nominated.[137] Swallowing his humiliation, the senator sent the nominee his congratulations. Taft, in victory magnanimous toward his former benefactor, replied in his primly slanting penmanship: "I have never ceased to remember that I owe to you my first substantial start in public life, and that it came without solicitation."[138]

Identified in the popular mind as an arch-foe of Roosevelt, Foraker also had gained a reputation as an equally tenacious friend of big business. It was hardly a comfortable distinction. He was derided as a tool of tycoons and targeted by the era's muckraking journalists. A leader of the "railroad senators," he assiduously defended the rail systems whose monopolistic power and extortionate ways increasingly alienated Americans.[139]

When Congress sought in 1906 to regulate the railroads, the Ohio senator assailed the legislation with a verbal fusillade of no less than seventy-eight speeches. In the subsequent enactment into law of what was known as the Hepburn Act, he was one of only three Senate dissenters and the lone Republican.[140] Roosevelt — never one to mute his opinion of others — called Foraker "one of the most unblushing servers and beneficiaries of corporate wealth within or without office that I have ever met."[141]

Foraker's association with big capital was to return to haunt him. William Randolph Hearst's rambunctious *New York World* leveled in 1908 the sensational charge that the senator had been employed secretly by the Standard Oil Company, the business trust then most notorious to Americans. The newspaper had unearthed a set of letters to Foraker from John D. Archbold, company vice president,[142] showing that during his first term the senator had been quietly hired by Standard Oil as a special counsel.[143] Such ties once had been accepted practice, but in the trust-busting environment of the day were political poison.

The revelation created an uproar. The many enemies whom the

vitriolic senator had accumulated over the years joined in the chorus of condemnation.[144] Foraker didn't deny the affiliation, but protested that his work for Standard Oil had been confined to advising the company on litigation in Ohio and complying with federal antitrust laws. In any event, he added, it had lasted barely a year and had ended seven years previously.[145]

He disclaimed any wrongdoing:

> My employment was legitimate; ... nothing I had to do had the slightest reference to any duty of any kind that I was charged with as a senator.[146]

But the storm of disapproval was not to be quelled. Foraker, up for reelection that year, declined to seek a third term.[147] He confided to a friend the painful "mortification of defeat."[148]

The man who had shaken the Senate chamber with his oratory and consorted with presidents departed Washington in disgrace. Not, however, in the eyes of one constituency: the people of color whom he had championed throughout his public career. Two days after leaving office, Foraker was feted by members of the capital's black community at a mass meeting at the cavernous Metropolitan African Methodist Episcopal Church. He was presented a giant silver loving cup in gratitude for his services to their race.[149]

Less publicly, a few others also were beginning to see Foraker as an unappreciated voice of the downtrodden. The president of Cornell University, Jacob G. Schurman, proclaimed to one of the Ohioan's former classmates: "Senator Foraker is a great champion of human rights, whether the rights of individuals, or of races, or of citizens of territories and states."[150]

The ex-senator returned to Cincinnati and resumed his law practice. He represented a clientele of major corporations, undeterred by the ruinous consequences of his connection with Standard Oil.[151]

The Foraker mansion back in Washington pulsated no more with the confidences of presidents, the banter of lawmakers, and the merry tinkle of bone china, crystal, and sterling. It was sold in 1913 to the widow of a Michigan lumber baron who had made a fortune—fittingly—supplying ties to the railroad industry so long accorded Foraker's Senate patronage.[152]

The political warhorse made one last race for public office. He tried in 1914 to reclaim his old Senate seat, seeking the Republican nomination in a three-way contest. He finished second to a promising former Ohio state legislator and lieutenant governor named Warren G. Harding.[153] Subsequently elected, Foraker's senatorial heir would achieve five years later the goal that had eluded his predecessor: the presidency.

In his enforced retirement from the public arena, Foraker cultivated the quieter satisfactions of private life. He lavished attention on his children and grandchildren.[154] He had the fatherly pleasure of sharing a law partnership with his eldest son Benson. While serving as a captain in Cuba during the Spanish-American War, the young man had contracted yellow fever from which he never fully recovered. He passed away in 1915.[155] Benson seems to have been closest to his father, and his loss left a painful void:

> For years I have cherished the thought that I had a strong staff to lean upon in my last days. Now it is broken, and the fond hopes and bright promise of a vigorous manhood are withered and scattered.[156]

True to his pious upbringing, he devoted much time to Bible study.[157] He also undertook a book of his own. He wrote his autobiography, *Notes of a Busy Life*, a two-volume review of the Foraker public record yielding scant glimpses of the inner man. It was published locally in 1916.[158]

The book was no best seller, but it did attract one reader of note. Foraker's nemesis Theodore Roosevelt plowed through the work and underwent a surprising metamorphosis. He tempered his judgment of his old Washington foe. After reading the memoirs, Roosevelt wrote to a presumably flabbergasted Foraker: "I admire your entire courage and forthrightness." The senator, he added, had been driven by a noble sense of duty: "to help people who had no champion."[159]

Following from afar events in his old bailiwick of Puerto Rico, as he assuredly did, Foraker would have been gratified to watch the territory settling smoothly into American rule under a government of his design. Most pleasing of all must have been the eventual fulfillment of a goal particularly close to his heart. Seventeen years after the senator had first advanced the idea, President Woodrow Wilson signed into law in 1917 legislation granting Puerto Ricans U.S. citizenship.[160]

Victory in this quest that he had pursued so long and hard seemed to release Foraker to depart in triumph from a lifetime of battling. Two months later, as springtime showers swelled the Ohio River and greened the enclosing hillsides he so loved, Foraker passed away. He was in his seventieth year.[161]

His widow Julia lived pluckily on, a redoubtable matriarch. Fifteen years later, at age eighty-four, she published her own autobiography. *I Would Live It Again: Memories of a Vivid Life* surpassed her husband's opus in naturalness and candor — enough so to merit reissuing for a later generation of readers in 1975.[162]

The yellow mansion in Washington proved less durable. Still filled with much of the original Foraker furniture, it was sold just before the 1929 stock market crash to the adjacent Foundry Methodist Church. The sumptuous parlors and suites were converted into prosaic Sunday School classrooms. The showplace built by prominent Methodists elicited from their churchly brethren no deference. The house was razed to the ground in 1960 for an annex to the Sunday School.[163]

7 — Senator Joseph B. Foraker

Long after his home had been reduced to rubble and his name largely lost to memory, Foraker received from the federal government belated commemoration. It vindicated the most lonely and maligned of his crusades for racial fairness. Under congressional prodding, the army in 1972 rescinded posthumously all the dishonorable discharges issued so peremptorily to African-American soldiers six decades earlier in what had come to be known as the Brownsville Affair.[164]

There remained one survivor. Eighty-six-year-old Dorsie W. Willis had been consigned by the stigma of his army dismissal to shining shoes for fifty-nine years at a Minneapolis barber shop. The following year Congress passed, and President Richard M. Nixon signed into law, legislation awarding him compensation of twenty-five thousand dollars. The hoary veteran, eyes glowing, remembered fondly the senator who had defended the soldiers with a courage never to be forgotten.[165]

8

Representative William A. Jones

First Congressional Reformer, 1899–1918

America's largest Caribbean acquisition changed more than just its sovereignty when it came under U.S. rule in 1898. Puerto Rico became "Porto Rico" and its inhabitants "Porto Ricans."

The proud old name[1] was corrupted, not so much out of high-handed linguistic imperialism, perhaps, as unwitting oversight. But guilelessness didn't make the bastardization any less offensive to Puerto Ricans — or revealing of their adoptive countrymen.

The mischievous respelling had begun, innocuously enough, with a clerical error: a mistake in the English translation of the Treaty of Paris formally ending the Spanish-American War. The blunder was then on the verge of being heedlessly perpetuated two years later as Congress framed a government for the new possession. The Foraker bill of 1900, its pages replete with "Porto Ricos," would have enshrined the anglicized term as the official designation.[2]

The mangling of the name, and the wounded sensibilities of those who bore it, stirred little discernible sympathy among the island's new American rulers. Save one.

There strode into the well of the House of Representatives during the debate a trim man who carried himself with the litheness of an athlete and the courtliness of an aristocrat. His features were refined and his air of gentility impeccably Virginian.[3] From this very effigy of the Old South issued a little speech of a sort hardly to have been expected.

He objected to emasculating Puerto Rico's name. More than mere carelessness, he charged, it was motivated by a chauvinism that demeaned the island's people.

"Ignorant of its derivation and meaning, and insensible to the wishes and the feelings of those who are attached to it," he asserted, his voice rising in agitation, the bill's authors "had arbitrarily and wickedly determined that it shall be so."[4]

The impassioned appeal rang upon deaf ears. Puerto Rico was to remain "Porto Rico" until a more receptive Congress finally restored the rightful name in 1932.[5]

Pleading the cause of an aggrieved racial minority of Americans, perched out on the nation's far perimeters, had fallen to an unlikely advocate. Congressman William A. Jones was a conservative Southern patrician who had fought for the Confederacy in the Civil War and devoted most of his political energies cultivating the introverted confines of tidewater Virginia.

But to those who had penetrated his sublime self-containment and got to know him, the crusade was no aberration. It conformed perfectly with the man's character.

His was a character shaped from birth by a life of privilege, coupled with a tenet, of *ancien régime* quaintness, that such advantages imposed an obligation to serve others.[6]

Representative William A. Jones, 1910 (Library of Congress).

William Atkinson Jones sprang from the young republic's gentry. The first English colonizers of the New World were still settling in at Jamestown when a Jones forebear headed up the James River and began to acquire land. The enterprising ancestor, Peter Jones, is said to have left his name on the Virginia town of Petersburg, south of Richmond.[7] A scion, a century later, honored the family name by serving as a captain in the Revolutionary War.[8] The Joneses by then were well established in tidewater Virginia as wealthy planters and civil leaders.[9]

The immediate lineage of William Jones, however, was a less parochial mixture of Virginian and Northeasterner. His father, Thomas, Jr., a tidewater country lawyer and local politician, had married his law partner's young governess, Anne Trowbridge, offspring of a Massachusetts family who had come south from her residence in Plattsburg, New York.[10] The couple made its home near the winding Rappahannock River in a town that had borne the quintessentially Virginian name of Richmond County Courthouse until, in a burst of sympathy with the Polish struggle for independence, recently renaming itself Warsaw.[11] There their only son was born six years later in 1849.[12]

The boy grew up amid the crescendo rumbles of approaching civil war. His father's native Southern loyalties were reinforced by cousinship and friendship with Robert E. Lee, the Confederate military commander.[13] Although fifty years old when hostilities broke out, Thomas Jones promptly enlisted in a local infantry company and campaigned across Virginia and Maryland.[14]

In the waning days of the conflict in the autumn of 1864, he enrolled his fifteen-year-old son as a cadet at the Virginia Military Institute in Lexington. The cadets forsook their war-torn campus later that year for presumably more peaceful quarters in Richmond, only to find themselves amid the Union forces' siege of the Confederate capital. Jones and his classmates exchanged their pens for rifles in its futile defense.[15]

William's father, showing a steadfastness to his ideals (or, others might venture to say, obstinacy) that he was to impart to his son, refused to lay down his weapon after the surrender at Appomattox. Instead, he joined a holdout remnant of greycoats mounting a doomed last-ditch resistance in North Carolina.[16]

The eventually pacified veteran returned from the war intent on giving his son the best available education. William boarded two years at a college preparatory school in Fredericksburg, and then at age nineteen took up studies at the University of Virginia, following his father's profession of law. He excelled in athletics and academics, graduating in 1870 with distinction.[17]

The graduate then made a career decision that defied the conventional wisdom of his peers. The war's shattering of the agrarian base of the southern way of life persuaded most of his perceptive contemporaries to abandon their rural roots for more promising prospects in their state's cities or to flee the Old Dominion altogether.[18] William, drawn by stronger local urges, returned home to pursue a future in his little pastoral shire.[19]

The Jones homeland was a gently rolling peninsula stretching between the Potomac and Rappahannock rivers into Chesapeake Bay. It was known, picturesquely, as the Northern Neck. The area cherished a proud history as the birthplace of three of the nation's first five presidents — Washington, Madison, and Monroe — and a succession of other luminaries from colonial entrepreneur Robert Carter, to Revolution theorist George Mason, to General Robert E. Lee.[20] National influence once had been matched by economic dynamism.[21] But agricultural decline and isolation from the shifting currents of commerce and culture had left the Northern Neck by the 1870s a torpid backwater.[22] The accompanying anomie and alienation bred another attribute: a streak of feisty independence.[23]

As uninviting as the place would seem for a young man of ambition, the Northern Neck evoked in William an ancestral loyalty and identification with its historical heritage.[24] He took his law degree straight home and set up practice with his father in Warsaw.[25] He showed an immediate proclivity, gaining a reputation as a canny criminal lawyer who seldom lost a case.[26]

The young jurist's workplace was the county courthouse, just across the street from his law office. The brick chamber with soaring chimneys and tall Palladian windows was an imposing relic of colonial times. And it served as something more than a seat of justice. As throughout rural Virginia at that period, it doubled as a countryman's theatre and public forum. "Court days" drew crowds of locals to watch the dramas unfolding before the bar, with lawyers as leading performers, and to ventilate politics in the corridors. Jones thus found himself thrust early into the political arena.[27]

Not unwillingly. Like so much else that impelled him, politics presented itself as an inherited family calling. A great-uncle had served many years in the state legislature and a term in Congress. His father and a string of other relatives had held assorted local elective offices.[28] His regard for politics was exalted, even for his own less cynical day. He was moved on occasion to extol the political profession in terms more often reserved for the priesthood. He once pronounced politics to be

> the highest of earthly pursuits and the politician the most faithful representation of true manhood.[29]

As apprenticeship for a life's work so ennobled, Jones began almost immediately upon his return to the Northern Neck to dabble in the affairs of the Conservative party. This Virginia party had been formed a decade earlier as a disparate alliance of antebellum Democrats, former Whigs, and renegade Republicans brought together by shared opposition to the postwar Reconstruction imposed by the Radical wing of the Republican party. While dominant in the state as a whole, the Conservatives remained the minority party in the Joneses' region. Both he and his father worked as local organizers.[30]

The younger Jones made his entry into elective politics just three years after coming home. He was elected at age twenty-four as commonwealth's attorney, or county prosecutor. It was a post that his father had held before the war. William's popularity among voters was to retain him the position in an otherwise Republican county for ten years.[31]

One lure of politics for Jones was the opportunity it offered to mobilize for his stagnant area an infusion of economic revitalization.[32] He was a tireless promoter of improvement schemes. He was instrumental in founding a newspaper to enhance regional communications, and a local telephone company. He pushed truck farming, and pursued quixotically for twenty years a railroad line.[33] Civic-spirited though they were, Jones's efforts for economic uplift weren't entirely disinterested. Even as a young man, he held an important personal stake in the Northern Neck as a major landowner and farm operator.[34]

Jones's political horizons were expanding beyond the bounds of his county. He attended the 1880 presidential nominating convention of the Democratic party, the partisan step-parent of Virginia's Conservative grouping. He then campaigned back home for its nominee, Winfield Scott Hancock, with vigor undiminished by the standard-bearer's notoriety in the South as a former Union general.[35]

When the Conservative party metamorphosed in 1883 into the Democratic party, Jones helped supervise the reorganization as chairman of the new party in the Northern Neck congressional district.[36] His rising prominence in party circles began to suggest him as a possible candidate for the congressional seat. He was mentioned for the post in 1884, when just thirty-five years old, and four years later bid for it unsuccessfully at the state party convention.[37]

Political matters were momentarily eclipsed, however, by personal ones. Jones had come to relish the company of a young woman who had moved to town from Williamsburg. Claude Douglass Motley shared a family background in law and politics. She was the daughter of a lawyer and niece of a U.S. senator. The couple married in the first days of 1889[38] and occupied a commodious Queen Anne house, with wraparound porch, built that year just up the road from the courthouse.[39] The pair soon became parents of a son and daughter.[40]

Jones's two decades in the public eye — in the courtroom, in meeting halls, on the hustings — had established an identity among Northern Neck folk as a patron appealing not so much to their passions as to their trust. He projected no magnetic personality. He had no capacity (or taste) for the politician's glad-handing gregariousness.[41] His face, with brow resolute and moustache arcing tightly downward, wore an expression of determination.[42] His manner was reserved to the point of coldness.[43]

He preferred to be known as someone who undertook important public goals, and fought for them tenaciously.[44] His hallmark was hard work rather than flamboyance; scholarship rather than sensation.[45] Yet in debate, Jones was a tiger. He could be vicious in arguing an issue, less often by rant than by cool reasoning that quietly demolished the opposition.[46] Colleagues remembered him as "aggressive" and "combative," but principally as persuasive. "He possessed in an unusual degree," recalled one, "the power of lucid and perspicuous speech."[47]

After two false starts, the time seemed propitious for Jones to run for Congress. The political landscape had become more inviting. Republicans, who had held sway in the Northern Neck's First Congressional District since the Civil War, approached the election of 1890 weakened by apathy and divisions.[48] And from his own party arose no serious rivals to Jones. He was nominated by acclamation.[49]

Political campaigns in this bypassed corner of Virginia still observed an Old South etiquette. Openly promoting one's own candidacy was shunned as unseemly self-serving. Jones scrupulously complied.[50] "He never by word or letter personally solicited a single vote," it was remarkably said of him.[51]

But such gentlemanly restraint made the contest no noticeably less strenuous. Jones campaigned indefatigably — pressing the issues, flailing the incumbent, and unspokenly commending himself to the voters. Drawing on his native physical vigor, the candidate laboriously crisscrossed by horse and boat a sprawling congressional district bereft of less arduous modes of transportation such as railways. He lavished two-hour orations upon knots of farmers and watermen.[52]

A segment of the constituency too sizable to be ignored by any candidate, as in much of the postwar South, was African-Americans. They nearly outnumbered white residents, in fact, in Jones's home county.[53] The black minority received from the Democrat treatment riven with inconsistencies reflective of his region's tortuous racial legacy. He sought to woo African-American voters from their traditional Republican sympathies during the 1890 campaign,[54] and later opposed literacy tests and other restrictions on black suffrage.[55] But he also voiced the denigrating racism of the southern elite of his day, once avowing himself "for the white voter."[56]

On election day, Jones's tactics and energy paid off. He defeated the two-term Republican incumbent, "reclaiming" the congressional seat, as jubilant Democrats were wont to phrase it, for the old antebellum party.[57]

The freshman congressman arrived in the Houses of Representatives in one of the most vehement partisan overturnings ever to sweep through the chamber. Republicans had lost, in a sudden voter uprising, not only their majority but nearly half their members. It was a welling up of national discontent that prefigured the angry grassroots democratization movement known as populism.[58]

Jones, for all his Bourbon pedigree, found himself in the vanguard of the movement. The *leitmotivs* of his political life were an odd combination of the traditional and the progressive. So seemingly contradictory, the two often conjoined.[59] His attachment to many of the ways of the bygone South arrayed him against the forces in society perceived to be threatening them: industrialization, urbanization, and their political by-products — big money's corrupting influence on elections and the rise of city political machines. These concerns allied the patrician with a swelling rabble of the disaffected across America.[60]

His speeches often carried a clarion populist ring:

> The tide of progress is rapidly spreading over the land. The people are demanding a larger share of their own government.[61]

Such proletarian rebelliousness had roots in the cranky independence of Jones's Northern Neck. It was a place that, despite long absences on Capitol Hill, remained his magnetic pole, politically and spiritually. He kept in unusually close touch with his constituents, attuning himself to their sometimes contrarian views. At first his ceaseless touring of a congressional district so recently plucked from the Republicans seemed a political necessity. But Jones continued the practice long after securing his grip on the seat simply to plumb local opinion.[62]

His fellow rural Virginians, he was keenly aware, felt woefully unburnished by the Gilded Age. Agriculture was mired in depression.[63] Resentment found an outlet in the Farmers' Alliance, an agrarian protest organization whose demands reached beyond agriculture to the full-throated populist agenda of trust busting and fair taxation. The Alliance became a potent political force which Jones embraced from the outset of his congressional career.[64]

The disaffection deepened when matters began to go amiss in his own chosen profession and party. The state Democratic party fell in the 1890s under the control of a political machine whose urban orientation, corporate coziness, and shady dealings were an anathema to the old-line country squire. The party boss, Thomas S. Martin, was a self-made railroad lawyer and apostle of the new style of autocratic, ward-heeler organizations then springing up across the country. Martin, who soon consolidated his power by appropriating a Senate seat, was to be a thorn in Jones's side for thirty years.[65]

Martin's rule was marked by squelching of dissent, voting irregularities, bribery — and unparalleled electoral success.[66] Jones vilified Martin as an "evil genius of honest politics"[67] and his organization as a "corrupt, vile, selfish, and miserable machine,"[68] and battled them relentlessly. The jousting brought not only little reward but retaliation. The party organization toppled him as head of the state's congressional delegation, and tried twice to undermine his political base by redrawing the boundaries of his district.[69] The unremunerated struggle was a bitter experience for the man who regarded himself as a steward of the idealism of the founding fathers whose native soil he represented. "It almost makes me lose faith," he once despaired, "in the honesty and stability of mankind."[70]

The search for remedies to redress the evils that seemed to so menace turn-of-the-century America had led Jones for years to espouse measures deemed in the more smug quarters of the republic dangerously radical.[71] While still a mere local party activist, he had begun advocating reforms to break up the new concentrations of power and make government more responsive to popular will. Afforded a more prominent platform in Congress, he came to be identified as a leading voice for corrective action.[72]

He pushed, over the years, a series of proposals that gradually gained respectability and became canons of the political program termed progressivism: regulation of corporations, a graduated income tax, popular election of state and local judges, limits on political campaign spending and disclosure of contributors.[73]

But the reform to engage Jones most fully was the direct election of senators. Members of Congress' upper house had been designated by the Constitution to be chosen by state legislatures, presumably more responsible than the ordinary voting riffraff. State legislatures, however, increasingly had come under the thumb of moneyed interests, to which their senators often were glaringly beholden.[74]

Jones's call for popular election of senators came early in the slow evolution of this idea — in 1897 — and baptized him in the maverick lot of a political reformer. It predated the senatorship of Martin, but certainly drew intensity from his foe's subsequent accession.[75] Jones led the campaign in Virginia to obtain voter selection of the senators whom the Constitution still obliged the legislature to formally elect.[76] The struggle was protracted. Seventeen years after he first had urged the reform, his party (then dominant in Virginia) agreed in 1904 to nominate Senate candidates by primary elections.[77]

Victory gave Jones fatherly pride. "I put it in motion...," he bragged a little to a political supporter, "and advocated it in season and out of season until it was finally adopted."[78]

The Constitution was amended nine years later to stipulate that all senators be elected "by the people." The other principal progressive reforms, one by one, also became the law of the land, their contentious past receding into today's casual acceptance.

The credit, however, must go elsewhere than to Jones. The congressman proved a better motivator than leader. The same qualities that attracted so many adherents — unswerving dedication to the cause, tempered by reluctance to dictate to others — rendered him unsuitable to lead them.[79] He resisted the compromise and concession so crucial in the legislative process. He refrained from forcing the natural course of events. He shunned organizing and directing his followers. For nimble leadership in the political hurly-burly, his stubborn independence just got in the way.[80]

In the bluster and bravado atmosphere of Capitol Hill in the Gilded

Age, there emanated from Jones ever a plaintive note of the outsider. His reserve and iconoclasm inhibited forming friendships among his colleagues.[81] Those in his select circle of congressional chums, however, were rewarded with warmth and unshakable loyalty. Said one: "He was slow to give his affections, but once given they were inflexible."[82]

Popularity, for Jones, ranked less important than principle. An early House assignment called for reviewing bills on federal pensions, most of them claims from individual members on behalf of constituents, usually war veterans. Traditionally the process had been an exercise in collegial rubber-stamping — but not for Jones. With typical tenacity, he scrutinized each bill and challenged many as unwarranted. The vigilance won him plaudits from the public but few friends among his fellow lawmakers.[83]

His field of endeavor expanded far beyond the Northern Neck of Virginia, or even the continental United States, when Congress in 1899 created committees to oversee the territorial spoils of the Spanish-American War. Jones was named ranking minority member of the new House Committee on Insular Affairs. The choice may have met a desire of Democratic leaders for a staunch anti-imperialist who would stand up to the ardent Republican empire builders than in triumphal reign on Capitol Hill.[84]

In Jones, the critics of imperialism had no stouter champion. He shared the indignant anti-imperialism of William Jennings Bryan, the Democrats' unsuccessful presidential candidate in 1896.[85] Caught up in 1898 in the fevered call to arms, which induced even Bryan to recruit a regiment of doughboys, Jones had voted for war against Spain.[86] But he had hastily recanted of the vote he had come to "bitterly regret,"[87] and redoubled his opposition. He spoke out against the war's land grabs, and allied himself with the vociferous Anti-Imperialism League.[88] Jones, observed a House colleague, "was not dazzled by the glamour of colonial empire."[89]

His aversion to imperialism was grounded on beliefs from the Virginia hearths of the founders: that government should be a consensual arrangement in which all participate freely as equals.[90] Wielding a scepter over people conquered by the sword, to Jones, violated American democratic ideals:

> The more our Constitution and Government are examined the less they will be found suited to aggressive war and foreign conquest. Their whole spirit and genius are opposed to them.[91]

He felt the United States should extend these principles overseas to the islanders whom war had placed under its protection. Americans, as he once said in another context, should show "a heart that was comprehensive enough to embrace humanity itself."[92]

The country's newly-won empire became for Jones — seemingly

incapable of executing any task by halves — a consuming interest.⁹³ It grew, remarked a committee colleague who worked closely with him, into "his great official life work."⁹⁴

The prime responsibilities of the new congressional overseers were the two largest acquisitions: the Philippines and Puerto Rico. The two places engendered sharply contrasting constitutional scenarios. The Philippines, where victory against Spain was degenerating into bloody insurrection against U.S. occupation, was the focus of a national debate whether to retain it or grant it independence. Puerto Rico, on the other hand, evidencing no discernible clamor for autonomy, was perceived by most everyone — even avowed foes of empire — as a permanent annexation. The exponents of a paradoxical preference to free the Philippines but keep Puerto Rico included Jones.⁹⁵

Incorporating Puerto Rico into the American motherland represented for Jones, the ex–Confederate guardian of the values of the Old South, something of an expurgation racially. The Virginian remained bound by many of the racially derogatory attitudes of his upbringing. He had opposed absorbing Hawaii in 1898 on grounds baldly racist. He wrote to a friend: "To complicate ... the race question further by fresh infusions of alien and inferior blood into the body politic seems like utter insanity."⁹⁶

Compared to many of his Southern peers, however, Jones's conduct on racial matters was decidedly moderate. He kept his prejudices discreetly private. And he showed a willingness to revise them. The acceptance — even advocacy — that he extended to Puerto Ricans contrasts with the racist contempt heaped on inhabitants of the country's overseas territories by some fellow lawmakers. Jones's Virginia colleague, Senator John W. Daniel, for example, during a debate in 1898 described Filipinos as a "witch's caldron" of races and an "Asiatic mess of pottage."⁹⁷

When the Foraker plan for governing Puerto Rico was plowing its way through Congress in 1900, the most spirited attacks came from Jones.⁹⁸ While there's no evidence that the disagreement was anything but legislative, one suspects that it may have been aggravated by personal disparities. As kindred custodians of the new empire, Foraker and Jones could hardly have been more fundamentally different. One a Union veteran, the other a Confederate. One an agent of corporate power, the other a defiant agrarian. One a machine politician, the other an arch-foe of the bosses. One a voracious empire builder, the other an anti-imperialist. One a flamboyant extrovert, the other a reserved loner.

His populism revealing itself, the Virginia congressman detected in the Ohio senator's territorial scheme an open invitation to corporate thievery. Jones's suspicions fell on the proposed "executive council," a super-arm of government, its members appointed by the president, serving as both the governor's cabinet and the legislature's upper house.[99] It would be empowered, among other things, to issue franchises for conducting business in Puerto Rico.[100] Here, Jones worried, was a wide portal for American corporate exploitation. He found the provision "offensive and repugnant."[101] His concerns went unheeded, but were soon to be justified as mainland business interests proceeded to grasp the island economy in a hammerlock.[102]

Jones tried again later in the year to restrain the rapacity of American companies. This time he targeted corporate land ownership. In a companion Foraker bill, he proposed to prohibit corporations in Puerto Rico from engaging in agriculture.[103] Otherwise, he warned,

> the great corporations of this country will own every single acre of the sugar and tobacco lands of this most fertile island [and] ... the condition of the population will, I believe, be reduced to one of absolute servitude.[104]

His efforts on this occasion met with more success. While an outright ban proved more than Congress was prepared to swallow, it agreed to limit a company's landholding to five hundred acres.[105]

When Democrats gained control of the House in 1911, the gadfly became policymaker. Jones moved up to chairman of the committee immersed in defining the country's new imperial role.[106]

Demanding attention most urgently was the biggest possession — and the most unruly: the Philippines. By the time he received the gavel of the committee, Jones had been urging the archipelago's independence for a decade.[107] Ever since Congress' first legislative embroilment, he had advised Americans, for reasons both strategic and philosophical, to (as he put it in 1901) "withdraw now and forever."[108]

Jones subsequently visited the Philippines, becoming one of the first congressional overseers to view an outlying dependency firsthand. The trip took a party of lawmakers and other public officials to the islands for two months in 1905. The group was escorted by William Howard Taft, recently promoted from the possession's first civilian governor to President Theodore Roosevelt's secretary of war. The junket was a transparent device to build support for the administration's plan for a long American presence in the Philippines.[109] But Jones, in his independent way, followed his own agenda. When possible, he skipped red-carpet receptions and show-window tours to interview ordinary Filipinos.[110] He also sought out insurrection leader Emilio Aguinaldo.[111] The traveler returned with his liberation convictions unshaken.

As incoming chairman of the committee, Jones's first order of business was to prepare legislation for the Philippines embodying these predilections. He set out to lighten the rod of empire. More governance would be entrusted to Filipinos — electing the previously appointive upper house of their legislature and filling many government jobs heretofore reserved for Americans. And the possession would be promised eventual independence.[112]

These were heretical notions in the jingoistic temper of the times.[113] Accomplishing the task took five years and the election of a sympathetic president. But in 1916 the supportive Woodrow Wilson signed into law Jones's liberalization of U.S. rule, committing the home country to setting the Philippines free "as soon as a stable government can be established." A son of the South, which at his birth had held in bonds four million African slaves, had negotiated the freedom of ten million Filipinos. Islanders were jubilant. Its author regarded the Jones Act as the achievement of his career.[114]

Next to feel Jones's reforming hand was Puerto Rico. The most vexing issue was one that had stymied the neophyte imperial power for two decades: whether or not to give Puerto Ricans U.S. citizenship. Although support seemed to be building for making the islanders American citizens, momentum was slowed by divisions in Congress and in the possession itself. Some islanders were reluctant to part with their Puerto Rican citizenship, either out of sentimentality or resistance to perceived American compulsion.[115] Lawmakers had come to favor U.S. citizenship, but were split over how best to grant it — individually to those wishing it (the preference of the Senate) or collectively to all (the choice of the House and the presidential platforms of both major parties).[116]

In resolving their conundrums, Congress and the dependency received regrettably little help from the grand old man of Puerto Rican politics, Luis Muñoz Rivera. The successful arbiter with pre-war Spain and leader of the territory's dominant political party, now the island's representative in Congress, seemed undecided himself. His counsel to his colleagues in Washington was frustratingly ambiguous.[117]

Barely had he warmed his new committee chair before Jones introduced legislation to re-christen Puerto Ricans at a stroke as American citizens. The administration of President Taft, the chairman's erstwhile traveling companion in the Philippines, promptly endorsed it.[118] But collective citizenship needed to be made more palatable to those desiring something less autocratic. A compromise was suggested by the agency in the Department of War delegated to look after the overseas possessions, the Bureau of Insular Affairs. The originator was a young law officer named Felix Frankfurter, whose legal acumen was to lead to New Deal social activism and a seat on the Supreme Court. Frankfurter proposed granting citizenship to all Puerto Ricans except those who declined it. His idea broke the stalemate.[119]

Compared to the watershed bestowal of citizenship, other features of Jones's revision of the imperial relationship were relatively modest. Puerto Ricans long had chafed at the limited participation permitted in their own government—"protesting and struggling against it," complained Muñoz Rivera, "with energy and without result."[120] Jones's remedies patterned those provided the Philippines. Members of the upper house of the legislature would no longer be appointed by the American president but elected by the Puerto Rican people. Washington's control would be reduced by cutting the number of presidential appointees at cabinet level in San Juan from eleven to three.[121]

The five-hundred-acre limit on corporate landholding, which Jones had pushed into law, had withstood concerted attempts — by the sugar industry, a president (Theodore Roosevelt), a war secretary, and several island governors — to weaken or repeal it.[122] But it had accomplished no more than mere survival. The law was a dead letter, unenforced and breached after seventeen years on the statute books by no fewer than 477 big landowners. It was lamely reincorporated into the new scheme.[123]

The reform plans gained impetus from one of the first inspection trips to Puerto Rico by a congressional overseer. The visitor in 1912 wasn't in this case Jones, however, but his Senate counterpart, John F. Shafroth of Colorado, Republican chairman of his body's committee dealing with the island. Illness may have prevented the Virginian from making the journey.[124]

The new governmental framework for Puerto Rico had been slow to piece together. But once assembled, it was put in place with dispatch. Since matters coalesced amid the approach of World War I, the action often is ascribed to wartime preparations — to shore up U. S. support in the Caribbean. The timing, however, appears coincidental. The United States had no need to cement the loyalty of Puerto Rico in the coming conflict by conferring constitutional concessions. The culmination, instead, seems to have arisen from the eventual emergence of a consensus.[125]

Sensing that conditions finally were ripe, Jones dusted off his reform package and in the opening days of 1916 put it before Congress. It breezed through his committee in January after just five days of hearings, and in May won approval from the House.[126] When the bill stalled in the Senate, intervention by the president became crucial. While Woodrow Wilson and Jones had no close personal ties, they had early political bonds. The congressman had worked hard for the New Jersey governor's presidential nomination in 1912 when the Virginia party machine opposed it. Such loyalty might help incline the president toward Jones's legislation.[127]

Wilson, who before entering the White House had espoused toward the overseas protectorates the paternalistic view that Americans "must be their tutors," was a late convert to broadening their autonomy.[128] And Puerto Rico ranked low on his presidential agenda. But once he had undergone a change of heart and disposed of other matters, the president took up the cause in earnest.

He dashed off a letter to Puerto Rico governor (and friend) Arthur Yager signaling his commitment:

> I fully appreciate the importance of the Puerto Rico Bill.... I shall try to interest myself continually in the matter until something is accomplished.[129]

And so he did. The president took the rare step of hieing himself to the Capitol to press for action on the legislation (as well as a few others).[130] He publicly denounced the existing arrangement with Puerto Rico as "not just," engendering among islanders "uneasiness" and "suspicious doubt" about American intentions.[131]

Pressure came not only from the White House but also from Puerto Rico. A commission of islanders, bipartisan and high ranking, traveled to Washington to lobby senators for approval.[132]

The Senate gave in, passing the bill in early 1917, and Wilson signed it into law.[133] The author of the legislation had another Jones Act to his credit.

The reception among Puerto Ricans was muted. While whipped to no frenzy of church bell pealing nor dancing in the plazas, islanders seemed to welcome the liberalization. They regarded it as an important advance toward the more complete self-government that they wished one day to achieve.

Muñoz Rivera, who failed to live to see the legislation clear the Senate, accepted the Jones plan with mixed disappointment and hope. "Meager and conservative as the bill appears...," he said, "we sincerely recognize its noble purposes and willingly accept it as a step in the right direction and as a reform paving the way for others."[134] His successor as the island's voice in Congress, Felix Cordova Davila, also deemed the new law a "step"—"the first step in the path of our liberty, which ... represents considerable progress in the recognition by Congress of our political rights."[135]

The mass of the Puerto Rican people tacitly ratified the revised relationship with their mainland sovereign by embracing the new nationality. Any islander wishing to opt out of U.S. citizenship, under the law's escape clause, had merely to go before a court within six months and so declare. Of the territory's more than one million residents, only 288 took the opportunity.[136]

The homeland extended a hand of paternal greeting. "We welcome the new citizen," Wilson proclaimed in an open telegram to the Puerto Rican public, "not as a stranger, but as one entering his father's house."[137]

Little fuss was made, either by Jones himself or his contemporaries, over the Virginia congressman's democratization of the country's links with Puerto Rico. The achievement tended to be overshadowed by the similar work for the Philippines which preceded it.[138] But Jones had given the possession the most sustained attention it had received in Washington since acquisition. And he had edged the relationship a little closer to the national ideals so dear to him.

In Jones, said his Puerto Rican colleague in the House, Cordova Davila, islanders had a devoted friend:

> It is not too much to say ... that during the tenure of his office as chairman of the Committee on Insular Affairs more was accomplished in this direction [setting policies for Puerto Rico] than in all of the preceding years of American occupation.
> From the Stygian darkness that surrounded the Porto Rico situation for nearly twenty years Congressman Jones did much to lead his country to the light.[139]

His thinning hair and moustache now a powdery grey but his form as erect as ever, Jones had become a fixture at the Capitol, as familiar to many as the tobacco leaves and corncobs carved atop the building's stone columns.[140] The congressional seat which he had wrested from a quarter century of Republican control had been transformed into one of the Democrats' most solid. The realignment owed much to Jones's tireless courting of a district already securely his.[141] Sometimes he faced no opponents, and at other times Republicans amounting to no more than token candidates.[142] The only serious electoral test had come from within his own party — a challenge for renomination in 1906 after the state Democratic machine had redrawn the boundaries of the district in vain hopes of ridding itself of a pesky foe.[143]

Party allies had sought for years to interest Jones in higher office. He passed up opportunities to run for governor in 1897, and for the Senate in 1899 and 1905.[144] While caution and indecision were factors in his choice, so was another proclivity. The man from the Northern Neck, evidence suggests, may have been one of those rare politicians who preferred advancing causes rather than his career.[145] When pressing for popular election of senators, he took pains to rule out "personal and selfish motives."[146]

But eventually Jones could stand aside no longer. Party boss Martin, whose Senate victory in 1905 the reform engineered by Jones had been gallingly unable to forestall, came up for reelection in 1911. Jones challenged him for the Democratic nomination. He targeted his campaign squarely against the Martin organization.[147] "The so-called machine or organization has long been in power," he charged. "In my opinion, much too long, and I believe the people of the State have become weary of the intolerable abuses which its unrestricted power has brought upon them."[148] But he was to learn, much to his disappointment, that Democrats weren't in fact weary of bossism. Martin trounced Jones by a margin of two to one.[149]

His faith in the electorate shaken but his idealism intact, Jones reconciled himself to serving out a career in the House. As one routine reelection succeeded another, he became in time the chamber's senior member, serving longer continuously than any of his colleagues.[150] His indefatigable constitution, meanwhile, had begun to flag.[151] Jones had just completed twenty-seven years in Congress when in the spring of 1918 he passed away. He was taken from Washington and buried where he had begun life sixty-nine years earlier, in the tidewater Virginia town of Warsaw, in so many ways always his home.[152]

Despite his roots deep in a rural fastness of the United States, the most effusive grief poured forth halfway around the globe. In the Philippines, the big American possession set by Jones on a path to independence, his passing occasioned national mourning.[153] The liberator from Virginia was hailed in the same breath as the martyred nineteenth century nationalist José Rizal. A Philippine leader who had helped draft the landmark 1916 law, Manuel L. Quezon, pronounced Jones's passing "the greatest national loss since Rizal was taken away from us."[154] Jones's name was affixed reverentially to one of Manila's principal bridges, and to streets and parks throughout the archipelago.[155]

The Philippine government commissioned a marble and bronze memorial rising twenty feet above his grave. Largely forgotten today beyond Virginia's Northern Neck, Jones is still commemorated in the Pacific nation whose promised freedom he legislated. Eighty years after his passing, in the centennial of the Spanish-American War in 1998, the wife of the Philippine president, Amelita Martinez Ramos, made a pilgrimage to Warsaw. She laid a wreath on the memorial that — like the antipodean worlds of Jones himself— lends to the simple Old Dominion churchyard a dash of foreign splendor.[156]

9
General Frank McIntyre
Military Administrator, 1905–1929

The ascendant decades of America's imperial adventure can be traced, rather remarkably, in the life of one man.

Navigators and warriors, statesmen and fortune hunters weave in and out of the colonial saga, but Frank McIntyre remains — a ubiquitous presence from the gun smoke of conquest to the scepter of empire.

The others touch one possession, perhaps a couple of them. He, like the knowing traveler who has been everywhere, encompasses them all.

McIntyre, the person, also stands distinctively apart.

Unlike the hard-charging military commanders who had won the island dependencies, he was deferential and retiring.[1] Albeit himself a general, he was the oddity of a general hopelessly incapable of inspecting troops.[2]

Among territorial founding fathers often distinguished by an abrasiveness that alienated those around them, McIntyre got along with practically everyone.

While others more assertive or egoistic imprinted on the protectorates their personal marks, McIntyre left no memorial, no local landmark emblazoned in his honor, no legislative act perpetuating his name. Yet he wielded perhaps greater sway upon the United States' little empire than all his more visible imperial colleagues.

It was just such a role of anonymous influence that McIntyre — anomaly that he was — desired.[3]

America's covey of overseas islands, never much of an allure for most of her countrymen, may have attracted McIntyre in part because he himself was only one generation removed from an isle across the sea. He was the son of Irish immigrants.

The mother of the future territorial administrator, Mary Gaughan, had been propelled to American shores, ironically, by a gesture of anti-colonial defiance. She came to join a brother expelled from Ireland for striking a British tax collector. She settled in Georgia.[4] There she met another Irish émigré,

Denis McIntyre.[5] The two were married, probably in the 1850s, and moved amid the ominous buildup of civil war, to Montgomery, Alabama.[6] The couple was acquiring a family, and in the closing days of the war, in January 1865, parented their fourth child, Frank.[7]

The McIntyres weathered the hardships of war and defeat, and prospered in their adopted homeland. The young husband landed a good job with a small railroad company, bought land, hired tenants to farm it, and began amassing wealth.[8]

Their son Frank showed himself to be a bright child. After breezing through the local schools, at age fifteen he won a mathematics scholarship at the University of Alabama.[9] His interest had been aroused, however, by a career as an army officer. The preparatory institution for the army's elite, the U.S. Military Academy, had no room for him. But when a vacancy arose at the close of his third year of studies, he eagerly transferred to West Point.[10]

For a seventeen-year-old who never had set foot beyond his native Alabama, a cosmopolitan life of learning and camaraderie on the palisades of the Hudson River proved a stimulating experience. He formed friendships with fellow cadets, including John J. Pershing and Peyton C. March, that were to endure for years to come. McIntyre graduated in 1886 ranked tenth in his class.[11]

The newly-commissioned lieutenant was sent west for a taste of foot soldiering. He served on the Rio Grande River and various posts in Texas.[12] Then came more studies, at the army's infantry and cavalry school at Fort Leavenworth, Kansas, where another officer destined for prominence in the country's overseas realm, General Nelson A. Miles, had just completed his command. Besides the martial skills, McIntyre also took the trouble there to gain a proficiency of unforeseen usefulness in his future calling: the Spanish language.[13]

After a brief assignment with his infantry regiment in Michigan,[14] the bookish young officer returned happily to the academy at West Point which he had left barely four years before. He taught mathematics for four years, while further studying Spanish, as well as French.[15]

The professional enjoyments at West Point were enhanced by personal ones. During his posting several years earlier in Texas, McIntyre's heart had been captured by a young woman. Mary Dennett was the daughter of a man who, like his own father, was a local railroad official. The relationship blossomed into marriage in 1892 in the bride's home state.[16]

A son, James Dennett, was born the following year at West Point, and another, Frank, Jr., shortly after leaving the ivied halls of academe for the austere barracks of Fort Wayne, Michigan. They were to be joined in coming years by a third son, Edward, and three daughters, Marie Dufilho, Margaret Hennett, and Nora.[17]

War, meanwhile, beclouded the family horizon.

The Spanish-American War, like all such conflicts, altered the lives of many, but few, perhaps, as much as that of McIntyre. It bore consequences never to be anticipated. The war was to initiate him in the challenges of subsuming people in other lands — an interest that would become his life's work.[18]

When war broke out, McIntyre's infantry regiment decamped from Michigan and steamed into the Atlantic to invade Puerto Rico. The thirty-three-year-old first lieutenant commanded a company of soldiers during the brief campaign, evidently taking no part in combat. Nor did the lowly junior officer seem to have come into contact with the expedition's commander, General Miles.[19]

The most memorable incident of the armed struggle, for McIntyre, had little to do with military action but much to tell about the affable young Irish-American who found himself drawn to the conquered people. Seeking shelter for his troops in the countryside one evening, McIntyre bivouacked them in the barn of a Puerto Rican farmer. He summoned forth the Spanish that he had been studying so assiduously and struck up a friendship with the *jíbaro*. It was to be no fleeting acquaintance. In ensuing years when McIntyre's job brought him back regularly to the island, he ritually revisited the farmer — and was feted by a fiesta.[20]

Shortly after hostilities ended, the lieutenant received his baptism in ruling dependent people. He was plucked from his regiment and sent to the southern Puerto Rican city of Ponce as an official in the local military government. He served as judge advocate and inspector general under General Guy V. Henry. When Henry became military governor of the entire island a few months later, McIntyre went with him to the capital at San Juan as aide de camp. But his first experience in territorial administration may have provided McIntyre an example less

General Frank McIntyre, 1918 (National Archives).

to emulate than to avoid. Henry was a hardened hero of the Indian wars whose tactlessness and chauvinism antagonized Puerto Ricans. The lieutenant soon left the governor's staff and returned to the mainland.[21]

He wasn't to remain Stateside for long. After an interlude of a few months at Camp Meade, Pennsylvania, he resumed his doughboy's tour of America's new overseas conquests. The next destination was the war's largest prize: the Philippines.[22]

The insurgency that pitted Americans against their former comrades in arms was an ugly coda to the war with Spain, especially for someone of McIntyre's sensibilities. The army's transformation from liberator to oppressor, together with the fratricidal violence, troubled the cerebral young infantryman. He would carry the emotional scars for the rest of his career.[23]

To the strife, he brought a conciliatory manner that succeeded in edging the warring sides a little closer together, earning from Filipino foes a grudging respect for himself and his country. Serving on the island of Cebu in the central Philippines, McIntyre, now a captain, countered guerrilla warfare by developing working relationships with Cebuano leaders, drawing on a shared Roman Catholic faith and his knowledge of Spanish.[24] He also schooled himself in the local tongue.[25] In his job as press censor, he plied the blue pencil lightly. The editor of the island's leading newspaper was astonished to find the American "not only courteous and patient but liberal, at a time when the armed resistance to the United States was still going on." The favorable impression would turn out to be of unexpected importance. The editor, Sergio Osmeña, was to enter politics and eventually become the last president of the Philippines under American rule.[26]

When U.S. forces finally crushed the Filipino insurrection in 1902, McIntyre returned with his unit to the United States.[27] But he never really left the outlying possessions behind him. They were increasingly to absorb his professional life.

The returnee trained recruits in California for a while,[28] but his army superiors rightly perceived him less suited to the drill field than a desk at headquarters. Rather than a leader of troops, with its aura of dash and glory, McIntyre was channeled into a career in one of the service's most maligned positions — an army bureaucrat.

While others might have been repulsed by the low esteem or the prospect of confinement in a stuffy office, McIntyre felt at home in the bureaucratic world of corridors and memoranda, and thrived in it. His temperament was well fitted. It was an odd combination of the approachable and the withdrawn. He was easygoing, with an open, fleshy face, cleft chin, and fuzzy moustache that seemed to invite a friendly word. Yet the small, guarded eyes suggested a deeper introversion, even secrecy. For all his ready fellowship,

McIntyre disliked socializing. He spoke rarely of himself, shunned publicity, and grew embarrassed if praised. He wrote no memoir, kept no diary of which anyone knows, and saved few personal papers. He preferred to toil quietly in the bureaucratic shadows.[29]

When the army reorganized itself under a general staff in 1902 (over the strenuous objections of his former Puerto Rico commander, General Miles, the service's commanding general), McIntyre was picked as one of forty-two junior officers to work at the new top echelon. Among his duties, he supervised the Philippine Scouts, a colonial militia of Filipinos under American officers.[30]

The administration of the swatches of American soil beyond the country's shores was, at the time, makeshift. While Congress promptly had formed committees for broad overview, day-to-day management remained dispersed. The acquisitions won by sea power — Guam and American Samoa — were ruled by the navy. Those conquered largely by ground forces — Puerto Rico and the Philippines — were tended by the army. Then, two years after the Spanish-American War, jurisdiction over Puerto Rico was snatched from the army and splintered among four federal departments.[31]

In the imperialistic fervor surrounding the war, many expected the United States to follow the practice prevailing in other capitals of empire by creating a major new arm of government to manage the possessions just gained and those anticipated to be added in the future. "This enterprising and expanding nation," enthused the *Washington Post* in 1899, "may [develop] a necessity for a Department of Colonies, which, presumably, will have for its head a Colonial Secretary, with a seat in the Cabinet.... [a] great department."[32] It was destined never to happen. Not through mere inattention nor departmental rivalry. The deeper reasons were philosophical.

The old-line European imperial powers administered their dependencies through central colonial offices, backed up by a corps of specialized civil servants.[33] So conspicuous an imperial apparatus was unacceptable in the United States. Having cast off the colonial yoke themselves not so long ago, Americans harbor an abiding ambivalence about possessing subservient territories of their own. While a string of flag colonies stirred within the British, French, Germans, Dutch, Portuguese, and Japanese a swaggering national pride, the same achievement leaves Americans feeling a little uneasy. The political manifestation has been to keep the country's imperialism as discreet as possible. Its possessions are known, not by the emotion-laden term "colonies," but by the euphemisms "territories" or "insular areas." And the instrument for administering them is shunted to the bureaucratic backwaters where it need twinge no consciences.[34]

The haphazard way in which the territories were looked after at the turn of the twentieth century bothered some. President Theodore Roosevelt, whose commitment to imperialism was matched by his desire for orderly government, sought authority to centralize the responsibility. He asked Senator Foraker, chairman of the chamber's committee on Puerto Rico and the Pacific islands:

> Cannot you get a rider on one of the pending bills authorizing the President to designate the Department which shall supervise or assume headship over all our island possessions? It is my experience that the lack of some supervising power in the Cabinet over our island possessions works ill. It is a disadvantage to me that I have not Porto Rico, for instance, under the Secretary of War. Guam and Tutuila [Samoa] should also be under him.[35]

While Roosevelt's request came to nought, the makings of something approaching a central colonial office already were to be found in an existing Washington agency. The Department of War, the civilian overlord of the army, had wasted no time after the Spanish-American War—just three days after the peace treaty was signed—to create an internal office to superintend the territories acquired by the victorious troops. Its first chief was a tall, sober young major recently returned from the Cuban front, McIntyre's West Point classmate Pershing. After a series of reorganizations and name changes, the agency emerged in 1902 as the Bureau of Insular Affairs.[36]

The bureau held jurisdiction over the two largest possessions: the Philippines and (except for a nine-year hiatus) Puerto Rico. It oversaw the other major former colony wrested from Spain — Cuba — during its four-year preparation for independence. The office also served as an informational center for all the dependencies, even those run by the navy.[37] Its powers, however, were only sketchily defined, an opening for adding new responsibilities as America's imperial fling forged ahead.[38] Secretary of War Elihu Root once marveled that the bureau had its fingers in so many tasks "which in other countries would be performed by a much more pretentious establishment."[39]

It was into this budding entity that McIntyre was about to be thrust. His deft touch in territorial matters had commended him to Root's successor as secretary of war, William Howard Taft, himself a colonial old hand as a former governor of the Philippines. Taft appointed the soldier in 1905 assistant chief of the insular bureau.[40]

One of his most vexing challenges lay not out in the islands but right in the office: coping with the inadequacies of his chief. Clarence R. Edwards was a colonel with crafty, hooded eyes and a pompous set to his jaw.[41] He shared with McIntyre combat experience in the Philippines, but there any similarity between the two men ended. Edwards owed his position less to any particular qualifications for dealing with the protectorates than to personal connections. He was an intimate of Taft, and his wife a favorite of Root, who had advanced from secretary of war to secretary of state. The placid McIntyre had to contend with his chief's cantankerousness. The unsociable assistant manned the office while the boss lounged at the Metropolitan Club, a convenient one-block stroll up the street, courting Washington bigwigs.[42] Edwards, in the view of one detractor, "was a very charming phony."[43]

The assistant chief was the bureau workhorse. He traveled as a troubleshooter to two Caribbean countries where the United States had intervened — Cuba in 1906 and the Dominican Republic in 1908.[44] He mounted inspection trips to Puerto Rico and the Philippines.[45] Keeping tabs on America's outlying extensions at that time was no jet-hopping jaunt. It entailed laborious journeys by train and steamship, in the case of the Philippines, a transpacific voyage of longer than two weeks each way.

The one-time mathematics scholar showed a knack for the complexities of territorial finances. He became the in-house fiscal authority, contriving, among other things, a new currency system for the Philippines.[46] He also found time to fill in as the agency's liaison with Congress, drafting a stream of legislation.[47]

In an army bureaucracy not often associated with intellectual ferment, McIntyre managed to find and cultivate men who shared his erudite interests. One was Felix Frankfurter, a bureau legal officer aged in his twenties, starting a public career that would lead to New Deal innovation and the Supreme Court. The two became fast friends. "He was a superior person," Frankfurter later remembered his old colleague, "a man of learning and understanding."[48]

McIntyre's capabilities did not escape notice. His commander-in-chief, Roosevelt, pronounced him "one of the finest men in the army."[49] (The esteem, however, may have been unreciprocated. McIntyre is said to privately have dismissed the brash Roosevelt, hardly his type, as a grandstander.)[50] Another fan was rising army star Pershing. He and McIntyre had palled together at West Point, fought on neighboring islands in the Philippines, and kept in touch over the years. Pershing is believed to have extolled to the army high command his friend's performance at the agency he once had headed.[51] McIntyre's prospects were aided by a seemingly instinctive likability. He was described at the time by the *Washington Post* as "one of the most popular men in military service."[52]

Such glowing estimations assured that the assistant would one day succeed Edwards. When the chief was given command of a fort in Wyoming in 1912, McIntyre took over the bureau.[53] He chose another West Point classmate as his assistant.[54] Promotion at work was accompanied by promotion in rank: from colonel to brigadier general. Nor was it an ordinary advancement, for McIntyre became, at age forty-seven, the army's youngest general.[55]

The bureau which the new general acquired was no career capstone. It was a bureaucratic Lilliput — not only by contrast with the mammoth colonial ministries of European powers, but even by Washington standards. The office lay tucked away in a few small rooms in the labyrinths of the State, War, and Navy Building, a bare-bones operation further attenuated by periodically exiling some employees to another building elsewhere in the city. The clerical staff in one early year numbered sixty-one, drawing a total payroll of sixty-six thousand dollars. Few Americans ever had heard of the agency.[56]

But the government had come to rely on the obscure little bureau, and particularly on the shrewd officer who ran it, in the alien task of tending a collection of scattered islands. The secretary of war in Taft's presidency, Henry L. Stimson, once confessed to McIntyre his "absolute confidence ... that I could leave the direction of the colonial work virtually entirely to you."[57]

Changeover at the insular bureau coincided with changeover at the White House. The newly-elected Woodrow Wilson, unlike his predecessors Roosevelt and Taft, had no personal exposure to the country's overseas kingdom and no clear policy. His new secretary of war, Lindley M. Garrison, was equally unversed in the empire whose management he had inherited. Like Stimson before him, the secretary happily delegated the protectorates to McIntyre.[58]

A major responsibility of the agency was choosing mainlanders to direct the territorial governments, and then supervising them. In that era of tight American control of its offshore satellites, expatriate civil servants ran much of the public sector. In the Philippines alone in the year of McIntyre's accession, 2,633 Americans worked in the insular government — more than a quarter of the roster. While most were selected at the territorial level, the upper tier throughout the dependencies was appointed in Washington — from governors down to postmasters and school superintendents. Once settled into cane seats in Manila or San Juan, they found the insular bureau casting a watchful eye over their shoulders. A cable signed "MC INTYRE" was to be disregarded at one's peril. Woe betide an appointee who lost the chief's confidence.[59]

Normally a model of tact, the general, in dealing with governors under his aegis, occasionally revealed a tougher side. Philippines Governor W. Cameron Forbes learned that he had been replaced in 1913 in a curt cable from McIntyre stating that his resignation "would be convenient."[60] A later governor of Puerto Rico, who had rashly circumvented the chief by corresponding directly with his patron in the White House, Warren G. Harding, was condemned to a tenure troubled and abbreviated.[61]

As the temper of the times regarding the territories grew less retentive, McIntyre became an intermediary in loosening the country's hold on its largest possession. He examined conditions in the Philippines at first hand on a forty-day visit in 1915, recommending sweeping Filipinization but stopping short of independence in the foreseeable future. Back in Washington, he worked closely but discreetly with Congressman Jones to revise the imperial relationship. His input may be detected in the ultimate legislation the following year extending a promise of eventual freedom at no specified date.[62]

By the time the Jones Act became law, the Great War had engulfed Europe and within a year it had drawn in the United States. Territorial matters were superceded by wartime demands. McIntyre was borrowed from the insular bureau by the army's general staff. He was put in charge of public relations for a war effort far from universally popular. Repeating a role performed eighteen years earlier as a young captain in the Philippines, he served as a press censor. As before, his leniency won favor among journalists. He took over as chief press censor from a fellow officer eager for action on the French front: Douglas MacArthur.[63]

When his old West Point chum Peyton March rose in 1918 to the army's top post, chief of staff, he picked McIntyre as his assistant. For a year and a half, he wielded the clout of the second most powerful officer in the army.[64] But the war had diminished some of the appeal of a quiet, if heady, life at headquarters. McIntyre the desk officer requested service in France. He was promised a command there, only to have the opportunity eclipsed by armistice in November 1918.[65]

Instead of sailing off to France, the general trudged down the War Department corridors back to the Bureau of Insular Affairs.[66]

Both he and the territorial domain that he resumed managing had emerged from the war subtly changed. His pate had grown bald and his moustache grey.[67] His purview, meanwhile, had grown. The expansive suzerain had picked up another acquisition: the U.S. Virgin Islands, purchased in 1917 from Denmark. (The new territory was assigned to the navy, however, only under McIntyre's peripheral overview.)[68] Not only was the fief larger, but a trifle freer. Woodrow Wilson, once his concept of home-style imperialism had come into focus, had fostered a climate of liberalization. The Philippines and Puerto Rico had been conceded greater autonomy.[69] But beneficence had not prevailed everywhere. Other places only informally part of the American orb had felt an iron rod. In the name of restoring public order, the U.S. military had occupied two nations sharing the Caribbean island of Hispaniola — Haiti and the Dominican Republic.[70]

The returning boss needed to reacquaint himself with his bailiwick. Hardly had he moved back into his office in 1920 before heading off to the Philippines. It was his fourth visit to the distant possession.[71] There he basked in the goodwill generated by the Jones Act's promise of independence and a governor (former New York congressman Francis B. Harrison) whose ardent championing of Filipinos made him the most popular ever sent.[72] McIntyre's own stature as an authority on the islands was increasingly recognized. "I don't know any American who knows more about conditions in the Philippines," declared the era's most prominent Filipino leader, Manuel L. Quezon, "than does McIntyre."[73] When the governorship fell vacant in 1927, he was mooted for the post. However flattering such speculation, the general's aversion to public life would have made him cringe from the job, which in any event went to Stimson.[74]

Not that the chief was missing out on professional advancement. He was elevated in 1921 to major general. Yet he was the most junior officer heading a bureau in the War Department.[75]

The Caribbean soon demanded the general's presence. The Arcadian Puerto Rico which had given the fresh-faced doughboy his first inviting glimpse overseas had become, twenty-seven years later, an island in distress. In the Roaring Twenties, all that was roaring in America's second largest possession were population growth, poverty, unemployment, the profits of U.S.–owned agricultural exporters, and the dependency's inability to feed itself.[76] In the year of McIntyre's 1925 visit, the son of a renowned island political leader whose mantle he would soon assume, Luis Muñoz Marín, observed caustically that "the story of Porto Rico is ... economically, the triumph of after-dinner delicacies — coffee, sugar, tobacco — over the dinner itself."[77]

The beggarly conditions were assuaged somewhat, for the visitor from Washington, by the remedial efforts of his island host, one of the War Department's most salutary gubernatorial choices for Puerto Rico. Horace Mann Towner had been well schooled in territorial matters as an Iowa congressman chairing the House insular affairs committee. As governor, he had reformed taxes to narrow the possession's gaping disparities of wealth.[78]

The visit produced a rare breach in McIntyre's wall of resistance to publicity. Somehow he was induced — the only known occasion in his life — to grant an interview to a magazine, the popular *Puerto Rico Ilustrado*.[79]

The inspection tour took the chief also to Haiti, the Dominican Republic, and Panama. He was accompanied by two daughters, then at the lively ages of about fourteen and twenty. His wife, Mary, was confined at home by frail health suffered since a difficult delivery of the youngest child.[80] The Caribbean trip was repeated three years later, with the same destinations and the same two daughters in tow.[81]

A regressive turn in political attitude toward the possessions during this period in Washington tested McIntyre's agility. Wilson's trio of conservative Republican successors — Harding, Calvin Coolidge, and Herbert Hoover — shared not his open-handedness. Harding opposed, as he had done as a senator, any commitment to set the Philippines free.⁸² Coolidge spurned extending Puerto Rico more self-government.⁸³ Hoover vetoed legislation giving the Philippines independence in ten years, and branded the Virgin Islands "an effective poorhouse."⁸⁴ To McIntyre fell the delicate task of tempering the harsh edges of sternness while mollifying resentment in the territories.⁸⁵

The Caribbean expedition marked his farewell to the dependencies. The general in 1929 reached the army's mandatory retirement age of sixty-four and was mustered out.⁸⁶ He had worn the uniform longer than the country had worn the robes of empire (forty-three years), and had helped rule its realm for nearly the life span of its version of a colonial office.

So steeped in offshore America, the retiree couldn't just walk away from it. Nor did his government, nor his friends in the islands, wish him to do so. The insular bureau which he had guided for two decades retained its departed chief as a consultant — partly official, partly voluntary on his part.⁸⁷ The Philippine government hired him as a lobbyist. Bestowed the grand and rather euphemistic title of Philippine trade commissioner, McIntyre rented an office in the equally grand Barr Building newly built overlooking Farragut Square in downtown Washington. The former colonialistic administrator of Filipinos now worked for their self-determination.⁸⁸

Old associates in the possessions also recruited him into the railroad business which once had occupied both his father and father-in-law. McIntyre chaired the board of the Philippine Railroad Company and served as a director of the Panama Railway Steamship Line.⁸⁹

He put aside his distaste for socializing to hold a membership in the Army and Navy Club in Washington and New York.⁹⁰

When pressure began mounting to switch supervision of the nation's dependencies from military to civilian hands, the retired general could no longer remain circumspectly quiet.⁹¹ He sallied forth to publicly defend the mission to which he had devoted his life. For the prestigious journal *Foreign Affairs*, he wrote in 1932 an article that reads like a valedictory.

> The theory that there is something in the education and training of military men which unfits them for dealing with civilians is not supported by the experience of the United States or by that of foreign countries....
> The work of the War Department in the Philippines, in Porto Rico, in the Canal Zone, in Cuba and elsewhere has been well done. If it has fallen short of perfection there remains the satisfaction of remembering that many expert critics predicted that it could not be done at all.⁹²

A shroud of sadness fell with the passing in 1935 of McIntyre's wife, after years of semi-invalidism.⁹³ Grief had darkened the family home tragically often. The couple had lost a son, the general's namesake Frank, Jr., in 1915 at the age of twenty.⁹⁴ Then, two years before Mrs. McIntyre departed, the middle daughter, Margaret, perished of a sudden illness in Denver, Colorado, at the age of twenty-four.[95] But consolation was to be found elsewhere in the family. The elder son, James, born propitiously at West Point, had followed his father into the army and advanced rapidly.[96]

The widower moved to the Washington home of his elder daughter, Marie.[97] After a long career negotiating the passages of the capital bureaucracy, McIntyre was ready for a complete change. He severed his ties the following year with his former agency and the Philippines, and left Washington altogether.[98] He reverted to his Southern roots. He returned to his hometown of Montgomery, Alabama, where another daughter and son resided.[99] There the urbane ex-general underwent an unlikely transformation into businessman and cattleman. He owned a warehouse company. And he bought and operated several farms, including one baronial spread of eight thousand acres, for breeding Hereford cattle.[100]

The busy retiree began taking trips every winter to Florida.[101] During one such pilgrimage to Miami Beach in 1944, he passed away at the age of seventy-eight.[102]

As if to confirm that McIntyre had been the very soul of the Bureau of Insular Affairs, the agency failed to survive him. The territories it managed were turned over in 1934 and 1939 to the Department of the Interior, and the office was disbanded.[103] An era of American imperial administration — in many ways, the McIntyre era — had ended.

10
Theodore Roosevelt, Jr.
Governor of Puerto Rico, 1929–1932

A Model A Ford clattered into a town somewhere in Puerto Rico, rounded the central plaza, and drew up in front of an old Spanish city hall. Out jumped an American. His slightness was belied by the face of a pugilist, with nose flattened crooked, and the aplomb of one born to lead.

He strode inside and summoned the mayor. Then he sent out word that he, the governor, was on hand, available to anyone wishing to speak with him. Although no one had been expecting the island's chief executive — these inspection visits were deliberately unannounced — townspeople began trooping in. Before long, two or three hundred crammed the building. The questions poured out. The small figure at the front of the room fielded them all gamely in a halting Spanish that left his hearers alternately bemused and impressed by his pluck. He even engaged the occasional sharpie in a bit of banter, to the mirth of his audience.[1]

The governor at times flashed a toothy smile that recalled one of the day's most famous and recognizable public figures, known even to many Puerto Ricans: Theodore Roosevelt. For before them stood his eldest son and namesake.

Theodore Roosevelt, Jr., bore the mixed benefits and burdens of wearing an eminent name.

He owed much to his father's pervasive example. The Puerto Rican inspections, for instance, patterned the celebrated surprise visits by the elder Roosevelt, as a New York City police commissioner thirty years earlier, to precinct stations and cops on the beat.[2]

But the son also strived mightily to prove his capabilities as a distinct individuality. In Puerto Rico, at least, he succeeded. In his own right, "Ted" Roosevelt was arguably the best governor from the mainland, in a line half a century long, whom the home country ever sent to the island.

Yet identification with the man whose name he carried was as inescapable as it was inevitable. It began in the most tender years of boyhood. No sooner had the toddler learned to walk than he took to trying on his father's shoes and tromping around the family house on Long Island, New York, acting out literally a role that he would perform metaphorically for the rest of his life. Another favorite pastime also presaged a future preoccupation: games of hide-and-seek with his father and siblings (eventually to number five) in the shadowy upper recesses of the Sagamore Hill mansion — searching for the elder Roosevelt, as in many ways he would find himself continuing to do ever after.³

Theodore Roosevelt, Jr., 1924 (Library of Congress).

The young Ted, like the young Theodore, endured a childhood of debility. His body was scrawny, his eyes slightly crossed, and his speech mildly impaired.⁴ As in his own oft-recounted youthful invigoration, the father prescribed for his son a regimen to nurture him physically as well as intellectually. Private tutoring at home was followed by study at the local one-room public schoolhouse, then boarding at prestigious Groton School in Massachusetts.⁵ The pint-sized kid displayed a pugnacity out of all proportion to his size. His father reckoned the tyke "a tougher, hardier little fellow" than he himself ever had been.⁶ Roughhousing at school was welcomed as a sign of growing robustness.⁷

He was exposed to the rugged outdoor life so valued by his father. Ted was sent to the cabin of naturalist John Burroughs in the upper Hudson River valley for a week of hiking, fishing, and bird-watching.⁸ As a teenager, he and brother Quentin were packed off by the senior Roosevelt — whose accession to the presidency prevented him from escorting them himself— on a hunting expedition in the Black Hills of what was then the Dakota Territory, site of his own wilderness epiphany years before.⁹ Noticing his eldest son's innate aggressiveness, his father introduced him to the Japanese martial art of jujutsu, in which he himself was taking lessons at the White House.¹⁰

Under the attentions of a father who was nothing if not engaged with his children — detractors were wont to ridicule Roosevelt as never having outgrown boyhood — Ted developed interests akin to those of his father. They would last a lifetime.

A penchant for matters military showed itself early. "Someday," Ted announced at the family dinner table one day at age nine, "I'm going to be a soldier."[11] Sparked, perhaps, by his own combativeness, the inclination was stoked by history lessons and fanned into glowing flame by his father. The boy loved to walk to work in Washington with his dad when assistant secretary of the navy, drinking in accounts of great military campaigns, the indulgent elder sometimes squatting to trace battle lines in the dust with his finger.[12]

A future outdoorsman was similarly bred. The game-hunting father read to him and Quentin stirring tales of hunting and introduced them to celebrated hunters.[13]

Ted also was drawn toward public life. The national press coverage lavished on the lively brood of Roosevelt children growing up in the White House accustomed Ted, from adolescence, to living in the spotlight.[14]

Scrappiness increasingly came to characterize the young Roosevelt's approach to life. It left its stamp on his education — and, more lastingly, on his visage. His career at Harvard University was punctuated by football mayhem, fistfights (as previously at Groton), and rebelliousness toward attending classes. Ted threw himself into intercollegiate football with reckless abandon. Competing in his first game against arch-rival Yale University as the lightest player on the field, he sustained a broken nose. It defied surgery to remain permanently disjointed.[15]

Ted took his college degree and escaped, briefly, the long shadow cast by his father in the White House. Foreswearing family connections, by his own efforts he found a job in a carpet mill near Hartford, Connecticut. Declining a family allowance, he subsisted on seven dollars a day. He wanted no favored treatment and got none, relegated at times to washing by hand newly-loomed carpets.[16] But the drudgery was relieved by romance.

The object of his affections was a young woman whom he had met soon after entering the work force. Eleanor Alexander was a demure product of New York City's society class. She beheld the world through wide, playful eyes that masked a keen intelligence and steely self-possession. Like Ted's mother, she embodied a paradoxical combination of independence and subservience to her mate's career. The two were married in 1910 in New York City.[17]

The bridegroom was no longer the anemic stripling of Sagamore Hill. While still small, at five feet seven inches tall, he had been transformed by "the strenuous life" espoused by his father into a specimen of sinewy vigor.[18] He didn't, however, really look much like his namesake. Without knowing that he was the son of Theodore Roosevelt, few people would have guessed so. The brow was more broad, the eyes spaced more widely, the face more bony, the lips more full. The blue eyes, unshielded by the pince-nez spectacles emblematic of his father, could penetrate coldly or radiate warmth. The smile was beguiling. It crinkled his face like a wad of paper.[19]

The newlyweds moved to the West Coast when the junior Roosevelt won promotion to the carpet company's office in San Francisco.[20] But the rug trade soon palled. Seeking something offering more dash and money, he returned east in 1912 to enter the securities business in Manhattan. The bond salesman and investment banker had attained enough success to become in 1914 a partner in a brokerage house in Philadelphia.[21]

The next generation of Roosevelts, meanwhile, was making its appearance. Theodore Roosevelt received his first grandchild two years after leaving the presidency, with the birth to Eleanor and Ted of a daughter, Grace. She was to be joined in coming years by three brothers.[22]

For Theodore, Jr., now in his twenties, the new career in the private sector blended with a new one in the public sector: politics. It was a calling manifestly closer to his heart than high finance. Indeed, his goal is said to have been to rake in enough money working for a few years in the financial markets to underwrite a life in politics.[23] Out in California, he had apprenticed as a political liaison for his father. The restless ex-president was then maneuvering for a return to elective politics. On his behalf, son Ted met with California Governor Hiram Johnson, who was to become his father's vice-presidential running-mate on the 1912 Progressive party ticket. He also arranged a speech by the elder Roosevelt at the Berkeley campus of the University of California. After relocating back east, he drew on his network of acquaintances among financiers — whom his father, no friend of Wall Street, jocularly termed "the plutocrats"— to drum up support for the former president.[24]

The junior Roosevelt's zest for military affairs impelled him into action as Europe became locked in a war beyond any previously known. His country might remain an aloof bystander, but he could not. The young man who once had hoped to attend one of the nation's military academies[25] inaugurated military instruction of his own. He and like-minded friends organized in the summer of 1915 a training camp for young businessmen at Plattsburg, New York. To head up the venture, they conscripted General Leonard Wood, Rough Rider Theodore Roosevelt's one-time commander in Cuba.[26] The throngs of volunteers — more than one thousand turned out — evidenced a pent-up readiness for war that rebuked the restraint of the Wilson administration.[27]

The eldest son of the eager volunteer in the Spanish-American War was the most avid among his offspring to fight in the world war. He soon got his chance. Just weeks after the United States entered the war against Germany,

Ted and his brother Archie were called to duty. Their training at the Plattsburg camp qualified them for positions that most doughboys would have relished: reserve officers. But the two Roosevelt would-be warriors were disappointed. They had been ordered back to Plattsburg Barracks, facing the bleak prospect of sitting out the war Stateside, drilling recruits.

For perhaps the only time in his life, the junior Roosevelt asked his father to intervene. The former president appealed to General John J. Pershing, commander of American forces. He asked if Ted and Archie might enlist in the regular army as privates and go to France with the first batch of U.S. troops. Pershing (and the secretary of war) consented, save for deeming the two young men to be underutilized as mere privates. The brothers sailed for Europe in June 1917 as commissioned officers, boning up on French en route.[28]

In the war zone, Ted again had to argue his way to combat duty. He refused a staff position, and instead took command of an infantry battalion on the front lines. One of Major Roosevelt's battalion captains was brother Archie. They received in full measure the battlefield action they had craved. They were gassed at Cantigny. They fought Germans hand-to-hand.[29]

But the horrors of war were assuaged by special family dispensations. Eleanor, ever the supportive wife, had followed her husband to Europe, helping the Young Men's Christian Association to establish canteens for servicemen on furlough. She set up house in Paris, where the Roosevelt brothers found periodic refuge from their trenches, just two hours away. Another brother, Quentin, was stationed at an aerodrome as a fighter pilot, and a fourth, Kermit, joined them in France after fighting with British forces in Iraq. Eleanor supplied Ted's pampered battalion with cases of soft drinks, pounds of tobacco, baseball equipment, and boxing gloves.[30]

Mindful of the scrutiny imposed by his famous name, Major Roosevelt exercised his command with leniency. Shunning the courts-martial used routinely by fellow commanders to enforce subordination, he relied on less harsh forms of discipline.[31]

The crucible of combat seemed to smelt his raw fighting spirit into something finer: military gallantry. He led a raid into enemy territory and rescued a wounded comrade under fire, earning several decorations. His brother Quentin was less fortunate, perishing in July 1918 in an air battle over Germany. Days later at Soissons, Ted himself was peppered by machine gun fire in a leg. Field ambulances scarce, he grittily hitchhiked his way to medical attention in Paris by artillery limber, motorcycle sidecar, and private auto. Disconsolate tamely recuperating on crutches as a training instructor behind the lines, the newly-promoted lieutenant colonel slipped away to resume command of his regiment.[32]

The junior Roosevelt emerged from the war with a demonstrated affinity for military life. His commander, Brigadier General Francis C. Marshall, wrote to his father on Armistice Day words that must have filled the former commander-in-chief with pride:

> I don't wish to be fulsome, but I do wish to tell you that your son is a magnificent soldier, and that his men love him almost to idolatry.[33]

While the eldest son hadn't marched off to war simply to measure himself against his father, his pursuits in life were underlain by a continual process of comparison — by himself as much as by others — to the outsized persona of TR.[34] A month after the letter of commendation from the front, Eleanor, just returned from France, called on her father-in-law, laid up in failing health at Sagamore Hill.

> "You know, Father," [she said,] "Ted has always worried for fear he would not be worthy of you." ...
> "Worthy of me?" [the elder Roosevelt replied.] "Darling, I'm so very proud of him. He has won high honor not only for his children but, like the Chinese, he has ennobled his ancestors. I walk with my head higher because of him."[35]

A week later, the patriarch, as daunting as he was fatherly, had expired. Archie's cablegram from home, "THE OLD LION IS DEAD," reached brother Ted in the post-armistice stillness near Koblenz on the German frontier.[36]

Colonel Roosevelt, soon to be demobilized, delayed his return to the United States to address the plight of the thousands of fellow veterans reentering a civilian life fraught with uncertainties. Several weeks of brainstorming with a score of other officers in Paris led to the birth of the veterans' organization known as the American Legion.[37]

Roosevelt himself was one returning serviceman whose homecoming was blithely unclouded by uncertainty. He knew precisely the next direction for his life. In the closing days of the war, his father had urged him in a letter to return home and "come forward in public life."[38] The advice probably was unneeded. His son had long been preparing, both cognitively and practically, to do just that. His outreaching, empathetic personality, and what his wife described as "a remarkable faculty of making one feel at one's best,"[39] were potential political commodities. More tangibly, he had amassed a war chest of half a million dollars to bankroll a try at politics.[40]

He set off at once running for public office. His first public appearance after returning home took place at a gathering of the local Republican party. Standing jauntily before the crowd, hands on hips, he declared, in a turn of phrase that might have sprung from his late father: "It's bully to be home again!" Despite already talk of higher office for the war hero with the famous name, the junior Roosevelt announced his candidacy for the low-rung post of state assemblyman.[41]

He campaigned with the hellbent tenacity he had displayed on the football field and the battlefield. The fog-horn voice, booming out from the incongruously small frame, drowned out all others. The political views were as firm as those of his father, but expressed in a manner more confrontational. Whereas the elder Roosevelt had a gift of arguing with intellectual force, the son often came across as merely dogmatic.[42] As a niece put it, her uncle was "lacking in subtlety."[43] On the campaign trail, as elsewhere, he seemed a rougher version of his namesake.

His local-lad popularity won Roosevelt election in 1919 by the largest margin in the history of the legislative district. The triumph was sweetened by the birth, on election day, of the couple's fourth child, a son Quentin.[44]

Assemblyman Roosevelt showed himself, like his father, politically conservative with a streak of independence. In his maiden speech, he startled many by arguing against expelling from the legislature five Socialists. He was outvoted. Forsaking his Wall Street ties, he also at times upheld the interests of labor over corporations.[45]

He was soon drawn into national politics by the unlikely lure of an intrafamily squabble. A distant cousin, Franklin D. Roosevelt, assistant secretary of the navy, had been nominated for vice president on the Democratic presidential ticket headed by James M. Cox, governor of Ohio, in the forthcoming 1920 election. Convinced that the Democrats, and the family nominee himself, were expropriating Theodore Roosevelt's good name for a party he had abhorred, the presidential son volunteered to barnstorm the country ostensibly setting the record straight. He did so with all the zeal of a defender of the family honor. "He is a maverick," he said of Franklin in Sheridan, Wyoming. "He does not have the brand of our family." The Cox-Roosevelt team lost the election to Republicans Harding and Coolidge, an outcome to which Theodore Roosevelt, Jr., may have had the satisfaction of having mustered a few votes. The antipathy between the Oyster Bay and Hyde Park branches of the family was to long endure.[46]

Whether on the hustings, in a trench on the western front, or at home, the junior Roosevelt, like his father, was a voracious reader. Not only did reading afford enjoyment, but it also reflected his ethic of turning every moment to productive use. Eschewing the theater and movie house, his favorite entertainment was a quiet evening at home in an easy chair, the surrounding floor strewn with books. On military leaves in Paris during the Great War, he would gather up books from around the house and read aloud. His tastes, like those of his father, ran to the classics, both new and old. The traveling library that he later took along on trips included a volume by the ancient Greek poet Theocritus.[47] He once asserted:

I read in bed. I read in my bath. I read in the train. I read in the subway. I would feel as desolate without a book in my pocket as I would if I had lost my trousers.[48]

The passion for books led before long to writing one of his own. He recounted his war experiences in a work entitled *Average Americans,* published in 1919.[49] It was his entrée into a lifelong avocation as an author.

The national political arena, into which Roosevelt had thrust himself during the 1920 presidential campaign, was to retain him for a spell. A grateful President Harding appointed him to a position that had become something of a Roosevelt family sinecure: assistant secretary of the navy. It had been held by his father twenty years earlier, and just vacated by his cousin Franklin.[50]

Returning to the capital city where he had spent many of his formative years, the junior Roosevelt enjoyed living in the nexus of political power and social networking. Poker games at his house frequently attracted the president himself.[51] But the energetic former field commander found his job dull. He complained to a friend of feeling "yoked to" his desk.[52] His chief assignment was a thankless rearguard fight to protect the navy from overly drastic cuts under a 1922 treaty reducing the world's battle fleets.[53]

The naval appointment was a diversion from his goal of higher elective office. He hankered to put himself again before the voters. The most logical post to pursue was, as before, one previously filled by his father: governor of New York. He began making exploratory trips to his home state to gauge the extent of his support.[54]

It was at that delicate political stage that the rising tide of corruption in the Harding administration spilled over on Roosevelt. His early navy responsibilities had involved him peripherally in a seemingly innocuous transfer of naval oil reserves at a place in Wyoming called Teapot Dome to the Interior Department (a switch that he had opposed as detrimental to national security). He had forgotten about it until the sensational disclosure that the public oil had been leased to private interests, to the profit of Interior Secretary Albert B. Fall and the Sinclair Oil Company. Roosevelt had been a Sinclair stockholder, but his wife fortuitously had sold the shares four months before the leasing deal. His brother Archie was a Sinclair vice president, but also a company whistle-blower who reported that his boss had bribed the interior secretary. Theodore, Jr., testified at the ensuing Senate investigation and won exoneration.[55]

An obstacle looming larger than Teapot Dome for the New York gubernatorial candidate in 1924 was the popularity of incumbent Alfred E. "Al" Smith. But when the Republican favorite, speaker of the state assembly, dropped out of the race sensing certain defeat, Roosevelt got his chance. The nomination was his. He campaigned strenuously, delivering as many as twenty speeches a day, most from the rear platform of a railway parlor car whistle-stopping through small towns. It was an uphill struggle.[56] He quipped: "I was supposed to be a beaten man at the start."[57]

His badgering of Franklin Roosevelt as a vice presidential candidate four years earlier was returned in kind. The latter's wife, who shared with his own the name Eleanor, toured the state in a car roofed with a gigantic papier-mâché "teapot" intended to tar the junior Roosevelt with the Teapot Dome scandal. (The stunt drew from her in later years a contrite apology.)[58]

In a race deemed by many to be hopeless, Roosevelt made a respectable showing, losing to Smith by one hundred thousand votes among three million cast. The outcome positioned the victor for the Democratic presidential nomination in 1928. But it effectively drove the loser out of elective politics.[59]

Theodore, Jr., drowned his disappointment in true Rooseveltian fashion: he trekked abroad to hunt big game. It was an expedition undertaken as much for the halls of science as for the trophy room. The Field Museum of Natural History in Chicago sponsored a search by him and his brother Kermit on the northern slopes of the Himalayas in central Asia for the rare wild sheep *Ovis poli*. They bagged eight of the sheep, then, joined by their wives, hunted in Kashmir.[60]

The involuntary respite from public life also afforded time for the quieter pastime of writing. There issued forth a series of books — on the Asian hunt (*East of the Sun and West of the Moon*, co-authored with Kermit), acts of heroism in the recent war (*Rank and File*), and life at Sagamore Hill (*All in the Family*).[61]

Another hunt for the Chicago museum followed. He and Kermit scoured northern Indochina for the giant panda, then little known to science. The quest succeeded, but its exertions killed two participants and left Ted a malarial skeleton.[62]

The junior Roosevelt increasingly found himself at pains to square his hunting with his image as a conservationist. He exulted in the natural world and sought to protect it unspoiled. As assistant secretary of the navy, he was proud to have convened a conference that set guidelines for federal recreation facilities.[63] "Many of us ... really have more naturalist in us than hunter," he explained to a friend. "I practically never shoot the same kind of game twice.... I have not shot a wild animal in North America for twenty years."[64]

From the depths of Indochina, the hunter was about to be plucked from political exile. In his absence, Roosevelt's wife and elder sister Alice had been busily lobbying on his behalf for a position in the incoming government of Herbert Hoover. Five years earlier, as rising stars in the Republican party, the two men had worked together vainly to arrest the rudderless drift of the

Harding administration.[65] Roosevelt later had harbored ambitions of becoming Hoover's vice presidential ticket-mate. His family now touted him for the plum job of governor of the Philippines, the country's largest possession. The only offer forthcoming, however, was governor of Puerto Rico.[66]

When the proposal reached the panda stalker, his first response — carried from the jungle by runner, like a scene from Kipling — was to reject it as unworthy of his qualifications. But his wife urged him to reconsider, and he changed his mind. He accepted the appointment to keep his public-service career alive.[67] "I have got to get into the line of officeholders again," he wrote to her, "or I am going to be forgotten."[68]

However unappealing the post, Roosevelt plunged into the preparation with intensity. On the long voyage home from the Far East, he cultivated a fellow passenger who spoke Spanish and borrowed his textbooks on the language. When the ship docked in New York, he had taught himself a working knowledge of the tongue of the Puerto Ricans whom he would soon be governing.[69] It was a gesture that would prove to be of incalculable value.

The new governor was inaugurated in San Juan on a bright October day in 1929 beneath a canopy of palm fronds erected at the front of the capitol to shade the ceremony from the glaring midday sun. When Roosevelt, in cutaway and top hat, opened his inaugural speech with the words "*Señores y señoras,*" there arose from the assembled crowd of straw-hatted and white-frocked islanders an astonished "Aaaaah!" Then applause and cheers. No previous governor, in thirty years of American rule, had deigned to address Puerto Ricans in their own language. He proceeded to plow through the entire *discurso inaugural* in Spanish.[70]

The island, he told them, held special meaning for him. His father was the only president to visit Puerto Rico, and the glowing accounts of the trip heard as a college student were etched vividly in his memory.[71]

The newly-installed chief executive confided to the press his desire to be a "people's governor."[72] He hoped "to go among the people personally, talk with them, and see [their lives] for myself."[73] Puerto Ricans were quick to welcome his interest. A delegation from the back country came calling to implore him to venture out of the governor's palace into the island beyond, visiting not just politicians and leading citizens but *jíbaros* (peasants) and other ordinary folk.[74]

He soon began doing just that. At least once a week, the governor would climb into his car, accompanied, as often as not, only by a driver, and set off — without fanfare or prior notice — into the island. He would stop at a school, a town hall, or a private house, look at conditions, and interview people in his stumbling Spanish. To reach mountain fastnesses unserved by passable roads, he rode horseback. Schoolteachers, or policemen, or mayors malingering were caught off guard and reported. Residents, surprised, ushered him into their shacks and huts, pressing him with gifts of eggs or oranges. The Puerto Rican populace, as word of the governor's visits spread, was delighted.[75]

Roosevelt traveled altogether to more than seventy towns, some never previously graced by the presence of a governor.[76]

A young Puerto Rican destined for future island leadership, Luis Muñoz Marín, wrote admiringly to Roosevelt of his "encounters with prominent and unprominent politicians, with poets, writers, beggars, mangoes, legislatures, *pasteles* [pies], points of view, Hispanic idiosyncracies, American garnishings."[77]

Consternation at the poverty that his inspection trips had revealed in the U.S. dependency resolved the governor to bring it to the attention of the American public.[78] He wrote a graphic exposé for the Sunday magazine of the *New York Herald-Tribune*:

> I have stopped at farm after farm where lean, underfed women and sickly men repeated again and again the same story—too little food and no opportunity to get more.... I have seen mothers carrying babies who were little skeletons. I have watched in a classroom thin, pallid little boys and girls, trying to spur their brains to action when their bodies were underfed.[79]

The article stirred a storm. Readers were shocked to learn of children starving under the American flag. Newspapers demanded action, chorused nationally in one two-week span in two hundred editorials. The War Department, alarmed, sought to silence Roosevelt. (He politely refused.)[80] The president was more sympathetic. Hoover sent a commission to investigate and requested three million dollars in aid.[81]

The governor initiated a crash program of his own to revitalize the impoverished possession. Its trademark was a level of personal, hands-on participation to which no governor of a state or territory today would dream of stooping.

To boost income from tourism by attracting more cruise ships, Roosevelt lent his services as celebrity host. He went to the docks to personally welcome disembarking passengers. Often they were then invited to a reception at the governor's palace. "Sometimes we had as many as four hundred and fifty at a time," recalled his wife Eleanor. "Ted would take time out to greet them, and [our housekeeper] and I would show them over the palace and the garden." Such exalted hospitality helped to increase the number of visiting cruise ships from nineteen in 1929 to thirty the following year.[82]

The moribund needlework trade got the same kind of personalized attention. This cottage industry once had been a proud mainstay of the island economy, outranked only by sugar. But mercenary middlemen, miserly remuneration, and inferior materials had reduced it to ruin. Lingerie and table linens from Puerto Rico lost their high reputation — and their mainland market. Reviving the industry became a crusade of the governor's wife. An old lunatic asylum was converted into a workshop where a hundred women, sewing under close supervision for fair wages, produced articles of marketable quality. Samples were distributed to farm families throughout the island for copying on a piecemeal basis. Eleanor became the sales rep. Drawing on her wide circle of acquaintances in New York City, she traveled there frequently (at her own expense) laden with suitcases of Puerto Rican needlework to show to buyers at department stores.[83]

The governor also took the less exceptional step of setting up an agency to lure business firms to the island. It was the forerunner of an industrialization campaign that was to transform Puerto Rico in the 1950s and 1960s into a Caribbean manufacturing powerhouse.[84]

The possession over which Roosevelt presided, however, was still an agrarian society run on mercantile lines. Cultivable land was monopolized by U.S.–owned corporations growing crops for export. The gargantuan sugarcane plantations, he was persuaded, prevented the island from feeding its people and tilling its own soil. He raised half a million dollars through bonds to buy up plantation acreage and redistribute it to the landless, first as leasers and eventually as purchasers, for growing vegetables and other foods. The resulting cornucopia was sufficient to permit export of vegetables to the mainland.[85]

Education, in Roosevelt's Puerto Rico, was made less academic and glamorous, but, in his view, more rational. Although hardly an anti-intellectual, the governor was dismayed to find young islanders routinely trained for highly-skilled fields in which jobs were scarce, while jobs in the trades went unfilled. He established a network of rural vocational schools teaching agriculture, selected trades, and manual arts. The latter, specified the apostle of practicality, were to indulge in "no articles of ornate uselessness."[86]

Roosevelt's most important contribution may have had less to do with tourist dollars, embroidery, or school buildings than with something more elusive: the Puerto Rican spirit. From General Miles's promise in 1898 of the "blessings of enlightened civilization"[87] to a Roosevelt predecessor's avowal in 1921 to infuse "Americanism,"[88] mainlanders had tended to regard Puerto Ricans as products of an inferior culture to be re-made in their own image. "We felt we could do no higher or nobler work," Roosevelt observed, "than to model these other people on ourselves."[89]

He preached a doctrine quite different. To islanders, the message was as inspirational as it was rare: cultural self-esteem. Since the first time he spoke to them — in his inaugural address — the governor encouraged *puertoricanos* to take pride in their Hispanic heritage and retain it. Don't, however, reflexively repudiate all mainland influences, he advised. Blend in those that can be beneficial.⁹⁰

> I told the people that they should be proud of their Spanish language and traditions and preserve both, but that they should learn English and acquaint themselves with Americans' method of thought. I explained to them that one did not eliminate the other, but that by adding the second to the first they were enriched, not impoverished.⁹¹

He took actions to try to slow the tide of Americanization. When efforts arose to scrap the traditional Hispanic Christmas observance of *Magos de Oriente* (The Three Kings) for that of the American Santa Claus ten days earlier, Roosevelt promptly proclaimed 6 January a public holiday.⁹² Enamored of poetry ever since memorizing verse at his father's knee, Roosevelt reveled in Spanish poetics, even composing some himself. He established an annual competition to award two medals for the year's best poem in Spanish and English.⁹³

As with Puerto Rican poetry, the governor took an interest in the island's natural setting. When his two eldest sons came from boarding school in Massachusetts to San Juan for the summer, he took them fishing and, much like his own father, sent them on field trips with a naturalist. One such outing even turned up a new subspecies of lizard, which they gladdened the heart of their mother by naming for her: *Ameiva metmorei eleanorae*.⁹⁴

For a man of privileged breeding, Roosevelt had a ward politician's instinct for the common touch. One of his first acts as governor was to dispose of the two gubernatorial limousines and chauffeurs. He traveled instead in his own Model A Ford, driven by one of the palace guards, to make himself less aloof from his constituents.⁹⁵ He and Eleanor enrolled the child living with them in Puerto Rico, the youngest, ten-year-old Quentin, at a local school for island boys.⁹⁶

When Roosevelt learned that public funds were being used to buy little American flags for schoolchildren to wave at appearances by the governor, he ordered the money spent instead for school breakfasts.⁹⁷

Nothing better exemplified the governor's plebeian inclinations, in the minds of Puerto Ricans, than his adoption of the local tongue. He always had found learning a foreign language difficult, but tackled Spanish with dogged determination.⁹⁸ To expand his vocabulary, every night before retiring he memorized twenty new words, then found a way to work them into conversation the next day.⁹⁹ He disciplined himself to speak Spanish exclusively to all Puerto Ricans except children, whom he wished to encourage to learn English.¹⁰⁰

The governor's Spanish never achieved flawless fluency, however, and he committed his share of gaffes.

> Once, when addressing a group of parents on school problems and desiring to impress them with my knowledge of the subject, I used a direct translation from English into Spanish of "I have four children myself." Unfortunately, the meaning is not the same. I found out that I had informed the startled audience that I had given birth to four children!¹⁰¹

Related the incident by Roosevelt at lunch afterward, the president of the island Senate was unruffled. He just lifted an eyebrow and replied laconically, "*Pero, Señor Gobernador, todo es posible en los tropicos* [But, Mr. Governor, everything is possible in the tropics]."¹⁰²

On another occasion, he bungled the introduction of his visiting supervisor from the War Department in Washington. Mentioning that the general was unmarried, Roosevelt mispronounced the Spanish word for "bachelor" and described him to the audience as a "tapeworm."¹⁰³

His populist instincts made Roosevelt a colonialistic ruler toward whom even the ruled could feel affection. He was that rare imperial satrap for whom Queen Victoria, doting empress of a far larger colonial realm, had yearned so disappointedly — one "liked and beloved by high and low."¹⁰⁴ Puerto Ricans took a shine to the disarming little New Yorker, dubbing him *"el jíbaro de La Fortaleza* [the peasant of the governor's palace]."¹⁰⁵

Peasant's quarters, however, La Fortaleza was not. A crenelated Spanish redoubt built in 1529 on a cliff one hundred feet above the sea, its stone walls, eight feet thick, embraced within them the opulent trappings of Madrid's vanished empire. No official residence of any other U.S. governor matched it in magnificence (nor does so today).¹⁰⁶

Aficionado of conquest and military lore that he was, Roosevelt loved it. His evident relish pervaded the letters dispatched to friends back home inviting them to visit:

> We are living in a splendid old Spanish Palace, within a mile of where [Sir John] Hawkins was buried by [Sir Francis] Drake. In the evening we sit on a terraced turret, under which Spanish treasure from the Indies used to be stored. Altogether, it is delightful.¹⁰⁷

The most eminent visitor whom the governor entertained at La Fortaleza was the president himself. Following in the wake of Roosevelt's father a quarter century before, Hoover became in 1931 the second U.S. chief executive to visit Puerto Rico. He steamed to the island aboard the battleship *Arizona* for a three-day inspection, after calling at the country's sister possession in the Caribbean, the Virgin Islands.¹⁰⁸

Already one of the most indigent corners of America, Puerto Rico bore throughout Roosevelt's governorship the added misfortune of the Great Depression. The territorial treasury ran low and local banks teetered on the brink of insolvency. Sometimes default was averted only by bailouts with the governor's own money. When the government couldn't meet its payroll at year's end in 1930, threatening to spoil the *Magos de Oriente* gift-giving for employees' families, Roosevelt was stirred by nostalgic memories of his own childhood Christmases at Sagamore Hill. He wrote a promissory note of two hundred thousand dollars to cover the payroll until the treasury was replenished. It represented half of his personal assets.[109]

In a bank panic the following year, the governor authorized the government to lend one hundred thousand dollars to a bank on the verge of closing, securing the loan with another personal note. He broadcast a radio message announcing his action and imploring public confidence. Matters stabilized.[110]

Wielding a scepter over people of another culture and language impelled Roosevelt, like many others before him, to ponder the problematical constitutional relationship between the United States and Puerto Rico—and how it might best evolve. He was troubled that the political arrangement had been thrust upon islanders without their consent. In a letter to Ernest H. Gruening, who would become three years later the federal government's chief territorial overseer, the governor urged that people in the dependencies choose for themselves their desired status:

> I am of the opinion that some day at an appropriate moment some individual in authority in the United States ought to announce publicly certain truisms insofar as Porto Rico or any Island and people so situated are concerned,—i.e., that their ultimate relation to our nation must be of their own determining.[111]

Although he kept his views discreetly private while governor, Roosevelt had formed his own opinion on the connection with Puerto Rico that might be most suitable. He ruled out statehood because of cultural and economic disparities. He rejected independence on grounds that the island couldn't afford to lose its economic lifeline to the mainland.[112] The option "best for both," he wrote later, was a self-governing "dominion" under American sovereignty.[113] And that, more or less, is what Puerto Rico was eventually to become under the rubric of "commonwealth."

The governorship, which Roosevelt initially had spurned, had been turned into something of a personal triumph. He had shown executive ability. He had won the hearts of the populace. He had attracted notice in the home country. A major Stateside newspaper acclaimed him "one of the finest, and perhaps the finest colonial governor in our history."[114] His career in public service had been revived.

His own self-evaluation was more modest. In meeting Puerto Rico's challenges, he reckoned that he had made only a start. Assessing his accomplishments in a letter to a clergyman, he quoted one of his favorite Biblical phrases:

The work here is stupendous and of course we will not be able to accomplish what we would wish, but at least we can feel that "a great door and effectual is open unto us."[115]

Roosevelt's performance in Puerto Rico persuaded the Hoover administration that he was ready for larger responsibilities. After two years on the island, the president elevated him at the beginning of 1932 to the position that previously had eluded him: governor of the Philippines.[116]

His work in the Pacific displayed many of the trademarks of his service in the Caribbean. He mounted inspection trips throughout the archipelago, logging more than 10,000 miles by boat, train, car, horse, and foot to visit 48 of its 49 provinces. He redistributed land to small farmers and expanded public education. He labored long hours at his Manila office — typically until nearly midnight — then relaxed by going hunting.[117]

The public reception, too, was equally rapturous.[118] The *Philippine Herald* applauded "a Governor General who does not mind being bitten by mosquitoes, who can fall into wild carabao [water buffalo] wallows and like it, who can drink Igorot [tribal] wine and lick his chops, who can be really human without losing his grin."[119]

Presidential politics intruded, however, on Roosevelt's Pacific adventure. Hoover was sternly challenged for reelection in 1932 by Theodore's cousin Franklin. The president invited the governor to return from Manila to campaign against his Democratic foe. While Theodore loathed his Hyde Park kin as much as ever — accusing him in a letter of having "sold his birthright" — he declined, pleading an obligation to the Philippine people.[120] But Franklin's subsequent election ensured a prompt end to Theodore's governorship. Asked by the Philippine press how closely he was related to the incoming president, he quipped: "Fifth cousin, *about to be* removed."[121] He cabled his resignation a day after Franklin's inauguration.[122]

The junior Roosevelt sensed that his life in public office was finished. The Philippine governorship "may well mark the end of my active career as a public servant," he wrote to his mother from Manila.[123] Later he added: "That chapter of our lives is definitely closed. I believe the chances of me 'coming back' politically are almost nonexistent."[124]

His search for new endeavor led him to a field of absorbing interest throughout his life: books. The reader and author branched into publishing. The Doubleday publishing family had been Oyster Bay neighbors, and scion Nelson Doubleday a Prohibition tippling companion. The publishing house lay conveniently near Sagamore Hill on Long Island. Roosevelt in 1933 joined Doubleday, Doran & Company, soon becoming a vice president.[125] The bibliophile was in his element. He told friends it was "the only work I have really enjoyed outside of politics."[126]

The first book of his own to issue from his new publishing home grew from his recent experience as a colonial administrator. He had the distinction of being the only person to have presided over the country's two largest dependencies. And retrospection had crystallized his thoughts on the whole provocative issue of America's foray into imperialism. He expostulated them in a series of lectures at London University in England. Then came the book *Colonial Policies of the United States*.[127]

His years abroad as an American viceroy had turned Roosevelt into an apostate. They had engendered views as averse to the conventional wisdom of his day as they were to the ardent imperialism of his father.[128]

As a nation, the parvenue imperialists whom the junior Roosevelt depicted were not the egalitarian internationalists that they often flattered themselves to be. In ruling others, he found Americans fundamentally handicapped by a superiority complex:

> We have one besetting sin in common with many other peoples, including the British. We think we are better than other people. Anyone who does things in a different fashion than us is either comic or stupid. We regard being a foreigner in the nature of a defective moral attribute. A little proper pride is good for a people and far from objectionable. What is objectionable is showing it.[129]

The constraints imposed by a people so "parochially minded" and by a system of government grounded on consent, in his opinion, rendered Americans poor colonialists.[130] "We are not ... fitted," he concluded, "to carry out any far-range colonial objective."[131]

Private citizen Roosevelt himself cut a figure assertively nonparochial. He lent his name and his time to promoting racial and religious toleration, an activity which in that era still carried a whiff of heterodoxy. It was a cause that he had prominently supported while in the public sphere. He had rebuked anti–Semitism as assistant secretary of the navy[132] and repudiated the support of the Ku Klux Klan in running for governor of New York.[133] Such probity externally was mirrored less consistently in his personal conduct. Roosevelt privately favored immigration quotas and in his diaries referred to Jews by street epithets.[134] But upon resettling in New York, he joined the boards of the National Association for the Advancement of Colored People, the predominantly black Howard University, and the Anti-Defamation League.[135]

Although Roosevelt seems to have reconciled himself to occupying no further elective offices,[136] he couldn't resist opportunities to continue skirmishing politically with the Roosevelt in the White House. He was a highly visible critic of Franklin's presidency, issuing statements and delivering speeches. The governmental activism of the New Deal was to him an anathema which threatened, he warned darkly, to "destroy democracy."[137]

Political frustration was offset by domestic fulfillment. Roosevelt and his wife never had acquired a permanent home, assuming that, as his father's eldest son and namesake, he would one day inherit the Sagamore Hill family seat. The expectation was thwarted by opposition from brother Archie. Ted took the closest alternative. He purchased in 1937 an apple orchard adjoining Sagamore and put his home there. His architect son-in-law designed a spacious Georgian house shot through, front to rear, by a long hallway. Hung with portraits of four generations of Roosevelts and artifacts from exotic travels, the hallway became a baronial family gallery. Books crowded the library, and spilled over into most other rooms.[138] In the parlors and on the lawns of Old Orchard, as he named the house, Roosevelt entertained new literary friends from the publishing world. Softball games drew teams captained by travel writer Lowell Thomas and playwright Thornton Wilder. Conversation was spiced by witticisms from Alexander Woollcott.[139]

Roosevelt had chosen to make his home in the very shadow of his father's in much the same way that he had coped all his life with the shadow of TR himself. Rather than either traffic shamelessly in his famous paternity, or dissociate himself from it, he accepted the varied perks and penalties with a sense of resigned obligation.

More than any of his brothers and sisters, he felt a duty to be custodian of his father's legacy.[140] (And "father," when the junior Roosevelt wrote it, invariably was accorded respectful capitalization.) He once enjoined a brother to "guard that good name."[141] He himself needed no such reminder, but living a life that honored his namesake proved anything but easy. To a journalist friend, he lamented:

> Half of the community bewail the fact that I in no way resemble my Father, and the other half abuse me roundly for imitating him. Many of my Father's most earnest supporters feel that somehow I am slurring his good name by endeavoring to perform public service, while most of the people who disliked him and opposed him during his life, and who feel that as he is dead it is not proper to say anything about him, take the feeling out on me.[142]

There were advantages, to be sure, of which someone bearing a name other than Theodore Roosevelt, Jr., couldn't avail himself. But, balancing out both sides, his wife Eleanor concluded that "the disadvantages of being a great man's son far outweigh the advantages."[143]

Keeping the flame of his father, in the view of the son, implied no political dynasty nor mantle of succession. He yearned to be seen not as Theodore Roosevelt's heir, but as an offspring credited with accomplishments of his own.

> I don't believe in "descendants of." I have somehow the feeling that this does not check with my conception of democracy. Though I have been in politics most of my life, I do not quote my Father in my speeches, and I do not speak at celebra-

tions in honor of his memory. This is not because I do not agree with what he advocated, and did, for I do emphatically.... I feel that I should be accepted and treated by the American people as merely an American who has himself done thus and so.[144]

The approach of a second world war gave the Rough Rider's son another opportunity to make his own mark in a setting where he seemed perhaps most at home: the battlefield.

The combat hero of World War I at first opposed American involvement in the new conflict engulfing Europe. He was disillusioned that the last war had led to depression and despotism.[145] "No one wins a war," he wrote to his wife in 1940, and the nation "might not survive another."[146] As U.S. participation began to look inevitable, however, he offered his public support for national preparedness, including conscription.[147]

Next he offered the services of himself. Still on the army's roster as a fifty-four-year-old reserve colonel, Roosevelt asked General George C. Marshall, the chief of staff, to restore him to active duty. Impressed by the colonel's performance in the previous war, Marshall agreed.[148] In the spring of 1941, with the advance of the German *Wehrmacht* fast dissolving American neutrality, Roosevelt resumed command of his old infantry regiment at Fort Devens, Massachusetts.[149] He was exhilarated. "He has got his teeth into something," said his wife, "he knows he can do supremely well."[150]

The United States' entry into the war later in the year effected a truce in the personal war between the Roosevelt cousins. Franklin promoted Theodore to brigadier general three days after war was declared, and the new general reciprocated by calling at the White House in a gesture of solidarity.[151]

Going off to war became once again a family affair. Son Quentin enlisted in his father's division. Eleanor soon followed, as she had twenty-five years before, to serve with the Red Cross in England.[152]

Notwithstanding the star now adorning his steel helmet, Roosevelt was not prepared to spend the war in a command bunker. He made himself one of the army's true fighting generals.[153] He was to be found on the ground with his troops — wading ashore in Tunisia and Sicily, then jouncing along the battle lines in a jeep labeled, on its bullet-pocked windshield, "Rough Rider."[154] His proletarian camaraderie bore out a conviction that "the essence of leadership lay in being genuinely fond of your men."[155] The attachment was mutual. Roosevelt became, among adoring GIs, a figure of almost mystical proportions.[156]

His superiors were less admiring. They saw the jaunty *esprit de corps* as laxity — "utter disregard of discipline, everywhere evident in [the] cocky division," in the view of General Omar N. Bradley. He and General George S.

Patton, once Sicily had been secured in 1943, relieved him and the senior divisional general from command.[157] Roosevelt told his wife he was "heartbroken."[158]

The demoted general retained enough favor, however, to be included in plans for the Allies' forthcoming invasion of occupied France. He was transferred to England, from whence Operation Overlord would be launched. Quentin, recuperated from wounds sustained in Algeria, was awaiting him.[159] Roosevelt characteristically asked to be sent ashore in the first wave of invaders. The request initially was denied. At age fifty-seven, the general would be the oldest participant, and a gammy hip compelled the assistance of a cane. But Bradley, despite his recent censure of Roosevelt, reckoned his presence with the landing forces would be "an inspiration." He was cleared to take part.[160]

The subsequent D-Day assault in June 1944 was fraught with unforeseen difficulty. Scrambling ashore on a stretch of Normandy coast designated by the military as Utah Beach, Roosevelt perceived at once that his men had been mistakenly landed nearly a mile south of their intended position. As German machine guns sprayed them, he escorted the soldiers, squad by squad, to the shelter of a sea wall. "We're going to start the war from right here," he announced. Leaning on a cane, oblivious to the bullets thudding the sand around him, he organized a counterattack.[161]

Coastal France was liberated, and Roosevelt was named interim military governor of Cherbourg. Unlike San Juan or Manila, this governorship came with no palace. His headquarters was a captured German truck rudimentarily fitted out with electric lights, a desk, and bed.[162] But preferment was on the way. The commander of Allied forces in Europe, General Dwight D. Eisenhower, elevated him in July to major general with command of a division.[163]

Roosevelt never saw the promotion orders. That night in camp he passed suddenly away. He was buried by a phalanx of fellow generals in the French town of Sainte-Mère-Eglise. The funereal strains of "The Son of God Goes Forth to War" from a military band were muffled by the distant rumble of battle.[164]

In his demise, Theodore Roosevelt, Jr., achieved an objective sought throughout his life: recognition as somebody more than just the namesake of a famous father. It became apparent that, by any standard, he had been an exceptional soldier. His courage under fire awed even his detractors. Bradley, asked years later to single out the most compelling act of bravery he had witnessed in wartime, replied without hesitation: Roosevelt's gallantry at Normandy.[165] Patton in his diary conceded Roosevelt to be "one of the bravest men I ever knew."[166]

The valor on Utah Beach earned the general, posthumously, the nation's highest military award, the Medal of Honor. When the smoke of battle gave way to statistical tallying, Roosevelt emerged as the war's most decorated soldier. He had won every combat medal available to American ground forces.[167]

Less accomplished than his father in the field of public service, he had surpassed him in another. While the senior Roosevelt had been "a dilettante soldier and a first-class politician," as journalist A.J. Liebling put it, perhaps a little unkindly, "his son was a dilettante politician and a first-class soldier."[168]

He had pursued the two callings headlong.[169] Meditating on the experience on the day before the Normandy invasion, in the introspection of approaching combat, Roosevelt wrote to his wife an unintended epitaph:

> We've had a grand life and I hope they'll be more. Should it chance that there's not, at least we can say that in our years together we've packed enough for ten ordinary lives.[170]

11
Paul M. Pearson
First Civilian Governor of U.S. Virgin Islands, 1931–1935

On the face of it, few were less qualified to be governor of one of the country's overseas possessions.

He was a professor of rhetoric at a small college. He had held no public office. He had ventured but once beyond the bounds of the American continent. His big fling at running an organization had ended in bankruptcy.

But Paul M. Pearson possessed attributes not enumerated on a job résumé. Countering the baser instincts of his time — and sometimes of himself — he held in respect people of other races. He empathized, through his own life of financial hardship, with those trapped in want. He was game to pioneer the untried and unsanctioned.

Choosing him to preside over an impoverished Caribbean protectorate was to prove hardly as fanciful as supposed.

For Pearson, the Antilles was just one more stop in the lifelong peregrinations of a dreamy optimist confident that he could improve the human condition. Rapt listeners to his recitations surely would be transported. Small-town America would discover the arts and undergo a Renaissance. His family would be catapulted, by his latest scheme, to financial security.

The pattern of a peripatetic existence was formed early. The toddler Pearson scarcely had begun to make the acquaintance of the world when, at the age of about five, around the year 1876, he was uprooted. Leaving the farm where he had been born, in the tablelands of southwestern Illinois near a hamlet called Gillespie,[1] he migrated with his parents and infant brother westward in that most storied of American conveyances — the Conestoga covered wagon. The Pearsons crossed the Mississippi River and clomped their way to Kansas.[2]

There his father exchanged farming for a livelihood more befitting his gentle temperament: clerking in a shop. Samuel M. Pearson succeeded sufficiently to acquire in time his own general store in the eastern Kansas town of Osawatomie and build an exuberant Queen Anne-style house with wraparound porch. Once the boy grew old enough, he helped his father in the store, peddling newspapers on the side to earn pocket money.[3]

His mother was a character altogether different. Ella Cameron, Scottish in extraction rather than English like her husband, was as stern as he was mild. Before marriage, she had wielded the rod of a schoolteacher. And she seemed to exert on her eldest son a stronger influence. To him she imparted two interests of hers never to be lost: education and elocution.[4]

The Pearsons' firstborn matured into a strapping lad, a footballer, but he bore the perversely girlish forename of Pearl. The name chosen by his parents, for reasons obscured by time, was to be retained stoically into young manhood.[5]

The childhood household was schooled only sketchily. Pearl's father had received the equivalent of a third-grade education. His mother had the distinction of having attended high school — among an elite of less than 3 percent of her contemporaries in post–Civil War America to have done so. But there is no evidence that the one-time schoolteacher completed her secondary education.[6] They aspired to better scholastic training for their children. At considerable financial sacrifice, the elder Pearsons sent both of their sons, Pearl and younger brother Andrew, known as Drew, to college. The boys attended Baker University, a carriage journey's distance to the north at Baldwin City.[7]

Baker was a frontier institute presuming to style itself a university, and its academic demands left Pearl ample time for campus social life, such as it was.[8] He plunged into the whirl of fraternity and sorority affairs, frequented the Methodist church, and joined its youth organization.[9]

The kid from Osawatomie emanated the sublime cocksureness of the conquering collegian. The steady gaze, the square jowls, the fixity of the cleft chin served notice that he intended to leave his mark on the world. It was a look of guileless ambition common to young people, but one that Pearson was never to outgrow.[10]

College activities brought him into the company of a female classmate who shared his interests in Greek-letter societies and Methodism. Heavy-lidded blue eyes and a mound of dark golden hair had denoted Edna Rachel Wolfe as something of a campus beauty, capable even of distracting lecturers. She was three years younger than Pearl and the offspring of a more affluent family. Her father in Humboldt, Kansas, was a professional man, a dentist. Friendship blossomed into romance, interrupted by Pearl's graduation in 1891.[11]

The nineteen-year-old graduate set off to begin his working life. For

Pearl, however, the rite wasn't as simple as just starting a career. He tackled multiple vocations simultaneously — an exercise in occupational juggling that would complicate his onward course nearly ever after.¹²

His workday job was teaching school at the small town of Cherryvale in the southeastern corner of Kansas. Hoping to command more respect from pupils little younger than himself by appearing older than his years, he grew a beard. (The model may have been his own bearded father.)¹³ Outside the

Paul M. Pearson, as governor of the Virgin Islands in the 1930s (courtesy Julie Lange Hall).

schoolhouse, he answered an ecclesiastical call. He was ordained as a Methodist minister, traveling a circuit extending fifty miles into the plains.¹⁴ "[I] married the love-lorn, buried the dead of all faiths," he remembered.¹⁵

The busy young man also began a pursuit lying perhaps nearest his heart. He had found, in college classrooms, maybe, or campus convocations, that he enjoyed reciting in public.¹⁶ "There is nothing so intoxicating," he enthused, "as the thrill of an audience."¹⁷ As his schedule of teaching and preaching permitted, he teamed up with a fellow Baker alumnus (and brother minister) to visit neighboring communities delivering lectures combining edification and entertainment.¹⁸ Pearson would continue doing "platform work" of various types — orations, readings, drama — for forty years.

The keen novice originated his own contribution to the genre: the "lecture recital." He would summarize the life of an author, evaluate his or her work critically, then recite excerpts.¹⁹ "Without the interpreting voice," he contended, "the printed page is as incomplete as the score without the orchestra."²⁰ The first to be brought to the Pearson platform was James Whitcomb Riley, the era's most popular poet, whose sentimental evocations of rural life the circuit preacher had been reading to a youth group he had organized.²¹ Riley was to be joined, in the repertoire of lecture recitals in ensuing years, by a pantheon of thirty other literary lights.

His success on the platform persuaded Pearson to make a career of public speaking. Little Cherryvale began to seem confining. After two years there, he left in 1893 for the throbbing midwestern metropolis of Chicago. He enrolled at Northwestern University's Cumnock School of Oratory, at that time the high temple in its field.[22] Elocution, however dated a discipline today, was then widely studied. Schools devoted to it thrived in the country's major cities.[23]

The courting of Pearson's college sweetheart, meanwhile, had continued from afar. While studying at Northwestern, he asked Edna, in her junior year at Baker, to marry him. She declined.[24] The sting of rejection perhaps sharpening his own natural gifts, he completed the two-year course on elocution in a single year.[25] Impressed, the university invited him to join the faculty.[26] Settling his affairs in Kansas to take up the position at Northwestern, Pearson called at Baker University to see Edna. The young woman who had rejected his marriage proposal a few months earlier now accepted. Her suitor was no longer a mere student but a faculty member with husbandly prospects.[27]

The fiancé was elated. On the platform, he began to conclude his recitals with a Riley paean to matrimonial love, "An Old Sweetheart of Mine."[28] "People must know that I read it well," he wrote to Edna, "because of the joy the poem brought into my life."[29]

The two were married in June 1896. They honeymooned, inauspiciously, at the desolate prairie railroad flag stop of Bangor, Kansas, at a hotel lacking so much as indoor plumbing — an occasion remembered thereafter with unfailing mirth. The rest of the summer, as another midwesterner possessed of formidable speaking talents, William Jennings Bryan, campaigned for president, the newlyweds spent in a manner that would become habitual: touring the Chautauqua circuit.[30]

Chautauqua was a peculiarly American phenomenon that flashed across the country's benighted hinterlands like a flaming lamp of learning during a period almost exactly contemporaneous with Pearson. From its genesis on the shores of Lake Chautauqua in upstate New York as a training camp for Methodist Sunday School teachers, three years after Pearson's birth, it developed quickly into something more mainstream. Religious instruction was supplemented with secular enlightenment — lectures to inform and educate — and with musical entertainment. The formula proved wildly successful. It appealed to a yearning for self-improvement and civic betterment then stirring within the nation, and Chautauqua assemblies sprang up across the land. Most were sited in spots of natural beauty, such as lakesides or mountain valleys. And most arose west of the Atlantic seaboard, whose cultural advantages the movement sought tacitly to spread inland. The number of Chautauqua summertime communities eventually exceeded two hundred, attracting audiences of twenty-five million.[31]

In illumining the lives of the American rural, the tents of Chautauqua have been extolled as "caravans of culture"[32] and "a traveling people's university."[33] But the movement also has been derided. Novelist Sinclair Lewis, for one, dismissed it as "nothing but wind and chaff and the heavy laughter of yokels."[34]

Pearson's expositions on literary themes were a natural for Chautauqua. His first connection with the movement that would become so important in his life came while still studying his craft. As a student at Northwestern, he procured a booking to address a Chautauqua assembly in the summer of 1894 in the Colorado foothills of the Rocky Mountains.[35] Longer engagements at Chautauqua gatherings two years later in Minnesota and Indiana occupied much of the bridal couple's first summer together.[36]

The responsibilities of marriage and a new job produced scarcely a pause in Pearson's burgeoning career on the speaker's platform. During the academic year at Northwestern, he shuttled to towns near Chicago to give evening recitals, absenting himself from the marital apartment in Evanston and returning by early-morning "milk trains" in time to teach eight o'clock classes.[37] Christmas holiday seasons and summers customarily were spent, sometimes with his wife, on speaking tours and the Chautauqua circuit.[38] Even his teaching duties led to the public platform. The precocious young instructor organized within the oratory school a drama group, and rehearsed it during lunch breaks. The Thalian Club, as it was called, was destined to break new ground in the prudish world of Chautauqua by introducing in 1899 the performance of drama.[39]

The pace of his speaking activity quickened further with the addition of another forum: the Lyceum movement. While sharing with Chautauqua a goal of edifying the bourgeoisie, the Lyceum system bore subtle differences. It was half a century older. It was more purely educational. And it met in wintertime. The latter offered Pearson a welcome opportunity for more platform work in the Chautauqua off-season, and he soon was busily booking himself and the Thalian Club.[40] His involvement was to generate a book about the Lyceum[41] and his rise, at the age of just twenty-four, to the movement's presidency.[42]

The prominence which Americans at the turn of the twentieth century accorded the art of speaking to an audience may nowadays seem puzzling. Making it one's life work, even more so. But in an era lacking radio, motion pictures, or television, public speaking served as an important medium of communication—a way for people rather isolated by today's standards to acquire information and ideas. There were books, newspapers, and magazines, of course, but a presentation from a platform offered the attraction of a live speaker in a sociable setting. Public speaking ranked behind only church and school in influencing public thought.[43]

For the practitioners of elocution who made the rounds of marquee tents and meeting halls, such as Pearson, their role exacted heavy demands.

Travel, to bookings often mere whistle-stops on the rail lines of a society devoid of automobiles, was an exercise in endurance. During one span of two months in 1906, Pearson spoke in eleven states, scattered as far westward as the Indian territory of Oklahoma.[44] On all such trips, a bundle of rail timetables was his trusty traveling companion.[45] Trains ran late, and audiences were entreated to wait.[46] He wore a cloak of coal soot.[47] "I have two hours of dirt and cinders on me," he complained to his wife in a letter written aboard one belching train.[48] To save money, he slept overnight in depots or on the seat of a coach car, rather than a Pullman berth, texts of his lectures propped beneath his head as a pillow.[49]

Technological progress that would outmode such travails was proceeding apace while Pearson labored back and forth across the country. A Packard automobile became in 1903 the first to traverse the continent. And the Wright brothers later the same year first coaxed an airplane into flight. But the car and plane arrived too late to benefit Pearson.[50]

The voice — the touring speaker's most valuable asset — was to be cultivated and looked after. It had to be kept strong enough to project, without aid of electronic amplification, to the rear of an open tent or echoey hall. Pearson exercised his voice daily. When on the road, he would seek out an empty church or wander into the prairie to practice booming out his recitals. More than just training, the regimen signified for him moral virtue.[51] "Management of the voice necessitates self-control," he maintained, "and self-control is morality."[52]

On the platform itself, other perils loomed. Appearances in Chautauqua tents were prone to distracting outdoor noise. "I did [poet Eugene] Field yesterday for 40 minutes," he reported to his wife from Elkhart, Indiana, "to the accompaniment of carpenters, puffing trains, and panting naphtha launches."[53] Foul weather could wreak havoc. Thunderstorms drowned out the voice. Cold temperatures shrank attendance. Blasts of wind collapsed tents.[54] The greatest test, however, was the audience. While applause was exhilarating, listlessness was humiliating. Each performance became a struggle for the listeners' approval.[55] As Pearson once wrote to Edna, "My work is on trial every night."[56]

Life on the road imposed hardships not only on him, but also his family. Frequent absences from home left his wife to bear household burdens heavier even than those of most homemakers of the day. Edna had given birth during the first three years of marriage to two sons, Drew and Leon.[57] As the only parent regularly present, she shouldered most of their upbringing. She was to endure a heart-breaking series of miscarriages — one a year for a decade, she later confided[58] — before the birth of two daughters, Barbara and Ellen.[59] The busy mother did get help from a succession of housemaids,[60] but made the home hers, to the point of tailoring the children's garments.[61]

The platform widow fought loneliness. "My dear Husband," she wrote to him during a three-week lecture tour,

> I have been feeling very blue and abused all day, in fact ever since you have left, because we are alone so much. It seems that a month is the longest you can stand it with us.... Of course it is mean of me, for you go to earn money, but all the same you love to go & that hurts.[62]

While away, Pearson dutifully wrote to his wife daily, and often twice a day.[63] Letters to "Sweetheart" or "My dear" filled reams of stationery collected from hotels where he had lodged. The missives issued from hotel dining rooms, hurtling trains, depot waiting rooms, posted with stamps whose exorbitant cost of two cents was sometimes begrudged.[64]

Despite the tribulations, Pearson clearly enjoyed circuit speaking, at least most of the time. But his rambles were impelled by more than personal stimulation and professional fulfillment. He was supplementing the family income. Finances posed a chronic worry.[65] The matrimonial letters chime a persistent refrain: "dreadfully pinched ... penniless again ... constantly hard up."[66] He begged his wife's sufferance with his shortcomings as a provider: "Though your 'usband is poor in money, he is poor in nothing else."[67]

The beleaguered breadwinner was forever searching for financial salvation. He invested in Canadian timberland.[68] He tilled new fields in public speaking. But most of his ideas for increasing the financial support of his family, such as joining the Lyceum circuit, necessitated more travel, thereby decreasing his in-person support at home.[69] No wonder Edna's sweet little mouth was slowly souring into a permanent scowl.[70] Through it all, Pearson remained serenely optimistic that El Dorado lay just around the corner. "Things are working our way, dear," he would assure his spouse. "Everything is going to be all right."[71]

Unconvinced by her mate's Pollyanna confidence, Edna turned her hand to earning money at home. Financial concerns were jarringly unfamiliar to this coddled daughter of a well-off father.[72] But she was talented at drawing and painting, and parlayed these gifts into a home business making wood crafts for a cooperative at Harvard University.[73] She also considered taking in sewing or boarders — schemes scotched by her husband.[74]

In addition to his financial circumstances, Pearson long had fretted about his education. In the refined world of academia, he felt his training to be inferior.⁷⁵ He sought to remedy the perceived deficiency. After teaching at Northwestern five years, he took a leave of absence in 1901 to study for a year at Harvard. There he delved into English literature and writing—the fount of so many of his platform recitals.⁷⁶

The most lasting consequence of his year in the East, however, was a new job. He took a position as assistant professor of rhetoric and public speaking at Swarthmore College, a small Quaker institution west of Philadelphia.⁷⁷ The move in 1902 from a cosmopolitan Chicago university to a pastoral campus still echoing the Quaker plain language of "thee" and "thou" was a cultural jolt. It also marked the Pearsons' sixth change of home in as many years of marriage.⁷⁸ But the affiliation with Swarthmore was to endure nearly thirty years.

Starting as rhetorician within the English department, the up-and-coming young professor soon oversaw the formation of a Department of Public Speaking and became its chairman.⁷⁹ The new position offered a soapbox for one of Pearson's professional campaigns: challenging the highly mannered style of public speech then in vogue. He and a small band of fellow rebels championed a delivery more conversational, a gesturing more natural. Their ultimate triumph was to relegate stilted elocution to the realm of historical curiosities.⁸⁰

The change of setting was accompanied by changes more personal. Pearson's baptismal name of Pearl had been gradually transposing into "Paul." Colleagues on the platform circuit began affixing the new name, and Pearson, finding he preferred it, just before moving to Swarthmore formally made the switch. (He was to remain Pearl, however, for a decade longer in signing letters to his wife.)⁸¹ Another change was less temporal. The Pearsons were a religious couple, Methodists intent on "inculcating religious truth" in their children (as the father once put it).⁸² The simple piety of the Quaker faith enveloping Swarthmore began to appeal to them, and both in 1907 joined the Society of Friends.⁸³

The Swarthmore professor retained his double life as a touring speaker. He had made sure, in his contract, that his teaching duties afforded ample time for speaking engagements. Besides the summer recess, he was permitted two months in winter and another month in spring.⁸⁴

After nine years on the footlights side of the public speaking business—on the platform as part of the troupe of marketable attractions known in the industry as "talent"—Pearson added a role backstage. He cast his eye on the leading trade magazine in the field. It was a publication called, appropriately, *Talent*, read by speakers, entertainers, agents, and the proprietors who booked the circuits. Seeking new horizons both professionally and financially, in 1903 he bought the magazine. He moved its offices from New York to

Philadelphia, and set himself up as editor.[85] "I am sure," he averred, "that I can be a successful editor."[86] He was. He boosted advertising, tripled the number of pages, introduced color. Subscriptions climbed.[87]

His new-found skills as an editor led Pearson two years later to launch a new magazine. *The Speaker* was a quarterly compendium of readings proven successful on the platform. The magazine sold well, and plowed welcome cash into the family coffers—as much as a thousand dollars a year. *The Speaker* was published eight years.[88] *Talent,* meanwhile, merged in 1907 with its chief competitor.[89]

Pearson also found another way to harness the printed word to serve the spoken word. He wrote two books on public speaking. As his magazine responsibilities lightened, he compiled in 1909 a collection of amusing yarns to draw laughter from an audience.[90] Three years later he issued a work on speaking off-the-cuff. Initially co-authored, *Extemporaneous Speaking* subsequently was revised by Pearson alone.[91]

Little Swarthmore College hardly bestrode the crosscurrents of national affairs, but Professor Pearson had ties with two students thereafter to make names for themselves. An early pupil of his, Mabel Vernon, rose to prominence in the women's suffrage movement.[92] A later student at Swarthmore in the 1920s—and performer on the Chautauqua circuit with one of the professor's daughters—was future author James A. Michener.[93]

Organizing a speech department and running two magazines had given Pearson a taste for turning his ideas into realities and then administering them. He was ready to undertake a project far more ambitious. To no cause was he more devoted than using the public platform to bestow "culture"— the books, poetry, drama, music, and art so enjoyed by him and his wife.[94] Although the mission was strenuously being fulfilled across the American heartland, he perceived a geographical void: the eastern part of the country. The Chautauqua and Lyceum movements seemed almost to have abandoned the seaboard where they had begun.[95]

To serve the neglected East, Pearson decided to found his own Chautauqua circuit. He began contracting with towns in Pennsylvania, Maryland, Delaware, and New Jersey, and lining up talent. Scraping together loans from every friend whom he could dun, he printed fliers and programs, bought tents and folding chairs, hired tent crews and straw bosses.[96] After two years of preparation, the Swarthmore Chautauqua made its debut on a June day in 1912 in Chestertown, Maryland.[97] Its three-week circuit took it to 41 towns.[98] It was a hit. As summer succeeded summer, the endeavor grew. By 1925, the peak year, Pearson's Chautauqua was conducting five separate circuits covering 987 towns in 15 states, entertaining in 33 tents a combined audience of 644,000.[99] The speakers whom the crowds flocked to hear included some of the day's luminaries: former president William Howard Taft, William Jennings Bryan, Senator Robert M. LaFollette, Congressman Champ Clark.[100]

The crop of dark, wavy hair had turned a gossamer white, and co-workers called him "Pop" Pearson.[101] But his shoulders were squared, as ever, for toiling tirelessly at a chosen task. "God has given me the disposition to work," he once mused.[102] And his face wore still the broad smile of youthful enthusiasm.[103]

The enterprise became, for the founder, a family affair, embracing the three eldest Pearson children. Drew worked on tent crews and wrecking crews, and as an advance man. Leon acted in plays and wrote two of his own. Barbara was her father's chauffeur and an actress.[104] Conspicuously less enthusiastic, however, was their mother. Edna Pearson displayed scant support for the Swarthmore Chautauqua, as with the magazine ventures preceding it.[105] In a letter to her during a Chautauqua tour in 1914, Pearson despaired: "You have lacked confidence in practically everything I have undertaken and have daily disapproved of my action."[106] Much of her tepidity may have been financial. Her husband's brainchild, however successful artistically, took three years to turn a profit and never earned much money.[107]

Edna's qualms may have been foresighted. Although hard to envision amid the thronged tents, the Chautauqua movement was nearing an end of its spectacular run. Its audience was ceasing to need it. The proliferation of family automobiles and better roads were diminishing the isolation of small towns. Motion pictures and radio were serving up information and entertainment in more accessible form. The Great Depression, shrinking the wallets of patrons and creditors alike, dealt the final blow.[108]

Pearson had an inkling of the threat, but believed Chautauqua would weather it and remain a permanent feature of American provincial life.[109] He strove to stave off doom. He booked bigger drawing-cards and more entertainers. He raised more loans. He docked his own salary. He tried setting up a charitable foundation to underwrite Chautauqua. His wife took a job operating a local tearoom. As the financial storm clouds thickened, he resorted to borrowing money from his own life insurance — and, eventually, selling the family house. To no avail. The Swarthmore Chautauqua, followed by its founder, plunged in 1930 into bankruptcy.[110] The downcast Pearson sought to comfort his associates (and himself): "What we did is not lost. Chautauqua has not failed; times have changed."[111]

He had left the college faculty, and found himself suddenly out of work.[112] But his Chautauqua credentials won Pearson prompt reemployment just a month after bankruptcy. He was hired to evaluate the potential for adult education at a recreation complex called Ogilbay Park near Wheeling, West Virginia. The quiet little back-country park was a faint echo of his once-vibrant Chautauqua circuit, but it offered welcome occupation in hard times.[113]

Just when Pearson's stage seemed to be constricting, unbeknownst to him it was about to widen beyond anything he might have imagined.

For all his zeal to broaden people's cultural horizons, Pearson himself was no citizen of the world. His thousands of miles of perambulating, the literary figures whom he popularized, his Chautauqua programming — all were rather parochially American. Yet there were glimmers of interest in what lay beyond the country's shores. He dreamed of traveling the globe. Letters to his wife fantasized about "our trip around the world."[114] During World War I, he dispatched Chautauqua performers to military training camps to entertain doughboys heading overseas.[115] He internationalized Chautauqua, marginally, extending one of his Swarthmore circuits across the border into Canada.[116] It inspired in him the vision of a movement eventually encompassing the earth.[117] Pearson even dabbled fleetingly in international affairs. As president of the International Lyceum Association in 1921, he took the lead in organizing a conference on "Public Opinion and World Peace." It precipitated the only trip he had made abroad, a visit to post-war Europe. The resulting conference in Washington drew no lesser personage than French statesman Georges Clemenceau.[118]

When Pearson's exhilarating ride as a platform headliner and impresario shuffled to a halt, depositing him in West Virginia to search for a new direction in life, the federal government in Washington, as it happened, also was conducting a search.

The United States, at the outset of its entry into World War I, had purchased the western side of the Virgin Islands, three isles lying forty miles east of Puerto Rico. The nuggets of green verdure and golden beaches awash in the blue Caribbean Sea had been, for two centuries, the Danish West Indies.[119] But Denmark's oceanic empire had been long moldering away, and the United States had been trying for fifty years to acquire the islands as a security precaution.[120] Alarm at German belligerency in the Great War then convulsing Europe, with a threat of the kaiser's army overrunning Denmark and gaining the Virgins, gave the American pursuit new urgency. A deal was clinched. (No bargain, however, for Americans. Too jittery to haggle, they quintupled the offer they had made fifteen years earlier, ringing up the most expensive overseas real estate transaction in the country's history.) The Danish possession became American in 1917 just before the nation went to war against Germany.[121]

Procured for national defense, the Virgin Islands at first were administered militarily, by the navy.[122] But dissatisfaction over naval rule intensified in the exigencies of the Great Depression. The Hoover administration's economic relief efforts ran afoul of the islands' procrustean naval government. Exasperated, the president in 1931 switched jurisdiction of the territory from military hands to civilian.[123]

Dethroning the navy necessitated installing a government of civilians, starting with a governor. But whom was the president to appoint? The name of Paul Pearson surfaced. There are two versions of precisely how the out-of-harness ex-professor came to the notice of the White House. Both accounts are plausible. And both illustrate the deplorably makeshift way in which the United States for decades chose the chief executives of its offshore satellites.

In one rendition, the wife of an official close to Hoover chanced to mention knowing some "fine people" in Swarthmore. The town's association with Quakerism may have struck a responsive chord with the Quaker president. An aide, Herbert D. Brown, was asked to follow up. Brown headed an agency called, quaintly, the Bureau of Efficiency, and he acted with fitting dispatch. He motored to Swarthmore in search of likely candidates. A local couple, Chester and Abby Mary Roberts, recommended Pearson.[124]

Another scenario attributes the appointment to the influence of Pearson's son Drew, who had become a Washington newspaper columnist syndicated nationally. He had personal and professional ties with the publisher of the newspaper with the largest circulation in the capital, Eleanor Medill "Cissy" Patterson, to whose daughter he had been married.[125] "Cissy arranged it," Drew's wife once told her sister-in-law.[126]

Whatever may have motivated his selection, Pearson in March 1931 was named the first civilian governor of the U.S. Virgin Islands.[127] The man who had devoted most of his life to edifying people in scenic settings set off for a new audience in a locale more exotic than any ever to grace the Chautauqua circuit.

The popular image of a Caribbean Shangri-la was breathtakingly fulfilled by Charlotte Amalie, the capital city awaiting the new governor on the island of St. Thomas. A turquoise harbor was cradled by three hills of feathery palms and leafy mahogany, punctuated by the orange and scarlet blooms of royal poincianas. Through the foliage peeked the red tin roofs of whitewashed buildings cascading toward the waterfront. Trade winds wafted the warmth like a lazy ceiling fan.[128]

Charm, alas, masked wretchedness. The Virgin Islands, never a land of plenty, had been reduced by the Great Depression to indigence. Half of the workforce lacked jobs. Income per capita had fallen below three hundred fifty dollars a year. Only one islander in ten could afford to pay taxes. Half of the children were reckoned to be undernourished. The Red Cross was feeding a quarter of the population of the island of St. Croix.[129]

Such were the inhospitable conditions that greeted Pearson after a four-day steamship voyage from the mainland to his new island domain. He wasted no time in tackling them. What he called the "critical economic problems" dominated his inaugural address, delivered in the white linen suit that was to become his vestment in the tropics.[130] His own lifelong struggle to make ends meet helped him empathize with the hardships facing islanders. "Together," he exhorted them, "we may accomplish anything."[131]

The new governor and the Hoover administration advanced a recovery plan. Its boldness belied the complacency of which the president was so roundly accused back home, and, ironically, foreshadowed the New Deal of his successor. The program called for parceling out homesteads to broaden the feudalistically constrictive ownership of land (60 percent of St. Thomas was owned by 15 persons, 70 percent of St. Croix by 14, and 80 percent of St. John by 12), reviving the sugar and rum industries under the aegis of a public corporation, organizing cooperatives, and providing employable skills through adult and vocational education.[132]

Congress ponied up a million dollars, and implementation began.[133]

Pearson barely had settled himself into the governor's mansion before being called upon to host an historical event: the first visit to the territory by an American president. A week after his appointee's inauguration, Hoover steamed to the islands aboard the battleship *Arizona*. His one-day inspection of prostrate St. Thomas left the president moved. Neither the tribulation of refugees in war-torn Europe nor the bread lines and soup kitchens of depression-gripped America had prepared him for the penury of the Caribbean possession.[134]

He bared his impressions to reporters at his next stop, San Juan, with more candor than discretion. He pronounced the Virgin Islands "an effective poorhouse."[135] The presidential denigration hardly endeared the United States to its newest subjects. Nor did it enhance reception of the new governor, although Pearson maintained a circumspect silence.[136]

A master of using the public platform to heighten people's awareness, the governor took to the airwaves to publicize the territory's adversity among mainlanders. He beamed radio broadcasts from New York, Washington, and Boston, highlighting the heart-rending woes of children. (Combined with similar efforts by his fellow governor in Puerto Rico, Theodore Roosevelt, Jr., American radio listeners were well briefed on the dire straits of their Caribbean possessions.)[137]

Pearson also solicited private aid. He sought corporate funding for vocational training of young people, and procured three thousand dollars from a foundation for school hot lunches.[138]

The recovery plan began gradually to ease the depression's grip. The island government bought sugar mills and three thousand acres of fallow cane fields on St. Croix, the comparatively flat southern island whose ruined stone windmills and empty smokestacks attested to the collapse of its sugar industry.[139] Homesteads were platted.[140] Two-room houses were built at a rock-bottom five hundred dollars each.[141] The government took over the rum industry, capped by Prohibition, renovating old distilleries and erecting new ones in readiness for the day of repeal.[142] His new role as purveyor of Demon Rum raised eyebrows among some of the Pearsons' Quaker communicants.[143] He tried to placate one inquirer: "Government House [the governor's residence] is 'dry.' Edna and I are 'dry' wherever we go."[144]

As immediate relief, four thousand islanders — close to half of able-bodied adults — were put to work on public projects. Nearly eleven thousand, or half the population, were rationed food.[145]

Behind the shroud of economic despair, the Virgin Islands possessed all the makings of a tourist mecca: the tropic sun and sunsets few could forget, spectacular coral reefs, colonnaded citadels of commerce swathed in the tinted plaster of their Danish past, and plantations in picturesque decay.[146] The naval government had been oblivious to the potential. And the depression had dried up most overseas tourism.[147] But the new civilian rulers glimpsed the possibilities.[148] The Pearson regime took the first modest steps to attract more visitors. The islands were better advertised.[149] The first big hotel, whose name of Bluebeard Castle evoked villainous visitors of old, was built atop a hill above St. Thomas harbor.[150] From such beginnings, the territory was to grow, beyond any of the early planners' wildest imaginings, by the 1960s into a place centered shamelessly (and, some would say, ruinously) on tourism.[151]

Pearson may have been alive to the tourism promise because he himself so reveled in the islands' allure. Once his wife and daughters joined him, at the end of the 1931 school year,[152] the gubernatorial family eased into a lifestyle taking full advantage of the glorious Caribbean setting. The days began, three or four mornings a week, in the sunrise coolness of quarter to seven, with father and daughters cantering off into the early light for a brisk jaunt on horseback. Days ended with a family swim and picnic at a sparkling beach.[153]

Their home was the West Indies villa of a northerner's fantasies. Government House reclined regally behind a two-story filigree verandah, halfway up Charlotte Amalie's central hill. A lone sentry, dapper in his tan uniform and puttees, paced in front. Inside, the mansion sported gilt chairs and, for state occasions, elegant Danish table china.[154]

Ever curious about his surroundings, as throughout his footloose life, Pearson enjoyed exploring his new neighborhood. Ambling down to the harbor, he watched steamships fueled at dockside by a procession of barefoot porters, both men and women. They lugged on their heads forty-five-pound baskets of coal for two cents per load.[155]

Not that Pearson indulged much in leisure. His managerial style was frenetic work. He drove himself so hard, in fact, that his superior in Washington, the secretary of the interior, worried that he might be over-exerting.

"You are not settling down," wrote Ray Lyman Wilbur after the governor's strenuous first seven months in office, "to a pace which a white man can keep up in a semi-tropical country."[156]

But Pearson didn't let up, introducing to his Antillean enclave innovations few islanders ever expected of those sent out to administer them. Many were the product of the governor's set of personal convictions. A few were simply idiosyncratic. Nearly all were tinged with the idealism of a born dreamer.

The navy's rule of the Virgin Islands, among its other deficiencies, had borne an ugly strain of racism. A populace nearly all black had been governed by a service at the time not only all white but infused by the racial contempt of a dominant echelon of officers from the segregated South. Relations were uneasy and occasionally violent.[157]

The new civilian governor brought a racial disposition far more tolerant. His life had evidenced toward Americans of African descent a quiet respect. Early in his career on the public platform he had introduced a lecture recital on the black poet Paul Laurence Dunbar.[158] On the road, he had been drawn to services at African-American churches.[159] Although himself not innocent of privately letting slip the epithet "nigger," he had admonished his children's use of racially derogatory language.[160] In the Virgin Islands, he sought to end the era of Jim Crow by treating islanders as equals. Assembling a government to replace the navy's, Pearson gave employment preference to islanders. The policy raised hackles in some quarters back home, and he was compelled to defend it. To a top official of the Republican party, he wrote:

> You will be interested to know that the people of the Virgin Islands produce lawyers and doctors and professional men of standing among their fellows, and that such men are chosen for positions whenever possible.... rather than bring in people from other countries.[161]

The Pearson administration wound up appointing islanders to three-quarters of government posts formerly filled by navy personnel.[162]

The territory presented a new frontier for its governor's lifelong crusade to elevate people through literature and the arts. He tried permeating the place with music — promoting music instruction in schools, shipping in musical instruments inveigled from donors on the mainland, and arranging concert tours by musicians from the home country.[163] He imported Chautauqua lectures, and reprised some of his own, including, fittingly, the one on Dunbar.[164]

Pearson's leadership was, in many ways, impolitic and quirkily personal. Yet it commanded support in Washington across a surprisingly wide political spectrum. Hoover remained staunchly complimentary, praising his appointee's "unselfish and zealous work in dealing with one of the most difficult problems which a man of humane spirit could undertake to cope with."[165] After two years in Government House, however, the president at whose pleasure he served was voted out of office. Hoover was succeeded by a chief executive, Franklin D. Roosevelt, who could hardly have been more different philosophically. Despite a sweeping overhaul of federal officialdom, the new president chose to retain Hoover's man in the Virgin Islands.[166] The governor's activism and willingness to experiment presumably won Roosevelt's favor.

While not active politically, Pearson's politics leaned Democratic (an inclination either unknown or unimportant to Republican Hoover). He reported having voted for Democratic presidential nominees six times. His wife served in Swarthmore on the party's local committee. Son Drew was a vociferous Democrat, although brother Drew was a financial contributor to the Republican party.[167]

Pearson's nondoctrinaire enthusiasm for the task in the Virgin Islands — "I am happy in this job," he once confided to Interior Secretary Wilbur[168] — enabled him to work remarkably smoothly with two presidents poles apart. Roosevelt came to be as admiring as Hoover. "I have followed closely the progress of our program under your leadership," he wrote in 1934, "and appreciate the splendid service which you have rendered."[169]

Repeating a role he had performed three years earlier for Hoover, Pearson hosted in March 1934 a visit by First Lady Eleanor Roosevelt. The governor managed to cram into her twenty-four-hour stopover two functions intended to break down island barriers of color and gender, causes which the guest of honor was only too pleased to support.[170] One event was a biracial reception of guests heretofore kept apart by race — as Pearson put it, "a natural mingling of persons who would, but for color, come together."[171] The other affair was a meeting of church women of all denominations, whom Mrs. Roosevelt addressed. The governor hoped the gathering would embolden island women to assume greater responsibilities outside the home.[172]

Four months later, Pearson again served as maître d' and tour guide for another visitor from the White House. The guest this time was the president himself, following in his wife's footsteps. Roosevelt motored across St. Thomas in an open touring car, the governor at his side, then took a three-hour look at St. Croix.[173] He was engulfed in a sea of beaming faces, cheers, and applause.[174] The welcome was marred only by the banner of a diehard partisan on St. Croix urging, "Give Us a Democratic Governor" (a gesture, Roosevelt later reassured Pearson, that left the president "not at all favorably impressed").[175]

The busy band of civilians running the Virgin Islands had set itself conspicuously apart from the sleepy custodial regimes so characteristic of the colonial West Indies. Confronting an economic crisis, the Pearson government had forced changes in the very structure of the society. The effort yielded much success — and much frustration.

The sugar industry was resuscitated, with more cane grown and sugar factories opened.[176] But the new lease on life was to prove brief, fickle rainfall ultimately rendering Virgins sugar uncompetitive.[177] The rum industry doubled its capacity and cashed in on the lifting of Prohibition, but short of the bonanza predicted.[178] Agriculture was made more egalitarian. Despite early recruitment problems, four hundred landless families were installed on homesteads — nearly tripling the number of farms in the islands.[179] The administrative vehicle for most of these initiatives, the state-owned Virgin Islands Company, became a major economic force, employing one resident in ten and nearly breaking even financially.[180]

More islanders were working, yet joblessness remained stubbornly high. Thousands migrated to the mainland, principally New York's Harlem.[181] Traffic of a different sort flowed in the opposite direction. Tourists visiting the islands more than quadrupled, the vanguard of future hordes.[182]

Patterns of life in the Virgin Islands had been altered. The changes had benefited many ordinary islanders. But they had raised a threat to those occupying traditional positions of power. As the leading protagonist of these reshapings, Pearson found himself growingly a figure of controversy. The have-nots embraced him. The labor movement paraded the streets of the capital on New Year's Day in 1934 waving banners proclaiming, "Governor Pearson Is Getting Us Better Education" and "Governor Pearson Is Giving Natives a Place in Their Own Government."[183] Moneyed interests, on the other hand, just as fervently opposed him.[184] The governor saw an underlying contest for dominance:

> It is definitely a class struggle.... All our plans look toward improving the conditions of the poorer people, which will increase their power and decrease the power and authority of the estate owners.[185]

Foes in the island barony, joined by disaffected former colleagues, agitated for Pearson's removal.[186] Gaining no sympathy from Roosevelt or his secretary of the interior, Harold L. Ickes, the opponents turned to Congress.[187] They succeeded in interesting the chairman of the Senate territorial committee in murky allegations of corruption and abuse of authority.[188] Chairman Millard E. Tydings of Maryland leapt at the opportunity to escalate a long-running feud with the governor's superior, Secretary Ickes. He launched an investigation. A team of inquisitors was dispatched in the spring of 1935 to the Antilles.[189]

Pearson, old thespian that he was, took perverse pleasure in the unfolding probe. "The truth is," he confessed to two confidants, "the drama of things appeals to me."[190]

His insouciance was justified by events. The investigation turned up nothing damaging. Roosevelt, perceiving a personal vendetta, secured its termination.[191] He congratulated Pearson that there had emerged "no facts that reflect upon your honesty, or integrity, or devotion to duty."[192]

Notwithstanding the exoneration, the passions that the governor aroused from opposing sides in the possession had divided the populace and undermined his effectiveness. Roosevelt grasped the political dynamics, and in July 1935 replaced Pearson.[193] Continuity of policies was assured by appointing as successor his trusted lieutenant governor, Lawrence N. Cramer.[194]

Pearson was not being sacked, only moved. He had earned a standing as a valued member of the New Deal team. Avowed Roosevelt: "I want you to continue to be a member of my Administration."[195] The departing governor's fan at the Interior Department, Ickes, had his eye on Pearson for a responsibility that bore little apparent resemblance to overseeing tropical islands yet drew upon his economic recovery work there. His help was wanted for a federal initiative tinged in the eyes of many Americans with radicalism: public housing. Thousands of people left by the depression without means for decent places to live were to be provided subsidized housing. Pearson was recruited to serve as Ickes's assistant director of housing, in charge of public welfare. Both the secretary and the president felt the assignment perfectly suited Pearson's psyche.[196] Roosevelt wrote to him:

> It will give you a chance to assist in the social rehabilitation of those under privileged fellow citizens of ours who, on account of economic conditions, have been forced to live in slum areas. I am sure that this is the sort of a task that will engage the interest of a man with your background and concern for humanity.[197]

Indeed it did. With the wonderment of those never having possessed much money of their own, Pearson was impressed by the financial scale of the operation which he would help to direct. He excitedly dashed off a radiogram from Washington to his wife back in St. Thomas that the budget amounted to two hundred million dollars.[198]

The new housing program commanded greater support monetarily than popularly. It met wide resistance in a country unaccustomed to the government serving as landlord to the poor, many from ethnic and racial minorities. With missionary zeal, Pearson helped to introduce public housing in major cities such as Chicago and bastions of racial segregation such as Charleston, South Carolina. The successes established a bridgehead for the oncoming battle to racially integrate the nation's housing.[199]

Some parts of America in the thirties banned public housing outright by law. One such place was California. Pearson set out to repeal the ban with a state law permitting public housing. He went to California in 1938 and prowled the corridors of the state capitol until legislators passed the bill.[200] The triumph was to be his last bow. Just as the legislation was being signed into law, Pearson passed away in San Francisco at the age of sixty-seven.[201]

He was not forgotten in the languid little Caribbean possession that he had guided so kinetically to civilian rule. Fourteen years later, there took place on St. Thomas a ceremony at which the celebrated guest was Pearson's son Drew, one of the country's most-read newspaper columnists. Ground was broken for, aptly, a public housing project named "Paul M. Pearson Gardens."[202]

Whether the imposing remembrance would have pleased the honoree is by no means certain. Quakerly humility asserting itself, he had instructed his family that he wished no memorial.

> If I am remembered for a time by some, that is sufficient. My life is a part of the eternal goodness which manifests itself in every man and cannot cease. Thus I shall live on even after I am forgotten.[203]

12

Anthony M. Solomon
*Inaugurated Acquiring
Northern Mariana Islands, 1963*

The names of the islands are seared in national memory as flash points of epic struggles for control of the Pacific in World War II: Saipan, Tinian, Truk, Kwajalein.

They had been swarmed from the skies by screaming Hellcats and thundering B-24 Liberators. Their beaches had been invaded by rollicking LSDs and waves of surf-splattered GIs.

Now, twenty years later, came a new and much different contingent of Americans. A delegation of civilians in business suits and tailored sport shirts swooped into coral airstrips and swooshed by seaplane into emerald lagoons. They were accorded the elaborate courtesies of honored guests by village elders and throngs of islanders.

The year was 1963. The event marked the beginning of a process that was to determine the future of these spoils of war in the world political order.

It wasn't to be easy. The undertaking, like so much in the history of these specks tossing in the western Pacific, was shaped from start to finish by occurrences unforeseen and beyond their control. Thrust unwontedly to world attention by war, their postwar destiny was shunted rudely into the shadows by the transiencies of the American presidency.

The announcement of the White House initiative to chart their future course was relegated, by hapless timing, a mere footnote to a presidential trip. The project was made public, not in Washington, but in New York amid the hoopla of a visit by President John F. Kennedy to dedicate a war memorial.[1] The press barely took notice. Buried in the columns of the *New York Times* on that day in May, deep on page 32 next to a flashy advertisement for Trans World Airlines, was a three-paragraph snippet: "Survey Group to Seek Ways to Spur U.S. Trust Islands."[2]

Much the same obscurity awaited the mission's subsequent findings.

They were to be all but lost in the upheaval attending the assassination of their presidential sponsor.

Preempted. Neglected. Yet never quite abandoned. Despite circumstances conspiring so perversely against it, the endeavor inaugurated a relationship with the islands known collectively as Micronesia that eventually generated for the United States its most recent overseas possession.

The portentous expedition to the far Pacific was headed by an economist by training, whose experience at the age of just forty-three years already spanned the worlds of business, academia, and government service. He displayed an acumen and tough-minded efficiency that would earn Anthony M. Solomon positions of trust for three presidents.

Anthony M. Solomon, circa 1963 (courtesy Anthony M. Solomon).

His role in widening America's embrace of people beyond its shores may owe something to a more inward aspect of the man. Solomon is the son of outsiders across the sea whom the country had taken in. Not, however, from the sunny reefs of Micronesia but the austere ghettos of czarist Russia.

There, in the opening years of the twentieth century, a twenty-one-year-old Jew named Jacob Solomon confronted a cruel choice. Either accept conscription into the Russian army, enduring the harsh persecution dealt Jews in the czar's armed forces, or procure an exemption by the drastic means of incapacitating himself. He resolved to have an eye put out. His fiancée, Edna, learning of it, intercepted him at the doorway of the doctor awaiting with his scalpel. She vowed never to marry Jacob if he carried out his scheme.

Edna proposed a less painful alternative: emigrate to the United States. When he protested that he knew no one in that alien land, she invited him to look up two elder half-sisters living there. She herself would follow.

Jacob took passage to New York. He shuffled through the immigration lines, hired a horse and buggy, and struck off westward. At nightfall, he found himself in New Jersey at a town north of Kearny called Arlington. He stayed overnight, and in the morning conceived an instant affection for the place.

He decided to settle right there. The good offices of Edna's half-sisters went wanting.

His betrothed joined him a year later, at age nineteen, and the two were married. The couple was to reside ever after at the New Jersey town where the émigré had chanced to spend his first night on American soil.

In his adopted homeland, the young bridegroom showed himself a plucky entrepreneur. He took up making leather goods for horses, and landed a lucrative contract outfitting the equestrian forces of Standard Oil Company of New Jersey. When motor vehicles (fueled by Standard Oil) supplanted the company's horses, Jacob Solomon turned to selling real estate.[3] But the business climate was deteriorating into depression. Solomon again switched fields, operating a restaurant and bar in downtown Newark.[4] The bar was busy enough to occupy five bartenders.

Children entered the Solomon household — first two daughters and then, in 1919, a son, Anthony Morton.[5]

The father of the family was a consummate man of commerce. "He was a businessman," remembers his son. "He had no other interests."[6] But his business sense was sorely tested by the exigencies of the Great Depression. The difficulties of his father, and the spectacle of idle workers, hungry neighbors, and hobos so emblematic of America in the nineteen thirties, deeply impressed Anthony Solomon.[7]

While still in high school in Arlington, where more common teenage absorptions were Brooklyn Dodgers baseball or Guy Lombardo's jazz, he became "intrigued" (to use his word) with the sober field of economics. He pondered the impact of economic forces on people and how government might ameliorate it.[8] At age seventeen, in 1937, he pursued his interest at the University of Chicago. He proved adept, graduating with Phi Beta Kappa honors.[9]

The opportunity to participate in governmental molding of economic conditions led the new graduate to take the civil service examination for federal economists. He tested so well — "I was told I had the second highest score in the country," he recalls — that Solomon was hired right off the campus. He was hustled to Washington in 1941 without so much as a farewell visit home to New Jersey.[10]

Rearmament for World War II had revived the nation's economy and generated inflationary pressures. Price controls were instituted, and the young economist was put to work setting ceilings on prices of iron and steel.[11]

Six months later came the Japanese attack on Pearl Harbor. Solomon volunteered for military service and was slotted for naval officer candidate school. The next day, however, a friend told him the government was seeking someone to help oversee the finances of Iran and Iraq, then virtual client states of the British Empire. The Department of War deferred his enlistment for service instead in the Near East.[12]

At the dewy age of twenty-two, Solomon became an imperial potentate. He hardly looked the part. He stood just five feet, eight inches tall to the topmost waves of his dark hair. He was built rather slight. His speech echoed the inflections of Gotham. His calm eyes emanated more empathy than command.[13]

With the imposing title of director-general of finance of southwest Iran, based at Ahwaz, he tended the till in a domain stretching at times into eastern Iraq, cavalierly appropriating "what powers I needed." He expedited food imports. He supervised expenditures for building a road to carry military supplies from the U.S. Lend-Lease program to the Soviet Union.[14]

After a couple of years there, he felt impelled to return to the United States and don a uniform in the ongoing war. But when word of Solomon's plan reached the British ambassador in Teheran, he wired Prime Minister Winston Churchill to help retain the American. Churchill is said to have appealed to President Roosevelt, arguing that Solomon would serve the war effort better in Iran than at the front. Improvements wrought in Iran, the prime minister claimed, had enabled Britain to reduce its military presence there by two army divisions. Solomon remained.[15]

When he did go back to the United States in 1946, the war had ended. The twenty-six-year-old was promptly drafted into the postwar army. But military duty once again was waived, this time on medical grounds.[16]

Solomon set out to deepen his professional knowledge through graduate studies in economics and public administration at Harvard University.[17] But after two years of classroom work — paling, perhaps, beside practical application in the perfumed East — the student found himself "bored stiff." Solomon fled to New York City and rented a tiny apartment in Greenwich Village.[18] The bracing, bohemian setting proved academically fertile. It nurtured a master's degree from Harvard in 1948, followed by a doctoral degree in 1950.[19]

The sojourn in Manhattan also brought forth a flowering of romance. Solomon was attracted by a young woman — a thoroughly "New York City girl," as he fondly describes her — who shared his interest in matters economic. Constance Kaufman had earned a bachelor's degree in business at New York University, and was working as a junior buyer at Bloomingdales department store. Connie and Tony became inseparable companions, and in the spring of 1950 were married.[20]

The bridegroom toiled in the trenches of the financial world as a securities analyst for the investment house Bache & Company.[21]

The newlyweds traveled to Mexico. Their host was a former colleague of Solomon's from his Persian venture, an American who had gone to live in the United States's southerly national neighbor. The place seduced them. "We fell in love with Mexico," Solomon says. The casual visit stretched into long-term residence.[22] The gringo economist, unversed in Spanish, partnered with a Mexican in a publishing business. The firm issued trade magazines and compiled the first directory of the country's industries.[23]

Then Solomon's trained eye spotted an enticing financial opportunity. A new food company in Mexico City had begun packaging dehydrated soups. "I saw the promise." He took over Rosa Blanca Products Corporation in 1953, built it into a booming enterprise, and sold it in 1961 to the giant American combine General Foods Corporation. The deal left Solomon a millionaire and his financial future secure.[24]

The expatriate couple became in Mexico the parents of three children: a son, Adam, and two daughters, Nicki and Tracy.[25] But not long after erecting a palatial home there, the country lost its hold on the Solomons just as swiftly as it had beguiled them ten years before. "We got bored," he relates, and left.[26]

The family resettled back in the United States. It was preparing for a vacation in Europe when Solomon unexpectedly received overtures from his postgraduate alma mater. A professor at Harvard approached him with an offer. Would he like to come and teach? The young man who had exiled himself from Cambridge not so long ago returned in 1961 as a lecturer on business administration.[27]

Although out of government service for fifteen years, Solomon still had admirers in Washington. His combined talents as an economist and a successful businessman in Latin America — not to mention the esteem of Roosevelt — commended him to the Kennedy administration when looking for an economic troubleshooter to send to South America. He was asked in 1963 to lead an expedition to evaluate the U.S. foreign aid program in the continent's poorest nation: Bolivia.[28] The resulting appraisal was received with such favor that it was to open an opportunity unimagined.[29]

Just a week after submitting his report, Solomon was to be offered a more important mission — to Micronesia.

Micronesia is a scattering of islands strewn across the empty horse latitudes of the Pacific between Hawaii and the Philippines, a watery kingdom as large as the continental United States. The volcanic lumps and coral atolls number nearly 2,000, of which fewer than 100 are inhabited, at the time by something over 80,000 people.[30]

The component island groups — the Carolines, Gilberts, Marianas, and Marshalls — since lapped by the tides of imperialism in the seventeenth century had been shuttled among five world powers. All except the Gilberts, a colony of Britain, were placed by the League of Nations after World War I under the administration of Japan.[31] Subsequently fortified, the islands were wrested from Japan in the ensuing world war by the United States at heavy cost. Combat on Micronesia's beaches and cliffs — among the war's most fierce — claimed the lives of over six thousand Americans and thousands more Japanese.[32]

Consecration by blood and valor resolved Americans, once the war was over, to hang onto the islands. "We fought for them. We've got them. We should keep them." Such was the temper of the times, blared forth in 1945 in Congress.[33] When the newly-created United Nations in 1947 divvied up the war's territorial orphans among foster nations, it obligingly assigned most of Micronesia to the trusteeship of the United States.[34]

The country had sought the islands primarily to bolster national security.[35] And its attentions to its new ward in the succeeding two decades had been myopically martial. A base of the Central Intelligence Agency had been plunked down on Saipan in the Marianas for spiriting clandestine Cold War operatives throughout Asia.[36] The extremities of the Marshalls had been co-opted for the equally dark work of testing nuclear weapons.[37]

The civic needs and possibilities of the region languished in neglect. The only discernible policy of the United States in its Trust Territory of the Pacific Islands during the nineteen fifties seemed to be cutting the budget. The wartime Quonsets of the territorial government moldered away. Its castoff navy vehicles sputtered unrepaired. Roads disintegrated. School curricula catered less to young islanders than to children of U.S. military families. Scrap metal from war debris ranked as the second leading export. The trust territory began to be referred to snidely as the "rust territory."[38]

It also became the target of charges more stinging. This bedraggled dependent, military pawn of its mainland master, opened the United States to accusations of colonialism in a postwar world rebelling against the imperial past. Leaders of the Soviet bloc turned the trust territory into a weapon against the United States in the propaganda battle for the support of ideologically nonaligned nations emerging in growing numbers from colonialism.[39] "Colonial tyranny," taunted the bombastic Soviet premier, Nikita Khrushchev. "Freedom to the American Pacific!"[40]

The swipe rankled the Kennedy administration, just settling into office and eager to project to the world an image of vibrant idealism.[41] "If we are to succeed anywhere," the president vowed to his cabinet, "we must succeed in the Western Pacific."[42]

Kennedy's interest went beyond presidential imagery or Cold War jostling. It was also personal. He had served during World War II in the Pacific, and the experience had left a lasting attachment. The raw, twenty-five-year-old scion of Boston privilege, commanding a navy patrol torpedo boat in 1943 in the Solomon Islands, had been shocked at the squalor he encountered there.[43] His sympathy for the islanders was cemented after his PT-109 was rammed by a Japanese destroyer and sank. Hospitable Melanesians helped arrange a rescue by the Australian navy.[44]

His sobering coming-of-age in the Pacific was never to be forgotten. Long after returning Stateside and putting off navy blues, Kennedy felt a national obligation to improve conditions in the islands.[45]

As president, he conceived a vision for Micronesia that reflected his wider dream for the nation as a whole. It embodied the soaring aspirations of those less jaded times. Kennedy envisioned a Pacific protectorate where American rule was more noble, just as he pictured a United States of greater economic and racial opportunity.[46] He wanted the government to stop "playing Viceroy," as he once put it, and show more concern for its island wards.[47] For skeptics, he had a simple justification: "Because it is the right thing to do."[48]

In nearly twenty years since the end of the war, it was the first time that a presidential administration had exhibited more than passing interest in the Micronesian outpost.[49] Some in Washington, accustomed by default to running the trust territory as a private fief, regarded the White House attention as excessive. The chairman of the House territorial committee, Representative Wayne N. Aspinall of Colorado, for one, felt Kennedy's interest "obsessive," and told him so.[50]

To begin transforming his vision into reality, Kennedy undertook a series of preliminary initiatives. He moved the capital of the trust territory from Hawaii—separated, against all logic, more than three thousand miles from its constituency. The government was relocated first to Guam, then to Saipan in the trust territory itself.[51] The territorial government was civilianized by halting participation by the navy.[52] Kennedy closed the CIA base, a curtailment that appealed to a president still smarting from the responsibility he ascribed to the agency in the failed invasion of Cuba at the Bay of Pigs in 1961. The hush-hush facility reopened as the very public seat of the territorial government.[53] Shutting down the CIA base negated the last rationale for keeping Micronesia off-limits to outsiders.[54] So Kennedy lifted twenty-year-old restrictions on entering the region.[55]

The years of parsimony were ended. The administration underwrote a program of improvements long overdue, notably in the sphere of education.[56] The president hailed it as "the beginning of a new era of progress for the Trust Territory and its inhabitants."[57] A new era of spending, it certainly was. Federal funding of the territory, which for a decade had averaged $5 million a year, tripled in 1963 to $15 million.[58]

But the long-range future of Micronesia in the global scheme of things remained unaddressed. The administration, its energies directed by special presidential interest to this distant sprinkling of islands, meant to settle the matter. Doing so required gathering knowledge of the place first hand. A small team of federal officials was dispatched to Micronesia in 1962 to start the process.[59] It was to be followed by a mission more thoroughgoing — experts in relevant fields, from within the government and outside it, to recommend a course of action. To lead the task force, the White House sought someone savvy of foreign cultures and deft at distilling complexities.[60]

Solomon's report on Bolivia, just submitted, lay on the desks of policymakers, its impressiveness fresh in their minds. A young Kennedy aide, Michael V. Forrestal, contacted Solomon. He was offered the Micronesian mission.[61]

The rest of the party was filled out in brainstorming between Solomon and the administration.[62] The seven other members comprised four federal officials, the education commissioner of the Virgin Islands, a professor of public administration, and a private consultant.[63] Getting the desired people entailed, in at least one case, hard bargaining. A gifted economist selected from the staff of the Council of Economic Advisers was so coveted that the White House initially refused to part with him even for a couple of months. He was grudgingly relinquished, and Richard N. Cooper began his rise to positions of high responsibility in Washington — and lasting friendship with Solomon.[64]

The group's commission was less than open-ended. Kennedy already had decided the geopolitical outcome he wanted for Micronesia: permanent ties of some sort with the United States. He had set forth his goal in a pair of internal "national security action memoranda" organizing the Solomon mission and its smaller predecessor.[65] The earlier directive foresaw a relationship described as "full association."[66] In private conversation, the president is said even to have gone so far as to predict that the islands eventually would become a state of the union.[67]

The Solomon task force appointees assembled in Washington, underwent briefings, and set off. They headed first to Paris, to tap the expertise of those in charge of the nearest equivalent Pacific regency — French Polynesia. Then they sped skyward to Oceania.[68]

The leap from the boulevards of Old Europe and marble canyons of Washington was transporting. Micronesia swallowed up the visitors in a universe of endless seas, vaulting skies, and hypnotic timelessness. Pines nodded over deserted beaches. Poinciana patiently daubed hillsides. Seaward cliffs stoically concealed the gun shell scars of warfare so forgetfully recent.

For six weeks in July and August, the Solomon mission hop-scotched from island to island across the trust territory, sampling opinion.[69] It met with governmental bodies, women's associations, missionaries, private individuals.⁷⁰ Each session took the same form. The mainlanders solicited views on the islands' future and asked questions.⁷¹ They also inspected roads, schools, and farms.⁷²

The exercise was accompanied by an effusion of pomp that Solomon, more comfortable outside the limelight, would have preferred to avoid. "Much panoply," he calls it. A touch of heraldry was added by the presence of a military aide-de-camp. And every stop became a public event, drawing a welcoming party of local leaders and a heavy turnout of villagers.⁷³ Such occasions evoke traditional Micronesian culinary hospitality. Roast pork and saffron rice fill long tables alongside chicken with coconut, sashimi with hot peppers, breadfruit, cucumber laced with ginger, and taro.⁷⁴

Having circuited the islands, the task force closeted itself in Saipan to write a report. Each member drafted a section in his field of specialization. They reassembled every evening for a week for roundtable discussions that were, by all accounts, spirited and frank. Solomon moderated the dialogue, and collated the resulting document.⁷⁵

The delegation returned to the States with a report that was to fill three volumes.⁷⁶

Casting a stern eye to the past, it issued a damning indictment of American stewardship. The report depicted an apathetic overseer leaving a society of vulnerable indigenes not merely static but in some respects measurably worse off than before:

> In the almost twenty years of U.S. control, physical facilities have further deteriorated in many areas, the economy has remained relatively dormant and in many ways retrogressed while progress toward social development has been slow. The people remain largely illiterate and inadequately prepared to participate in political, commercial and other activities of more than a rudimentary character.⁷⁷

Islanders were earning, the visitors were chagrined to discover, barely a third as much per capita as before World War II under the rule of their old enemy, the Japanese.⁷⁸

Despite long neglect, the Solomon mission reckoned the situation to be salvageable. It accepted the prevailing wisdom that Micronesia should be retained in American hands. "Essential to the United States," it agreed, "for security reasons."⁷⁹ To redeem Americans' past performance and enhance acceptance of their longer-term presence, the report proposed a crash program.

The place would be plied with federal attention and money the likes of which it never had known. Derelict public services — notably education and health care — would be renovated to an acceptable standard by pouring in financial aid, erecting new facilities, retraining staff, and arranging exchanges with American counterparts. The age-old Micronesian economy based on fishing and gathering coconuts and other fruit would be made more productive to boost family incomes. The United States would lavish upon its suddenly rediscovered ward assistance worth as much as three hundred dollars a year per islander — nearly quadruple each's current income.[80]

The largess would be less than purely magnanimous. It was calculated to impress Micronesians so favorably that they would embrace a closer and more lasting relationship with their benefactor.

An "effective capital investment program" was prescribed "to give Micronesians a sense of progress to replace the deadly feeling of economic dormancy."[81] But merely helping islanders wasn't enough. The program must pack "maximum political impact."[82] The political goal would be the one envisioned by the mission's presidential mentor — what the report called "permanent affiliation."[83] Loss of their sovereignty, however nominal it might be, would be compensated by a gain in self-government. The trust territory government was reproached as a lordly "quasi-colonial bureaucracy."[84] It would be replaced by a chief executive who was Micronesian and an American-style legislature elected by the people.[85]

But liberality extended only so far. The Solomon task force had seen "clear limitations on the present-day ability of Micronesians to govern themselves."[86] It recommended an approach that might strike many as bordering on duplicity: give the islands only "a reasonable appearance of self-government," while retaining for the United States "adequate control."[87] American interests would continue to be safeguarded by a high commissioner sent out from Washington, as under the trust territory setup.[88] And the full constitutional rights enjoyed by mainlanders would wait until later.[89]

Once Micronesians had witnessed American indulgence financially and (to all appearances) politically, they would be asked to vote on linking up with the United States constitutionally.[90] Although unstated in the report, such a plebiscite would represent a major concession in U.S. territorial policy. Belying its fervent avowal of democratic ideals, the country long had resisted letting the inhabitants of its overseas possessions vote on whether they actually wanted to be part of the United States. And none ever had been given an opportunity to cast ballots on the question before acquisition.[91] The outcome of the Micronesian plebiscite, however, was never to be in doubt. U.S. munificence was designed to "insure" a tally that was "favorable."[92] The Solomon mission set a brash goal to be achieved by 1968: "Winning the plebiscite and making Micronesia a United States territory."[93]

It would be no cakewalk. Islanders were hardly clambering to become Americans. Most appeared to not only care little about their political future, but to be "not even aware of it as a question."[94] They were dimly conscious merely that the "Japanese time" had been succeeded by the "American time."[95]

Moreover, they were far from a cohesive territory-in-waiting. The disparate Carolinians, Mariana Chamorros, and Marshallese rarely identified themselves as "Micronesians," a label affixed by nineteenth century Europeans. And they harbored no emotional attachment to this artificial grouping and putative U.S. territory.[96]

Further dampening prospects for American affiliation, the trust territory officialdom was said to be stubbornly still espousing a political goal of independence. Such dissent within the overseer's own ranks posed an obstacle "hard to overcome."[97]

In the outside world, the U.S. scheme would be a tough sell. The era of imperialism was fast receding. Empires were dissolving. Colonies were battling or bargaining for their independence. Anticolonialism was in full cry. Annexing an overseas appendage would put the United States in the awkward position of bucking world opinion.[98] The country long had been a proud participant in the new order, refraining since World War I from acquiring territory abroad. Now, the report cautioned, the United States would be publicly "breaching its own policy."[99]

Colonies taken under the wing of the United Nations had followed a path different from the one plotted for Micronesia. All had either won their independence or merged with a nation contiguous to them. None had gone the suspiciously colonialistic route of absorption by the administering power, as would the American trust territory.[100]

The Solomon program faced domestic hurdles, too. The United States would be taking on an effective charity case — what the report diplomatically called "a deficit area."[101] Micronesia would need to be subsidized by its adoptive national parent for "the now foreseeable future."[102]

To start chipping away at the barriers while the financial and political incentives took hold, the task force proposed a grab-bag of hearts-and-minds measures. Station an American publicist, or "information officer," in each of the trust territory's six districts. Americanize schooling by introducing "United States oriented curriculum changes and patriotic rituals." Increase U.S. college scholarships for Micronesians. Send island leaders Stateside for visits. Assign sixty Peace Corps volunteers to the islands.[103]

Notwithstanding the difficulties confronting his plan, Solomon was confident that it could be accomplished. He assured the president, in a letter, that incorporating Micronesia into the United States as a territory was "definitely attainable." The islanders, he sensed, were ready. "The Micronesian inhabitants recognize that they cannot stand alone."[104]

Its work finished, the task force dispersed, its members returning to their separate callings. Solomon remained in Washington to introduce the report to an awaiting government.

A thirty-two-page summary was submitted in September to Kennedy.[105] It came highly recommended by his staff. The assistant who had conscripted Solomon, Michael Forrestal, wrote in a covering memorandum to the national security adviser, McGeorge Bundy:

> If the President is doing any reflective reading this weekend, or while he is flying around next week, you might want to put it with his papers. I think it is worth reading and at some point we need to get a nod from the President.[106]

Solomon went to the White House a month later to meet with Kennedy.[107] Evidently having previously escaped his eyes, the president proceeded to read the summary of the report as Solomon and Secretary of the Interior Stewart L. Udall sat before him in the Oval Office. It was a feat of quick comprehension that Solomon never would forget. Kennedy plowed through the thirty-two pages in ten minutes, grasping all salient points. "He amazed me."[108]

The president gave the plan his blessing.[109] To jump-start implementation, the three decided to send to Micronesia the assistant interior secretary who had led the preliminary mission the previous year.[110]

Wasting no time, Kennedy followed up the next day with another of his national security action memoranda. This one directed federal agencies to begin carrying out the report's recommendations.[111] The president focused special attention on the plebiscite. An attached note said Kennedy was eager to learn of plans for "the fixing of a date ... and the public announcement thereof."[112]

The president was quietly preparing a more splashy demonstration of his interest in Micronesia. He would go there on an official visit. Kennedy had broached the idea to a delegation of islanders visiting Washington earlier in the summer while the Solomon expedition was still being organized. The findings of the mission seemed to crystallize the plan in his mind. The day after meeting with Solomon, the president told the cabinet that he would visit Micronesia by the end of the year or early 1964.[113]

Solomon and his team had provided Kennedy what he wanted. The mission corroborated the president's goal for the islands and laid out a plan for reaching it. In a letter to Solomon at his home in Georgetown, Kennedy pronounced the enterprise "a fine job."[114]

The reception elsewhere in Washington, however, was less cordial. The Department of the Interior — which, despite its name, administers the country's external territories[115] — appeared a little resentful of a band of outsiders intruding on its jurisdictional turf. A department official called the Solomon recommendations "mischievous."[116]

The Solomon plan encountered resistance in Congress, too. Powerful lawmakers felt it gave Micronesians too much latitude too soon. The chairman of the Senate committee overseeing the territories, Henry M. Jackson of Washington, a chum of the president's from his senatorial years, was supportive.[117] But his counterpart in the House, Aspinall, objected that islanders were unqualified to assume more of their governance or even vote on their political future. They might be "ready," he suggested, in fifty years.[118]

Solomon and the Kennedy administration were pushing a timetable far more hasty. The leader of the mission had advised the president, in a letter, that for a plebiscite "optimum timing ... would be early 1968."[119] Two federal departments, State and Defense, wanted the vote even sooner—in 1967 and 1966, respectively.[120]

When Solomon appeared before the House committee to discuss his report, Aspinall curtly ruled out any plans for a plebiscite at all. "There's no point to even talking about a plebiscite," he told him. Solomon, squirming, could maintain no respectful silence.

> Mr. Chairman, are you telling me that [you've] closed your ears? You won't even hear a report? You have no objectivity? You don't want to know the facts of the situation?

Aspinall retreated. "Oh, no," he replied. "I'm perfectly willing to listen."[121]

As the recommendations of the Solomon mission floated out to Micronesia, they won a wide welcome. Clan chiefs, trading company businessmen, and the younger set of trust territory administrators (although conspicuously not their more skeptical seniors) offered preliminary approval.[122]

A public health scare, meanwhile, showed Kennedy's continuing personal regard for the region. Polio, a disease fast disappearing on the mainland, had broken out in the Marshall Islands, claiming eleven lives.[123] The president was incensed at what he interpreted as Americans' failure to adequately protect islanders entrusted to their care. "I am shocked," he scolded Udall in a blistering memo. "This is inexcusable.... I would like a complete investigation."[124]

Kennedy would get no investigation of the Pacific polio outbreak. Nor would he track the progress of the master plan that he had commissioned. Nor visit Micronesia. Eighteen days after firing off the memo to Udall—during one of those "flying around" appearances mentioned so lightly by his Solomon go-between—the president was assassinated in Dallas.

The ensuing turmoil of a sudden change in national leadership, which threw into uncertainty so many Kennedy initiatives, enmeshed also the scheme for Micronesia. It immediately short-circuited the mission sent to the islands to begin implementing the plan.[125] Then, in the new climate in Washington, a shroud of secrecy fell upon the Solomon report. Unsensitive portions—those devoid of political and military implications—at first had been freely made public.[126] But within a month of the assassination, even the seemingly inoffensive volume on social and economic matters was slapped a security classification of "confidential," banning its dissemination.[127]

The man who had crafted the plan for Micronesia began to worry that it was adrift. Stamping the report as classified, Solomon feared, might be a convenient way of shelving it.[128] Implementation was spotty.[129] The follow-up actions of holdover Kennedy officials diminished as the government shifted into the hands of presidential successor Lyndon B. Johnson. Kennedy appointees gradually left office.[130] The informal working group of Micronesia authorities in key agencies broke up.[131] Congress dallied. Attention focused increasingly on war in Vietnam.[132]

Solomon watched with dismay from Foggy Bottom, where he had taken a position at the State Department, helping supervise aid to Latin America.[133] The unpretentious appointment — a deputy assistant secretary of state — would extend over the years into a string of nine stints of service at the State and Treasury departments, all in the fields of international affairs and trade.[134]

Although he no longer held official responsibilities in the Pacific, Solomon couldn't forget Micronesia. To try speeding up the plan for the islands, he mooted the idea of prodding appropriate administration officials by memo. But one of the department's Far East hands dissuaded him.[135] The busy young office-bearer found he could do no more. "I had too much on my plate."[136]

The concerns of Solomon, who admits to being a "pretty impatient guy,"[137] may have been exaggerated. Fitfully and often imperceptibly, many of the mission's recommendations were finding their way to Micronesia and effecting changes. By the close of the nineteen sixties, federal spending there approximated the increased level that the plan had proposed.[138] The economic stimulus had quickened business activity, modernized communications, and launched the islands' own airline, Air Micronesia.[139] Schools were humming.[140] The first region-wide legislature had been elected.[141] One American influence far from subtle was the Peace Corps. The Solomon report's modest suggestion of sixty volunteers had ballooned to an invasion of nine hundred, at its peak, saturating the islands.[142]

The political blueprint for these developments, under wraps for years, suddenly was flung open to the public. Not, however, by government censors in a burst of repentance. The most sensitive parts of the Solomon report were leaked in 1971 by enterprising Pacific journalists — a student newsletter at the University of Hawaii and a weekly newspaper in Micronesia.[143]

While welcoming an end of secrecy, the man whose name the report bore was hardly pleased by the reaction that his newly-unveiled plan aroused in the region. The ready approbation of the nineteen sixties had given way in the seventies to hard questioning. The very changes that American planners were engendering in the islands seemed to work against them. More exposure to the rest of the world, bringing mixed blessings economically and socially, and protracted discussion of the constitutional future, had bred greater political sophistication. American motives were being challenged. Among some islanders, particularly the well-educated young, they were openly mistrusted.[144] The newsletter of Micronesian students in Hawaii lambasted the Solomon program as "a ruthless five-year plan to systematically Americanize Micronesia into a permanent association in clear and conscious defiance of [the United State's] trusteeship obligations."[145]

The target of such criticism took it philosophically. Solomon was "amused," he says, to be portrayed as "a sinister maneuverer." The report contained "nothing *that* sinister," in his judgment, but offended advocates of Micronesian independence. He was struck by the irony of being faulted in the islands for proposing too little autonomy, and in Congress for proposing too much.[146]

Solomon was now little more than an interested spectator of events in Micronesia. He was occupied filling a succession of high-level governmental assignments in the sphere of international economics. As assistant secretary of state for economic affairs in the late sixties, he persuaded foreign steelmakers to curb exports to the United States and helped reform the global monetary system.[147] Then a fellow alumnus of the Kennedy and Johnson administrations, Robert S. McNamara, the former secretary of defense who had become president of the World Bank, recruited Solomon. He set up a public corporation to spur western business development in Yugoslavia.[148]

His capacities were earning for Solomon a name as a financial sage and administrator. Even among those whom politics might be expected to cast as foes. Politically, Solomon was a Democrat who had served only Democratic presidents. But the administration of Republican Richard M. Nixon held him in sufficient regard to consider nomination to an important international post. He was touted highly to the president by his national security assistant, Henry A. Kissinger:

> Solomon is ... extremely vigorous, a first-class administrator, businessman, and economist.... was outstanding [at the State Department].... a tough, no-nonsense operator who earned an excellent reputation on Capitol Hill.... Also stands very high with the U.S. business community.[149]

While no appointment emerged from the Nixon administration, that "excellent reputation on Capitol Hill" noted by Kissinger generated work there. Solomon lent to the lawmaking process his expertise on trade as an adviser to the chairman of the committee that writes the nation's tax laws, the House Committee on Ways and Means.[150]

Professional fulfillment was darkened, however, by personal tragedy. The younger of his two daughters, Nicki, at the age of twenty-one in 1975 was murdered in her apartment in Washington. The pain of loss was slow to heal.[151]

The search for solace led Solomon to discover within himself a new interest far removed from the hard-figures world of high finance. As part of a catharsis to help him (in his words) "stop brooding" about his daughter, he took up a hobby of sculpting. In a studio at his farm in Great Falls, Virginia, a glen of rusticity across the Potomac River from the clamor of Washington, he began creating semi-abstract artifacts in wood, bronze, and terra-cotta.[152]

He also created something more. From the amateur sculptor sprang an eminent collector. Strolling one day past an antique shop in London, his eye was caught by the sculpture of a Chinese figure. It was a tomb sculpture, art fashioned solely for burial — and buried away, too, from the attentions of scholars and collectors. Solomon bought it, and began studying the neglected art form. He purchased more over the years.[153] His troupe of engaging clayware depictions of humans and animals, dating back as much as two thousand years, grew into the largest and finest private such collection in the West. It was to wind up donated to Harvard, and the subject of museum exhibitions there and in New York.[154]

Far away in the Pacific, meanwhile, Micronesia's political future was taking shape. But not in the way envisaged by Solomon and his fellow American strategists. The United States and Micronesia finally had begun negotiating in 1969, but the talks were stymied by tensions within the islands.[155] A geopolitical entity never knit together more than loosely, the place was breaking up.

The fragmenting force came from the Northern Mariana Islands. A cluster of reefed green lumps at Micronesia's northwestern end, adjoining Guam, the Marianas lie a little apart from the rest of the region, not only geographically but also economically and temperamentally. In large measure because of their perceived value as the most militarily useful portion of the region, they had been accorded within the trust territory favored treatment. An infusion of dollars for military installations there, the CIA base on Saipan, and the trust territory headquarters had left the Marianas better off financially than the rest of Micronesia.[156] The American-spawned development, in turn, reinforced Mariana islanders' self-image — resented throughout the region — as regarding themselves as somehow superior to other Micronesians.[157]

The separatist impulses coalesced in 1971 into action. The catalyst appears to have been a new territory-wide tax, imposed by the Micronesian congress, that would have channeled revenue from wealthier districts such as the

Marianas to underwrite programs in poorer islands.[158] The Mariana legislature angrily voted to secede.[159] Informal feelers went out to Americans in the stalled status negotiations, and the United States and the breakaway Marianas opened separate, bilateral talks. Their shared objective: to make the Marianas a U.S. territory.[160]

Three years of bargaining culminated in 1975 in an agreement and a truncated version of the plebiscite proposed a decade earlier. Mariana voters — all 5,005 of them — endorsed union with their mainland overseer by an emphatic majority of nearly eighty percent.[161] Congress ratified annexation the following year.[162] The country had acquired territory overseas — albeit its smallest ever — for the first time in sixty-nine years.[163]

The process which the Solomon mission had set in motion years previously had, tardily and clumsily, planted the American flag in Micronesia. But for the man who had got things underway, observing from afar, any sense of accomplishment was tempered. The splintering of Micronesia left Solomon "disappointed." If the American government had acted with greater dispatch, he feels, it never would have happened. He had found island leaders, in the sixties, ready to affiliate with the United States as a unified Micronesia. "They would have been content," he recalls, "with my arrangement." Then Americans held back. The culprit, to him, was Congress. Lawmakers dawdled, and "time," he says, altered forever the outcome.[164]

But Solomon had little opportunity, at that juncture, to indulge in such ruminations. The country had elected in 1976 a new president, Democrat Jimmy Carter, and members of his party with experience in government found their services in demand. At the time that the Marianas were taking their place in the U.S. constitutional family, Solomon was taking a new place of his own in the federal hierarchy.

Carter's secretary of the treasury, W. Michael Blumenthal, had worked with Solomon in the nineteen sixties on trade negotiations. The two men — both trained economists who had succeeded in business and then branched into government via the State Department — took a liking to each other. Blumenthal picked Solomon as the third-ranking officer in his Treasury Department.[165]

When the increasingly uncompetitive U.S. steel industry came under renewed pressure in 1977 from foreign rivals, the new undersecretary for monetary affairs was called upon for help. The president reassured the public: "I've got one of the best people in government working on it." His trust wasn't misplaced. As he had done a decade before, Solomon finagled for American steelmakers trade protection.[166]

His prowess as a global bargainer was reaffirmed during talks in China reopening economic relations between the two countries estranged for a quarter of a century. Americans wanted the Chinese to ante up more compensation for holdings that the communist government had nationalized. Against all expectations — including his own — Solomon persuaded the Chinese to pay twice as much as they had offered.[167]

One of the most important posts in the nation's central banking system fell vacant in 1980. It was the presidency of the doyen of the Federal Reserve banks — the one in New York, standing watch over that city's world financial hub. Solomon was appointed. The self-possessed New Yorker rode herd on the sometimes tumultuous realm of stock tickers and market indexes with the serene aplomb of one whose breadth of experience had fit him for anything.[168]

To those expecting pontification, Solomon sometimes seemed as inscrutable as one of his tomb sculptures. As throughout his public life, he was reserved and careful to a fault in his utterances.[169] He faced interrogators from behind the cover of a bristly, closely-cropped beard and moustache, and curls of smoke from a smoldering pipe.[170] But the reflective manner masked iron resolution. Commented one banker:

> When he sits back and smokes that pipe, he looks like an academician.... Then all of a sudden he comes out with a statement, and it becomes obvious that there's real steel there.[171]

The position at the Fed capped Solomon's public career. He left at the government retirement age of sixty-five,[172] and sidestepped into the private sector, chairing the American operations of the London-based merchant bank S. G. Warburg.[173]

Today Solomon's domain has shrunk. The borderless orb of banking and monetary policy has contracted to the intimacy of the study of a penthouse apartment on Manhattan's Upper East Side. Books on history, travel, and the arts share their shelves with family photographs. A grey miniature poodle scampers in and out.

A decompressed life has its compensations. Family can be devoted the attention that occupational demands never permitted. Solomon has had the satisfaction of watching his son follow him into a career in finance. Adam co-founded and chairs an investment firm in New York. He visits his father twice a week, often bearing news of his two grown sons, the elder man's only grandchildren.[174] Daughter Tracy resides at the opposite end of the country, north of San Francisco. She continues the family entrepreneurial tradition as a business executive.[175] Their mother, Solomon's wife of forty-eight years, Connie, passed away in 1998.[176]

Retirement also has enabled Solomon to cultivate his artistic side. His living room isn't so much the room of a home as a sculpture gallery. A galaxy of ancient Chinese figures and modern abstractions on pedestals renders furniture almost an intrusion. He briefly resumed sculpting of his own. Then, with the encouragement of his daughter-in-law, a painter, he began creating small, abstract watercolors.[177]

Solomon's collection of Eastern art includes no Micronesian latte stones, the carvings symbolic of the early Chamorros.[178] Nor has he become a Micronesia aficionado. The islands came his way at the outset of a long career in government, and have since receded to the periphery, much like their geographical isolation. Any attachment to the place also may be diminished by disappointment over its political disintegration.

But the instrumental role that he played in incorporating these islands into the world community is brought home to him from time to time. When Micronesia's new sovereign states last negotiated renewal of their U.S. economic aid a few years ago, they asked Solomon to represent them. He was flattered, but compelled by a bout of illness to decline.[179]

The relationship between Solomon and the region has remain distanced. Not just his ties to independent Micronesia, but even the segment that fulfilled his aspiration of becoming an American territory. The journey he once made to Oceania for a president fixated by a far corner of the Pacific hasn't been retraced. The islands have yet to lure Solomon back for a visit.[180]

Chapter Notes

The shortened citations refer to books and articles by the author's last name. They are fully cited in the Bibliography following.

1. Charles Wilkes

1. Writing at the same period (1849), Herman Melville describes a South Pacific where, for "a thousand miles, stretched north and south an almost endless Archipelago, here and there inhabited, but little known; and mostly unfrequented, even by whalemen, who go almost every where." Melville, 9.
2. Strauss, 107.
3. Strauss, 107.
4. Rutland, 213, 220, 253.
5. Captain Edmund Fanning, who had been plying the Pacific for two decades, proposed an expedition to Madison in 1810 and again in 1812, and was rewarded with command of the two ships that never sailed. Strauss, 107; Silverberg, 16.
6. Strauss, 107.
7. Richardson, vol. 2, 312–313; Strauss, 107–108; Henderson, 29; Silverberg, 17; Van Buren, vol. 1, 194–195.
8. Adams, an ardent home gardener, also took an active part in founding the Smithsonian Institution in Washington. Nagel, 311, 357, 366–367.
9. Cook's three voyages (1768–71, 1772–75, 1776–80) blazed the way for the Union Jack most notably in Australia and New Zealand. The former became a British penal colony only eighteen years after the explorer's departure. Moorehead, 134–167.
10. Strauss, 108.
11. Adams's proposed voyage to the Northwest perished in a House of Representatives committee, and his endorsement of a more ambitious expedition approved by the House two years later was rejected by a Senate committee. Strauss, 108–111; Henderson, 29; Silverberg, 24–25; Nagel, 296.
12. Henderson, 30.
13. Henderson, 4.
14. Wilkes, *Autobiography*, 2; Henderson, 3–4, 6. The Wilkes family in England had amassed a fortune in brewing.
15. Wilkes, *Autobiography*, 2; Henderson, 6. Mary Seton was sister of Elizabeth Seton, who founded the American Sisters of Charity religious order and was beatified as a saint by the Roman Catholic church in 1963. Silverberg, 22.
16. Henderson, 4.
17. Henderson, 8.
18. Silverberg, 22.
19. Charles's father eventually discarded his Toryism and became a patriotic American. Henderson, 6.
20. Henderson, 5–6.
21. Henderson, 8.
22. Wilkes, *Autobiography*, 16.
23. Henderson, 10.
24. Henderson, 10. Commodore Matthew C. Perry commanded the warships that in 1853 opened Japanese ports and initiated the gradual ending of the country's long closure to outsiders.
25. Wilkes, *Autobiography*, 16.
26. Henderson, 10.
27. Wilkes, *Autobiography*, 17.
28. Henderson, 10.
29. Wilkes, *Autobiography*, 16–17; Henderson, 11; Silverberg, 22–23. The ship was the *Hibernia*, owned by Captain Craig & Brothers.
30. Wilkes, *Autobiography*, 19–35; Henderson, 11.
31. Wilkes, *Autobiography*, 19–37; Henderson, 12–13.
32. Wilkes, *Autobiography*, 37; Henderson, 13.
33. Henderson, 13; Wilkes, *Narrative*, vol. 1, frontispiece. The portrait was executed by the painter Thomas Sully.
34. Wilkes, *Autobiography*, 17.
35. Wilkes, *Autobiography*, 37; Henderson, 13. The French minister in Washington also had used his good offices to help procure Wilkes his midshipman's commission.
36. Wilkes, *Autobiography*, 38; Henderson, 13–14.
37. He sailed aboard the frigate *Guerriere* to Minorca, then a two-year journey aboard the *Franklin* to Chile and Peru. Wilkes, *Autobiography*, 41, 49–107, 109–166; Henderson, 16–25.
38. Henderson, 20–21.
39. Wilkes, *Autobiography*, 106–107; Henderson, 22.
40. Jeanie Jaffrey (later Renwick) of Lochmaben, Scotland, inspired in 1790 Burns's poem "I Gaed a Waefu' Gate Yestreen." Burns, vol. 3, pt. 1, 102; Henderson, 21.
41. Wilkes, *Autobiography*, 106.

Notes — Chapter 1

42. Henderson, 22; Wilkes, *Autobiography*, 106.
43. Wilkes, *Autobiography*, 226; Henderson, 27. Henderson states that the promotion preceded the wedding.
44. Henderson, 21, 30.
45. Wilkes, *Autobiography*, 105.
46. Wilkes, *Autobiography*, 106.
47. Henderson, 22; Silverberg, 23.
48. Henderson, 3–4.
49. Henderson, 30.
50. Henderson, 30; Strauss, 122.
51. Wilkes, *Autobiography*, 324.
52. Strauss, 111; Silverberg, 25. The expedition was led by Antarctic explorer Nathaniel B. Palmer.
53. The *Beagle* circumnavigated the globe from 1831 to 1836.
54. Those laying the legislative groundwork included the indefatigable Edmund Fanning, who had first proposed the idea to President Madison twenty-five years earlier; writer and lecturer Jeremiah N. Reynolds; and former naval secretary Southard, who had become, usefully, chairman of the Senate committee on naval affairs. Strauss, 108–113; Silverberg, 26.
55. Henderson, 32; Strauss, 113; Silverberg, 26–27.
56. Henderson, 30.
57. Wilkes was the second person to head the three-year-old office. Henderson, 32; Strauss, 113, 122; Silverberg, 27.
58. Henderson, 33–34; Strauss, 113; Silverberg, 27–28.
59. Wilkes, *Autobiography*, 337–339; Henderson, 32; Silverberg, 29–30. The navy secretary was Mahlon Dickerson.
60. Wilkes, *Autobiography*, 324–336; Henderson, 34.
61. Strauss, 113–114.
62. Strauss, 114. The only former president to sit in the House of Representatives, Adams served with distinction there seventeen years.
63. Wilkes, *Autobiography*, 338; Strauss, 114; Henderson, 35; Silverberg, 31–32.
64. Strauss, 114; Henderson, 35; Wilson, *Van Buren*, 176. The navy secretary who lost responsibility over the expedition was Dickerson, a holdover from Jackson's cabinet and an old friend of Van Buren's. Cole, 89, 250, 286.
65. Poinsett found the plant in Mexico in 1825 while serving as his country's first minister there. Henderson, 35; Strauss, 114; Silverberg, 32; Wilson, *Van Buren*, 181.
66. Among those declining to command the expedition was Wilkes's boyhood acquaintance Matthew C. Perry, the future commodore. Wilkes, *Autobiography*, 341–343; Strauss, 114–115; Henderson 36, 43; Silverberg, 32–33.
67. Wilkes, *Autobiography*, 340.
68. Henderson, 37; Strauss, 115–116.
69. Wilkes, *Autobiography*, 343–344; Henderson, 37; Silverberg, 33; Bixby, 12.
70. Wilkes, *Autobiography*, 373.
71. Henderson, 37.
72. The *Vincennes* had made pioneering voyages to the South Pacific in 1829 (under the command of Captain William C. B. Finch) and 1835 (under Commander J. H. Aulick). Wilkes, *Autobiography*, 351–352; Henderson, 39; Strauss, 88–92; Silverberg, 36.
73. Several of the scientists later achieved renown in their fields. Wilkes, *Autobiography*, 381–382; Henderson, 41–42; Bixby, 9; Silverberg, 37.
74. Wilkes, *Autobiography*, 353; Henderson, 43; Strauss, 117; Wilson, *Van Buren*, 176.
75. Henderson, 43, 45; Strauss, 123; Wilkes, *Autobiography*, 350, 355–356, 377; Silverberg, 34, 38; Bixby, 3.
76. Wilkes's other two children were nine-year-old Jane and five-year-old Edmund. Wilkes, *Autobiography*, 373; Silverberg, 13.
77. Wilkes, *Narrative*, vol. 1, 3.
78. Wilkes, *Autobiography*, 396; Henderson, 54; Strauss, 124; Silverberg, 47. The offending commodore was John B. Nicholson.
79. Wilkes, *Narrative*, vol. 2, 298; Henderson, 3–4, 64. Cooper was a friend of Wilkes's father.
80. Wilkes, *Narrative*, vol. 1, 135–139.
81. Wilkes, *Narrative*, vol. 1, 137.
82. One of the expedition's schooners, *Flying Fish*, reached 70° 14' south latitude, just short of Cook's 71° 10' in 1774. Wilkes, *Autobiography*, 443; Henderson, 67–68; Silverberg, 59, 61–62; Bixby, 22–23, 29.
83. Wilkes, *Autobiography*, 322; Henderson, 73.
84. Henderson, 116.
85. Wilkes, *Narrative*, vol. 1, xxiii.
86. Henderson, 74.
87. Silverberg, 13; Bixby, vi.
88. Wilkes, *Autobiography*, 391.
89. Henderson, 75; Strauss, 125; Bixby, 8. Such heavy punishment was to provoke court-martial charges when the expedition returned.
90. Strauss, 123.
91. The island depicted is Minerva or Clermont de Tonnerre in the Tuamotu or Pearl Islands west of Tahiti. Wilkes, *Autobiography*, 423; Henderson, 77; Silverberg, 70.
92. Henderson, 77–79; Silverberg, 72–74; Bixby, 38–42.
93. Wilkes, *Autobiography*, 423. Charges of cruelty later brought against Wilkes in the incident came to nothing.
94. Henderson, 79, 188, 205; Strauss, 126; Silverberg, 71; Bixby, 44.
95. Henderson, 83.
96. Wilkes, *Autobiography*, 424.
97. Wilkes's disciplinarian instincts seem to have been softened by the appeal of a chief for clemency on grounds that white sailors' infractions against islanders usually went unpunished. In any case, exile from Samoa was regarded locally as a severe sentence. The murderer, named Tuvai, was deposited on Wallis Island. Henderson, 84–85; Strauss, 127; Silverberg, 81–82; Bixby, 50–52, 55–56.
98. The chief, Opotuno, had escaped another navy search four years before and was wreaking havoc throughout the island of Savai'i, whose other chiefs participated in the Wilkes expedition's attempts to

find him. Wilkes, *Narrative,* vol. 5, 32–33; Wilkes, *Autobiography,* 434–436; Henderson, 85; Strauss, 127; Bixby, 52–54.
99. Silverberg, 78–81.
100. Wilkes, *Autobiography,* 436.
101. "From this event," writes diplomatic historian George Herbert Ryden, "may be dated the official relations between Samoa and the United States." Ryden, 21; Strauss, 127; Bixby, 50, 53.
102. Wilkes, *Narrative,* vol. 2, 115–154.
103. Strauss, 113 n. 19.
104. Strauss, 127.
105. Wilkes, *Narrative,* vol. 2, 130; Strauss, 126; Gray, 48.
106. Wilkes, *Narrative,* vol. 2, 126.
107. Wilkes, *Narrative,* vol. 2, 127.
108. Wilkes, *Autobiography,* 436–445; Henderson, 87–90; Strauss, 127–128.
109. Wilkes, *Autobiography,* 447; Henderson, 97–98.
110. The peaks were reported seen from aboard three ships on 16 January 1840. Wilkes, *Autobiography,* 447; Henderson, 100–101; Silverberg, 93; Bixby, 66–67.
111. Henderson, 103, 113; Silverberg, 109–110.
112. Any errors may have been attributable to the unusual refraction of light in Antarctica. Henderson, 125–132, 137; Bixby, 95, 176–178.
113. Henderson, 139–140, 213; Silverberg, 94–95, 99, 102–105; Bixby, 68–69, 77–78, 91–92, 95.
114. Wilkes, *Autobiography,* 443.
115. Wilkes, *Autobiography,* 448; Henderson, 114–115.
116. The expedition surveyed Tonga and the Ellice Islands in Polynesia, Fiji in Melanesia, and the Gilbert and Marshall islands in Micronesia. Wilkes, *Autobiography,* 456–477; Henderson, 149–157; Strauss, 128–131. Two vessels, under Hudson's command, also returned to Samoa. Wilkes, *Narrative,* vol. 5, 20–34; Henderson, 181; Strauss, 141; Bixby, 3.
117. Wilkes, *Autobiography,* 469–472; Henderson, 163; Strauss, 135–137; Silverberg, 129–133; Bixby, 109–123.
118. The territory covered the eventual states of Oregon, Washington, and Idaho, as well as parts of Montana and Wyoming. It was settled then chiefly by Native Americans and fur traders on the coast, with a few pioneering farmers inland. Wilkes, *Autobiography,* 501–506; Henderson, 172–175; Silverberg, 149–152, 156–158; Bixby, 140–145.
119. Wilkes, *Autobiography,* 506.
120. Whereas the schooner *Sea Gull* had vanished with all hands on board, the *Peacock*'s crew was saved. Wilkes, *Autobiography,* 503; Henderson, 71, 184–186; Strauss, 125, 141; Silverberg, 63–65, 152–154; Bixby, 147–152.
121. Henderson, 187; Strauss, 142; Silverberg, 159.
122. Henderson, 199–200; Strauss, 142; Silverberg, 161–166; Bixby, 163–166.
123. Henderson, 200; Silverberg, 160; Bixby, 162. The island, midway between Hawaii and Guam, today contains an air force installation.
124. Strauss, 145; Wilson, *Van Buren,* 179.
125. Silverberg, 166; Henderson, 43.
126. The samples of fish, reptiles, insects, crustaceans, shells, and corals were accompanied by more than 2,000 drawings. Henderson, 207; Strauss, 143.
127. A third ship, the supply vessel, had been sent home early as too sluggish. Of the original 342 seamen, 15 perished at sea, 47 deserted, and 59 were discharged. Replacements were recruited along the way. Silverberg, 13, 41, 136; Bixby, 7.
128. Wilkes, *Autobiography,* 517–519; Henderson, 203; Strauss, 143.
129. Strauss, 144–145; Silverberg, 168.
130. Wilkes, *Autobiography,* 519–527; Henderson, 203; Strauss, 144. Van Buren, a somewhat reluctant patron of the expedition, later took pride in its accomplishments. "The discovery of a new continent," he boasted, "is one of the honorable results of the enterprise." Wilson, *Van Buren,* 179.
131. Wilkes, *Autobiography,* 521–522; Henderson, 203–204. Tyler, now a detractor, once had been a party ally and advocate of Van Buren. Cole, 156, 350.
132. Henderson, 205.
133. Strauss, 144; Silverberg, 169.
134. Writing the story of the expedition was to have been farmed out to Department of State official Robert Greenhow, who had authored a history of Oregon and California. Wilkes, *Autobiography,* 521; Henderson, 214–215, 218; Cole, 320.
135. Henderson, 205.
136. Wilkes, *Autobiography,* 525–527; Henderson, 205.
137. Despite precautions, some of the exotica fared badly in Washington. Careless handling ruined certain specimens or lost necessary identification, while pilferers stole others. Wilkes, *Autobiography,* 529; Henderson, 201–202; Strauss, 144; Silverberg, 176–177.
138. Wilkes, *Autobiography,* 525–527; Henderson, 205–206; Strauss, 142–143. The senator praising the expedition was William C. Preston of South Carolina.
139. The charges ranged from insubordination and speaking abusively to destroying a requisition for medical supplies. Strauss, 143.
140. The principal accuser was Assistant Surgeon Charles F. B. Guillou, one of the officers against whom Wilkes had preferred charges. Wilkes, *Autobiography,* 523–524; Henderson, 203–204, 208.
141. The most severe sentence was administered Guillou. He was suspended from the navy — only to be reinstated later by President Tyler. Strauss, 143–144, 146 n. 37.
142. The charges included oppressing fellow officers, disobeying orders, and using excessive force against native people. Wilkes, *Autobiography,* 523–524; Henderson, 209–211; Strauss, 144; Silverberg, 173. The reprimand was read, ironically, by Wilkes's old acquaintance Captain Matthew Perry, in the former's absence.
143. He also branded Upshur's conduct "most disgraceful and unpatriotic." Wilkes, *Autobiography,* 449.

144. Jack's proper name was John, that of Charles's father and of his dissident ancestor. Wilkes, *Autobiography*, 519; Henderson 220.

145. Wilkes, *Autobiography*, 740; Henderson, 220.

146. Audubon urged publication of findings "collected by so many scientific men in no less than four years of constant toil and privation." Wilkes, *Autobiography*, 521, 523; Henderson, 214–215 (Audubon quotation, 215); Strauss, 144.

147. Wilkes, *Narrative*; Wilkes, *Autobiography*, 531–548; Henderson, 216–217.

148. Wilkes, *Autobiography*, 532.

149. Henderson, 216.

150. Henderson, 217.

151. The five-volume edition was succeeded a few years later by a one-volume version that increased its popularity. Silverberg, 180.

152. Henderson, 215, 217, 218, 272; Silverberg, 178.

153. The war was fought from 1846 to 1848. Henderson, 223, 226.

154. Henderson, 225–226.

155. Wilkes remarried in October 1853. Wilkes, *Autobiography*, 733; Henderson, 225–226. Edmund, his wife, and children are said to have been the first non-Mormon family in Utah.

156. Henderson, 226.

157. Wilkes, promoted to commander in 1843, was advanced to captain in 1855. Henderson, 226; Silverberg, 174.

158. Henderson, 229–230.

159. Henderson, 229.

160. Henderson, 229–230.

161. Henderson, 231.

162. The seized Confederates, James M. Mason and John Slidell, were seeking European aid in the war effort. Wilkes, *Autobiography*, 767–775; Henderson, 235–242; Silverberg, 182–184; Sandberg, 359–369.

163. Navy Secretary Welles offered praise as fulsome as it was fleeting: "Your conduct was marked by intelligence, ability, decision, and firmness, and has the emphatic approval of this department." Wilkes, *Autobiography*, 775; Henderson, 242; Sandberg, 362 (Welles quotation).

164. Wilkes, *Autobiography*, 776–778; Henderson, 244–245.

165. Wilkes, *Autobiography*, 777.

166. Henderson, 246, 248.

167. Wilkes's squadron did capture thirty vessels carrying goods to the South. The blockade runners most sought in the 1862 operation were the famed *Alabama, Florida,* and *Georgia.* Wilkes, *Autobiography*, 783–804; Henderson, 248–261; Silverberg, 185.

168. Wilkes's defense lawyer was an old Illinois associate of Lincoln's, Orville H. Browning, who had discussed the case with the president. Lincoln, 182; Sandberg, 276; Wilkes, *Autobiography*, 831–843; Henderson, 246–247 (Welles quotation), 269; Silverberg, 185–186.

169. Wilkes, *Autobiography*, 840.

170. Henderson, 271.

171. The third of the final volumes, besides the two by Wilkes, was one on botany. Nine other planned works were canceled. Henderson, 272; Silverberg, 178.

172. Wilkes, *Autobiography*, v, 929.

173. Wilkes, *Autobiography*, 927.

174. Henderson, 270.

175. Wilkes, *Autobiography*, 930; Henderson, 273; Silverberg, 187. Mrs. Wilkes outlived her husband by twenty-nine years, passing away in Florence, Italy, in 1906.

176. Henderson, 273.

177. Henderson, 182.

2. Richard W. Meade III

1. The life of Richard W. Meade, Jr., was adventuresome from the start. He was born in Spain, where his father, the original Richard W. Meade, a wealthy Philadelphian, served as the American government's financial agent. He imprudently lent much of his fortune to King Ferdinand VII, and when some went unreturned he sought reimbursement from the United States — initiating several generations of sometimes contentious relations between Meades and their government. Obituary, 566. His son, Richard W. Meade III, was born 9 October 1837 in New York City. Navy, biographical summary; Garraty and Carnes, vol. 15, 218.

2. The real Robinson Crusoe — the marooned Scottish sailor Alexander Selkirk whose experiences inspired the novels of Daniel Defoe — has a link with one of Samoa's fellow U.S. possessions in the Pacific. After his rescue in 1709 from four years of isolation on the island of Mas a Tierra in the Juan Fernandez Islands west of Chile, Selkirk on his journey home visited Guam. Souhami, 160; Beardsley, 141–142.

3. Garraty and Carnes, vol. 15, 218.

4. Obituary, 566.

5. The letter of 28 February was written to President Polk's navy secretary John G. Mason. Meade, letters.

6. After a change of administration, the letter of 25 March (as well as another) was sent to his successor under President Zachary Taylor, William B. Preston. Meade, letters.

7. Sketchy enrollment records in the archives at Mount St. Mary's College show Meade departing in June 1850, presumably to enter the naval academy. Navy, biographical summary; obituary, 658; Garraty and Carnes, vol. 15, 218.

8. Navy, biographical summary; Garraty and Carnes, vol. 15, 218.

9. Callahan, 374.

10. Garraty and Carnes, vol. 15, 218.

11. Navy, biographical summary; Grant, vol. 23, 138 n; Garraty and Carnes, vol. 15, 218.

12. General Meade commanded the Union's victorious Army of the Potomac. Grant, vol. 23, 138 n; obituary (Meade, Jr.), 566.

13. Obituary, 566–567.

14. Garraty and Carnes, vol. 15, 218; *National,* vol. 4, 180.
15. Meade served at the naval academy from 1865 to 1868, and published his text in 1869. Navy, biographical summary; Garraty and Carnes, vol. 15, 218.
16. Garraty and Carnes, vol. 15, 218.
17. Meade surveyed coastal Alaska with the gunboat *Saginaw* in 1868–69. Garraty and Carnes, vol. 15, 218.
18. Meade, "Winter Voyage," photograph opposite 141, 142.
19. The *Narragansett* was a single-masted sailing ship equipped with a steam-powered propeller. Twelve years old, it had spent the Civil War patrolling the Pacific and then lain decommissioned two years before resuscitated for Meade's voyage. Navy, *Dictionary,* vol. 5, 12–13; Garraty and Carnes, vol. 15, 218.
20. Garraty and Carnes, vol. 15, 218.
21. The expedition departed in March 1871. Navy, *Dictionary,* vol. 5, 12–13.
22. Meade, "Winter Voyage," 141.
23. The popular mooring spot in the strait was Byron's Island Bay. Meade, "Winter Voyage," 139.
24. Obituary, 566.
25. Meade, "Winter Voyage," 139.
26. The ship left San Francisco in December 1871. Navy, *Dictionary,* vol. 5, 12–13.
27. The Pacific Mail Steamship Company of New York shipping magnate William H. Webb inaugurated service from San Francisco in 1871 using four Civil War surplus side-wheel steamers. Gray, 57; Rigby, 76; Ellison, 41; Ryden, 50. The steamship line's commercial designs on Samoa also enjoyed the active support of the U.S. minister in Hawaii, Henry A. Peirce. Ryden, 69; Gray, 58.
28. Ryden, 54–55; Gray, 56; Paullin, 350.
29. The letter was written in January 1872 to Navy Secretary George M. Robeson. Paullin, 350.
30. Rieman, 1.
31. Rieman, 6.
32. Rieman, 13.
33. The tattooing noted by Wilkes remained prevalent into the twentieth century. "The men are tattooed with an elaborate pattern from the waist to the knees and round the wrists; the women on the arms and thighs with little crosses rather far apart," observed writer W. Somerset Maugham in 1916. Wilkes, *Narrative,* vol. 2, 141; Maugham, *Notebook,* 39–40. Flowers graced both men and women. Maugham, *Notebook,* 40.
34. Gray, 53; Wilkes, *Narrative,* vol. 2, 140.
35. Gray, 5.
36. Gray, 49; Robson, 19.
37. Gray, 56; Robson, 22–23.
38. The safe channel bears to this day the name Narragansett Passage. Gray, 58.
39. The pirate, evidently a gregarious and generous rogue popular among his neighbors in Apia, is reported to have benefited from canny local legal advice. Rigby, 77; Robson, 42–44.
40. The regulations are alleged to have accorded the Webb steamship line preferential treatment. Ryden, 69; Paullin, 351.
41. "Meade," asserts Ellison, "was of an impetuous nature." Ellison, 41 n. 36.
42. Paullin, 351; Rigby, 77–78; Garraty and Carnes, vol. 15, 218.
43. The flag carried a stripe for each of the archipelago's nine inhabited islands and four stars. It wound up outlasting the transitory alliance of chiefs. Ryden, 65; Rigby, 77–78.
44. Ryden, 67; Paullin, 351.
45. Ryden, 67.
46. Quoted in Ryden, 67.
47. Quoted in Ryden, 66, 67.
48. Gray, 58; Paullin, 351; Kennedy, *Samoan,* 8–9.
49. Gray, 58.
50. Paullin, 350.
51. The petition was signed 9 April 1872. Ryden, 69–70.
52. Garraty and Carnes, vol. 15, 218; Meade, "Winter Voyage," 142; Navy, *Dictionary* (accessed on Internet). Christmas Island, now renamed Kiritimati (pronounced "Kiritimas"), south of Hawaii, was turned over to the new island nation after the British protectorate of the Gilbert Islands became the independent country of Kiribati in 1979.
53. Quoted in Garraty and Carnes, vol. 15, 218.
54. The agreement was transmitted to the Senate 22 May 1872. Grant, vol. 23, 134–135; Richardson, 168–169. The Samoan chiefs may have acted under authority as shaky as that of Meade. Gray, 58.
55. Ellison, 43–44; Kennedy, *Samoan,* 9; Garraty and Carnes, vol. 15, 218.
56. The pact is regarded as the first formal agreement between Samoans and Americans. Gray, 58. "Though not ratified by the Senate," Ellison states, "the Meade agreement marked the beginning of close relations between the United States and Samoa." Ellison, 43–44.
57. "To the decisive action of Meade," Paullin goes so far as to say, "the United States owes its present possession of Samoa." Paullin, 352; Garraty and Carnes, vol. 15, 218; Kennedy, *Samoan,* 14.
58. Using the pseudonym "A Naval Officer" or "Reform," Meade penned articles not only for military periodicals but also the *New York Herald.* Garraty and Carnes, vol. 15, 218.
59. Garraty and Carnes, vol. 15, 218.
60. Canadian-American ties had been frayed by a fishing dispute. The cruise extended from 1879 to 1882, during which Meade in 1880 won his captaincy. Garraty and Carnes, vol. 15, 218–219.
61. The torpedo that Meade recommended in 1882 was the eventual naval standby, the Whitehead. After testing the *Dolphin* in 1885–86, Meade pronounced it sound structurally but weak in design and workmanship. Redesigned, from its decks President Cleveland in 1893 reviewed assembled U.S. and foreign naval ships at New York as part of the Columbian Exposition. Garraty and Carnes, vol. 15, 219; Navy, *Dictionary,* vol. 2, 82.
62. Meade worked for the railroad from March 1884 to November 1885. Navy, biographical summary; Garraty and Carnes, vol. 15, 219.
63. Garraty and Carnes, vol. 15, 219.

64. Obituary, 658; Garraty and Carnes, vol. 15, 219.
65. Garraty and Carnes, vol. 15, 219.
66. Navy, biographical summary; Garraty and Carnes, vol. 15, 219.
67. Obituary, 658.
68. Meade is said to have been vexed particularly by another admiral with whom he long had been on bad terms. Obituary, 658; Garraty and Carnes, vol. 15, 219.
69. Obituary, 658; Garraty and Carnes, vol. 15, 219.
70. Obituary, 658.
71. Navy, biographical summary; obituary, 658; Garraty and Carnes, vol. 15, 219.
72. Meade, "Winter Voyage," 142.
73. He expired 4 May 1897 at the age of fifty-nine. Navy, biographical summary; obituary, 658; Garraty and Carnes, vol. 15, 219.
74. The high estimation of the voyage comes from the sober *Army and Navy Journal*. Obituary, 658.
75. Garraty and Carnes, vol. 15, 219.

3. Albert B. Steinberger

1. See any of the myriad Gauguin biographies, such as Sweetman.
2. Ball, 99–123.
3. Morris, *Heaven's Command,* 320.
4. Connell, thick of beard and of Irish brogue, called on the surprised Wilkes while charting Fiji. Morris, *Heaven's Command,* 363; Silverberg, 122–123; Strauss, 8, 11, 12.
5. Strauss, 16–18; Gray, 27; Robson, 19.
6. Robson, 16.
7. Stathis, 87; Torodash, 51. Steinberger's father is said to have been the first American to operate a blast furnace smelting iron with anthracite coal.
8. Stathis, 88.
9. Stathis, 88.
10. Steinberger's name is not to be found among the records of army enlistments or veteran pensions at the National Archives.
11. However gifted a soldier, Justus Steinberger seemed prone to career obstacles requiring intervention by his old friend Grant. When Steinberger was summarily mustered out of the army in 1864, Grant wrote from his Virginia battlefront headquarters a letter to the secretary of war asserting that the colonel "possesses qualities which would have made him now one of our best Citizen Generals had his lot been cast in the East... instead of on the Pacific Coast." Steinberger's command was restored. After the war, Steinberger's nomination as army paymaster was stalled until Grant again rode to the rescue, dispatching in 1867 a letter to the foot-dragging Senate committee. Steinberger was confirmed. Grant, vol. 10, 367 (quotation), vol. 17, 56–57; Torodash, 42; Gilson, 294; Stathis, 103.
12. Stathis, 88; Torodash, 52.
13. Stathis, 88; Torodash, 52. Steinberger's father-in-law, Alfred Ely, served in the House of Representatives from 1859 to 1863. In an interview in the *New York Times* in 1876, Steinberger promoted him to senator.
14. Gilson, 294.
15. Stathis, portrait opposite 86; Torodash, 52; Robson, 46.
16. Ellison, 50; Gilson, 296; Robson, 45. The Robson book contains much erroneous information about Steinberger.
17. Rigby, 79; Stathis, 87–89; Grant, vol. 23, 137; Gray, 57; Ryden, 42. Webb's steamer line between California and Australia had secured a subsidy from New Zealand and Grant's endorsement of a U.S. mail subsidy. But the unprofitable service soon was abandoned.
18. Ellison, 46–47; Grant, vol. 23, 137.
19. Grant, vol. 17, 56–57.
20. Stathis, 88; Grant, vol. 23, 101; Ellison, 48 n. 5.
21. "A thin strip of silver beach rising quickly to hills covered to the top with luxuriant vegetation" is W. Somerset Maugham's description in perhaps his best-known short story, "Rain," set in Pago Pago. Maugham, *Stories*, 2.
22. The missionary boats are pictured by Robert Louis Stevenson, a later resident of Samoa, in *The Beach at Falesá*, his short novel based in the islands. Stevenson, 61.
23. Stathis, 90; Robson, 47.
24. Samoans of the era are depicted through the observant eyes of Maugham in his notebook. Maugham, *Notebook*, 39–40.
25. Robson, 46; Gray, 53.
26. Robson, 48.
27. Ellison, 50; Stathis, 90.
28. Steinberger's instructions from Secretary of State Fish confined his assignment to "the sole purpose of obtaining full and accurate information." Stathis, 90.
29. Ellison, 52.
30. Stuart, 116, 260.
31. Rigby, 79; Gray, 57; Ryden, 44; Grant, vol. 23, 137–138.
32. Robson, 37.
33. The commercial agent was replaced by appointment of the first U.S. consul in Samoa. But the supplanted commercial agent appears to have continued to discharge his office in the western part of the archipelago, leaving American interests in the hands of rival officials in Apia and Pago Pago. Grant, vol. 23, 138; Rigby, 76; Robson, 41. The senator who effected the replacement was Cornelius Cole. Rigby, 76.
34. Gilson, 294.
35. Rigby, 79.
36. Rigby, 80; Gray, 60–61; Torodash, 53. Despite having installed as consul in Samoa the manager of a land speculation company, Secretary of State Fish recommended that Steinberger "caution [the chiefs] against making grants of their land to individual foreigners." Stathis, 90.
37. Robson, 42; Gray, 57.
38. Stathis, 90; Gray, 60–61; Ellison, 53.
39. Robson, 46–47, 49–53, 56–57; Torodash, 53.
40. Steinberger's visit extended from 7 August to 7 October 1873. Stathis, 90; Torodash, 53.

41. Stathis, 91 (quotation); Gray, 61; Ellison, 55.
42. Stathis, 91.
43. Stathis, 90.
44. Torodash, 51; Stathis, 91; Ellison, 55. Torodash esteems Steinberger's *Report on Samoa or Navigator's Islands* "an excellent, comprehensive, informative, and still useful document."
45. Stathis, 91.
46. *New York Daily Tribune*, 9 May 1874.
47. Stathis, 92; Torodash, 54; Gray, 62. While commending Steinberger's report, the *Tribune*, for example, argued editorially that the American system of government had "no place for protectorates or colonies." *Tribune*, 11 May 1874, quoted in Stathis, 92.
48. Stathis, 92.
49. Rigby, 82; Strauss, 83–85.
50. Rigby, 97. Grant's secretary twice had been appointed a government agent to the Dominican Republic during the administration's unsuccessful attempt to annex the country.
51. Torodash, 50 n. 6, 54; Stathis, 93.
52. Rigby, 82. The undated note specifically addresses financial arrangements, but the prognostication carries wider relevance.
53. Rigby, 82; Stathis, 92; Grant, vol. 23, xiv.
54. Rigby, 83.
55. Two days before departure in June 1873, he telegraphed Grant from San Francisco rather peevishly: "There being no communication, I have been compelled to furnish my own means of conveyance." Grant, vol. 23, 101.
56. Torodash, 55; Robson, 56–58.
57. The *Tuscarora* was touched with Civil War distinction. It was the sister ship of the USS *Kearsarge* that in June 1864 off the coast of Cherbourg, France, sank the famed Confederate raider *Alabama*. Torodash, 55; Navy, *Dictionary*, vol. 7, 363–364.
58. Stathis, 95; Gray, 62.
59. Stathis, 95.
60. Ellison, 59–60. The new Samoan flag looked more like its U.S. counterpart. The stripes (decreased in number from Meade's nine to seven) were colored red and white, and a white star placed in a field of blue.
61. Stathis, 94.
62. Stathis, 95; Torodash, 54, 55; Robson, 56–57.
63. Stathis, 95.
64. Gray, 63.
65. Stathis, 95; Gray, 63.
66. Gray, 98.
67. Stathis, 95; Gray, 63.
68. Steinberger acknowledged the problem. In his Independence Day letter informing Secretary of State Fish, he pledged as a U.S. citizen to accept "no pay, emoluments, or title of nobility," and asked the department's help in procuring congressional legislation authorizing his foreign premiership. Stathis, 95–96.
69. Press criticism ranged from allegations of commercial improprieties to misguided imperialism. Stathis, 96–97.
70. Stathis, 96; Gray, 63.
71. Stathis, 94, 99; Torodash, 54; Robson, 55.
72. Ellison, 83; Stathis, 97; Ryden, 147; Kennedy, *Samoan*, 9.
73. Stathis, 97; Robson, 65.
74. Stathis, 97; Robson, 65.
75. : "It was *his* government," stated a congressional report on the episode in 1888. "All [foreign residents] agree that he had practically absolute power in the islands." Congress, *Samoa*, 142–143.
76. Congress, *Samoa*, 142; Gray, 63.
77. Stathis, 97.
78. Stathis, 97.
79. Congress, *Samoa*, 143; Stathis, 97.
80. A possible explanation of the missionaries' change of heart may be that they had hoped to control Steinberger through their influence with the king, only to have him become an admirer of the premier. Robson, 67.
81. Rigby, 85; Gray, 63.
82. Torodash, 57; Gray, 63; Stathis, 97; Robson, 40. Torodash calls Foster "a thoroughly unsavory character."
83. Stathis, 97–98; Gray, 63–64.
84. The missionary participating in the plans, the Reverend George A. Turner of the London Missionary Society, only two years earlier had extolled Steinberger's "honest, kindly spirit" and legacy of "esteem and love." Stathis, 91.
85. It emerged that Steinberger had purchased his two-masted sailboat with an $8,500 loan from the German trading company. Stathis, 91.
86. Stathis, 93–94; Gray, 63–64; Torodash, 54; Kennedy, *Samoan*, 9.
87. Stathis, 94.
88. Stathis, 92–93; Torodash, 54. President Grant also was aware of what he termed, in a letter to Secretary of State Fish, Steinberger's "short visit to Europe." Quoted in Stathis, 92.
89. Stathis, 98–99 (quotation); Robson, 71–79.
90. Stathis, 99; Gray, 63–64; Congress, *Samoa*, 143; Kennedy, *Samoan*, 9; Robson, 71–79. Steinberger served as premier seven months, from 4 July 1875 to 8 February 1876.
91. Stathis, 99; Gray, 63–64; Congress, *Samoa*, 143; Kennedy, *Samoan*, 9.
92. Stathis, 99; Gordon-Cumming, 156; Robson, 84–85. Casualty figures for the fracas on 13 March 1876 differ in some accounts. Estimates of the wounded range as high as thirty.
93. Stathis, 99; Robson, 87.
94. Ellison, 72 n. 57.
95. The compassionate gesture was reported later by Steinberger. Torodash, 58.
96. Cole's life reads like a work of South Seas fiction. Having run away from home at age fourteen, he was shipwrecked as a cabin boy on a whaler three years later in Samoa. There he married into the Malietoa royal family, followed by five other relatively formalized unions generating eighteen recognized children. Some, like Emma, were to help shape the region's history. While one of his best friends was an infamous buccaneer, Cole was a successful and respected trader. Criminal charges trumped up against him in the Steinberger episode

subsequently were dropped in the United States. Robson, 12–16, 30, 82–83, 91; Stathis, 99.

97. Stathis, 99.

98. An English woman living in Fiji at the time, Constance F. Gordon-Cumming, may have expressed the prevailing sentiment in calling the seizure of the Samoan premier "rather embarrassing" and the clash of arms "senseless." Gordon-Cumming, 156; Stathis, 100; Gray, 64; Ellison, 74; Robson, 68.

99. *New York Daily Tribune*, 9 May 1874, quoted in Stathis, 92.

100. *New York Herald*, 26 March 1876, quoted in Stathis, 101.

101. *New York Sun*, 12 March 1876, quoted in Stathis, 101; Stewart and Tebbel, 77. It was the *Sun* that, in opposing Grant's reelection in 1872, gave American politics the refrain: "Turn the rascals out!"

102. *New York World*, 20 April 1876, quoted in Stathis, 100.

103. *New York Times*, 5 May 1876, quoted in Stathis, 100.

104. Stathis, 100; Gilson, 332–334.

105. Steinberger sought damages of $2 million, but Britain claimed to be absolved of responsibility because the premier's apprehension had been requested by the U.S. consul and Samoan king. Torodash, 59; Stathis, 100.

106. Gray, 64; Stathis, 100; Robson, 87.

107. Gray, 64; Stathis, 100; Kennedy, *Samoan*, 9.

108. Robson, 87. Robson reports that Steinberger was accompanied by a brother, Dr. C. M. Steinberger, a physician evidently residing on the West Coast, who had rushed to the South Pacific when learning of his brother's plight.

109. Stathis, 101–102.

110. Robson, 87.

111. Stathis, 100–101.

112. Stathis, 103.

113. Congress, *Samoa*; Karnow, 10, 82–83, 136.

114. Ellison, 83; Torodash, 59; Stathis, 103.

115. Stathis, 102.

116. Gray, 64; Stathis, 102; Gilson, 332.

117. Stathis, 102; Robson, 87.

118. Robson, 87, 95, photo following 128.

119. Stathis, 102.

120. *New York World*, 16 March 1876, quoted in Stathis, 102.

121. Torodash, 52; Stathis, 102.

122. Ellison, 83; Torodash, 52; Stathis, 103.

123. Steinberger is depicted by Rigby as a product of the Grant administration's climate of corruption, through his relationship with the president's private secretary Babcock, "one of the most sinister and deceitful figures ever to serve in the White House." Babcock later faced criminal charges. Rigby, 83–84; Stathis, 100.

124. Ryden, 147; Kennedy, *Samoan*, 9; Stathis, 103.

125. Congress, *Samoa*, 142; Gray, 63; Kennedy, *Samoan*, 9; Stathis, 91; Robson, 65.

126. Ellison, 83.

127. The assessment comes from Gilderoy W. Griffin, who succeeded Steinberger foe Foster as U.S. consul. Torodash, 59.

128. Ryden, 110–111; Ellison, 55; Kennedy, *Samoan*, 9; Stathis, 91.

129. Ellison, 83; Stathis, 104.

4. Henry Glass

1. An American fleet under Rear Admiral George Dewey sank all but one of twelve Spanish vessels in a five-hour battle on 1 May 1898. The Spanish suffered 380 dead or wounded, and the Americans just 8 sailors injured. Karnow, 102–105; Traxel, 137. The *Charleston*, reposing decommissioned in San Francisco nearly two years, was hastily refitted. The squadron departed Honolulu on 4 June. Glass, "Guam," 151; Navy, biographical summary; Navy, *Dictionary*, vol. 2, 82; Karnow, 119; Rogers, 109; Carano and Sanchez, 170–171.

2. Photograph of Glass aboard the *Charleston* in 1898, accompanying Boehm.

3. Glass is said to have relished combat—to have been happiest "when any fighting was in prospect." "Rear-Admiral Glass."

4. Glass, "Guam," 151.

5. The order of 10 May 1898 came from navy secretary John D. Long. Navy, "Seizure," 151.

6. Glass, "Guam," 151.

7. "What about Guam and where is it anyway? And what do we want of it?" asked the men aboard the ships, as one remembered. In their geographical ignorance, they weren't alone. Their commander-in-chief, President McKinley, at the time of Dewey's victory in Manila Bay, was hazy about the location of the Philippines. Traxel, 138–139, 219. See also Rogers, 109.

8. The board's members included influential strategist Alfred Thayer Mahan. Rogers, 109; Pomeroy, *Pacific Outpost*, 7; Musicant, 544.

9. Paternal ancestors had come to Norfolk in 1765. "Admiral Glass."

10. He was the son of an elder Henry Glass and his wife Martha. A naval record attributes to the younger Henry Glass a middle initial "E.," but he refrained from using it. Navy, biographical summary; Navy, *Dictionary*, vol. 2, 119; *Who Was Who*, vol. 1, 400.

11. Navy, biographical summary.

12. He became a midshipman in 1860. Navy, biographical summary.

13. Glass became an ensign in May 1863. *Who Was Who*, vol. 1, 400.

14. He saw action in Charleston harbor, Stone River, North Edisto, and Georgetown. Navy, biographical summary.

15. "Rear-Admiral Glass."

16. He served several years aboard the *Powhatan*, the flagship of Commodore Perry in 1854 when opening Japanese ports to world commerce. Thereafter he commanded a sloop and a side-wheel gunboat. Navy, biographical summary; Navy, *Dictionary*, vol. 4, 416–417, vol. 5, 365, vol. 8, 13–14.

17. See chap. 3. Glass served on the ship in 1869. Navy, biographical summary; Navy, *Dictionary*, vol. 7, 362–364.

18. The territory had been purchased thirteen years earlier from Russia. Navy, biographical summary.
19. Glass commanded two vessels in the region in 1881–82 and 1886–88. Navy, biographical summary.
20. Glass's *Marine International Law* was published in 1885, covering in its 270 pages everything from blockade to piracy to war. Glass, *Marine;* obituary; *Who Was Who,* vol. 1, 400.
21. Navy, biographical summary; Navy, *Dictionary,* vol. 2, 119, vol. 7, 114–115.
22. The volunteers were being trained, ironically, at the old Spanish garrison known as the Presidio. Karnow, 118.
23. Karnow, 119.
24. The transports carried the vanguard of the Eighth Army Corps — infantrymen from California and Oregon, artillerymen, and a band — as well as four hundred tons of ammunition for Admiral Dewey. Musicant, 544; Traxel, 218; Glass, "Guam," 151; Navy, *Dictionary,* vol. 2, 82; Rogers, 109; Beardsley, 191.
25. Beardsley, 105–111; Thompson, 5.
26. No bigger islands are to be found in those ten million square miles of ocean until its westerly waves wash the shores of Japan, the Philippines, and New Guinea. Thompson, 18–20; Beardsley, 28.
27. Thompson 21; Beardsley, 20.
28. Pomeroy, *Pacific Outpost,* 3–4; Beardsley, 179–187.
29. Beardsley, 105–106; Thompson, 91.
30. The Ladrones were rechristened in 1668 by a Jesuit priest instrumental in introducing Christianity in Guam, Padre Diego de Sanvitores, in honor of Maria Anna, widow of Spanish King Felipe IV — the royal couple that had sponsored his missionary work there. Beardsley, 124–127; Thompson, 58 n, 91.
31. The official navy account of Glass's actions, in fact, is entitled "Seizure of the Ladrone Islands." Navy, "Seizure," 151.
32. The officer who shared his useful knowledge of Guam was Thomas A. Hallet. Rogers, 109; Glass, "Guam," 153.
33. Glass, "Guam," 151; Rogers, 109; Beardsley, 19, 22, 191.
34. Glass, "Guam," 151–152; Beardsley, 191.
35. Beardsley, 21, 22.
36. Glass, "Guam," 152.
37. Glass, "Guam," 152; Beardsley, 22, 192; Carano and Sanchez, 171.
38. Glass, "Guam," 152.
39. Glass, "Guam," 152; Rogers, 109.
40. The *Charleston* was armed with two eight-inch guns and six six-inch guns. Navy, *Dictionary,* vol. 2, 82; Glass, "Guam," 152; Beardsley, 192; Carano and Sanchez, 171.
41. Glass, "Guam," 152; Beardsley, 192.
42. Glass, "Guam," 152; Beardsley, 192; Carano and Sanchez, 172.
43. Glass, "Guam," 152; Beardsley, 192; Carano and Sanchez, 172.
44. Glass, "Guam," 152.
45. Congress's authorization of war against Spain, on 11 April in distant Washington, occurred too late to reach the Pacific steamer arriving in Guam a few days later. Glass, "Guam," 152; Carano and Sanchez, 171; Pomeroy, *Pacific Outpost,* 4; Perkins, 300; Karnow, 436.
46. Beardsley, 192; Pomeroy, *Pacific Outpost,* 3; Perkins, 300.
47. Glass, "Guam," 152; Beardsley, 192; Carano and Sanchez, 172.
48. Glass, "Guam," 152.
49. The governor claimed Spanish law forbade him from boarding foreign vessels in the harbor. Glass, "Guam," 152; Beardsley, 192; Carano and Sanchez, 172.
50. Navy, portrait.
51. Glass, "Guam," 152.
52. Glass, "Guam," 152.
53. Glass, "Guam," 152; Carano and Sanchez, 174.
54. Glass, "Guam," 152; Musicant, 545; Beardsley, 193; Carano and Sanchez, 176.
55. Glass, "Guam," 152; Carano and Sanchez, 175.
56. Carano and Sanchez, 175.
57. Glass, "Guam," 153; Carano and Sanchez, 175.
58. Glass, "Guam," 153; Beardsley, 193; Carano and Sanchez, 176.
59. Glass, "Guam," 153; Rogers, 111; Beardsley, 193.
60. Glass, "Guam," 153; Carano and Sanchez, 176; Beardsley, 193; Rogers, 111.
61. Glass, "Guam," 153.
62. Glass, "Guam," 153; Musicant, 545; Carano and Sanchez, 176; Beardsley, 193; Rogers, 111.
63. Fort Santa Cruz, Glass decided, wasn't even sufficient threat in enemy hands "to expend any mines in blowing it up." Glass, "Guam," 153; Carano and Sanchez, 176–177; Musicant, 545; Pomeroy, *Pacific Outpost,* 4.
64. Glass, "Guam," 153; Carano and Sanchez, 176–177.
65. Rogers, 111; Beardsley, 193.
66. Navy, "Seizure," 151.
67. Dewey's fleet was laying siege to the Philippines with its ammunition bunkers only 60 percent filled. Traxel, 133.
68. Glass's orders were silent on any provision for administering Guam after he left. Navy, "Seizure," 151; Beardsley, 193–194.
69. Intermingling with Spaniards, Filipinos, and others, together with migration, epidemics, and colonial extermination, had left no pure, original stock Chamorros. Thompson, 5–6, 32–36; Beardsley, 133–135, 157.
70. Portusach's first name also is given, in some sources, as Frank or José. His descendants remain active in island affairs. His grandson served in recent years as mayor of Agana Heights. Rogers, 110; Farrell, 260–261; Stuart, 320 n. 24.
71. Perkins, 300; Beardsley, 193–194.
72. The Americans arrived 20 June and departed 22 June, "having completed the duty assigned," as Glass laconically put it. Glass, "Guam," 153.
73. Beardsley, 191.

74. "Admiral Glass."
75. "Rear-Admiral Glass."
76. Overwhelmed by Japanese invaders in the two days following the attack on Pearl Harbor in December 1941, the small American garrison on Guam put up token resistance for twenty-five minutes and then surrendered. The human cost ran higher than in 1898: 17 American defenders killed, succeeded by a brutal wartime occupation and 1,283 U.S. casualties in recapturing the island in 1944. Pomeroy, *Pacific Outpost*, 3, 158–160; Carano and Sanchez, 308; Stuart, 303, 309, 325 n. 52.
77. Excluding lesser islands with no indigenous population. Guam was preceded by U.S. annexation of Johnston and Sand atolls in the Pacific in 1858, the Caribbean navigational island of Navassa in 1865, and the Midway Islands in the Pacific in 1867. Beardsley, 191; Stuart, 18 n. 25.
78. Puerto Rico was wrested from Spain in August, and the Philippines were surrendered by treaty in December. See chap. 5; Karnow, 130.
79. Rogers, 109.
80. McKean advocated "a Pacific Gibraltar," but had to settle for modest shoring up of island defenses. He later became assistant chief of naval operations. Pomeroy, *Pacific Outpost*, 36, 51–53.
81. Musicant, 554, 564; Traxel, 218; Navy, *Dictionary*, vol. 2, 82.
82. Musicant, 556–557, 562–564, 566; Traxel, 216–219.
83. Musicant, 575–576; Navy, *Dictionary*, vol. 2, 82.
84. Manila fell on 13 August. Musicant, 583; Traxel, 223–225; Karnow, 123–124.
85. *Who Was Who*, vol. 1, 400.
86. Karnow, 139–140.
87. Glass apparently gave up command of the *Charleston* in December 1898. *Who Was Who*, vol. 1, 400; Navy, *Dictionary*, vol. 2, 82; Musicant, 562–563.
88. The ship ran aground 2 November 1899. Navy, *Dictionary*, vol. 2, 82.
89. Germany owned the Marshall Islands to the east. Britain held the Gilbert Islands farther eastward. Spain controlled the Mariana Islands except Guam. France and the Netherlands both had lesser dependencies in the area. Beardsley, 194; Musicant, 557–558.
90. Germany agreed secretly 10 September 1898 to buy from Spain the Caroline islands of Kusaie, Ponape, and Yap. Pomeroy, *Pacific Outpost*, 13–14; Beardsley, 194.
91. Beardsley, 195, 197; Thompson, 64.
92. President McKinley had assigned the navy to administer Guam. Beardsley, 195.
93. Captain Richard P. Leary took office 10 August 1899 proclaiming "the blessings of good government ... under the Free Flag of the United States," and issuing a stream of executive orders. Leary; Thompson, 64–67; Beardsley, 196–204.
94. Navy, biographical summary.
95. *Who Was Who*, vol. 1, 400; "Admiral Glass"; funeral notice.
96. Glass became rear admiral in October 1901, while at Mare Island. Navy, biographical summary; *Who Was Who*, vol. 1, 400.
97. The admiral is described in a posthumous tribute on the editorial page of the *San Francisco Chronicle* as "exceptionally popular" and "a genial companion." "Rear-Admiral Glass"; "Admiral Glass"; obituary.
98. He was sixty-four years old. Obituary; Navy, biographical summary; *Who Was Who*, vol. 1, 400.
99. Boehm; Beardsley, 236–237.

5. Nelson A. Miles

1. The Stars and Stripes was hoisted by an unusually high-ranking set of standard-bearers — a quintet of Miles's staff officers, comprising a general and four colonels. Miles, *Serving*, 297.
2. Musicant, 529; Davis, 282.
3. Volunteer militamen carried single-shot Springfield rifles, and regular army troops the newer Krag-Jorgensen carbines using five-shell magazines. Traxel, 142; Wooster, 217.
4. Martin Dooley was a fictitious Irish-American Chicago saloon keeper created by Finley Peter Dunne whose trenchant social comments bemused millions, first in newspapers and then in books. Dunne, xiii, 34 (quotation); Traxel. 31.
5. Nelson Appleton Miles was born 6 August 1839, having an older brother and two sisters. Wooster, 1–2; Johnson, 3.
6. Johnson, 3.
7. His father was a selectman, property assessor, and member of the school committee. Wooster, 2–3; Johnson, 3–4; Miles, *Serving*, 6, photographs opposite 8; Miles, *Recollections*, engraving, 20.
8. His mother's family name was Curtis. Johnson, 3; Wooster, 2; Miles, *Serving*, photograph opposite 8.
9. Westminster lies about fifty miles west of Boston. The Miles homestead on Turnpike Road still stands. Wooster, 2; Johnson, 3; Miles, *Serving*, 4, photograph opposite 8.
10. Miles, *Serving*, 5.
11. Miles, *Serving*, 4 (quotation); Miles, *Recollections*, 20; Wooster, 2.
12. Miles, *Serving*, 4. See also Miles, *Recollections*, 20.
13. The storied ancestors were the Reverend John Myles, great-grandfather Daniel Miles, and grandfather Joab Miles. King Philip's War pitted American colonists against a confederation of Native Americans under a leader called King Philip. Johnson, 4; Wooster, 2, Miles, *Serving*, 7; Miles, *Recollections*, 21–23.
14. Miles, *Serving*, 9.
15. Miles was a rebellious, much-disciplined, desultory student. Johnson, 3, 5; Wooster, 3.
16. Wooster, 3; Johnson, 4.
17. His two sisters had married. Wooster, 3.
18. Wooster, 3; Johnson, 5; Miles, *Recollections*, 23.
19. Boston was then a city of 177,800 people. Wooster, 3.

20. His mother's brothers George and Nelson Curtis lived in Roxbury, and another, John, was a proprietor of the crockery shop. Wooster, 3; Miles, *Recollections*, 1.
21. Wooster, 4; Johnson, 5.
22. Wooster, 5; Miles, *Serving*, 12–19.
23. Miles, *Serving*, 10.
24. Wooster, 3.
25. Johnson, 5.
26. Wooster, 5; Miles, *Serving*, 10; Miles, *Recollections*, 24; Johnson, 6.
27. Miles was given one thousand dollars by his father and borrowed the rest from an uncle. Within six weeks of Bull Run, the company had enlisted seventy volunteers. Wooster, 5; Miles, *Serving*, 25–26.
28. State militias at the time elected their junior officers. Thirty-five years later, the denial of the captaincy (by Governor John A. Andrew) still rankled Miles as "unwarranted and harsh in the extreme." Traxel, 144–146; Wooster, 5; Johnson, 6–7; Miles, *Serving*, 25–26; Miles, *Recollections*, 30 (quotation).
29. A volunteer regiment's valedictory procession to Washington through throngs of adulating citizenry is depicted in Stephen Crane's *The Red Badge of Courage*, 6.
30. The Massachussans saw the capital in September 1861. Their regimental commander, Colonel Henry Wilson, later became a senator and vice president in Grant's second term of office. Johnson, 7; Wooster, 50; Miles, *Recollections*, 31.
31. Miles, *Serving*, 27; Johnson, 8.
32. Wooster, 7.
33. Johnson, 8.
34. Wooster, 8; Miles, *Serving*, 28; Johnson, 9, 183. During this time, Miles stood up for another territorial forefather, Captain Charles Wilkes, who in 1861 had intercepted the British steamer *Trent* and seized two Confederate emissaries on board. Of their subsequent release, Miles commented in a letter to an uncle and aunt: "It looks a little cowardly." See chap. 1 and Wooster, 10.
35. Wooster, 10; Miles, *Serving*, 33; Johnson, 10–11.
36. Miles's friend and fellow future general Francis C. Barlow asserted that "he possesses in a more than ordinary degree that power of taking advantage of circumstances and localities which renders a man an efficient commander in battle." Johnson, 11, 14 (Barlow quotation); Wooster, 37.
37. Wooster, 10–11; Miles, *Serving*, 31 (quotation).
38. Johnson, 23.
39. Miles aptly described the Civil War as "a death grapple of giants." Miles, *Recollections*, 29.
40. "His troops," Wooster writes, "knew that he would be at the forefront of any engagement." Wooster, 18; Johnson, 12.
41. At Antietam, Miles took over a New York regiment after the two senior officers were wounded, one fatally. A regiment numbered about one thousand men. Wooster, 13; Traxel, 150; Johnson, 16–17; Miles, *Serving*, 40–46 (quotation, 45).
42. The battle at Spotsylvania, Virginia, took place in May 1864. Wooster, 20, 24–25; Miles, *Serving*, 67–68.

43. Of his eleven commissions as an officer, Miles said Lincoln's was the one that "I prize . . . far more than all the others." Miles, *Serving*, 67, 98 (quotation); Wooster, 25; Johnson, 21.
44. Miles inherited command of the six-thousand-man New York division in August 1864 from his ailing friend Barlow. Wooster, 29–30; Johnson, 23–24; Miles, *Serving*, 71–72, 78.
45. He commanded the Second Army Corps at engagements in April 1865. Miles, *Serving*, 79, 84–85, 88–89; Wooster, 30, 35–36.
46. Miles was hit by bullets in the throat at Fredericksburg in December 1862 and in the hip at Chancellorsville in May 1863. The Medal of Honor followed twenty-nine years later in 1892. Wooster, 14, 17–18, 32; Johnson, 18, 19–20; Miles, *Serving*, 49, 55–56.
47. Miles had been promoted to colonel after distinguishing himself at Antietam. Wooster, 15; Miles, *Serving*, 48.
48. Miles eventually won brigade command through army admirers, Barlow and General Winfield Scott Hancock. Wooster, 20.
49. Johnson, 25; Wooster, 37.
50. Miles, *Serving*, 93.
51. At Fredericksburg, Miles's regiment lost 108 of its 432 men, and at Spotsylvania his brigade 600 of 2,200. Wooster, 15, 25.
52. Wooster, 15, 18; Johnson, 12.
53. Johnson, 58–59; Wooster, 37.
54. Wooster, 21.
55. Wooster, 37.
56. Miles, *Recollections*, 34.
57. Miles evidently met Grant just once during the war, at a dinner occasion in 1864 arranged by General Hancock. The Union commander penned his commendation in a letter to General George G. Meade. Wooster, 27–28, 35 (quotation), 37.
58. Wooster, 21, 31.
59. Johnson, 28.
60. Wooster, 47.
61. Wooster, 38–39.
62. Davis's fellow captive was former Confederate senator and envoy to Canada Clement C. Clay. Miles's esteem for most Confederate leaders and fellow combatants did not extend to Davis, but he alleviated some of his confinement conditions, such as padding the hallway outside the Confederate's cell so the sentry's footsteps wouldn't disturb the prisoner's sleep. Johnson, 29.
63. Davis was imprisoned in May 1865, shortly after Lincoln's assassination the previous month, amid speculation that he might be put to trial over the crime. Wooster, 38–39, 40.
64. Miles's instructions came from Assistant Secretary of War Charles A. Dana. The term "light anklets" appears in a letter to Secretary of War Edwin Stanton. Wooster, 40–41 (quotations); Johnson, 29.
65. So distasteful was the affair that Miles excluded it altogether from his first autobiography. Wooster, 44; Johnson, 29–30.
66. Miles, *Serving*, 100.
67. Wooster, 47–50; Johnson, 31–32.

68. Wooster, 50.
69. Mary Sherman was described at the time by the daughter of North Carolina Governor William Holden as "handsome, middle-sized, rather thin, [with] brown eyes and hair, straight nose, and an exquisite mouth. Her manners are gentle, and polished; I take her to be a perfect lady." Wooster, 50, 51 (quotation); Johnson, 33, 43.
70. Miles, *Serving*, 33–34.
71. Sheridan substituted as best man for General Alfred Terry, whom military duties prevented from attending, as also generals Barlow and Hancock. The wedding took place 30 June 1868 at Cleveland's Trinity Church. Wooster, 51; Johnson, 34.
72. Wooster, 54.
73. Wooster, 46.
74. The Fortieth Infantry Regiment was recruited in Washington, D.C., and vicinity. Wooster, 47–50; Johnson, 31–32.
75. Miles was proud to have established 240 schools for freed slaves, and urged in a report in 1867 extending them "every advantage for enlightenment and improvement." The colonel served concurrently as an assistant commissioner of the Freedmen's Bureau, an agency of the War Department. Wooster, 47, 54–55; Miles, *Serving*, 104 (quotation).
76. Miles also feuded with General Meade over some regimental duties, and was disappointed in his desire for a brigadier generalship. Wooster, 52–54, 272.
77. Miles took command of the Fifth Infantry Regiment in March 1869. Wooster, 54.
78. Johnson, 37–38.
79. Wooster, 73.
80. Miles, *Serving*, 111; see also Wooster, 64.
81. Johnson, 38.
82. Garraty and Carnes, vol. 15, 447.
83. Wooster, 73.
84. Wooster, 73.
85. Miles, *Recollections*, 218.
86. Wooster, 61–64, 69; Johnson, 45–72.
87. The campaign followed the defeat of troops under Miles's friend Lieutenant Colonel George A. Custer at the Little Bighorn River in June 1876. Wooster, 59, 77; Johnson, 41–42, 83–84; Miles, *Recollections*, 198–211. During the winter pursuit, Miles became known among the tribes as "Bear Coat" because of his heavy overcoat with a collar of bear fir. Wooster, 80–93; Johnson, 110–170 (quotation, 110); Miles, *Recollections*, 219.
88. From a letter of 6 September 1874, quoted in Johnson, 54.
89. Johnson, 58–59, 154.
90. Miles, *Serving*, 122.
91. Wooster, 73.
92. Wooster, 128.
93. In another instance, an outbreak of violence in 1875 in New Mexico territory, Miles spurned the use of troops and met with chiefs, settling the matter peaceably by endorsing most of their grievances. Wooster, 72, 104–106, 151–153; Johnson, 202–205, 247–251; Miles, *Serving*, 169–181, 226–227; Miles, *Recollections*, 275, 525–527.

94. The bungled affray in South Dakota cost the lives of 151 Sioux, many of them women and children, and 25 soldiers. Miles, as divisional commander, blamed his subordinate in the field, Colonel James W. Forsyth. "I have never heard of a more brutal, cold-blooded massacre," Miles declared in an 1891 letter. Wooster, 176–190, 194 (letter); Johnson, 264–267, 295.
95. Miles, *Serving*, 117. In his other autobiography, he hails a West "redeemed from a wild state and its control by savage tribes, and given to civilization." Miles, *Recollections*, 320.
96. From a letter in 1874, quoted in Wooster, 68.
97. From a letter of 31 March 1877 from his Montana encampment (with the adjective rendered "wiley" in the rampant misspelling in his correspondence that seems a legacy of Miles's abbreviated schooling). Quoted in Johnson, 167–168.
98. He delineated his approach in a report in 1875. Wooster, 70, 74.
99. Early in his career as an Indian fighter, an experience with a Cheyenne chief left upon Miles a sobering impression. After the Red River War, he sought to prevent the chief Grey Beard from being banished to Florida. He failed, and en route Grey Beard was fatally shot by a guard. Wooster, 72, 74; Johnson, 72, 180.
100. The surrender in October 1877 evoked from Chief Joseph the still stirring words: "Hear me, my chiefs. I am tired; my heart is sick and sad. From where the sun now stands I will fight no more forever." Wooster, 109–110, 206; Johnson, 205 (surrender oration), 207, 211.
101. Miles had acquiesced in sending the Apache to Fort Marion, Florida, because the destination had been negotiated by Geronimo. He expressed his concerns in a letter of 27 August 1886. Wooster, 151, 152, 160; Johnson, 243, 244 (quotation). He also agitated to improve squalid conditions at a reservation in Arizona in 1887. Wooster, 165; Johnson, 254–255.
102. Miles, *Serving*, 139, 149, 281 (quotation); Miles, *Recollections*, 226; Johnson, 118.
103. Miles's efforts on behalf of the Nez Percé continued long after he had left the West. Miles, *Serving*, 181 (quotation); Wooster, 109; Johnson, 207.
104. Miles, *Recollections*, 527 (quotation); Wooster, 152; Johnson, 229, 248.
105. "If they can be treated fairly," Miles contended in a note to General Sherman in 1877, Indians "will rank as loyal friends of the govt. as they have been dangerous enemies." Wooster, 109 (Sherman note), 124, 194 (Short Bull letter in 1892).
106. Miles later devoted three chapters of his first autobiography to discussion of Native Americans. Wooster, 124, 192; Johnson, 183.
107. The guiding spirit of the progressive Indian school at Carlisle, Pennsylvania, Captain Richard H. Pratt, felt that Miles would do "justice to the Indians." Wooster, 125–126.
108. Miles, *Recollections*, 351.
109. Wooster, 125–126, 138, 140, 161, 192–193.

110. Later at Fort Keogh, Montana, the Miles family had the services of an African-American servant from Kentucky. Wooster, 59, 123.

111. Mary later told a magazine interviewer of the anguish of waiting day after day "with the dull pain still at my heart, and the ever present question uppermost: 'Will today bring the news that he has been killed?'" From an undated article in *Harper's Bazar,* quoted in Johnson, 138. See also Wooster, 112.

112. Wooster, 59; Johnson, 42, 179.

113. Wooster, 112.

114. The trip to the army camp on the Tongue River proved an adventure of its own. One of two steamers carrying Mary, her sister, and dependents of other officers, the *Don Cameron,* sank en route in the Missouri River near Sioux City. Mary's sister Elizabeth next year married the senator from Pennsylvania for whom the unfortunate vessel was named. Lizzie Cameron later was to long receive the amorous attentions of historian Henry Adams. Wooster, 94–95, 113; Johnson, 178–181, 228; Miles, *Serving,* 166 (quotation); Garraty and Carnes, vol. 4, 258. The Cameron-Adams relationship is chronicled in O'Toole.

115. Miles, *Serving,* 107.

116. Wooster, 114.

117. Johnson, 51, 77, 164.

118. Miles had long honored his parents' religious faith by remaining (with his wife) a devout Baptist and sending money to the church in Westminster. Wooster, 59, 71, 73.

119. Wooster, 134; Johnson, 225.

120. Wooster, 123.

121. The expedition occurred in October 1879. In a subsequent hunt in 1893 for grizzly bears, guests luxuriated in a private railroad car. Wooster, 123, 197. The latter trip is recounted in Remington, 89–100.

122. He reckoned that in the period 1874–79 over five million buffalo had been killed. Johnson, 45–46; Miles, *Recollections,* 134, 158–160.

123. Wooster, 31.

124. Wooster, 50.

125. The generals consulted were his patron Hancock and John M. Schofield. Wooster, 59–60.

126. The nephew was George Miles. Wooster, 124.

127. Less successful was a housing venture with Senator Sherman in the Columbia Heights section of the capital. Wooster, 137.

128. Remington, whom Miles long had cultivated, wrote a flattering account of the episode for *Harper's Weekly.* Wooster, 161, 177, 239, 271; Remington, x.

129. Wooster, 74–75, 128, 271.

130. Wooster, 108–109, 158; Johnson, 204–205, 210, 229, 251–254.

131. Wooster, 97, 118, 270–271.

132. The advice came in an 1888 letter, quoted in Wooster, 166–167. Sherman once grumbled, in a letter to Sheridan, that Miles "constantly implies that because he married my niece whom I love very much that I approve his ambitious views." Wooster, 118. On another occasion, he recommended (in a letter to Mary) that Miles "say little and write less, but create success." Wooster, 188.

133. Wooster, 128.

134. After interviewing Miles, Harrison approved his promotion (to major general) anyway. From a letter of 3 April 1890, quoted in Johnson, 262.

135. Cadet Johnson C. Whittaker of South Carolina, however, was spared by the court-martial an earlier sentence of one year at hard labor. The entire proceeding underwent harsh criticism in 1882 by the army's judge advocate general, and the decision was voided by President Chester A. Arthur. Wooster, 131–132.

136. Wooster, 200; Johnson, 304; Miles, *Serving,* 251–258; Brodsky, 332–346.

137. Miles, *Serving,* 252.

138. Wooster, 199; Johnson, 304.

139. From a letter of 18 July 1894, quoted in Johnson, 308. Miles warned his superiors that Chicago contained "more anarchists and socialists than any city on earth" and faced "a reign of terror." Wooster, 200. The eventual toll of strike violence was twelve persons killed and hundreds injured. Brodsky, 345.

140. Wooster, 174.

141. Miles had commanded the army's department of Columbia (Pacific Northwest and Alaska) in 1880–85, department of Missouri in 1885, department of Arizona in 1886–88, division of the Pacific in 1888–90, and division of Missouri (most of the plains) in 1890–94. Wooster, 131, 133, 139, 163, 169, 175; Johnson, 221, 226, 254, 257, 264.

142. Miles had become a (one-star) brigadier general in 1880 and a (two-star) major general in 1890. Wooster, 131, 133, 174; Johnson, 221.

143. Wooster, 201; Johnson, 309.

144. Wooster, 201–202; Johnson, 308. Miles's hitherto sickly son Sherman also was blooming into robust health, much to his father's relief.

145. The 1896 book was burdened by a title as cumbersome as its contents: *Personal Recollections and Observations of General Nelson A. Miles, Embracing a Brief View of the Civil War; or, From New England to the Golden Gate, and the Story of His Indian Campaigns, with Comments on the Exploration, Development, and Progress of Our Great Western Empire.* Wooster, 203–204; Johnson, 309.

146. Miles succeeded another distinguished Civil War commander, General John M. Schofield. Wooster, 204–205, 242; Johnson, 309.

147. Pershing had been a favorite of Miles since serving as a young lieutenant under the general in the 1880s in the department of Arizona. Wooster, 164, 205.

148. Miles's grasp of the army's needs seemed little bettered by a tour of eight European nations in 1897, a trip that generated the following year another book, *Military Europe: A Narrative of Personal Observation and Personal Experience.* Wooster, 207–209; Johnson, 304, 313–314.

149. Wooster, 205; Johnson, 313; Crichton, 287; Dunne, 32 (quotation).

150. Wooster, 210, 215, 220; Johnson, 317, 335.

151. The standing army of career soldiers was increased from 30,000 to 61,000, and short-term volunteers from 60,000 to 125,000. Camps were opened at Washington, D.C., Tampa, Mobile, Chickamauga (Tennessee), New Orleans, San Antonio, and San Francisco. Wooster, 215–216.

152. "God willing ...," McKinley complained, "we shall end the war before the General would have us begin operations." For military advice, he came to rely on the retired Schofield and Adjutant General Henry Corbin. Miles, *Serving*, 268–269; Wooster, 212, 215–217 (quotation, 217); Johnson, 310, 314–317.

153. Miles argued repeatedly for initially invading Puerto Rico, joined by Admiral Mahan and presidential adviser Schofield. Wooster, 220–221; Johnson, 320; Musicant, 518–520; Traxel, 222.

154. Pershing, for one, detected "a fear that Miles might become too strong politically after the war." Shafter also may have benefited from being a fellow Michigander of War Secretary Alger. Wooster, 218 (quotation); Johnson, 319.

155. "Great confusion" is Miles's description of conditions at the Tampa camp. Among those enduring the hardships there were Theodore Roosevelt and his Rough Riders. Miles, *Serving*, 275 (quotation), 276; Wooster, 220–223; Johnson, 321, 324, 347; Remington, 331.

156. The peril of tropical disease during Cuba's rainy season — "the sickly season," as he called it — had been a recurring concern of Miles. Roosevelt was second in command (to Colonel Leonard Wood) of the unit formally known as the First Volunteer Cavalry Regiment. Musicant, 518–519 (quotation); Miles, *Serving*, 293–294; Traxel, 211–212; Wooster, 223–224; Johnson, 325–326, 334; Remington, 331–344; Davis, 279, 305.

157. Miles also took action against the fever epidemic, quarantining the ill and burning infected buildings. The American expeditionary force had landed 22 June, and the Spanish defenders surrendered 17 July. Wooster, 224–225; Miles, *Serving*, 285–293; Johnson, 327, 330–332.

158. Puerto Rico scarcely turned up in official and unofficial discussions leading up to the war. One rare mention was a reference by U.S. Ambassador Stewart Woodford in Madrid when trying to keep commerce flowing between the two feuding nations. Musicant, 516–517; Morales Carrión, 137.

159. Spain extended in November 1897 to both Cuba and Puerto Rico an autonomy of exceptional liberality. It included self-government and even the power to make treaties with foreign countries. Morales Carrión, 120, 138–139; Musicant, 517.

160. Quoted in Musicant, 517.

161. Muñoz Rivera's to-the-death vows were short-lived. He worked closely with the conquering Americans, even flirting briefly with statehood for Puerto Rico, and served five years as the island's representative in Congress. He is the father of Luis Muñoz Marín, who dominated Puerto Rican politics during the middle of the twentieth century. Musicant, 521 (quotation); Morales Carrión, 161, 188; Stuart, 344, 414.

162. Johnson, 334; Wooster, 225.

163. The island even was rated, in one quarter, a prize more desirable than Cuba. Steel magnate Andrew Carnegie cabled Miles — ever receptive to advice from such a worthy — that victory in the larger island was "worthless," but winning Puerto Rico "would tell heavily [in] Spain and Europe." He conveyed his views to the general on 7 July amid the fighting in Cuba. Miles, *Serving*, 274; Wooster, 225 (quotations).

164. The invasion was approved 26 June to take place "with the least possible delay." Wooster, 224 (quotation), 226; Johnson, 334.

165. Musicant, 521; Miles, *Serving*, 296; Johnson, 334–335.

166. The first contingent left American shores 8 July, and the assembled convoy departed Cuba 21 July. Musicant, 521; Wooster, 225–226, 229; Miles, *Serving*, 296; Johnson, 334–335; Traxel, 219.

167. Miles described the "remarkable journey" in a letter to a friend, quoted in Wooster, 227. See also Musicant, 520–521.

168. The army's spy was Lieutenant Henry Whitney. Puerto Rico's first city at the time had a population of about 37,500. Miles was later to charge (in an interview in the *Kansas City Star* eleven days after the armistice) that the War Department had leaked to the press the plan to land at Point Fajardo. Musicant, 516, 523–524, 527; Miles, *Serving*, 298; Johnson, 335–336, 343–344; Wooster, 226, 230–231.

169. The convoy was commanded by Captain Francis J. Higginson. An escort ship, the cruiser *Dixie*, was left at Point Fajardo to direct subsequent troop carriers to Guánica. Wooster, 226 (quotation), 227; Miles, *Serving*, 296–297.

170. Miles's secrecy left his superiors with a perplexity that he may have intended. "Conflicting reports here as to your place of landing," Alger wired him. "Why did you change?" The general replied tersely: "Circumstances were such that I deemed it advisable." Wooster, 227.

171. The convoy arrived off Guánica at dawn 25 July 1898. Musicant, 529; Wooster, 227; Johnson, 336–338; Miles, *Serving*, 297–298; Davis, 277 (photograph).

172. The brigade landed were volunteers from Massachusetts, New York, and Illinois under Brigadier General George A. Garretson. Musicant, 529; Davis, 285; Johnson, 336–337.

173. Wooster, 227, 229

174. The port surrender was received 28 July by Lieutenant Greenlief Merriam of the *Dixie*. Musicant, 531–532; Wooster, 228; Johnson, 338.

175. Major Reber, a West Point graduate, was his future bride's second cousin. He later parlayed his Signal Corps experience into a successful career with the Radio Company of America (RCA). Johnson, 334–335, 351; Wooster, 237; Musicant, 531.

176. Freidel, 260 (painting by Howard Chandler Christy), 266, 267; Wooster, 228; Johnson, 338; Traxel, 167.

177. Miles, *Serving*, 299–301 (quotation, 300). Miles's arrival in Ponce had been attended by a ges-

ture of possible imperialistic portent. The Stars and Stripes was borne from the general's boat by a soldier who, while serving in the French Foreign Legion, also had been first to carry the French tricolor ashore in the conquest of Indochina. Traxel, 222–223.

178. The fire wagons and their century-old firehouse, the Parque de Bombas, a visual fire alarm of a building emblazoned in red and black, remain today a landmark on the city's tree-lined central plaza. Musicant, 532. Mr. Dooley's version of the capture of Ponce:

Th' nex' day th' army moved on Punch; an' Gin'ral Miles marched into th' ill-fated city, preceded be flower-girls sthrewin' r-roses an' geranyums befure him. In th' afternoon they was a lawn tinnis party, an'at night the gin'ral attinded a banket at th' Gran' Palace Hotel. At midnight he was serenaded be th' Raymimber th' Maine Banjo an' Mandolin Club. (Dunne, 37–38)

179. The bandstand had been appropriated as a campsite by army provost guards. Davis, 298, 302; Musicant, 532.

180. The proclamation was promulgated 28 July in Ponce. Miles, *Serving*, 301–302; Cabranes, 19; Musicant, 532–533; Wooster, 228; Johnson, 339.

181. Johnson, 337; Wooster, 228

182. General Brooke, a veteran of the Civil War, had served with Miles fighting Indians in the West. Musicant, 533–534; Wooster, 228; Johnson, 340.

183. Wooster, 228, 260; Musicant, 534; Johnson, 339–340.

184. Davis, 316; Traxel, 223.

185. Quoted in Musicant, 536.

186. Davis, 280; Johnson, 337; Knightley, 56–57; Wooster, 230.

187. Action at Guyama took place 5 August; near Cayay, 8 August; at Coamo, 9 August; the winning of Mayagüez, 10 August, and its occupation, 11 August. The clash (at Hormigueros) that opened the Puerto Rican campaign included cavalry for the only time in the Puerto Rican campaign. Musicant, 536–539; Wooster, 228; Miles, *Serving*, 302; Johnson, 340; Freidel, 272, 276.

188. Davis, 280. "Porto Rico" was the United States' officially anglicized misspelling of the name of the island until 1932. Stuart, 361–362. Another journalist in Puerto Rico was Stephen Crane, author of the Civil War novel *The Red Badge of Courage*. Knightley, 56–57; Traxel, 212, 223.

189. Wooster, 229; Musicant, 539.

190. The push across the island began 31 July when General Schwan's left-flank column of regulars landed at Guánica and set off for Mayagüez. It ended 13 August with the ambush by an advance guard also from Schwan's contingent. The armistice had been signed 12 August, followed by an immediate wire from McKinley to U.S. troops that "all military operations against the enemy be suspended." Wooster, 228; Musicant, 537 (McKinley telegram), 539; Johnson, 341; Traxel, 225, 264.

191. Johnson, 341.

192. Quoted in Musicant, 539. See also Traxel, 225.

193. "A clean-cut, scientific campaign," wrote Richard Harding Davis, marked by "good management and good generalship." Davis, 283–284. He challenged Mr. Dooley's jocular characterization of the campaign as a "gran' picnic." "The reason the Spanish bull gored our men in Cuba and failed to touch them in Porto Rico was entirely due to the fact that Miles was an expert matador; so it was hardly fair to the Commanding General and the gentlemen under him to send the Porto Rican campaign down to history as a picnic." Davis, 276–277. Even one of the general's congressional foes, Senator Redfield Proctor, was led to concede: "Not a lisp of criticism." Quoted in Wooster, 229. See also Wooster, 228, 231; Musicant, 539.

194. Miles's assessment extended to the Spanish-American War as a whole. Miles, *Serving*, 304. See also Musicant, 539; Johnson, 341.

195. Musicant, 539.

196. Wooster, 229–230.

197. Musicant, 540.

198. Johnson, 343; Wooster, 232.

199 Miles departed Puerto Rico 1 September and arrived in New York 7 September 1898. Johnson, 342; Wooster, 232.

200. Undated article in *New York World,* quoted in Johnson, 342.

201. Johnson, 342; Wooster, 232.

202. Johnson, 343, 344.

203. Wooster, 233.

204. Roosevelt, for his part, contrasted Miles with "broken-down and aged brigadier generals, men who never commanded three companies before"— an invidious reference to Cuba commander Shafter. Wooster, 233.

205. The commission to which Miles testified in December 1898, chaired by retired General Grenville M. Dodge, had been formed to investigate allegations raised largely by the former concerning the war. Wooster, 233–234; Johnson, 345–346, 348 (quotation).

206. The headline quoted in Brands, 320, is undated. Others exclaimed: "Food Spoiled and Thrown Away Because of a Faulty System" and "'Embalmed' Beef Found by Surgeon." *Journal,* 21 and 30 December 1898, 7 and 3.

207. In an incident oddly symbolic of his fallen standing with the McKinley administration, Miles soon afterward suffered the embarrassment of being thrown from his horse in front of the president while leading a parade before the White House. All that was harmed, for horse and rider, was decorum. Crichton, 287; Wooster, 234–235.

208. Brands, 319.

209. The Dodge commission and a second body set up by the War Department both concluded in early 1899 that Miles's charges (in the words of one) "had no sufficient justification." He was censured for failing to report his suspicions to the secretary of war. The commissary general was censured for purchasing prepared beef without adequate testing. Wooster, 236–237; Johnson, 349; Brands, 320 (quotation).

210. Sinclair brought to public attention scan-

dalous practices in the Chicago meat packing trade in his 1906 novel *The Jungle*. Brands, 319.

211. Strained relations with his superiors did not deprive Miles of gaining in 1901 the third star of a lieutenant general. Son Sherman, despite blurred vision in one eye, that same year became a cadet at West Point. Wooster, 237–238, 240–244; Johnson, 350–351, 353.

212. A previous slight, Miles's condescending suggestion during presidential speculation in 1895 that Roosevelt serve as the general's vice presidential running-mate, evidently had left Roosevelt unruffled. Wooster, 239 (quotation), 241, 243.

213. While commanding army operations in the Pacific Northwest, Miles in 1883–85 dispatched four exploring expeditions to Alaska. He also envisioned U.S. absorption of British Columbia. Wooster, 135–136, 269; Johnson, 353.

214. Accompanied by his wife, Miles on his Philippine trip also visited Hong Kong, China, Japan, Russia, Germany, France, and Britain. He pleaded in vain for the release of Mabini, revered today in his native land. Miles, *Serving*, 306; Wooster, 244–246; Johnson, 356–357.

215. "I trust that the office which Scott and Sherman held with so much distinction will not be destroyed while any of their comrades and friends still survive," Miles implored. While the office couldn't be rescued, its demise was delayed until Miles retired. Wooster, 242 (quotation), 243, 247.

216. Johnson, 357–358; Wooster, 247.

217. Wooster, 247. See also Johnson, 358.

218. Within a week, the commanding generalship was abolished. Roosevelt made his vow in a letter to Senator Henry Cabot Lodge, quoted in Wooster, 248.

219. In addition to ventures in his native Westminster, Miles had accumulated investments in many places where he had served across the country—from real estate in Washington, D.C., Missouri, California, and Washington state, to oil fields in Louisiana and Texas. Wooster, 250; Johnson, 360.

220. Wooster, 250.

221. Johnson, 351.

222. Mary passed away 1 August 1904. Johnson, 360; Wooster, 252.

223. Miles played chess almost daily at the Metropolitan Club in Washington and belonged to the Union League Club in New York. He spent winters at the Hotel Somerset in Boston. Wooster, 254, 263; Johnson, 360.

224. Sherman married Yulee Noble, daughter of the general's personal secretary William E. Noble. Miles's son rose eventually to the grade of major general. Wooster, 255, 265; Johnson, vii.

225. Wooster, 263.

226. Miles's brother Daniel, a bank president and businessman in Westminster, passed away in 1912 while visiting Washington. Wooster, 255. Westminster's most famous son rates no monument today in his hometown, save for a brass plaque honoring Spanish-American War veterans on a rock at the town hall. A large portrait of Miles, however, adorns the local library. And the town has assembled a collection of memorabilia—his Civil War overcoat and boots, saddle and saddle blanket, the silk headquarters flag from the Puerto Rico campaign, swords, and his lieutenant general's uniform.

227. Wooster, 254.

228. Miles's collection of scalps, headdresses, blankets, rugs, and weapons of famous chiefs eventually was donated by his children to the Museum of the American Indian in New York City. Wooster, 263, 265; Johnson, 353.

229. Miles served as chief technical adviser for the 1913 motion picture, filmed mostly at Pine Ridge, South Dakota, with government support that later was withdrawn. The film is known by the title "The Last Indian Wars for Civilization" and variations thereof. Wooster, 164, 177, 181, 187, 256–259; Johnson, 278–279.

230. The Spanish surrendered on 14 September 1898, Miles argued, not the 17 September to be posted on markers. Wooster, 264.

231. The book and its excerpts in *Cosmopolitan* magazine drew unflattering reviews. Wooster, 254.

232. Miles had dabbled in presidential politics by helping his uncle-in-law Senator John Sherman to seek, unsuccessfully, the Republican nomination in 1888 and 1892. Wooster, 196, 234; Johnson, 256–257.

233. Wooster, 3, 49, 113, 133, 251; Miles, *Recollections*, 232 (quotation).

234. Wooster, 250–252.

235. Wooster, 253 (quotations).

236. Miles resigned in December 1905. Wooster, 253; Johnson, 360.

237. Wooster, 254.

238. Leaving the political mainstream, he veered briefly into hard-right conservatism, helping found an anti-Catholic, anti-immigrant group known as the Guardians of Liberty. Wooster, 255.

239. Wooster, 256.

240. From an undated article in the *New York Times*, quoted in Wooster, 260.

241. Wooster, 261.

242. Wooster, 262; Johnson, 362.

243. The Sherman statue stands southeast of the White House on Fifteenth Street in the spot where the general in 1865 had reviewed his victorious troops. The elder of the namesake grandsons, Miles Reber, graduated from West Point military academy in 1923 before the proud eyes of his grandfather, and continued the family success in the army. Johnson, 361; Wooster, 263, 265.

244. The date of Miles's demise was 16 May 1925. Wooster, 264; Johnson, 363.

245. In addition to the presidential presence, eulogies came from Pershing and the acting secretary of war, Dwight F. Davis. Wooster, 264, 266; Johnson, 364.

6. B. F. Tilley

1. Blackwell, 44; Gray, 127–128.
2. Gray, 129–130.

Notes — Chapter 6

3. Blackwell, 44.
4. Tilley was born 29 March 1848. Navy, biographical summary; *Who Was Who,* vol. 1, 1240.
5. Navy, biographical summary; *Who Was Who,* vol. 1, 1240.
6. *Who Was Who,* vol. 1, 1240.
7. Tilley entered the academy in 1863. Navy, biographical summary; *Who Was Who,* vol. 1, 1240.
8. He served on the *Franklin,* flagship of the European fleet, in 1867–68, and the *Lancaster,* flagship of the South Atlantic fleet, in 1869–72. Navy, biographical summary; *Who Was Who,* vol. 1, 1240.
9. Two years after becoming an ensign in 1869, Tilley rose to command lieutenant. Navy, biographical summary; *Who Was Who,* vol. 1, 1240. The nickname appears in Blackwell, 23.
10. Tilley went charting aboard the *Pensacola* after shore duty in the hydrographic office in 1873. He evidently had returned to the Atlantic by the time of Steinberger's passage in 1875. Navy, biographical summary; Navy, *Dictionary,* vol. 5, 265; chap. 3 of this book.
11. The couple wed 6 June 1878. *Who Was Who,* vol. 1, 1240.
12. Tilley served at the naval academy in 1879–81, 1885, 1893, and 1896, and at the navy yard in 1889–90. At least one of the children attended the academy's primary school. Navy, biographical summary; *Who Was Who,* vol 1, 1240; obituary; Navy, photographs, son, 1892.
13. He had advanced to commander in September 1896. Navy, biographical summary; *Who Was Who,* vol. 1, 1240.
14. Tilley became commandant of the Norfolk Navy Yard in 1898. *Who Was Who,* vol. 1, 1240.
15. The tripartite commission met several months in Samoa and signed an agreement in November 1899. Britain settled for acquisitional rights in the Solomon Islands and west Africa. Gray, 100–102; chap. 2 of this book.
16. President McKinley in February 1900 directed the navy to "take such steps as may be necessary to establish the authority of the United States, and to give the islands the necessary protection." Gray, 107; Keesing, 128.
17. Tilley was selected in March 1899 in evident anticipation of the outcome of the ongoing trilateral talks on Samoa. Navy, biographical summary.
18. Navy, portrait, NH 43893.
19. Navy, portrait, NH 67313.
20. Daudet, 76.
21. The site had been chosen in 1889 and bought (for $5,241) from Samoan and resident American landowners. Gray, 105–106.
22. Navy, *Dictionary,* vol. 1, pt. A, 11; Blackwell, photograph opposite 26.
23. The *Abarenda* departed Norfolk 30 April and anchored at Pago Pago 13 August 1899. Navy, *Dictionary,* vol. 1, pt. A, 11; Gray, 105. On Pitcairn Island, see Ball.
24. Gray 10–12; Navy, photographs; author's observance.
25. The entire territory covers about seventy-seven square miles of land. Gray, 9. Pago Pago in 1900–01 may be glimpsed in Navy, photographs, NH 1514.
26. The island of Aunu'u lies off Tutuila's eastern tip; the three Manu'a islands, about sixty miles to the east; the two atolls comprising Rose Island, seventy miles beyond. Gray, 9, 119.
27. Gray, 163.
28. The staff or *to'oto'o* of a chief symbolizes authority, and the fly switch or *fue,* wisdom. Both later were to be incorporated into the territorial seal. Gray, 53; Maugham, *Notebook,* 39–40.
29. See chaps. 1–3 of this book.
30. Gray, 108, 110, 114 (quotation); Keesing, 129.
31. The deed of cession is reproduced in Gray, 112–117 (quotation, 114–115).
32. It was signed 2 April 1900. Gray, 116–117.
33. The American flag was raised 17 April 1900, the anniversary of which was to be celebrated thereafter in the territory as Flag Day. Gray, 111; Keesing, 129; Navy, photographs, NH 91728.
34. The high chief of Manu'u acknowledged U.S. sovereignty, but resisted formal cession. The American flag was hoisted 5 June 1900. These islands eventually were ceded in 1904, and a deed of cession signed the following year. Gray, 110, 130, 156–157.
35. Gray, 125.
36. The International Land Claims Commission had been created at a tripartite conference on Samoa in 1889 in Berlin. Gray, 92.
37. The order chronologically was the fourth to be issued by Tilley. Gray, 125–126.
38. Today all but a few acres of the territory are native owned. Perkins, 262; Gray, 125–126.
39. Gray, 126; Keesing, 201.
40. Olsen, 18; Keesing, 200.
41. Olsen, 17–18; Gray, 159.
42. Tilley's practice was followed by most of his successors. Gray, 126.
43. From a letter of 10 February 1902, quoted in Olsen, 17–18. See also Keesing, 200–201.
44. Tilley, 85.
45. Olsen, 21.
46. Gray, 25.
47. The Tutuila chief, the Mauga, offered his view in 1928. Gray, 123, 132–134. The courtroom is pictured in Navy, photographs, NH 1516.
48. The *Abarenda* had brought fifteen marines to Samoa. Blackwell, 23.
49. The force began in June 1900 with fifty-eight recruits. It was a contingent of the guardsmen who rowed the governor's surf boat to visit villages. Gray, 127–128; Olsen, 21; Navy, photographs, USMC 56078.
50. The road ran from Leone on the west to Fagaitua on the east. Gray, 128.
51. Gray, 128.
52. Remodeled and enlarged over the years, Government House (as it is now known) was built at a cost of $18,651, according to a territorial government visitor information brochure. Gray, 129–130; Navy, photographs, NH 57707, NH 63095 (*Abarenda*), NH 90163 (residence).

53. Navy, *Dictionary,* vol. 1, pt. A, 11.
54. The government copra fund, in its first year of operation (1901–02), brought the government over $10,000, its chief source of income. Gray, 54, 151–152, 153.
55. Gray, 164.
56. Forty of the schools were operated by the London Missionary Society, thirteen by Roman Catholics, three by Mormons, and one by Methodists. Gray, 173.
57. The navy turned down a second request in 1902. Gray, 174.
58. The school at Fagatoga opened in 1903 with sixty-two pupils from throughout American Samoa. Gray, 174.
59. Gray, 166.
60. Blackwell, 41.
61. A census of American Samoa in 1902 counted 5,060 indigenous islanders and 20 outlanders. Gray, 150.
62. The *fale,* a traditional dome-roofed, open-sided Samoan house, is pronounced "folly." The humble medical complex served as the territory's hospital until supplanted by a permanent dispensary — and larger *fale* — in 1906. It eventually grew into today's Lyndon B. Johnson Tropical Medical Center. Gray, 166–167; Stuart, 185.
63. Blackwell, 44.
64. Gray, 127.
65. English translation of a petition dated 18 December 1900 (parenthetical phrase in original), quoted in Olsen, 22–23.
66. Letter from Ebenezer V. Cooper dated 8 November 1901, quoted in Olsen, 24.
67. Evans, 13.
68. Tilley, 87.
69. Gray, 152; Olsen, 36.
70. Tilley's accuser remains anonymous. A letter in a woman's handwriting was sent to Secretary of the Navy John D. Long, who snipped off the signature before circulating it for investigation. Dr. Blackwell claimed to know the identity but refused to divulge it. Evans, 17–18; Blackwell, 51–52; Gray, 135.
71. Navy, biographical summary; Olsen, 23; Blackwell, 51.
72. The *Wisconsin* departed in October 1901 from San Francisco. Navy, biographical summary; Blackwell, 52.
73. Blackwell had given the same response earlier to the assistant navy secretary in Washington. Blackwell, 51, 52.
74. Evans reports having known Tilley "for many years." His account of the court-martial circumspectly mentions no names. Evans, 9, 12.
75. The court-martial met 9–12 November 1901. Evans, 17; Blackwell, 52; Olsen, 23 n. 5; Gray, 139.
76. The court-martial, he complained, was called "practically on an anonymous letter." Evans, 17–18.
77. Blackwell, 52.
78. Blackwell, 52.
79. Evans deplores "the injury to the reputation and feelings of the officer, who up to that time had enjoyed a fine reputation." Evans, 17–18; Navy, biographical summary.
80. Navy, biographical summary; *Who Was Who,* vol. 1, 1240
81. Navy, biographical summary; *Who Was Who,* vol. 1, 1240.
82. Navy, biographical summary.
83. He was promoted 24 February 1907. Navy, biographical summary.
84. He expired 18 March 1907. Navy, biographical summary; *Who Was Who,* vol. 1, 1240.
85. His wife, daughter, and another son also survived him. The family home evidently remained in Washington. Obituary; *Who Was Who,* vol. 1, 1240; Navy, photographs, Benjamin F. Tilley, Jr., 1914.
86. Navy, biographical summary.
87. The historian, ironically, was the direct professional descendant of Dr. Blackwell. Captain J. A. C. Gray served as the navy's last medical officer in the territory before its administration was transferred to the Department of the Interior in 1950. Gray, 139.

7. Joseph B. Foraker

1. Walters, 5–6; Johnson and Malone, 502.
2. The paternal grandparents moved in 1820 from Bombay Hook Island in Delaware Bay, and the maternal grandparents around the same time from Virginia. Walters, 5–6; Johnson and Malone, 502; *National,* vol. 3, 144. The westward migration was to continue in succeeding generations. Foraker's brother Creighton moved in 1882 to the territory of New Mexico, eventually serving as U.S. marshal. Foraker letter to Theodore Roosevelt, 16 December 1905, Foraker Papers.
3. Foraker was born 5 July 1846 at a farm near Rainsboro. Johnson and Malone, 502; Walters, 5; Foraker, *Live,* 53; *Who Was Who,* vol. 1, 410.
4. *National,* vol. 3, 144. Joseph Benson (1749–1821) was an eminent English Methodist clergyman.
5. The farm and mills were acquired when Ben was a two-year-old infant. Johnson and Malone, 502; Foraker, *Live,* 53–54.
6. Foraker, *Notes,* vol. 2, 10; Foraker, *Live,* 54; Johnson and Malone, 502.
7. Frémont's exploring expedition to California in 1843 had revealed its vast resources and earned him the nickname "the Pathfinder." His presidential candidacy in 1856, under the slogan "Free Soil, Free Speech, and Frémont," also attracted another budding politician. Abraham Lincoln delivered fifty speeches on his behalf. Despite such support, the Republican was defeated by Democrat James Buchanan. Foraker, *Live,* 53.
8. Foraker, *Notes,* vol. 1, 10–11.
9. Foraker, *Notes,* vol. 1, 9.
10. Johnson and Malone, 502.
11. The quotation and other recollections of his reading come from his wife. Foraker, *Live,* 54–55; Johnson and Malone, 502.
12. Johnson and Malone, 502.
13. Foraker enlisted 14 July 1862 in the Eighty-

ninth Regiment of the Ohio Volunteer Infantry. He was commended for bravery in carrying news of the capture of Savannah in 1864 to the Union fleet offshore, and cited for delivering a call for reinforcements at Bentonville in 1865. Johnson and Malone, 503; Walters, 15; *Who Was Who*, vol. 1, 410.

14. Foraker, *Notes*, vol. 1, 178; Weaver, 28. Warfare itself, however, held little appeal. In the daily journal he kept during the conflict, Foraker wrote: "Don't like fighting enough to make a profession of it. War is cruel...." Quoted in *National*, vol. 3, 144.

15. Of over 1,000 volunteers in the regiment, only 231 came home. Foraker, *Notes*, vol. 1, 34–35, 79.

16. Walters, 15; Johnson and Malone, 503.

17. Julia Bundy, of New England stock, was born 17 June 1847. Foraker, *Live*, 11–12; Walters, 15.

18. The log farmhouse in which Julia had been born was replaced in 1860 by an imposing structure suitable to receive local dignitaries. Foraker, *Live*, 5–6, 20.

19. Bundy, a Lincoln elector in 1864, served in the House of Representatives in 1865–67, 1873–75, and 1893–95. Foraker, *Live*, 34, 43; Congress, *Biographical Directory*, 700–701; *Who Was Who*, vol. 1, 410.

20. He studied at Ohio Wesleyan in 1866–68. Walters, 16; Johnson and Malone, 503; Foraker, *Live*, 65; *Who Was Who*, vol. 1, 410.

21. They were married 4 October 1870. *Who Was Who*, vol. 1, 410; Walters, 15.

22. Foraker served on the bench in 1879–82. *Who Was Who*, vol. 1, 410; *National*, vol. 3, 144.

23. Walters, x; Leech, 41.

24. Walters, 22, 25; Johnson and Malone, 503; *Who Was Who*, vol. 1, 410.

25. Foraker, *Live*, 141.

26. The ousted incumbent was a fellow ex-judge named George Hoadley. Johnson and Malone, 503; Leech, 41.

27. Foraker, *Live*, 100.

28. Foraker, *Notes*, vol. 1, 240–242; Johnson and Malone, 503 (quotation); Brodsky, 190–194.

29. *National*, vol. 3, 144.

30. Leech, 41; Walters, 3, 249; "Joseph B. Foraker"; Morris, *Theodore Rex*, 479 (Ohio boy's trek).

31. Foraker served as governor from 1886 to 1890. He was defeated by Democrat James E. Campbell. Walters, x; Johnson and Malone, 503; *Who Was Who*, vol. 1, 410; *National*, vol. 3, 144.

32. Foraker, writes Walters, "came to feel ... a genuine conviction of the righteousness of big business." Walters, 3–4.

33. Foraker, *Live*, 144.

34. The eldest son was his father's namesake and the youngest daughter was named Julia. Ranged between them were daughters Florence and Louise, and son Arthur. Foraker, *Live*, 146–148.

35. Foraker, *Live*, 146.

36. At the time of his defeat, McKinley was majority leader, chairman of the Ways and Means Committee, and a member of the Rules Committee. Leech, 37, 44.

37. McKinley proceeded to win two terms as governor. Leech, 50; Foraker, *Live*, 190.

38. Both he and McKinley had been suggested as possible presidential or vice presidential candidates. Leech, 41.

39. The senator, who had represented Ohio in the Senate since before the Civil War, was brother of Union General William Tecumseh Sherman and uncle-in-law of General Miles. Leech, 41–42, 50; chap. 5 of this book.

40. Leech, 64.

41. Leech, 71–72.

42. Before taking to the hustings, Foraker indulged himself in an excursion to Europe. Foraker, *Live*, 190; Leech, 77, 86, 94; *Who Was Who*, vol. 1, 410.

43. Foraker succeeded Senator Calvin S. Brice, a Democrat who had declined to seek reelection. Brice had the unhappy distinction of having managed the unsuccessful 1888 presidential reelection campaign of Grover Cleveland. Leech, 64; *Who Was Who*, vol. 1, 410; Congress, *Biographical Directory*, 668; Brodsky, 226, 237.

44. Ohio's appointed junior senator was duly elected later in the year. Walters, 137; Weaver, 56; Leech, 99–101, 138.

45. Walters, frontispiece photograph, 249; Morris, *Theodore Rex*, 460, 479.

46. Walters, 249.

47. Walters, 3; Leech, 25, 493; Johnson and Malone, 504; Morris, *Theodore Rex*, 460; "Joseph B. Foraker."

48. Leech, 25, 26, 36, 38–39.

49. Letter to Joseph G. Butler, Jr., 9 March 1911, Foraker Papers. Mrs. Foraker pronounced McKinley an "old friend." Foraker, *Live*, 190.

50. McKinley had grown up in the rural Ohio settlements of Niles and Poland, and, like Foraker, earned a battlefield commission in the Civil War. Leech, 4–7, 66–69, 138, 493–494.

51. Leech, 344–345; Pratt, *Expansionists*, 326.

52. Leech, 175, 326; Pratt, *Expansionists*, 233–252.

53. Walters, 4, 146; Johnson and Malone, 503; Leech, 118 (inaugural quotation), 175, 187, 192–193.

54. Walters, 4.

55. Remarks in *Cleveland Press*, 8 October 1898, quoted in Walters, 153.

56. The future state was annexed by Congress 7 July 1898. Walters, 152; Leech, 145–147. For a full account, see Pratt, *Expansionists*, 34–229, 317–326.

57. An earlier version of the Hay-Pauncefote Treaty had been rejected by the Senate in 1899. Leech, 504–514; "Joseph B. Foraker."

58. "Hawaii and the Danish islands both belong within our sphere of influence and ... should not be allowed to fall into the hands of any other great power," Foraker reasoned. Foraker, *Notes*, vol. 2, 422. A treaty to purchase the Danish West Indies for $5 million cleared the Senate, only to be defeated by the Danish parliament. A similar treaty in 1867 had met the same fate in reverse actions by the two bodies. Foraker, *Notes*, vol. 2, 423; Stuart, 149 n. 1.

59. Foraker, *Notes*, vol. 2, 66.

60. In the so-called Teller Amendment (of Senator Henry M. Teller of Colorado), Congress in April

1898 had pledged that the nation "disclaims any disposition or intention to exercise sovereignty, jurisdiction, or control over [Cuba], except for the pacification thereof, and asserts its determination, when that is accomplished, to leave the government and control of the Island to its people." U.S. occupation forces departed in 1902. In the Philippines, armed resistance to the Americans continued until the same year. Leech, 188–189, 393; Cabranes, 2 n. 4.

61. "The civil rights and political status of the native inhabitants hereby ceded to the United States," the treaty stated, "shall be determined by the Congress." Foraker, *Notes,* vol. 2, 76; Cabranes, 20.

62. Quoted in Cabranes, 36. See also Foraker, *Notes,* vol. 2, 75.

63. Americans were less generous with legal entitlements than the old imperialism that they took pride in liberalizing. The British Empire granted its subjects the full constitutional rights of any Englishman. Morris, *Pax Britannica,* 195; Cabranes, 36.

64. Morales, 153; Leech, 395, 493.

65. People in the new American protectorates "have not yet been educated in the art of self-government," Root wrote in 1899. "They would inevitably fail without a course of tuition under a strong and guiding hand. With that tuition for a time their natural capacity will, it is hoped, make them a self-governing people." Root, 163, 165. See also Morales Carrión, 149.

66. The War Department had considered the idea of an assembly, but concluded it should be postponed. Leech, 395.

67. Cabranes, 30, 40–41.

68. Leech, 493.

69. Foraker, *Notes,* vol. 2, 66.

70. Morales Carrión, 120, 138–139; Cabranes, 2 n. 5; Stuart, 331.

71. Foraker, *Notes,* vol. 2, 81; Leech, 493; Cabranes, 22 n. 70.

72. Foraker, *Notes,* vol. 2, 82.

73. The Danish West Indies possessed local legislative bodies, but severe restrictions on sex, age, residence, and income reduced eligible voters to a token few. Stuart, 331–332, 351.

74. A congressional inquiry recently had examined conditions in Puerto Rico. Foraker, *Notes,* vol. 2, 72; Leech, 395.

75. The exemption continues today. Foraker, *Notes,* vol. 2, 73–74.

76. Foraker's original bill had made the commerce duty free. Cabranes, 35; Foraker, *Notes,* vol. 2, 73–74; Leech, 487–488, 491, 495.

77. Foraker, *Notes,* vol. 2, 81. McKinley biographer Margaret Leech agrees. Leech, 500.

78. Cabranes, 14.

79. Cabranes, 21–22; Morales Carrión, 156.

80. The first Foraker bill of 1900 granted collective U.S. citizenship to former Spanish subjects (except those opting to retain Spanish nationality) as of the war's end and their progeny continuing to reside in Puerto Rico. Cabranes, 36.

81. Quoted in Cabranes, 37.

82. Cabranes, 23–24, 60.

83. Cabranes, 41–42.

84. American citizenship for Puerto Ricans had been steadfastly opposed by Secretary of War Root. Leech, 395; Cabranes, 21, 23.

85. "I ... did everything I could to have it enacted but a majority of the Senate thought it was then premature," Foraker wrote later. The compromise language was "a phrase I framed and substituted when I found I could not do better." Foraker, *Notes,* vol. 2, 84. See also Walters, 166; Cabranes, 41.

86. Leech, 493–494.

87. Letter from Charles Foster, 4 April 1900, Foraker Papers.

88. Leech, 493–494.

89. Leech, 498.

90. Quoted in Leech, 494. Foraker biographer Everett Walters rates the legislation "the most important of his senatorial services." Walters, 161.

91. Handed down just months after a reelection of McKinley widely interpreted as ratification of expansionism, the decisions drew Mr. Dooley's observation: "Whether th' Constitution follows th' flag or not, th' Supreme Court follows th' iliction returns." Cabranes, 44–51; Leech, 502–503 (Dooley quotation).

92. Quoted in Walters, 171. Allen, appointed by McKinley, had been Theodore Roosevelt's successor as assistant secretary of the navy. Leech, 254, 395.

93. Stuart, 383.

94. Letter, 27 November 1906, Foraker Papers. It was written, the senator was flattered to notice, as a matter of evident priority on the very day of the president's return.

95. Quoted in Morales Carrión, 159. On Muñoz Rivera, see also chap. 5 of this book.

96. The visitors, "three of their foremost citizens," appreciated most the return of civilian rule and the opportunity for local participation in the new government. The visit is undated. Foraker, *Notes,* vol. 2, 85.

97. Leech, 502, 581.

98. The Puerto Rican Senate previously had been appointed by the president and doubled as an executive council. Morales Carrión, 200.

99. Foraker, *Notes,* vol. 2, 82.

100. Foraker pushed the measure in 1903 and in the subsequent Congress. Cabranes, 56–57.

101. Roosevelt called for citizenship in his annual message to Congress in 1905, and then personally lobbied lawmakers. Cabranes, 57–60; Walters, 84–85.

102. Letter, 26 March 1906, Foraker Papers.

103. Roosevelt reiterated his endorsement in 1907 and 1908. Taft urged citizenship in 1909 and 1912. GOP platforms backed it in 1908 and 1912. Cabranes, 61, 67, 70; Foraker, *Notes,* vol. 2, 84–85.

104. Walters, 161.

105. Foraker, *Notes,* vol. 2, 66.

106. The Foraker bills would have administered the two possessions through the navy or another federal department of the president's choice. Guam got a statutory government in 1950. Samoa's lack of

one is partly by preference. Its "unorganized" government, however, follows the Puerto Rican pattern. Walters, 195; Olsen, 33; Stuart, 335–336.
107. Goode, 121.
108. Foraker, *Live*, 190; Goode, 121.
109. The plot occupied the northwest corner of Sixteenth and P Streets. Goode, 121. The name of the presidential residence at the foot of Sixteenth Street was changed by Theodore Roosevelt. Leech, 605.
110. The architect was Paul J. Pelz, whose Neoclassical Library of Congress building had opened earlier that year. Goode, 121.
111. Walters, 251–252.
112. The house was an architectural potpourri of indigenous Colonial Revival and assorted imported French styles. Goode, 121; Walters, 250.
113. Walters, 250; Goode, 121.
114. Dinners included as many as thirty guests. Goode, 122; portrait of Mrs. Foraker, Weaver, 46.
115. Foraker, *Notes*, vol. 2, 125.
116. Foraker, *Live*, 204.
117. Foraker, *Notes*, vol. 2, 10, photograph of senator fishing.
118. A less altruistic motive in Foraker's opposition to excluding Chinese workers may have been to replenish this source of cheap labor for American industry, particularly railroads. Walters, 189; Foraker, *Notes*, vol. 2, 172–180 (quotation, 172).
119. Letter to Foraker, 21 June 1905, Foraker Papers.
120. Morris, *Theodore Rex*, 472.
121. They succeeded in getting the African-American Mississippian elected. Foraker, *Notes*, vol. 1, 34–35, 179; Morris, *Theodore Rex*, 459.
122. While Roosevelt often is credited with first entertaining a black person at the executive mansion, Grover Cleveland fifteen years earlier had hosted African-American civil rights leader Frederick Douglass. Morris, *Theodore Rex*, 459; Brodsky, 484 n. 4.
123. Quoted in Morris, *Theodore Rex*, 464. The full extent of the disagreement is aired in an exchange of telegrams between Roosevelt and Foraker, 26 and 27 September 1906, and a letter from Roosevelt to Foraker, 28 September 1906, Foraker Papers.
124. The fracas had taken the life of one townsman and injured two others, including the police chief. Discharged were three companies (a fourth being away on assignment) of the Twenty-fifth Infantry, Colored, based near the racially tense town. Morris, *Theodore Rex*, 453–454, 462–463.
125. Foraker's interest first had been stirred by a memorandum from an organization called the Constitution League, whose lawyer, an African-American, had been turned away at the White House. Morris, *Theodore Rex*, 471.
126. Foraker, *Notes*, vol. 2, 231–327; Foraker, *Live*, 276; Collier, 133; Morris, *Theodore Rex*, 472. Roosevelt, paradoxically, had been a vocal supporter of African-American soldiers in the Spanish-American War. Traxel, 276, 319.
127. Foraker, *Notes*, vol. 2, 298. See also Foraker, *Live*, 277.
128. Morris, *Theodore Rex*, 472, 474.
129. Morris, *Theodore Rex*, 478–480; Foraker, *Notes*, vol. 2, 152 (quotation); Weaver, 127.
130. Morris, *Theodore Rex*, 482, 546–547; Goode, 123.
131. Morris, *Theodore Rex*, 511.
132. "I listened to the War Department, and I shouldn't," Roosevelt confessed at the time to a friend. Quoted in Morris, *Theodore Rex*, 474–475. See also 471.
133. Walters, 199.
134. "Joseph B. Foraker"; Morris, *Theodore Rex*, 471; Walters, 256–272.
135. "My debt to you," wrote Taft in a letter of thanks on 31 January 1887, "is very great." Foraker Papers. See also Foraker, *Notes*, vol. 1, 238.
136. Walters, 256–272.
137. Morris, *Theodore Rex*, 526–527.
138. Letter, 19 June 1908, Foraker Papers.
139. Walters, 254.
140. The Hepburn Act, approved by the Senate 77 to 3, authorized the Interstate Commerce Commission to set rates and otherwise regulate the railways. Walters, 218–224; Morris, *Theodore Rex*, 438, 446–447.
141. Letter to Senator Henry Cabot Lodge, 27 September 1906, in Roosevelt, *Letters*, vol. 5, 429.
142. The Archbold letters, written to Foraker between 1900 and 1903, had been bought by Hearst from thieves in 1904 and 1905. Letters from Archbold, 21, 22, and 27 January and 17 February 1902, and replies from Foraker, 25 January and 14 February 1902, Foraker Papers; Walters, 4, 274; Weaver, 140.
143. Foraker had been employed by the oil company from December 1898 to early 1901. Foraker, *Notes*, vol. 2, 344.
144. Walters, 4.
145. Foraker, *Notes*, vol. 2, 344.
146. Foraker, *Notes*, vol. 2, 344.
147. "If it had been any company except the Standard Oil Company, which, at that particular time was being arraigned by the Government upon charges that made it exceedingly unpopular, I might have been reelected," he claimed. "But however that may be, with President Roosevelt and President [-to-be] Taft both against me, it is no wonder I was defeated." Foraker, *Notes*, vol. 2, 348.
148. Letter to Jacob G. Schurman, 20 March 1909, Foraker Papers.
149. The engraved cup towered nearly two feet on its ebony base. Foraker, *Notes*, vol. 2, 320; Weaver, 155. "The Negroes of this country," eulogized the *Memphis Sentinel* newspaper upon his retirement in 1909, "have not had such a faithful champion of their rights since the days of Charles Sumner" (the abolitionist Massachusetts senator and architect of much of the nation's Reconstruction program). Quoted in Weaver, xxii.
150. Letter from Schurman to John A. Rea, 23 January 1908, Foraker Papers. Schurman was a bit player in America's imperial saga, having headed a presidential commission dispatched in 1899 to the Philippines to advise McKinley in setting policies for the new acquisition. Karnow, 150–153, 163.

151. Walters, 288.
152. Mrs. Delos A. Blodgett moved from Grand Rapids, Michigan, to Washington to educate her daughters at boarding schools in the capital. Her late husband's lumber business also had profited from the rebuilding of Chicago after its disastrous fire in 1871. Goode, 123–124.
153. Walters, 291–293. The victor graciously wrote to the former senator of "the one regret that is in my heart, that is — I had to acquire it [the Senate nomination] in a contest against you." Letter, 20 August 1914, Foraker Papers.
154. Walters, 294–295.
155. Walters, 98; Foraker, *Live,* 221–222, 333.
156. Foraker, *Notes,* vol. 2, 125. Julia Foraker felt that Benson's passing hastened her father's. Foraker, *Live,* 333.
157. Walters, 294–295.
158. Walters, 294.
159. Letter, 28 June 1916, Foraker Papers. See also Roosevelt, *Letters,* vol. 8, 1081.
160. The proposal so unacceptable in Foraker's day passed practically by acclamation. "We are conferring on them what they ought to have had years ago," one leading House Republican stated rather apologetically. Cabranes, 5, 12–16, 80–95 (quotation, 94).
161. He expired 10 May 1917. "Joseph B. Foraker"; Walters, 295; *Who Was Who,* vol. 1, 410.
162. She passed away in the year after its publication in 1932. The work was reprinted by Arno Press in New York.
163. The church is now known as Foundry United Methodist. Goode, 123–124.
164. The army acted under a threat of preemption by Congress in legislation of Augustus F. Hawkins, representative of California. Weaver, xiv, xvi.
165. Willis, son of a Mississippi sharecropper, passed away in 1977 at age ninety-one. Weaver, 209–212.

8. William A. Jones

1. The name is derived from the reported effusion of the first Spanish governor, Ponce de Leon, in 1508 upon sailing into the harbor at what is now San Juan: *"¡Que puerto rico!"* ("What a rich port!"). Waugh, 272; Stuart, 390 n. 1.
2. Cabranes, 1 n. 1; Clark, 7; Perkins, 135.
3. Congress, *Jones,* 27.
4. Jones added, for good measure, "that there does not even exist the pretext of changing the name to Americanize it, since *porto* is not an English but a Portuguese word." Quoted in Cabranes, 1 n. 1.
5. The insular legislature had petitioned Congress to correct the misspelling. Perkins, 135; Cabranes, 1 n. 1.
6. Shelton, iii, iv, 6, 13.
7. The family patriarch settled in Charles City County sometime before 1653. Shelton, 13–14.
8. Joseph Jones was William's great-grandfather. The family name of his wife, Jane Atkinson, provided the middle name of the great-grandson. Shelton, 14; Congress, *Jones,* 13.
9. Shelton, 13–14.
10. Thomas Jones had turned to law after a brief stint as a circuit-riding Presbyterian preacher. He and Anne Trowbridge were married in 1843. Shelton, 14–15; Congress, *Jones,* 13–14, 27.
11. The town became Warsaw in 1831, according to information at the Richmond County Museum.
12. William was born 21 March 1849. Shelton, ii, 13.
13. The elder Jones's mother, Mary, had been a Lee, daughter of former Virginia governor Richard Lee. Shelton, 15.
14. During the course of the war, he rose from sergeant to captain. Shelton, 15.
15. Richmond was contested from December 1864 until evacuated in April 1865. Shelton, 16–17.
16. Captain Jones lent his support to the diehards of General Joseph E. Johnston. Shelton, 15.
17. He attended Coleman's School in Fredericksburg and earned his law degree at the University of Virginia in two years. Shelton, 15, 17; Congress, *Jones,* 14.
18. Shelton, iii, 18–19.
19. Shelton, iii, 13, 17.
20. Congress, *Jones,* 27; Shelton, iii, 6.
21. Shelton, 3–4.
22. Shelton, abstract (n.p.), ii–iii, 2, 7–13, 20.
23. Shelton, 82.
24. Shelton, iii.
25. Shelton, 17.
26. Shelton, iv, 68.
27. Shelton, 12–13. Built in 1748, the courthouse is one of the country's oldest still in use as a hall of justice.
28. Great-uncle Willoughby Newton served as a Whig in the House of Representatives from 1843 to 1845. Shelton, 18.
29. Jones articulated his lofty estimation in 1893. Quoted in Shelton, 265.
30. Shelton, 35–36, 67–68, 71–72.
31. Congress, *Jones,* 15; Shelton, 15, 68.
32. Shelton, 28.
33. The weekly newspaper established in 1879, the *Northern Neck News,* continues to be published today. The phone company followed in 1896. Shelton, 20–26, 100.
34. Shelton, 22, 74, 100.
35. Despite the efforts of Jones and his father, Hancock carried neither their county nor the country in his election loss to Republican James A. Garfield. Shelton, 68–70.
36. Shelton, 74–76.
37. Shelton, 77, 86.
38. They were wed 23 January 1889. The bride's senatorial uncle was Richard Coke of Texas. "Marriage in the Hill City"; *Who Was Who,* vol. 1, 651; Shelton, 138.
39. The house was built on the site of the family home where Jones had been born, a structure said to have been burned by Union forces in the Civil War. The 1889 house, with wrought iron fence and gazebo, remains owned by the Jones family. Ryland, 102–103.

Notes — Chapter 8

40. Shelton, 138.
41. Shelton, 107.
42. Congress, *Jones*, frontispiece engraving.
43. Shelton, 67.
44. Shelton, 67, 108.
45. Shelton, 107, 146, 222.
46. Congress, *Jones*, 19, 68; Shelton, 67, 107, 120, 269.
47. The recollections come from Representatives Finis J. Garrett of Tennessee, Walter A. Watson of Virginia, and Edward W. Saunders of Virginia, respectively. Congress, *Jones*, 31, 19, 46.
48. Shelton, 70–71, 72, 75, 90–95.
49. Shelton, 86.
50. Shelton, 76, 162, 209.
51. Remembrance of Representative Andrew J. Montague of Virginia, a former governor and ally of Jones. Congress, *Jones*, 17.
52. The First Congressional District, while based in the Northern Neck, extended westward to Fredericksburg, southward across the Rappahannock River to an adjoining peninsula, and eastward across Chesapeake Bay to Virginia's Eastern Shore. Shelton, 71–73, 96–100, 210, 224–225.
53. Shelton, 72.
54. Jones portrayed his Republican opponent as insufficiently supportive of the congressional candidacy of a black Virginia party colleague. Shelton, 97.
55. Jones aligned himself against educational and property qualifications for voting as undemocratic but also, less admirably, as racially ineffective. Shelton, 178, 185.
56. Letter of 30 April 1906, quoted in Shelton, 226.
57. Jones outpolled incumbent T. H. Bayley Browne, 14,767 votes to 12,001. Congress, *Jones*, 16; Shelton, 100, 132.
58. Republican forces were reduced from 166 to 88, against 235 Democrats and 9 Populists.
59. Shelton, 245.
60. Shelton, iv–v, 145–146, 245.
61. From a speech in 1911, quoted in Shelton, 246.
62. Shelton, 108, 224, 269.
63. Shelton, 100, 103.
64. The Alliance, whose Virginia affiliate sprang up two years before Jones ran for Congress, later became a leading component of the Populist party. Shelton, 97–108; Brodsky, 347–349.
65. He was elected senator in 1893. Shelton, 83–84, 142–170.
66. Shelton, 143, 175, 235–236.
67. From a speech in 1911, quoted in Shelton, 254.
68. Quoted in Shelton, 256.
69. Jones was ousted as head of the congressional delegation in 1899. Shelton, 189. Redistricting efforts occurred in 1902–03 and 1906. The first was vetoed by the governor. The second added new territory but failed to prevent Jones's reelection. Shelton, 223–224.
70. Letter of 4 January 1911, quoted in Shelton, 241.
71. Shelton, 245.
72. Shelton, abstract (n.p.), 146.
73. Jones endorsed curbing trusts in 1890 (Shelton, 98 n, 244); the income tax in 1892 (Shelton, 114–115, 146, 243); popular election of judges and the campaign reforms in 1911 (Shelton, 252).
74. Shelton, 146–147.
75. Shelton, 147.
76. Congress, *Jones*, 17–18; Shelton, 146–173, 187–189, 191.
77. Shelton, 199.
78. Letter of 30 April 1906, quoted in Shelton, 226.
79. Shelton, abstract (n.p.), 221.
80. Jones, concludes Shelton, "was not an effective political leader." Shelton, abstract (n.p.) (quotation), 137, 184, 211, 214, 218, 266; Congress, *Jones*, 68.
81. Shelton, 67, 120.
82. Representative Andrew J. Montague of Virginia, in Congress, *Jones*, 19.
83. Shelton, 119–120, 267–268. Cracking down on pension abuses was an interest shared with the president, fellow Democrat Grover Cleveland. Brodsky, 183–184, 187–189.
84. Congress, *Jones*, 29; Shelton, 211, 269, 272.
85. Jones had endorsed Bryan before the state party machine did so, and headed the Virginia delegation to the party convention in Chicago that nominated Bryan. Shelton, 145. He was to remain a Bryan loyalist for twelve years. Shelton, 205–206, 212, 232.
86. Shelton, 271–272. On Bryan, see Karnow, 137.
87. From a speech in 1911, quoted in Shelton, 271.
88. The League's high-profile adherents included former president Grover Cleveland, industrialist Andrew Carnegie, and writer Mark Twain. Congress, *Jones*, 33, 41; Shelton, 277; Karnow, 109–110, 136.
89. Representative James L. Slayden of Texas, in Congress, *Jones*, 32–33.
90. Shelton, 222.
91. Letter of 8 May 1898, quoted in Shelton, 273.
92. Jones was describing an admired quality of a colleague. From an undated speech, quoted in Shelton, 296.
93. Shelton, 108, 169, 272.
94. Representative Finis J. Garrett of Tennessee, a fellow Democrat who ranked just below Jones on the panel and eventually succeeded him as chairman. Congress, *Jones*, 29.
95. "The sentiment in the United States seems to be practically unanimous," Jones stated at a congressional hearing in 1914, "that Porto Rico is to remain permanently a part of the United States." Quoted in Cabranes, 75. See also Shelton, 276.
96. Letter of 8 May 1898, quoted in Shelton, 274.
97. Daniel, revered by many Virginians in his day, served as senator from 1887 until his passing in 1910. He uttered his sentiments in the debate over ratifying the Treaty of Paris. Quoted in Brands, 332, 333. On Daniel, see Shelton, 107, 111, 132–133, 155.

98. Morales Carrión, 156.
99. Lewis, *Puerto Rico*, 107–108; Clark, 9–10.
100. Morales Carrión, 156.
101. Quoted in Morales Carrión, 156.
102. Lewis, *Puerto Rico*, 88.
103. The vehicle for Jones's proposal was legislation temporarily extending military rule until the new civilian government could take over. Morales Carrión, 157.
104. Quoted in Fernández Méndez, 168.
105. Specifically, the law provided that "every corporation hereafter authorized to engage in agriculture shall by its charter be restricted to the ownership and control of not to exceed five hundred acres of land." Quoted in Fernández Méndez, 167.
106. Jones succeeded, as chairman, Representative Henry A. Cooper of Wisconsin. Congress, *Jones*, 39; Shelton, 291.
107. Congress, *Jones*, 14, 32; Shelton, 276, 279–283.
108. From a speech in 1901, quoted in Shelton, 282.
109. Shelton, 213, 283–288.
110. Shelton, 287.
111. Jones called Aguinaldo, demonized by many Americans, a "distinguished Filipino," and continued the dialogue with him later by mail. Shelton, 285–291. The quotation comes from Jones's journal of the trip, quoted in Shelton, 287.
112. Congress, *Jones*, 21, 23, 59; Shelton, 281, 291–293; Karnow, 241–243.
113. No other Western imperial power had yet extended a colony autonomy, let alone pledged independence. Karnow, 242, 247.
114. Karnow, 246–247; Congress, *Jones*, 69; Shelton, 294–295.
115. Puerto Rico's House of Delegates told Congress in 1914 of its "opposition to being declared, in defiance of our express wish or without our express consent, citizens of any country whatsoever other than our own beloved soil." Quoted in Cabranes, 77. See also Morales Carrión, 187.
116. Both Republicans and Democrats had pledged Puerto Ricans collective citizenship in their 1908 platforms. Morales Carrión, 191; Cabranes, 66–67.
117. Since becoming resident commissioner in 1911, Muñoz Rivera had variously endorsed Puerto Rican citizenship; reported others' reservations on U.S. citizenship while dissociating himself from them; expressed preference for collective over individual citizenship; deferred to Jones's committee on the entire matter. Cabranes, 73–79.
118. The bill was introduced in January 1912. Morales Carrión, 185, 190–191; Cabranes, 68, 70, 73.
119. Frankfurter, later as a professor at Harvard University law school, prepared New Deal legislation regulating the securities industry, then was appointed by President Franklin D. Roosevelt to the Supreme Court. Morales Carrión, 187; Cabranes, 70.
120. Morales Carrión, 162–163, 187; Lewis, *Puerto Rico*, 106–107; speech by Muñoz Rivera in House of Representatives, 5 May 1916, quoted in Wagenheim, 127.
121. The president would no longer appoint the eleven members of the executive council, but choose the possession's attorney general, auditor, and education commissioner. Morales Carrión, 200; Lewis, *Puerto Rico*, 108.
122. The provision came under attack from Roosevelt in 1905 and President Taft's war secretary in 1910. Fernández Méndez, 169–174.
123. Morales Carrión, 157, 216–217; Lewis, *Puerto Rico*, 91–92.
124. Morales Carrión, 190–191.
125. Research by legal scholar and federal judge José A. Cabranes concludes that "nothing in the annals of Congress would suggest that the collective naturalization of the Puerto Ricans was a matter connected in any way with military concerns." Cabranes, 17. A differing interpretation may be found in Morales Carrión, 173, 193, 198–199.
126. Morales Carrión, 194–195; Cabranes, 80–91.
127. Shelton, 261–262.
128. Wilson had written in 1901, while a professor at Princeton University, that territorial people "must first take the discipline of law, must first love order and instructively yield to it…. We are old in this learning and must be their tutors." Quoted in Morales Carrión, 186.
129. Letter, 27 November 1916, Wilson, *Papers*, vol. 40, 90–91.
130. Morales Carrión, 195.
131. Annual message to Congress, 5 December 1916, Wilson, *Papers*, vol. 40, 159.
132. The commission was headed by Antonio R. Barceló, president of the Puerto Rican Senate and chairman of the ruling Union party. Morales Carrión, 196–197; Cabranes, 92.
133. The bill received Senate approval on 20 February and the president's signature on 2 March. Morales Carrión, 198.
134. Speech in House of Representatives, 5 May 1916, quoted in Wagenheim, 128. Muñoz Rivera passed away six months later, 15 November 1916. Cabranes, 91.
135. An assessment of the act in 1918, in Congress, *Jones*, 63.
136. Cabranes, 97; Clark, 24, 27.
137. Telegram to Governor Arthur Yager, 1 April 1917, Wilson, *Papers*, vol. 41, 515–516.
138. Congress, *Jones*, 65.
139. Congress, *Jones*, 64–65.
140. Congress, *Jones*, frontispiece engraving.
141. Shelton, 108, 224.
142. Shelton, 224, 227.
143. Shelton, 223–227.
144. Shelton, 135–137, 137–138, 157–158, 169–170, 207.
145. Shelton, 138, 158.
146. Letter of 1 September 1897, quoted in Shelton, 160.
147. Shelton, 240–260.
148. Statement of 14 January 1911, quoted in Shelton, 243.
149. The vote was 65,317 to 31,428. Shelton, 260.
150. Congress, *Jones*, 5; Shelton, 264.
151. Shelton, 234, 262, 295–296.
152. He expired 18 April 1918. "Congressman Jones"; Shelton, 296. His wife survived him.

153. Shelton, 296.
154. Quezon, who had been the possession's resident commissioner in Washington, was to serve as first president of the Philippines' transitional commonwealth government from 1935 to 1944. Congress, *Jones*, 25. See also Karnow, 242, 246.
155. Karnow, 241, 247; Shelton, 296.
156. Designed by Spanish architect Mariano Benillure, the memorial depicts a barefoot Filipina admiringly lifting a tablet bearing her country's coat of arms toward a bust of Jones, beneath the outspread wings of a bronze eagle. The base is inscribed:
To William Atkinson Jones
A Tribute of Undying Gratitude
of the
Filipino People
The memorial was built in 1924 and dedicated in 1926. It adjoins the brick, colonial style St. John's Episcopal Church, dating to 1835, where Jones long served as a vestryman. The dedication was attended by his widow and two grown children. Jones's son and grandson both perpetuated the family tradition of public service. William A. Jones, Jr., like his father and grandfather, served as commonwealth's attorney. William A. Jones III was a decorated aviator in World War II. The Philippine visitor was the wife of president Fidel Ramos. Richmond County Museum; Karnow, 241; Shelton, 296.

9. Frank McIntyre

1. Biedzynski, 1–2.
2. Biedzynski, 3.
3. Biedzynski, 1.
4. Biedzynski, 8; *Who Was Who*, vol. 2, 361.
5. Denis McIntyre had come, under no known compulsion in his case, from Killybegs, on Donegal Bay in the northwest corner of Ireland. *National*, vol. 32, 333.
6. Biedzynski, 8–9.
7. He was born 5 January 1865. Biedzynski, 9; *Who Was Who*, vol. 2, 361.
8. Biedzynski, 10–11; *National*, vol. 32, 333.
9. Biedzynski, 11–12; *Who Was Who*, vol. 2, 361; "Gen. M'Intyre."
10. McIntyre studied at the University of Alabama from 1880 to 1882. Biedzynski, 12–13; *Who Was Who*, vol. 2, 361; "Gen. M'Intyre."
11. Pershing was a member of McIntyre's class, while March was an underclassman two years below. Biedzynski, 15, 17; *Who Was Who*, vol. 2, 361; "Gen. M'Intyre."
12. McIntyre served with the Nineteenth Infantry Regiment in Texas from 1886 to 1887. Biedzynski, 18–20; *Who Was Who*, vol. 2, 361.
13. McIntyre studied at the army school from 1887 to 1889. Biedzynski, 20–23; *Who Was Who*, vol. 2, 361. Miles had commanded the army's Missouri River department, based at Leavenworth, from 1885 to 1886. Wooster, 139.
14. McIntyre was posted in 1890 to Fort Brady, Michigan. Biedzynski, 23.
15. McIntyre taught at West Point from 1890 to 1894. Biedzynski, 23–24; *Who Was Who*, vol. 2, 361.
16. McIntyre met his future wife while stationed at Fort Sam Houston. They were married 12 July 1892. The wedding site is variously reported as Dallas or San Antonio. Biedzynski, 24; *Who Was Who*, vol. 2, 361; *National*, vol. 32, 334.
17. Marie was born in 1905, Margaret in 1908, and Nora in 1911. Edward's birth date is unknown. Their father rejoined his infantry regiment in Michigan from 1894 to 1898. Biedzynski, 24–26; *National*, vol. 32, 334; *Who Was Who*, vol. 2, 361.
18. Biedzynski, 37.
19. Biedzynski, 43; *Who Was Who*, vol. 2, 361.
20. Biedzynski, 43.
21. McIntyre joined the military government in Ponce in September 1898, after the armistice the previous month, and shifted to San Juan in December. He went back to his regiment in March 1899 and left Puerto Rico the following month. Biedzynski, 44–46; *Who Was Who*, vol. 2, 361.
22. McIntyre's regiment was sent to the Philippines in July 1899. Biedzynski, 46; *Who Was Who*, vol. 2, 361.
23. Biedzynski, 48.
24. Biedzynski, 64–70; "Gen. M'Intyre."
25. "Popular Official Promoted," *Washington Post*, 6 July 1912, 6.
26. Osmeña, editor of Cebu's *El Nuevo Dia (The New Day)*, served as president in 1944–46. Biedzynski, 66–67 (quotation, 67).
27. Biedzynski, 71; "Gen. M'Intyre."
28. Biedzynski, 71.
29. Biedzynski, 1–2; photograph, "Gen. M'Intyre."
30. Biedzynski, 90–91; *Who Was Who*, vol. 2, 361. On Miles's opposition to the general staff, see chap. 5 of this book.
31. When Puerto Rico came under civilian government in 1900, the governor reported to the U.S. Department of State and other top officials to three other departments in Washington. General Services, 1, 3.
32. "To Care for Colonies," *Washington Post*, 12 March 1899, 20.
33. The Dutch had administered their possessions through a Department of Colonies since 1840, the British through a Colonial Office since 1854, the French through a Ministry of the Colonies since 1894, and the Germans formed a Colonial Office in 1907. Pomeroy, "Colonial Office," 521; General Services, 2.
34. As early as 1905, a proponent of a central colonial office noted "all the opposition to 'imperialism.'" Arthur W. Dunn, "A Colonial Department," *Washington Post*, 16 July 1905, B7. See also Stuart, 1–16; Pratt, *Colonial Experiment*, 2–3.
35. Letter, 30 March 1904, Foraker Papers. Roosevelt formalized the recommendation two years later in a message to Congress. Pomeroy, "Colonial Office," 524. His successor, Taft, harbored similar ambitions for centralization, also unfulfilled. "For Insular Department," *Washington Post*, 25 July 1909, 3.

36. The Department of War is today's Department of the Army. Its Division of Customs and Insular Affairs, formed in December 1898, became the Division of Insular Affairs two years later. General Services, 1; Pratt, *Colonial Experiment,* 154; Pomeroy, "Colonial Office," 525. Pershing headed the agency less than a year before resuming combat duty in the Philippines. Pomeroy, "Colonial Office," 531.

37. The bureau's supervision of Puerto Rico, surrendered to a quartet of federal departments in 1900, was restored in 1909. The agency managed postwar Cuba from 1898 to 1902. General Services, 1–2; Pratt, *Colonial Experiment,* 154–155.

38. "It may be truly said," the agency's chief told the secretary of war in 1901, "that every question involved in the conduct of governmental affairs lies within the possible scope of examination by this division." Quoted in Pratt, *Colonial Experiment,* 155. See also Biedzynski, 95–96.

39. Annual Report for 1901, quoted in Pomeroy, "Colonial Office," 525.

40. Taft served as first civilian governor of the Philippines, 1901–04. Biedzynski, 93–94; *Who Was Who,* vol. 2, 361; "Gen. M'Intyre."

41. Photograph, *Washington Post,* 30 December 1906, SM9.

42. Frankfurter, 61; Biedzynski, 93–94, 102.

43. The characterization is that of former bureau colleague Felix Frankfurter, 61.

44. The United States resumed rule in Cuba at the request of an island government in turmoil in 1906, set up a provisional government, held new elections, and departed in 1909. The U.S. military maintained an active role in the Dominican Republic from 1905 to 1939, including occupation from 1916 to 1924. General Services, 1–2; "Many Want Annexation," *Washington Post,* 16 October 1906, 12.

45. Biedzynski, 43, 170.

46. Frankfurter, 61.

47. Frankfurter, 64.

48. Frankfurter, 61. See also Karnow, 243.

49. Letter to Eugene A. Philbin, 18 March 1908, quoted in Biedzynski, 119.

50. McIntyre's low opinion of Roosevelt is attributed to a daughter. Biedzynski, 119.

51. Already a general through field promotion in the Philippines, Pershing went on to command U.S. forces in Europe in World War I. Biedzynski, 17 (touting McIntyre); "May Be a Brigadier," *Washington Post,* 23 May 1903, 4; Karnow, 194.

52. "Popular Official Promoted," *Washington Post,* 6 July 1912, 6.

53. Edwards became commander of Fort Russell, Wyoming. "To Succeed Gen. Edwards"; *National,* vol. 32, 334; *Who Was Who,* vol. 2, 361; "Gen. M'Intyre."

54. Classmate Charles Walcutt served as McIntyre's right-hand man for twelve years. Biedzynski, 17.

55. Biedzynski, 111, 127–131.

56. Biedzynski, 2; records of the Office of Preservation, Architecture, and Construction, Executive Office of the President; "Bureau of Insular Affairs,"

Washington Post, 26 July 1902, 4 (clerical figures). The structure that housed the agency is now known as the Old Executive Office Building.

57. Letter to McIntyre, 3 March 1913, quoted in Biedzynski, 97.

58. Karnow, 243; Biedzynski, 4.

59. General Services, 4; Clark, 59; Hahn, 152 (Philippine figures).

60. He was replaced by Wilson with Francis B. Harrison, a New York congressman more receptive to Philippine independence. Hahn, 150–151. Forbes's pique made him one of McIntyre's rare denigrators. He called the general "one of those weather vanes of mediocre ability and poor character ... more or less a wire puller." Quoted in Biedzynski, 157.

61. The hapless governor was E. Montgomery Reily, 1921–23. Clark, 59, 74; Morales Carrión, 205–206; Murray, 22, 336–339.

62. Biedzynski, 126, 149, 163–164, 168–169, 170–173, 350, 355; chap. 8 of this book.

63. Biedzynski, 209–210; "Gen. M'Intyre." On MacArthur's exploits in World War I, see Karnow, 260–261.

64. The West Point buddies both had served in the Philippines war, McIntyre as a conciliator and March as the grisly slayer of the fabled nationalist general Gregorio del Pilar. Biedzynski, 212–213; *Who Was Who,* vol. 2, 361; "Gen. M'Intyre"; Karnow, 158–159.

65. Biedzynski, 215.

66. McIntyre had been on leave from the insular bureau from July 1918 to the end of 1919. *Who Was Who,* vol. 2, 361.

67. Photograph, *National,* vol. 32, 334.

68. O'Neill, 34–35; Lewis, *Virgin Islands,* 351; Stuart, 294.

69. Biedzynski, 149.

70. Haiti was occupied from 1915 to 1930, and the Dominican Republic from 1916 to 1924. Pratt, 141–149, 150–152, 315.

71. Biedzynski, 223, 353; "Gen. M'Intyre."

72. Karnow, 244.

73. President of the Philippine Senate at the time, Quezon served as president of the island commonwealth from 1935 to 1944. "Filipino Leaders Back M'Intyre for Governor," *Washington Post,* 11 September 1927, 12.

74. The governorship opened up with the passing of Leonard Wood, Harrison's successor. Stimson thereafter left Manila to become President Herbert Hoover's secretary of state. Hahn, 166; "Filipino Leaders Back M'Intyre for Governor," *Washington Post,* 11 September 1927, 12; Biedzynski, 4.

75. Biedzynski, 225.

76. Clark, 106–120; Morales Carrión, 209.

77. Those three export crops dominated the island economy. From an article in *The Nation* magazine, quoted in Clark, 109. Muñoz Marín, son of Luis Muñoz Rivera, was to become the leading figure in Puerto Rican politics during four terms as governor from 1948 to 1964.

78. Morales Carrión, 209.

79. Biedzynski, 265–266.

80. Biedzynski, 120, 265.
81. Biedzynski, 301.
82. A member of the Senate insular committee, Harding had fought the Jones bill. He warned that promising independence threatened "national disgrace" by releasing Filipinos "to walk alone when they had not been taught fully to creep." Karnow, 249 (quotation); Pratt, *Colonial Experiment,* 315–316; Biedzynski, 223.
83. The president twice rejected formal entreaties from Puerto Ricans (one a commission that included Governor Towner) seeking greater participation in their affairs. Clark, 100–102.
84. The lame-duck president's 1933 veto was promptly overridden by Congress. Karnow, 254. On his Virgin Islands censure, see O'Neill, 49–50; Pratt, *Colonial Experiment,* 285–286.
85. As pacifier, McIntyre drew thankless assignments such as receiving a delegation of Filipino legislators who came to Washington in 1922 with a futile demand for complete and immediate independence. Untitled photograph, *Washington Post,* 14 June 1922, 19.
86. He retired in January 1929, succeeded by Brigadier General Francis Le Jau Parker. Biedzynski, 306; *Who Was Who,* vol. 2, 361; "Gen. M'Intyre."
87. Biedzynski, 3.
88. Biedzynski, 315.
89. *National,* vol. 32, 334.
90. *Who Was Who,* vol. 2, 361; *National,* vol. 32, 334.
91. Civilianizing the task had been proposed as early as 1927. Pomeroy, "Colonial Office," 527.
92. McIntyre, 303. See also Biedzynski, 336.
93. Funeral notice, *Washington Post,* 4 August 1935, 6; Biedzynski, 335.
94. Biedzynski, 169.
95. "Gen. McIntyre Returns from Daughter's Rites," *Washington Post,* 31 January 1933, 5.
96. James had risen to colonel at the time of his father's passing. Obituary, 740.
97. Biedzynski, 335.
98. Biedzynski, 3, 315.
99. Biedzynski, 336; *Who Was Who,* vol. 2, 361; obituary, 740.
100. *National,* vol. 32, 334.
101. Biedzynski, 340.
102. He departed 16 February 1944, and was buried at Arlington National Cemetery. Biedzynski, 340; *Who Was Who,* vol. 2, 361; "Gen. M'Intyre"; obituary, 740.
103. The bureau lost Puerto Rico to a newly-created division of the Interior Department in 1934, and the Philippines five years later. President Franklin D. Roosevelt called the reorganization "a functional transfer of obvious desirability." Pomeroy, "Colonial Office," 529 (quotation); Pratt, *Colonial,* 155; General Services, 1, 2, 4; Van Cleve, 8–9.

10. Theodore Roosevelt, Jr.

1. Roosevelt, *Colonial,* 100, 122–123; Roosevelt, *Day,* 230, 243.
2. Early in his political career, as president of the city's board of police commissioners in 1894–96, the senior Roosevelt had instituted nighttime inspection "rambles." Collier, 94–95.
3. He was born 13 September 1887 in Oyster Bay, New York, the first child of Theodore Roosevelt and his second wife, Edith Kermit Carow. Garraty and Carnes, vol. 18, 835; Collier, 77–78.
4. Collier, 77–78; Loosbrock, 88–89.
5. The junior Roosevelt enrolled at Groton, northwest of Boston, in 1900 as he turned thirteen years of age. Collier, 78; Renehan, 12, 67.
6. Letter to Mrs. Ellen L. Gray, 31 March 1897, Roosevelt Papers; Loosbrock, 88.
7. Collier, 85; Loosbrock, 88.
8. The influential nature writer and conservationist had camped with the elder Roosevelt in the Yellowstone region of the Rocky Mountains. Renehan, 73.
9. Collier, 124; Renehan, 73.
10. The president had become attracted to jujutsu through friend and Japanese cultural connoisseur William Sturgis Bigelow. Roosevelt set up in the White House a "Judo Room," and shared literature on the art with his son. Benfey, 66–67, 239, 245.
11. Quoted in Jeffers, 19.
12. Collier, 78, 124, 127.
13. Collier, 124.
14. Collier, 116, 124.
15. The president's son earned a degree at Harvard in 1905–08, under the constant scrutiny of newspaper reporters. To help make amends for the askew nose, Ted's crossed eye was corrected at the same time. Collier, 22, 140–141. The one-hundred-twenty-six-pound footballer, also nursing a broken ankle and two broken ribs, gave up the sport after his freshman season. Pearlman, 69.
16. Five dollars of his seven dollars in weekly wages from the Hartford Carpet Company in Thompsonville were consumed by room and board. Collier, 161–162; Loosbrock, 89.
17. Roosevelt, *Day,* 35; Collier, 162–163; Renehan, 118.
18. Collier, 22, 417.
19. Jeffers, photographs following 176; Roosevelt, *Day,* 263, 281.
20. Loosbrock, 90.
21. The Philadelphia brokerage in which he became a partner, Montgomery, Clothier & Tyler, had a family tie: Tyler was a cousin of his mother. Renehan, 66; Loosbrock, 90; Collier, 164, 183.
22. Grace was born in 1911, followed by Theodore III in 1914, Cornelius in 1915, and Quentin in 1919. Collier, 163, 181.
23. By 1915, Ted was earning the then-opulent sum of one hundred fifty thousand dollars a year. Snyder, 96.
24. The former president sought unsuccessfully to wrest the Republican nomination from William Howard Taft, before running under the banner of his own Progressive party in the 1912 election won by Democrat Woodrow Wilson. Collier, 164, 183, 186; Loosbrock, 90.
25. He had been dissuaded by his father, who felt

that most career officers suffered thwarted ambitions. Loosbrock, 88; Collier, 140.

26. The Business Men's Camp supplemented one which the army was conducting for college students. Jeffers, 84–85; Collier, 183–184; Loosbrock, 90–91; Renehan, 107–109.

27. Wife Eleanor, for her part, assembled a Women's Battalion that marched in a Preparedness Parade the following year in New York City sporting white uniforms and carrying symbolic lanterns. Collier, 186; Renehan, 117–119.

28. Roosevelt's request fell on receptive ears. He and Pershing had served together in Cuba, then as president he had promoted Pershing in 1906 from captain to brigadier general over 862 officers more senior. Collier, 197; Loosbrock, 91; Renehan, 131–132.

29. Collier, 198, 207, 225; Loosbrock, 92.

30. The three Roosevelt children were left with Eleanor's mother. The townhouse in Paris belonged to an aunt. Collier, 197, 210; Loosbrock, 91; Renehan, 152, 177.

31. Collier, 211; Renehan, 136.

32. Roosevelt was awarded the Silver Star, Croix de Guerre, Distinguished Service Cross, and Distinguished Service Medal. Garraty and Carnes, vol. 18, 835; Collier, 225, 231, 233, 239; Snyder, 96; Loosbrock, 92.

33. Letter of 11 November 1918, quoted in Roosevelt, *Day*, 112.

34. Collier, 197; Roosevelt, *Day*, 52.

35. Roosevelt, *Day*, 118

36. The former president passed away 6 January 1919. Collier, 243; Renehan, 222.

37. Another leading participant was Colonel William J. Donovan, whose undercover Office of Strategic Services during the subsequent world war was the progenitor of the country's intelligence community. Collier, 258; Jeffers, 123–126; Garraty and Carnes, vol. 18, 835; Loosbrock, 92.

38. Letter of 27 October 1918, quoted in Collier, 240.

39. Roosevelt, *Day*, 35.

40. Collier, 197.

41. Collier, 259; Snyder, 97.

42. Collier, 278; Roosevelt, *Day*, 45, 279.

43. The assessment of Archie's daughter Nancy Roosevelt Jackson, quoted in Collier, 278.

44. Collier, 259.

45. Collier, 278; Snyder, 97; Jeffers, 129–130; Garraty and Carnes, vol. 18, 835.

46. Theodore, Jr., and Franklin were fifth cousins. Collier, 258–260 (quotation, 260); Snyder, 97, 99; Burns, 24, 76. The target of Ted's vendetta, ironically, had been altogether complimentary of him and Archie during the war. He met them on an inspection visit to France as assistant secretary of the navy and praised their "really splendid records." Loosbrock, 92.

47. Roosevelt, *Day*, 59–60, 98, 262, 405.

48. Quoted in Roosevelt, *Day*, 371.

49. Roosevelt, *Day*, 122. Roosevelt ultimately would write four books on his own, co-author three others, and compile two collections of poetry.

50. The navy post was to remain in the Roosevelt family at the departure of Theodore, Jr. He was succeeded by a cousin, Teddy Robinson, son of his aunt Corrine Roosevelt Robinson. Collier, 296.

51. Collier, 279–280.

52. Letter to Philip Bancroft, 10 April 1923, quoted in Pearlman, 213. See also Pearlman, 212.

53. Collier, 281; Snyder, 97.

54. The elder Roosevelt served as governor in the two years before elected vice president in 1900. Collier, 285.

55. The junior Roosevelt before World War I had been a director of Sinclair Oil Company, which his banking firm had helped to finance. He had procured Archie his job there in 1919 through friendship with oilman Harry F. Sinclair. The scandal brought the resignation of Navy Secretary Edwin Denby and the imprisonment of Fall and Sinclair. Collier, 286–289, 295; Roosevelt, *Day*, 148; Snyder, 97–98.

56. The leading Republican candidate who withdrew was Assembly Speaker H. Edward Machold. During one stretch, Roosevelt gave two hundred speeches in eighteen days. Collier, 296–297, 299; Roosevelt, *Day*, 164; Snyder, 98.

57. Letter to Frank W. Buxton, 10 March 1938, Roosevelt Papers; Snyder, 98.

58. The former First Lady recanted in 1961: "In the thick of political fights one always feels that all methods of campaigning are honest and fair, but I do think this was a rough stunt and I never blamed my cousin when he retaliated in later campaigns against my husband." Roosevelt, *Autobiography*, 143. See also Collier, 299; Jeffers, 145–148; Snyder, 97–98.

59. The unsuccessful Republican candidate carried all of the state's sixty-two counties except those of New York City and Albany. Collier, 300; Roosevelt, *Day*, 165; Burns, 94–95.

60. The nearly year-long outing also yielded two thousand other specimens of mammals, reptiles, and birds. Collier, 302, 306–307. His father had gone big-game hunting in Africa after leaving the presidency in 1909. Pakenham, 157–159, 162–163.

61. *East of the Sun and West of the Moon* appeared in 1926, *Rank and File* in 1928, and *All in the Family* in 1929. Collier, 322; Roosevelt, *Day*, 326.

62. The expedition helped scientists to identify the panda as a relative of the raccoon. Kermit left the trip early, but Ted staggered into Saigon at the end a wasted figure who had lost forty-two pounds. Roosevelt, *Day*, 207–225; Collier, 324–326.

63. Pearlman, 193–194.

64. Letter to John Macrae, 10 September 1930, Roosevelt Papers.

65. Roosevelt also had traveled the country in the 1928 election campaign attacking Hoover's opponent, his old nemesis Al Smith. Collier, 284, 323.

66. Collier, 325.

67. The governorship was tendered in May 1929, his term to begin when Roosevelt returned from Indochina and regained health. Collier, 325; Roosevelt, *Day*, 209.

68. Letter to wife, quoted, undated, in Collier, 325.

69. Roosevelt, *Day*, 225.
70. The address was given by paragraphs alternately in English and Spanish, as in the past. But rather than the Spanish version being read by a translator, Roosevelt delivered both. Roosevelt, inaugural address, 7 October 1929, Roosevelt Papers; Roosevelt, *Day*, 227; Collier, 326; Jeffers, 179.
71. "Much personal sentiment," in the English version. President Roosevelt had visited the island in 1906. Roosevelt, inaugural address, 7 October 1929, Roosevelt Papers; Stuart, 353–354.
72. Quoted in Collier, 326.
73. Roosevelt, inaugural address, 7 October 1929, Roosevelt Papers.
74. Roosevelt, *Day*, 229.
75. Roosevelt, *Colonial*, 122–123; Roosevelt, *Day*, 229–230.
76. Roosevelt, *Day*, 229–230.
77. Muñoz Marín, who would come to dominate island politics during four terms as governor from 1948 to 1964, was then a young man of thirty-three years. Letter, 8 April 1931, Roosevelt Papers.
78. He had undertaken his first six weeks of inspections. Roosevelt, *Day*, 231.
79. *New York Herald-Tribune*, "This Week" magazine, 8 December 1929; typewritten manuscript, Roosevelt Papers; quoted in Roosevelt, *Day*, 231–232.
80. Newspapers also carried four hundred news reports on conditions in Puerto Rico. Governor's annual message, 9 February 1931, Roosevelt Papers; Roosevelt, *Day*, 231–232; Collier, 331.
81. The study which the president requested by the American Child Health Association confirmed Roosevelt's findings. Congress appropriated the desired two million dollars for farm loans and one million dollars for roads. Jeffers, 181; Roosevelt, *Day*, 232. The governor thereafter repaired frequently to Washington seeking relief. "I arrive there, booted and spurred like Paul Revere," he wrote to a friend, "trying to 'spread the alarm through every Middlesex village and farm' in Congress." Letter to Franklin D'Olier, 3 April 1930, Roosevelt Papers.
82. Collier, 331; Roosevelt, *Day*, 237 (quotation); Jeffers, 183.
83. Fair wages, at a time when most Puerto Rican families were earning $150 to $200 a year, meant $1 a day. Roosevelt, *Day*, 237–239; Collier, 331.
84. Roosevelt's Bureau of Commerce and Industry foreshadowed the later "Operation Bootstrap." In keeping with the independent Republican's affinity toward organized labor, he also created a Department of Labor. Roosevelt, *Colonial*, 121; Roosevelt, *Day*, 129, 237; Snyder, 99; Stuart, 40–41.
85. Roosevelt, *Colonial*, 121; Roosevelt, *Day*, 233; Snyder, 99.
86. Roosevelt, *Day*, 234–235 (including quotation); Snyder, 99.
87. Post-invasion proclamation, 28 July 1898, Miles, *Serving*, 301–302. See also chap. 5 of this book.
88. The credo of Governor E. Montgomery Reily, 1921–23. Clark, 52–53 (quotation), 74, 141; chap. 9 of this book.

89. Roosevelt, *Colonial*, 85.
90. "As Americans, add your culture to that of America," he said at his inauguration, "but do not lose that which you have inherited." Roosevelt, inaugural address, 7 October 1929, Roosevelt Papers.
91. Roosevelt, *Colonial*, 119.
92. Roosevelt, *Day*, 236.
93. Press announcement, 12 March 1930, Roosevelt Papers; untitled Spanish poem, 16 October 1930, Roosevelt Papers. Like his siblings, young Ted memorized poetry for recitation, including delivering "The Ballad of East and West" for a visit by its author, Rudyard Kipling. Collier, 78.
94. Sons Teddy and Cornelius were boarding at the Roosevelt family training ground, Groton School. The lizard was discovered on the island of Caja de Muertos off Puerto Rico's south coast. Roosevelt, *Day*, 246.
95. Roosevelt, *Day*, 243.
96. Rather than attend an American school in San Juan, Quentin went to a military boarding school in Rio Piedras with American teachers and Puerto Rican pupils, coming home on weekends. The youngster soon was spouting Spanish like a native. Roosevelt, *Day*, 245.
97. Jeffers, 183.
98. Roosevelt, *Colonial*, 100, 119.
99. Roosevelt, *Day*, 230.
100. Roosevelt, *Day*, 230.
101. Roosevelt, *Colonial*, 119–120.
102. Roosevelt, *Colonial*, 120.
103. Roosevelt had confused *soltero* (bachelor) with *solitaria* (tapeworm). The victim of the governor's slip was Brigadier General Francis Le Jau Parker, chief of the War Department's Bureau of Insular Affairs. Roosevelt, *Colonial*, 120; Roosevelt, *Day*, 230.
104. Quoted in Pakenham, 11.
105. Roosevelt, *Day*, 230. Roosevelt adopted the nickname to sign a Spanish poem he had written. Untitled poem, 16 October 1930, Roosevelt Papers.
106. Jeffers, 180.
107. Letter to John T. McCutcheon, 27 October 1929, Roosevelt Papers.
108. Governor's annual report, 14 September, 1931, 28, Roosevelt Papers; Jeffers, 185.
109. Jeffers, 183.
110. Jeffers, 186; Collier, 331; Roosevelt, *Day*, 250. Despite the hard times, Roosevelt managed to balance the government's budget in 1931 for the first time in seventeen years. Roosevelt, *Colonial*, 121; Roosevelt, *Day*, 250.
111. Letter of 14 November 1931, Roosevelt Papers. Gruening, then editor of a newspaper in Portland, Oregon, was appointed in 1934 the first director of the Department of the Interior's territorial office. He later served Alaska as governor and senator. Stuart, 396 n. 42. Puerto Ricans had to wait twenty more years to vote on their constitutional status, at a plebiscite in 1951.
112. Roosevelt, *Colonial*, 116–117.
113. Roosevelt, *Colonial*, 117. Puerto Rico became an autonomous commonwealth in 1952.

114. *Baltimore Sun*, quoted, undated, in Collier, 331. See also Roosevelt, *Day*, 234.
115. Letter to the Right Reverend Thomas Nicholson, 13 March 1930, Roosevelt Papers. The citation comes from 1 Cor. 16:9.
116. Roosevelt may have tipped Hoover's hand by making it known that he was considering resigning the Puerto Rican governorship — a prominent defection from his administration that the beleaguered president could ill afford. Collier, 331.
117. Collier, 332; Roosevelt, *Day*, 277, 279, 280–281; Garraty and Carnes, vol. 18, 835.
118. "Men who have had many years in the islands," commented the *New York Times*, "say no other governor has achieved such quick popularity." Quoted, undated, in Collier, 333.
119. Quoted, undated, in Roosevelt, *Day*, 278; Collier, 332.
120. Collier, 333. The jibe at Franklin came in a letter to Ernest H. Gruening, 29 March 1931, Roosevelt Papers. He told another that Franklin's "official garments are pretty well soaked with Tammany filth." Letter to Nicholas Murray Butler, 24 October 1930, Roosevelt Papers.
121. Quoted in Collier, 337.
122. Collier, 337. He was succeeded by Frank Murphy, governor of Michigan and future Supreme Court justice.
123. Letter of 19 September 1932, quoted in Collier, 334–335.
124. Letter of 14 October 1932, quoted in Collier, 334–335.
125. Roosevelt, *Day*, 371; Jeffers, 201–203; Collier, 389.
126. Letter to Mr. and Mrs. Henry Beston, 25 September 1935, Roosevelt Papers; Snyder, 99.
127. Roosevelt, *Day*, 397; Collier, 393.
128. Even President Roosevelt, however, near the end of his tenure may have begun to harbor doubts about retaining the Philippines. Traxel, 315.
129. Roosevelt, *Colonial*, 83.
130. Roosevelt, *Colonial*, 195–196.
131. Roosevelt, *Colonial*, 197–198. In his introduction, journalist Walter Lippmann called the book "a confession that the imperialistic dream of 1898 has proved to be unrealizable, that the management of an empire by a democracy like the American democracy is impossible" (xiii). See also Renehan, 227.
132. In his navy post, Roosevelt reprimanded an editor of the naval academy yearbook for publishing the photograph of the lone Jewish graduating cadet edged with perforations to facilitate its removal. Collier, 281.
133. "Americanism," retorted Roosevelt in rebuffing the Klan's overtures, "never goes masked." Collier, 286 (quotation); Pearlman, 199–200.
134. Pearlman, 199; Collier, 281.
135. Renehan, 227; Roosevelt, *Day*, 369; Collier, 389.
136. Collier, 389.
137. Collier, 387–388 (quotation, 387); Snyder, 100.
138. The architect was William McMillan, husband of daughter Grace. Collier, 322–323, 391; Jeffers, 207–208; Roosevelt, *Day*, 405.
139. Collier, 391–392. Another writer friend was novelist Edith Wharton, who complimented the prose in one of his Philippine gubernatorial reports, "which I admire as a woman of letters." Roosevelt, *Day*, 303.
140. Collier, 277–278.
141. Letter to sister Alice containing instructions for Kermit, 11 July 1924, quoted in Collier, 305.
142. Letter to Edward Sanford Martin, 27 April 1931, Roosevelt Papers. See also Roosevelt, *Day*, 164; Collier, 296–297.
143. Roosevelt, *Day*, 52.
144. Letter to G. A. Cleveland, 12 November 1917, Roosevelt Papers; Snyder, 95. At another time, he despaired: "I will always be known as the son of Theodore Roosevelt, and never as a person who means only himself." Quoted, source unidentified, in Jeffers, 174.
145. Collier, 392–393; Snyder, 100.
146. Letter, 1940, quoted in Roosevelt, *Day*, 418. See also Snyder, 100.
147. Snyder, 101; Pearlman, 246–248; Garraty and Carnes, vol. 18, 835.
148. As an aide to Pershing, Marshall had written to Roosevelt: "Your record as a fighting man [was] one of the most remarkable in the AEF [American Expeditionary Force]. ... among the finest examples of leadership, courage, and fortitude that came to my attention during the war." Letter, about 1920, quoted in Loosbrock, 92, and Pearlman, 71.
149. His unit was the Twenty-sixth Infantry Regiment. Fort Devens lay just a few miles south of the Groton School where Roosevelt had boarded in boyhood. Collier, 399; Snyder, 101; Renehan, 228.
150. Letter to Alexander Woollcott, quoted, undated, in Collier, 399.
151. Snyder, 101; Collier, 401.
152. The three family members were together in England briefly, although there was little contact with Eleanor in Salisbury, before father and son sailed to North Africa. Collier, 405; Renehan, 233–234.
153. The army's top brass believed a general belonged at his command post, not at the front lines. Collier, 418; Roosevelt, *Day*, 442.
154. The general reportedly was dubious about the "Rough Rider" name on the jeep, lest it seem to trade on his father's fame, but didn't wish to offend his driver who had painted it to please his commander. Roosevelt, *Day*, 448; Collier, photograph following 288.
155. Letter to a Major Philipps, 1 June 1922, Roosevelt Papers; quoted in Pearlman, 176.
156. Collier, 418. There were heroics, too. Roosevelt parleyed the surrender of the city of Oran in Algeria through sheer persuasion, and averted impending defeat at El Guettar by rallying his demoralized troops. Collier, 406–407; Roosevelt, *Day*, 440; Snyder, 101–102.
157. Roosevelt was convinced that the impetus underlying his demotion was Patton's chagrin at having indecorously taken Roosevelt's place in a fox-

hole during a German air raid in North Africa. Collier, 418–419. In any event, the high command's ire appears to have been directed chiefly at Roosevelt's superior, Major General Terry Allen. Snyder, 102 (including Bradley quotation).
158. Letter, quoted in Collier, 419.
159. Collier, 407, 420; Renehan, 234.
160. Collier, 422; Snyder, 102 (including Bradley quotation).
161. In a letter to his wife on the day before the invasion, he wrote: "It steadies the young men to know that I am with them, to see me plodding along with my cane." Quoted in Roosevelt, *Day,* 454. See also Jeffers, 3–6, 241–252; Renehan, 236–238; Collier, 422; Garraty and Carnes, vol. 18, 836 (quotation). Quentin, a captain who was landed several miles away, also survived the invasion unscathed. The two Roosevelts are believed to have been the only father and son participating together in the assault. Renehan, 238; Collier, 422.
162. Collier, 423.
163. Collier, 423.
164. He expired 12 July 1944. Renehan, 239; Garraty and Carnes, vol. 18, 835–836; Collier, 424.
165. Collier, 422.
166. Quoted in Snyder, 103.
167. Collier, 422, 424; Snyder, 103; Renehan, 239.
168. Quoted in Collier, 424.
169. He once vouchsafed a personal credo to students graduating from high school in Puerto Rico: "Work hard, play hard, stand for what you believe to be right, regardless of criticism or abuse." Address, June 1930, Roosevelt Papers. See also Roosevelt, *Day,* 45.
170. Letter, 5 June 1944, quoted in Jeffers, 3. Eleanor survived her husband sixteen years, publishing in 1959 her reminiscences. She passed away the following year at age seventy-one. The Old Orchard home is now part of the Sagamore Hill National Historic Site. Collier, 471–472; Renehan, 243.

11. Paul M. Pearson

1. He was born 22 October 1871. Godfrey, 3; *Who Was Who,* vol. 1, 950. Gillespie lies nine miles west of Litchfield.
2. The family may have settled initially near Coffeyville in Kansas's southeastern corner. "Dr. Paul Pearson"; Godfrey, 3.
3. Godfrey, 3, photograph opposite 3 (house); "Dr. Paul Pearson."
4. Godfrey, 3.
5. The middle name — Martin — was shared with his father. Godfrey, 3; *Who Was Who,* vol. 1, 950.
6. Godfrey, 3, 11.
7. Godfrey, 3; *Who Was Who,* vol. 1, 950.
8. The university, its distinguished alumnus Pearson wrote later, "was hardly the equivalent of a preparatory school of today." Quoted in Godfrey, 4.
9. His fraternity was Delta Tau Delta. Godfrey, 4–5.
10. Godfrey, photographs facing 6, 30, 50, 64, 273, 310; "Dr. Paul Pearson" (photograph).
11. She was born in April 1874. She lost her mother nine months later and was raised by a grandmother and nurse until, in her third year, her father remarried. Godfrey, 4, 36, photographs facing 64, 65, 106, 122, 226, 269.
12. Godfrey, 4; *Who Was Who,* vol. 1, 950.
13. Godfrey, 4; "Dr. Paul Pearson"; *Who Was Who,* vol. 1, 950.
14. Godfrey, 4.
15. Family chronology by Pearson, 1943, quoted in Godfrey, 4.
16. "Dr. Paul Pearson."
17. Letter to wife, 1899, quoted in Godfrey, 60–61.
18. "Dr. Paul Pearson"; Godfrey, 4.
19. Godfrey, 4.
20. Editor's introduction, *The Speaker,* December 1905, quoted in Godfrey, 149.
21. Godfrey, 4.
22. Godfrey, 5; *Who Was Who,* vol. 1, 950.
23. Godfrey, 43.
24. Godfrey, 5.
25. Pearson studied at Northwestern in 1893–94. Godfrey, 5.
26. Godfrey, 5; *Who Was Who,* vol. 1, 950.
27. Godfrey, 5.
28. "'As surely as the vine / Grew 'round the stump,'" the poem rhapsodizes, "she loved me — that old sweetheart of mine." Riley, 28–29; Godfrey, 5.
29. Letter, quoted, undated, in Godfrey, 5.
30. They were wed 11 June 1896. Godfrey, 6; *Who Was Who,* vol. 1, 950.
31. The "Mother Chautauqua" was organized in 1874 by Methodist bishop John H. Vincent. The figures for Chautauqua assemblies and attendees refer to 1906 and 1924, respectively. Godfrey, 8–12, 323.
32. John T. Flynn, "This Quaker Professor Entertains Millions of People," *American Magazine,* September 1926, 58–59, quoted in Godfrey, 323.
33. Godfrey, 322.
34. Quoted in Godfrey, 22.
35. He made his Chautauqua debut at Palmer Lake, Colo. Godfrey, 5.
36. The new husband and wife attended Chautauqua sessions at Waseka, Minn., and Winona Lake, Ind. Godfrey, 6.
37. Godfrey, 7.
38. Godfrey, 7, 23, 27, 257.
39. The club comprised students and faculty members. Godfrey, 6–7, 11–12, 19.
40. The movement came in 1826 from England to New England, where its early speakers included Ralph Waldo Emerson, Henry David Thoreau, Oliver Wendell Holmes, James Russell Lowell, and Horace Greeley. From the Lyceum movement is said to have sprung the public library system. Godfrey, 31–33.
41. *Who's Who in the Lyceum* was written by Paul

Pearson, financed by his brother (and nominal co-author) Drew, and published privately by them in Philadelphia in 1905. Godfrey, 31.

42. He headed the International Lyceum Association in 1905. Godfrey, 147, 165.

43. Godfrey, 7, 248.

44. Godfrey, 33.

45. Godfrey, 83.

46. Godfrey, 39, 90, 123, 280, 283.

47. Godfrey, 91–93, 113.

48. Letter to wife, 23 August 1905, quoted in Godfrey, 146.

49. Godfrey, 62, 92, 217.

50. Godfrey, 102.

51. Godfrey, 9, 38, 43–44.

52. Editorial, *Talent,* July 1905, quoted in Godfrey, 111.

53. Letter, quoted, undated, in Godfrey, 46.

54. Godfrey, 46–49.

55. Godfrey, 44–46.

56. Letter, quoted, undated, in Godfrey, 52.

57. Andrew Russell was born in 1897 and Leon Morris in 1899. *Who Was Who,* vol. 1, 950; *Current Biography* (1941), 658–659; Godfrey, 7, 23.

58. Godfrey, 133.

59. Barbara Wolfe was born in 1910 and Ellen Cameron in 1913. *Who Was Who,* vol. 1, 950; Godfrey, 213–214, 219, 287.

60. Godfrey, 40, 71, 103, 229.

61. Godfrey, 335.

62. Letter, late 1902 or early 1903, quoted in Godfrey, 77.

63. Godfrey, preface.

64. The letters were sprinkled with phrases of fractured German, presumably drawn from midwestern German immigrants whom Pearson held in high regard. Godfrey, 17, 88, 123.

65. Godfrey, 2, 229.

66. The portrayals appear in letters to his wife, 22 August 1899, late 1902, 1903, quoted in Godfrey, 19, 78, 128, respectively.

67. Letter to wife, 6 August 1911, quoted in Godfrey, 256.

68. Godfrey, 234.

69. Godfrey, 141.

70. Godfrey, 256.

71. Letter, 18 August 1910, quoted in Godfrey, 240. See also 161, 251.

72. Godfrey, 6.

73. She burned designs into wood with a heated steel lancet, most of her output being replicas of the Harvard seal. Godfrey, 76–78, photograph opposite 107, 335.

74. Godfrey, 97, 292.

75. "It is very embarrassing," he once lamented to his wife, "for I have not studied at Harvard or [Johns] Hopkins or anything of that kind...." Letter, June 1900, quoted in Godfrey, 36. See also 40.

76. Godfrey, 58–60.

77. Godfrey, 62–67; *Who Was Who,* vol. 1, 950.

78. Godfrey, 65, 67.

79. Godfrey, 73. He became Dr. Pearson in 1908 when conferred an honorary doctorate by Baker University as "an interpreter of literature." Godfrey,

197. Organizing the new department was to be followed in 1910 by Pearson's founding of the Speech Association of the Eastern States, a professional group now known as the Eastern Communications Association. Godfrey, 315.

80. The renegades — most, like Pearson, products of the Northwestern school of oratory — opposed the formalism espoused by the Brahmins of rhetoric in Boston. Godfrey, 320.

81. Godfrey, 54, 55, 66, 68, 253.

82. Letter to wife, 1904, quoted in Godfrey, 129.

83. Godfrey, 129; *Who Was Who,* vol. 1, 950.

84. Godfrey, 2, 78.

85. Godfrey, 107; *Who Was Who,* vol. 1, 950.

86. Letter to wife, late 1903, quoted in Godfrey, 107.

87. Godfrey, 110, 116.

88. The magazine, like his Lyceum book, was published in Philadelphia by the Pearson brothers. Its contents were valued enough to have been reissued twice in bound volumes — first during his lifetime in 1925 (by the New York publisher Noble & Noble) and again in 1972 (by Books for Libraries Press of Freeport, N.Y.). Godfrey, 148, 150; *Who Was Who,* vol. 1, 950.

89. *Talent* combined with *Lyceumite,* assuming the joint titles, with offices in Chicago. Godfrey, 182–184.

90. *The Humorous Speaker, a Book of Humorous Selections for Reading and Speaking* (New York: Hinds, Noble & Eldridge, 1909). The book was reissued in 1971 by Books for Libraries Press of Freeport, N.Y.

91. The book was published in 1912 by Hinds, Noble & Eldridge of New York, with co-author Philip M. Hicks. The revised edition was issued in 1930 by Noble & Noble, New York. *Who Was Who,* vol. 1, 950.

92. The 1907 graduate of Swarthmore was jailed ten years later for brandishing a banner advocating female franchise in front of the White House. She later became a national organizer of the forerunner of the National Women's Party. Godfrey, 249–250.

93. Valedictorian of the 1929 graduating class, Michener acted as leading man opposite an unspecified Pearson daughter, presumably Barbara. He rated himself "a frightfully bad actor." Kunitz, 665; Michener, "About the Author" (quotation).

94. Godfrey, 149, 320, 334.

95. Godfrey, 288.

96. Godfrey, 286, 288, 308.

97. Godfrey, 286; *Who Was Who,* vol. 1, 950.

98. Godfrey, 288, 320.

99. Godfrey, 318, 320; "Dr. Paul Pearson."

100. Bryan, thrice nominee for president, at the time was Woodrow Wilson's secretary of state. Clark was Speaker of the House of Representatives. Godfrey, 288, 297, 317.

101. Godfrey, 322, photographs opposite 311, 319, 322.

102. Letter to wife, 31 December 1903, quoted in Godfrey, 115.

103. Godfrey, photograph opposite 319.

104. Pearson also inaugurated for children a

Notes — Chapter 11

Junior Chautauqua program. Godfrey, 291, 301, 313, 320.
105. Godfrey, 147, 309, 313.
106. Letter, 28 July 1914, quoted in Godfrey, 309.
107. Godfrey, 286, 288, 308.
108. Godfrey, 325, 327.
109. Godfrey, 325.
110. Pearson was to owe money to creditors for the rest of his life. Godfrey, 325–326.
111. Letter, 1 April 1930, reproduced in Godfrey, 327.
112. Pearson served as an emeritus-like "honorary lecturer" from 1925 until departing the college in 1930, according to Swarthmore records.
113. He worked in West Virginia from May to November 1930. Godfrey, 332.
114. Letter, 17 August 1910, quoted in Godfrey, 240. See also letter nine days earlier, 233.
115. He was joined by other Chautauqua managers, the Young Men's Christian Association, and a theater chain. Godfrey, 321.
116. Chautauqua branched out to Canada's maritime provinces and Nova Scotia. Godfrey, 321.
117. Godfrey, 322.
118. On his visit to Berlin, then closed to civilians, Pearson practiced a bit of foreign intrigue, posing as a Red Cross captain to gain entry. He failed, however, to secure the kaiser's participation in the 1922 conference. Godfrey, 322. Pearson also had headed the Lyceum in 1905.
119. Lewis, *Virgin Islands*, 4–7, 25–27; O'Neill, 18–28.
120. Treaties ratifying the purchase, negotiated in 1867 and 1902, foundered in 1870 and 1903 in the U. S. Senate and Danish parliament, respectively. O'Neill, 34–36.
121. The United States purchased the islands for $25 million, or $290 per acre. Transfer occurred on the eve of entry into the war in April 1917. O'Neill, 37.
122. Lewis, *Virgin Islands*, 51–59; O'Neill, 40–46.
123. The Hoover administration had surveyed the grim conditions in the islands in 1929–30 and pressed remedies upon resistant naval administrators. The dispute pitted the architect of the rescue plan, Herbert D. Brown, director of Hoover's Bureau of Efficiency, against the islands' governor, Captain Waldo Evans. Hoover, by executive order, transferred control from the navy to the Department of the Interior. Lewis, *Virgin Islands*, 68–69; Pratt, *Colonial*, 217.
124. Mr. and Mrs. Roberts recounted the interview with Brown in a letter to Pearson a year later. Letter, 4 January 1932, Pearson Papers. See also letter from Pearson to Brown, in response to "your request for some facts about myself," 14 January 1931, Pearson Papers; Lewis, *Virgin Islands*, 72–73; Pratt, *Colonial*, 217.
125. Although Drew Pearson's three-year marriage to Patterson's daughter, Countess Felicia Gizycka, had ended in divorce in 1928, he remained at the time on friendly terms with his former mother-in-law, publisher of the *Washington Times-Herald*. Stewart and Tebbel, 463–466.
126. Quoted in Godfrey, 333.
127. "Dr. Paul Pearson."
128. Photographs, Pearson Papers; author's observance.
129. Letter to Lawrence N. Cramer (lieutenant governor for St. Croix), 13 January 1932, Pearson Papers; letter from R. B. Stafford and Lucy Gillette (commissioners of public health and public welfare, respectively), 27 November 1932, Pearson Papers; report, 1 May 1935, Pearson Papers; Pratt, *Colonial*, 285; O'Neill, 48; Lewis, *Virgin Islands*, 59.
130. Inaugural address, 18 March 1931, Pearson Papers. On tropical attire, see photographs and letter to Paul Alger (a Swarthmore friend), 27 November 1931, Pearson Papers.
131. Inaugural address, 18 March 1931, Pearson Papers.
132. The population of the islands at the time was about twenty-two thousand. Summary, 10 March 1934, Pearson Papers; Pratt, *Colonial*, 286–287; O'Neill, 48, 51–52; Lewis, *Virgin Islands*, 68–71; Godfrey, 339; "Dr. Paul Pearson."
133. O'Neill, 53; Pratt, *Colonial*, 286–287.
134. Hoover had supervised U.S. relief for civilian victims of World War I. He was accompanied to the Caribbean by Secretary of the Interior Ray Lyman Wilbur. O'Neill, 49–50.
135. The president dourly called into question the nation's fourteen-year-old purchase of the Virgins: "When we paid $25 million for them, we acquired an effective poorhouse, comprising 90 percent of the population.... The people cannot be self-supporting either in living or government without the discovery of new methods and resources. Viewed from every point except remote naval contingencies, it was unfortunate that we ever acquired these islands." Quoted in O'Neill, 49–50.
136. "Dr. Paul Pearson."
137. Letter, no addressee, 14 December 1932, Pearson Papers. On Governor Roosevelt's appeals, see chap. 10 of this book.
138. The governor pursued educational funding from the Carnegie Corporation. Letter to F.P. Keppel, 11 September 1933, Pearson Papers. The school lunch money came from the Golden Rule Foundation. Letter to J.H. Dilliard, 22 December 1931, Pearson Papers.
139. Letter from Franklin D. Roosevelt, dated only 1934, Pearson Papers. The Danish company which dominated sugar production on St. Croix had closed in 1929. O'Neill, 47–48, 53; Pratt, *Colonial*, 285.
140. Lewis, *Virgin Islands*, 70.
141. Report, 1 May 1935, Pearson Papers.
142. The national experiment outlawing liquor lasted from 1919 to 1933. O'Neill, 45.
143. Godfrey, 335.
144. Letter to Sue Yerkes, 28 March 1934, Pearson Papers.
145. Report, 1 May 1935, Pearson Papers.
146. O'Neill, 4–5; Stuart, 205.
147. O'Neill, 59–60.
148. "Dr. Paul Pearson."
149. Godfrey, 335; letter to Boyd J. Brown, 29 March 1932, Pearson Papers.
150. Letter from Franklin D. Roosevelt, dated

only 1934, Pearson Papers; report, 1 May 1935, Pearson Papers; Godfrey, 335.
151. Lewis, *Virgin Islands*, 14, 17–18; O'Neill, 4–5, 7.
152. Edna remained in Swarthmore while daughter Ellen completed her senior year of high school. The incoming governor's interim hostesses in Charlotte Amalie were two nieces. The family was reunited there in June 1931— along with three visiting sorority sisters of Barbara, who was studying drama at Yale University. Godfrey, 333–334.
153. Letter to Paul Alger, 16 July 1931, Pearson Papers; Godfrey, 130.
154. Journal account, 6 October 1933, Pearson Papers; Godfrey, photograph opposite 332.
155. Letter to Paul Alger, 16 July 1931, Pearson Papers.
156. Letter, 8 October 1931, Pearson Papers. The secretary mistakenly classified the islands as semitropical rather than tropical.
157. Lewis, *Virgin Islands*, 51; Stuart, 247–248.
158. Godfrey, 7.
159. Godfrey, 94.
160. Godfrey, 119.
161. Letter to Robert H. Lucas, 10 March 1931, Pearson Papers. Lucas was executive director of the Republican National Committee.
162. Report, 1 May 1935, Pearson Papers. Privately, however, Pearson waxed less than sanguine on the prospects for the islands to govern themselves. "Their people," he opined to the director of the federal territorial office, "are as yet unfitted by education, by franchise, and taxation systems, and by the body of laws under which they have grown up, to participate to any large extent in self-government." Letter to Ernest H. Gruening, December 1934, Pearson Papers.
163. Pearson envisioned "a music group in every school." Letter to George F. Peabody, 24 January 1933, Pearson Papers. The infusion of musical instruments, the governor hoped, might inspire an annual music festival in the territory. Godfrey, 335. Soprano Louise Stallings concertized in the islands in July 1932, at her own expense. Letter to her, 28 November 1932, Pearson Papers. A string quartet visited later. Radio address, 31 January 1934, Pearson Papers.
164. Godfrey, 335; letter to Paul Alger, 16 July 1931, Pearson Papers.
165. Letter from Hoover to Mrs. Everett O. Fisk, 30 November 1932, Pearson Papers.
166. O'Neill, 53.
167. His votes spanned presidential elections from 1892 to 1920. Memorandum, undated, Pearson Papers.
168. Letter to Ray Lyman Wilbur, 19 October 1931, Pearson Papers.
169. Letter from Roosevelt, dated only 1934, Pearson Papers.
170. Mrs. Roosevelt, who had visited Puerto Rico before calling at the Virgin Islands, bestowed Pearson the compliment of describing depression conditions in his domain as "slightly better" than those in his western neighbor. Roosevelt, *Autobiography*,

185. The First Lady also inspected new housing in St. Croix. Photograph, Pearson Papers.
171. Letter to Walter White, 9 March 1934, Pearson Papers.
172. The meeting was said to have been the first of its kind in island history. "The women here are not active in anything," Pearson despaired, "being entirely over-shadowed by the men." Letter to Walter White, 9 March 1934, Pearson Papers.
173. The president visited the Virgin Islands in July 1934 on a Caribbean trip which also included stops at Puerto Rico and the Panama Canal. Letter to George F. Peabody, 28 July 1934, Pearson Papers; photographs, Pearson Papers.
174. Pearson described "a glorious, enthusiastic, spontaneous welcome and a grateful shouting, applauding expression of the joy of the people." Letter to George F. Peabody, 28 July 1934, Pearson Papers.
175. Letter from Roosevelt, dated only 1934, Pearson Papers.
176. Cane cultivation increased between 1931 and 1935 by one-quarter and two sugar factories reopened. Report, 1 May 1935, Pearson Papers.
177. Yields in the U.S. Virgin Islands ran a third or less of those in the wetter British West Indies, and a quarter or less of those under irrigation in Puerto Rico. O'Neill, 54.
178. Seven distilleries were built or rebuilt. The label for bottles of the island government's "Government House" brand of rum had an eminent, if unlikely, designer. President Roosevelt, perhaps as a respite from the burdens of economic depression and imminent war, sketched a design of the white mansion overlooking a blue harbor where a schooner lay at anchor. Report, 1 May 1935, Pearson Papers; O'Neill, 54; Van Cleve, 111 (presidential rum label).
179. The program was hampered by disinterest among many landless laborers and unaffordability of homestead ownership, even at nominal terms. Report, 1 May 1935, Pearson Papers; Lewis, *Virgin Islands*, 82; O'Neill, 51–52.
180. The public corporation employed in 1935 nearly one thousand islanders in a population of twelve thousand, and eventually doubled its roster. Report, 1 May 1935, Pearson Papers; O'Neill, 53–55.
181. Adult education had been introduced, but vocational training had faltered. Report, 1 May 1935, Pearson Papers; Lewis, *Virgin Islands*, 81; O'Neill, 52, 54–55.
182. A cooperative had been established for hand crafts, helping increase sales to visitors six-fold. Report, 1 May 1935, Pearson Papers; Godfrey, 335.
183. Letter to Oscar L. Chapman (assistant secretary of the interior), 2 January 1934, Pearson Papers.
184. O'Neill, 53.
185. Letter to Harold L. Ickes (secretary of the interior), 22 March 1934, Pearson Papers.
186. Among the alienated ex-allies was former Hoover aide Herbert D. Brown. He and Pearson had parted ways over Brown's recommendations on territorial appointments and other matters. "Dr.

Paul Pearson"; background paper, dated only 1935, Pearson Papers.
187. Lewis, *Virgin Islands,* 79; "Dr. Paul Pearson."
188. Pearson's personal bankruptcy, resulting from his Chautauqua venture and declared in 1934, was exploited to discredit his executive competency. Letter to Harold L. Ickes, 28 February 1934, Pearson Papers.
189. Pearson called the investigators' visit to the islands in April 1935 "fire works" ignited by "wild charges." Letter to Harold M. Buckman, 29 April 1935, Pearson Papers.
190. Letter to Boyd J. Brown and Lawrence N. Cramer, 20 January 1934, Pearson Papers.
191. "Dr. Paul Pearson."
192. Letter from Roosevelt, 23 July 1935, Pearson Papers.
193. "Dr. Paul Pearson."
194. Lewis, *Virgin Islands,* 69–70; Godfrey, 338.
195. Letter from Roosevelt, 23 July 1935, Pearson Papers.
196. Letter from Roosevelt, 23 July 1935, Pearson Papers; "Dr. Paul Pearson"; Godfrey, 336.
197. Letter from Roosevelt, 23 July 1935, Pearson Papers.
198. Radiogram, summer 1935, Pearson Papers.
199. Godfrey, 336.
200. Godfrey, 336.
201. He expired 26 March 1938. "Dr. Paul Pearson"; *Who Was Who,* vol. 1, 950; Godfrey, 337–338. Edna survived her husband four years, deceasing 15 April 1942. Family tree, Pearson Papers.
202. Pearson Gardens, on Long Bay, today anchors the eastern side of the harbor at Charlotte Amalie. Pearson, "Virgin Islands"; Godfrey, 336; photograph, Pearson Papers; *Current Biography,* 658.
203. Letter to Drew Pearson, 15 May 1929, quoted in Godfrey, 337.

12. Anthony M. Solomon

1. The memorial in Battery Park that so diverted attention from the Pacific initiative, ironically, commemorated American servicemen who during World War II had lost their lives at sea, many of them in those very islands.
2. "Survey Group."
3. The parental history comes from Solomon, interview.
4. Solomon, interview; Bennett, "Anthony Solomon."
5. He was born 17 December 1919. Federal Reserve.
6. Solomon, interview.
7. Solomon, interview.
8. He attended the local public schools. Solomon, interview (including quotation); Farnsworth.
9. He earned a bachelor's degree in economics. Solomon, interview; Federal Reserve; Farnsworth.
10. Solomon, interview.
11. Solomon, interview; Farnsworth.
12. Solomon, interview. The United States sent to Iran a financial mission of sixty members. A grateful Churchill, in a letter to Roosevelt in 1944, praised its work as "a very necessary but a long, arduous, and thankless task." Letter, 21 May 1944, in Roosevelt, *Roosevelt and Churchill,* 500.
13. Solomon, interview.
14. Solomon, interview (including quotation); Harvard, "Harvard's"; Federal Reserve; Farnsworth.
15. Solomon, interview; Harvard, "Harvard's."
16. Solomon, interview.
17. Solomon, interview; Federal Reserve.
18. Solomon, interview (including quotation).
19. Federal Reserve; Harvard, "Harvard's"; Farnsworth.
20. They were wed 7 April 1950 in New York City. Solomon, interview (supplementary electronic mail).
21. Farnsworth.
22. The friend in Mexico was Bradley Murray. Solomon, interview.
23. The industrial directory project took three years, producing two thick volumes. Solomon, interview.
24. Solomon, interview (including quotation); Bennett, "Anthony Solomon"; Farnsworth; Federal Reserve; Harvard, "Harvard's."
25. Solomon, interview; Farnsworth.
26. The homeowner calls the house a "mansion." Solomon, interview.
27. He taught at Harvard Business School from 1961 to 1963. Solomon, interview; Harvard, *Directory,* 208; Harvard, "Harvard's"; Federal Reserve; "Survey Mission."
28. It was a small mission of three members. Solomon, interview; Harvard, "Harvard's"; "Survey Group."
29. Solomon, interview; Willens and Siemer.
30. Micronesia means "tiny islands." McHenry, 6 n; *Report,* S-1; Roff, 47; Trumbull, 14.
31. The region had been dominated variously by Spain, Germany, Britain, Japan, and the United States. *Report,* S-9; McHenry, 5, 234; Roff, 47.
32. The conquest in 1943–44 was predominantly a U.S. military operation. Pomeroy, *Pacific Outpost,* xix; Stuart, 312–313; McHenry, 54; Roff, 48.
33. Representative F. Edward Hébert of Louisiana, who thirty years later had an opportunity to implement his sentiments as chairman of the House Armed Services Committee when Micronesia's political fate was being decided. Quoted in McHenry, 66. See also Pomeroy, *Pacific Outpost,* xix.
34. The transfer excluded Britain's Gilbert Islands. McHenry, 6, 232; *Report,* S-1.
35. The United States succeeded in having its charge — alone among the eleven original UN trust territories — designated a "strategic" trust, enabling militarization and restricted access. McHenry, 5–6; Roff, 56–58; Trumbull, 14–15.
36. The secret CIA base, masquerading as the Naval Technical Training Unit, between 1951 and 1962 schooled hundreds of foreign provocateurs for service in China, Vietnam, and other arenas behind the bamboo curtain. McHenry, 57–58; Stuart, 298.
37. The United States conducted between 1946

and 1958 at Bikini and Eniwetok atolls sixty-six known nuclear tests, including detonating in 1954 its largest-ever hydrogen bomb. Hayes, Zarsky, and Bello, 69, 72, 239–240; Trumbull, 43–48; Roff, 55.

38. Trade in scrap metal for many years trailed only that in the copra extracted from the coconut that comprises Micronesia's predominant crop. Maga, 14–15; Webb, 87; Nevin, 23; McHenry, 7–8; Roff, 59; Trumbull, 21, 100–102, 128.

39. Maga, 10.

40. Khrushchev's gibes came in a speech in January 1961 and a subsequent statement to the Western press, respectively, both quoted in Maga, 10.

41. Maga, 10; Willens and Siemer, 3–4.

42. Unspecified date in 1961, quoted in Maga, 10.

43. The lieutenant, junior grade, was exposed to the primitive living conditions most prominently at Tulagi, the island near Guadalcanal where he was based. Perret, 106; Maga, 16; Willens and Siemer, 6.

44. The boat was sunk in August 1943 with the loss of two of its crew of ten. Kennedy had been in command four months. Perret, 109–114; Maga, 16–17.

45. Maga, x, 16–17.

46. Maga, 17.

47. Memorandum to Robert S. McNamara (secretary of defense), 1 February 1961, quoted in Maga, 21.

48. Memorandum to Wayne N. Aspinall (chairman of the House territorial committee), 20 March 1962, quoted in Maga, 25.

49. Maga, 20.

50. Letter to Kennedy, 20 March 1962, quoted in Maga, 16.

51. The government was moved to Guam, geographically within the Northern Marianas but jurisdictionally outside the trust territory, in 1961, and to Saipan the following year. Willens and Siemer, 11, 34–35; McHenry, 14; Maga, 26.

52. Maga, 26.

53. The site of the former espionage base, on a promontory behind the town of Garapan, quickly became known as Capitol Hill. Willens and Siemer, 32; Maga, 26; Stuart, 298.

54. Access to Micronesia had been restricted by a wartime presidential executive order in 1941 and by fencing off Saipan and Tinian to shield the CIA base in 1952. As Saipan served as port of entry to the whole region, the latter ban effectively had shuttered all of Micronesia. McHenry, 56–57; Nevin, 78; Farrell, 496.

55. He issued the executive order 23 August 1962. Kennedy, *Papers*, vol. 2, 640–641.

56. The program was enacted in July 1962. Kennedy, *Papers*, vol. 2, 564–565; Willens and Siemer, 31–32; Maga, 26–27; Kluge, 17.

57. Statement upon signing the legislation into law. Kennedy, *Papers*, vol. 2, 564–565.

58. McHenry, 15; *Report*, S-22.

59. The delegation, set up by Kennedy's *National Security Action Memorandum 145* of 18 April 1962, consisted of representatives of the departments of State, Defense, Interior, and Health, Education, and Welfare. It was chaired by Assistant Interior Secretary John A. Carver, Jr. McHenry, 15–16; Maga, 26; Roff, 60.

60. The "U.S. Government Survey Mission" was to "review the major political, economic and social problems facing the people" and advise on "a greatly accelerated rate of political, economic and social development." *National Security Action Memorandum 243*, 9 May 1963, National Security Files, box 341; Roff, 60–61; Farrell, 552.

61. Solomon, interview. This son of the nation's first secretary of defense, James V. Forrestal, crops up frequently in Halberstam. See especially 376–377.

62. Solomon, interview.

63. Solomon's cohorts were Richard N. Cooper of the Council of Economic Advisers; Donald C. Lindholm and Howard Schnoor of the Bureau of the Budget; Paul Daly of the Peace Corps; Dr. Pedro Sanchez, Virgin Islands education commissioner; Professor Gerard J. Mangone of Syracuse University; consultant Cleo Shook. A de facto member of what is generally described as a nine-man mission was Richard Taitano of the Department of the Interior's territorial office. Cover letter, *Report*; Willens and Siemer, 40; McHenry, 232; Maga, 29.

64. Solomon, interview. Cooper soon moved to the Department of State, serving as deputy undersecretary for international monetary policy in 1965–66 and undersecretary for economic affairs in 1977–81. He chaired the National Intelligence Council in 1995–97. He is now professor of international economics at Harvard.

65. *National Security Action Memorandum 145* of 18 April 1962 and *NSAM 243* of 9 May 1963. McHenry, 15; Maga, 29; Willens and Siemer, 27–31; Roff, 60–61; Kluge, 17.

66. *National Security Action Memorandum 145*, quoted in Maga, 29; *Report*, S-2; Roff, 61–62.

67. Maga, 32. A prominent recent precedent made such a notion anything but far-fetched at the time. Another group of Pacific islands — Hawaii — had attained statehood just a few years before, in 1959.

68. Willens and Siemer, 40.

69. Solomon, interview; Willens and Siemer, 40; McHenry, 16.

70. The task force spoke with seven local assemblies, eight legislative committees, seven municipal councils, three women's associations, twenty-five missionaries, and forty-five individual islanders. *Report*, S-4; Willens and Siemer, 40.

71. Solomon, interview.

72. *Report*, S-4.

73. Solomon, interview (including quotation). The escort was Commander Charles Chamberlain of the navy's Pacific command. Cover letter, *Report*.

74. Kluge, 147.

75. Willens and Siemer, 41.

76. The report went to the president 9 October 1963. *Report*, S-1; Farrell, 552; McHenry, 16.

77. *Report*, S-2; McHenry, 16.

78. *Report*, S-10.

79. *Report*, S-2; Maga, 31.

80. The mission proposed a spending program of

a minimum of $34 million to a maximum of $43 million for the four fiscal years of 1965–68. Islanders' per capita income at the time was estimated at $80. *Report,* S-24; McHenry, 17; Maga, 32–33; Willens and Siemer, 41–42; Nevin, 24.
81. *Report,* S-10–S-11.
82. *Report,* S-22.
83. *Report,* S-13.
84. *Report,* S-7, S-27.
85. *Report,* S-18; letter from Solomon to John F. Kennedy, 20 September 1963, National Security Files, box 342; Farrell, 552.
86. *Report,* S-7.
87. *Report,* S-18.
88. *Report,* S-18.
89. A backward step even from the unsavory imperialism of the past. The old British Empire had bequeathed to its subjects the entirety of Mother England's constitutional rights from the moment of acquisition. Morris, *Pax Britannica,* 195; *Report,* S-19; Maga, 30.
90. *Report,* S-5; McHenry, 17; Willens and Siemer, 43.
91. The United States had been an overseas suzerain more than half a century before consenting to its first referendum on constitutional status — in 1951 in Puerto Rico. The aversion to plebiscites was to persist into the closing decades of the twentieth century, and to this day for American Samoa. Stuart, 10–11, 408–413.
92. *Report,* S-4.
93. *Report,* S-5.
94. *Report,* S-7.
95. *Report,* S-7.
96. *Report,* S-12; Maga, 30. The name Micronesia first was appended to the region in 1847.
97. *Report,* S-7.
98. The plan was conceded to be "moving counter to the anti-colonial movement." *Report,* S-6.
99. *Report,* S-6.
100. *Report,* S-6.
101. *Report,* S-6.
102. The stipend might be seen, in the report's words, as "strategic rental." *Report,* S-6.
103. *Report,* S-16, S-17.
104. Letter, 20 September 1963, National Security Files, box 342.
105. *Report,* S-6.
106. Memorandum, 20 September 1963, National Security Files, box 342.
107. The meeting occurred 24 October 1963. Solomon, interview; Willens and Siemer, 46.
108. Solomon learned later that the president had studied speed reading. Solomon, interview.
109. Solomon, interview; Willens and Siemer, 46.
110. The official to be sent was John A. Carver, Jr. Solomon, interview; Willens and Siemer, 47.
111. The executive branch was "requested to develop and carry out necessary plans and programs to carry out recommendations in the report that are feasible and acceptable for implementation." *National Security Action Memorandum 268,* 25 October 1963, National Security Files, box 342; Willens and Siemer, 46.
112. Memorandum from Michael V. Forrestal, 25 October 1963, National Security Files, box 342; McHenry, 20.
113. Kennedy spoke of such a trip to visiting Micronesians in June and to the cabinet on 25 October 1963. Maga, 34.
114. "I deeply appreciate the efforts of you and your colleagues," the president added, "in doing a thorough study of this area, which is of such importance to the United States." Solomon resided at 3316 Volta Place, N.W. Letter, 4 November 1963, National Security Files, box 342.
115. When the department began in 1873 supervising the nation's territories, they were indeed interior. All lay within the shorelines of North America. Stuart, 369.
116. Quoted in McHenry, 18.
117. Willens and Siemer, 48. "Scoop" Jackson had played sandlot softball with Kennedy at Volta Park in Georgetown, where both resided. Don Shannon, "Saving Volta Park," *Georgetown & Country,* March 1997.
118. Aspinall later opined that Solomon "messed up things because he set up certain unapproachable goals." Quoted in McHenry, 192–193.
119. Letter, 20 September 1963, National Security Files, box 342.
120. Perhaps significantly, the Interior Department, unlike its two cabinet colleagues, never formally recommended a plebiscite date. Willens and Siemer, 48.
121. The exchange is quoted in Willens and Siemer, 47–48.
122. Maga, 32–33.
123. The epidemic of 212 cases occurred in January 1963. McHenry, 14.
124. Memorandum, 4 November 1963, National Security Files, box 342, with accompanying report (undated) from Assistant Interior Secretary Carver.
125. The assassination caught the Carver mission in the midst of its work in Micronesia. It stayed only a week. Solomon, interview; Willens and Siemer, 47.
126. Maga, 33.
127. Confidentiality had been requested by the Department of State, with the consent of Interior. Memorandum from Charles E. Johnson, 18 December 1963, National Security Files, box 342; Roff, 61. Even today, the warning "Confidential" remains menacingly inscribed at the top and bottom of each page.
128. Willens and Siemer, 49.
129. "A mixed success," in Solomon's words. Solomon, interview.
130. McHenry, 20; Farrell, 552.
131. McHenry, 20.
132. McHenry, 20.
133. He served concurrently as deputy assistant secretary of state for Latin America and deputy assistant administrator of the Agency for International Development from 1963 to 1965. Harvard, "Harvard's"; Federal Reserve.

134. Bennett, "Anthony Solomon."
135. An assistant secretary of state for the Far East convinced him that the matter would best be left to normal governmental processes. Solomon, interview.
136. Solomon, interview.
137. Quoted in Willens and Siemer, 47.
138. The government spent $39 million in fiscal year 1969 in the trust territory, right on target with the Solomon recommendation of $34 million to $43 million for fiscal years 1965–68. *Report*, S-24; Roff, 69.
139. Roff, 69.
140. Albeit in a provincially American mode. Nevin, 26–27, 33–34. On earlier under-funding, see Trumbull, 128.
141. The largely consultative Council of Micronesia was vested with lawmaking powers and transformed into the Congress of Micronesia. Letter from Solomon to Kennedy, 20 September 1963, National Security Files, box 342; Roff, 65; Farrell, 552.
142. The Peace Corps "oversold itself enormously," declares author Kluge, himself a corps volunteer in 1967 in Saipan. Kluge, 17; Nevin, 132–134; *Report*, S-17; Roff, 69.
143. The two volumes initially released and then classified in 1963 subsequently were cleansed of sensitive passages and declassified. A summary of the still-confidential political volume was leaked by the publications *Young Micronesian* in Hawaii and *Micronitor* in the Marshall Islands. McHenry, 16; Roff, 61.
144. McHenry, 88; Roff, 61.
145. *Young Micronesian*, quoted in McHenry, 19.
146. Solomon, interview (including quotations).
147. The voluntary steel pact was forged in 1968. Solomon was one of a task force of five financial authorities chosen by Johnson to redesign the international monetary system. He was assistant secretary of state from 1965 to 1969. Federal Reserve; Harvard, "Harvard's."
148. Solomon headed the International Investment Corporation for Yugoslavia, based in London, from 1969 to 1972. Federal Reserve; Harvard, "Harvard's"; Farnsworth.
149. Solomon was being considered to lead the United Nations Development Programme, evidently in November 1970 (the memo is undated). Memorandum, National Security Council Files, box 299, Agency Files, vol. 5.
150. He advised long-term chairman Wilbur D. Mills of Arkansas from 1972 to 1973. Farnsworth; Federal Reserve; Harvard, "Harvard's."
151. Farnsworth; Solomon, interview.
152. Solomon, interview (including quotation); Farnsworth. Of his sculpting, he also has said: "All my life, I have manipulated people and money, and I just felt I had to get into a more creative relationship." Quoted in Farnsworth.
153. Solomon, interview.
154. The collection has been bequeathed to Solomon's alma mater gradually over a ten-year span that began in 2003. Seventy-five of the objects were exhibited in 2002 and 2003 at Harvard's Arthur M. Sackler Museum and the Asia Society museum in New York. Solomon, interview; Harvard, "Harvard's."
155. McHenry, 94, 127; Maga, 34–35.

156. Such economic partiality toward the Marianas was criticized as early as 1961 by a United Nations visiting mission as "financial discrimination." McHenry, 13, 57–58, 130; Nevin, 145.
157. "Mariana Islanders tend to look down on other Micronesians," writes McHenry, "–even on the Palauans, who are said to look down on everyone." McHenry, 130. See also 57–58.
158. McHenry, 103.
159. "By force of arms if necessary," vowed the resolution of February 1971. Quoted in McHenry, 103.
160. Negotiations began in 1972. McHenry, 132–163; Roff, 69, 72.
161. Ninety-three percent of eligible voters cast ballots, 3,945 of them favoring affiliation and 1,060 opposing it. McHenry, 164–168; Roff, 72.
162. Roff, 72. The rest of Micronesia opted later for independence as three sovereign nations — the Federated States of Micronesia and the Republic of the Marshall Islands in 1986, and the Republic of Palau in 1994. They continue, however, to receive military protection and financial aid from the United States. Stuart, 6, 138, 422.
163. McHenry, 9, 222. The last previous acquisition was the Virgin Islands, purchased in 1917. The Commonwealth of the Northern Mariana Islands, with little more than 13,000 inhabitants when joining the United States, long ranked as the least populous possession. But its fast-growing population, now estimated to exceed 80,000, has surpassed that of American Samoa (reckoned at 58,000).
164. "I never imagined that our delaying so long," he laments, "would produce such a result." Solomon, interview (including all quotations).
165. Farnsworth; Federal Reserve; Harvard, "Harvard's."
166. Bennett, "Anthony Solomon" (including quotation).
167. The settlement was increased from $40 million to $80 million. Solomon, interview.
168. Solomon was appointed in January 1980 and took office 1 April, succeeding Paul A. Volcker. Bennett, "Federal Reserve" and "Anthony Solomon"; Federal Reserve.
169. Bennett, "Anthony Solomon"; Farnsworth.
170. Photograph, Bennett, "Federal Reserve"; photograph, Federal Reserve.
171. The unidentified chairman of a leading New York bank, quoted in Bennett, "Anthony Solomon."
172. He retired from the Fed on 31 December 1984. Federal Reserve.
173. He served as chairman of S. G. Warburg (U.S.A.) from 1986 to 1989. Harvard, "Harvard's."
174. Solomon, interview. Solomon Lewis LLC was founded in 2004.
175. Solomon, interview.
176. She departed on 15 May 1998. Solomon, interview (supplementary electronic mail).
177. Solomon, interview.
178. These capped monoliths adorn the flag of the Northern Marianas and the U.S. postage stamp issued to commemorate the new territory.
179. Solomon, interview.
180. Solomon, interview.

Bibliography

"Admiral Glass Reaches Last Harbor." *San Francisco Chronicle,* 2 September 1908, 1.
Ball, Ian M. *Pitcairn: Children of Mutiny.* Boston: Little, Brown & Co., 1973.
Beardsley, Charles. *Guam Past and Present.* Rutland, Vt.: Charles E. Tuttle Co., 1964.
Benfey, Christopher. *The Great Wave: Gilded Age Misfits, Japanese Eccentrics, and the Opening of Old Japan.* New York: Random House, 2003.
Bennett, Robert A. "Anthony Solomon: New Man at the Fed," *New York Times,* 28 September 1980, F1.
———. "Federal Reserve Names Solomon N.Y. Chief," *New York Times,* 22 January 1980, A1.
Biedzynski, James Christopher. "Frank McIntyre and the Philippines." Ph.D. diss., Ohio University, 1990.
Bixby, William. *The Forgotten Voyage of Charles Wilkes.* New York: David McKay Co., 1966.
Blackwell, Edward Maurice. *Blackwell Genealogy.* Vol. 2. Richmond, Va.: Old Dominion Press, 1948.
Boehm, Kerry. "Breakwater named for U.S. Navy captain." *Pacific Crossroads* (Agana, Guam), 16 August 1991, 13.
Brands, H. W. *The Reckless Decade: America in the 1890s.* New York: St. Martin's Press, 1995.
Brodsky, Alyn. *Grover Cleveland: A Study in Character.* New York: St. Martin's Press, 2000.
Burns, James MacGregor. *Roosevelt: The Lion and the Fox.* New York: Harcourt, Brace & Co., 1956.
Burns, Robert. *The Complete Works of Robert Burns.* Vol. 3, pt. 1. Philadelphia: Gebbie Publishing Co., 1896.
Cabranes, José A. *Citizenship and the American Empire: Notes on the Legislative History of the United States Citizenship of Puerto Ricans.* New Haven, Conn.: Yale University Press, 1979.
Callahan, Edward W., ed. *List of Officers of the Navy of the United States and of the Marine Corps from 1775 to 1900.* 1901. Reprint, New York: Haskell House Publishers, 1969.
Carano, Paul, and Pedro C. Sanchez. *A Complete History of Guam.* Rutland, Vt.: Charles E. Tuttle Co., 1964.
Clark, Truman R. *Puerto Rico and the United States, 1917–1933.* Pittsburgh, Pa.: University of Pittsburgh Press, 1975.
Cole, Donald B. *Martin Van Buren and the American Political System.* Princeton, N.J.: Princeton University Press, 1984.
Collier, Peter, with David Horowitz. *The Roosevelts: An American Saga.* New York: Simon & Schuster, 1994.
"Congressman Jones Dead." *New York Times,* 18 April 1918, 13.
Crane, Stephen. *The Red Badge of Courage: An Episode of the American Civil War.* 1895. Reprint, New York: W. W. Norton & Co., 1982.
Crichton, Judy. *America 1900: The Turning Point.* New York: Henry Holt & Co., 1998.
Current Biography. New York: H. W. Wilson Co., 1941.
Daudet, Alphonse. "Letters from My Mill." In *The Works of Alphonse Daudet.* Translated by Katherine Prescott Wormeley. Vol. 19. Boston: Little, Brown & Co., 1900.
Davis, Richard Harding. *The Cuban and Porto Rican Campaigns.* London: William Heinemann, 1899.

"Dr. Paul Pearson Dies in California." *New York Times,* 27 March 1938, sec. 2, 7.
Dunne, Finley Peter. *Mr. Dooley in Peace and in War.* Boston: Small, Maynard & Co., 1899.
Ellison, Joseph W. *Opening and Penetration of Foreign Influence in Samoa to 1880.* Corvallis, Ore.: Oregon State College, 1938.
Evans, Robley D. *An Admiral's Log.* New York: D. Appleton, 1910.
Farnsworth, Clyde H. "Behind-the-Scenes Monetary Power," *New York Times,* 22 January 1980, D11.
Farrell, Don A. *History of the Northern Mariana Islands.* Saipan: Public School System, Commonwealth of the Northern Mariana Islands, 1991.
Federal Reserve Bank of New York. "Anthony M. Solomon." *About the Fed.* http://www.ny.frb.org/aboutthefed/ASolomonbio.html, n.d. (accessed 14 March 2005).
Fernández Méndez, Eugenio, ed. *Portrait of a Society: Readings on Puerto Rican Sociology.* Rio Piedras: University of Puerto Rico, 1972.
Foraker, Joseph B. *Notes of a Busy Life.* 2 vols. Cincinnati, Ohio: Stewart & Kidd Co., 1916.
_____. Papers. Library of Congress, Washington, D.C.
Foraker, Julia B. *I Would Live It Again: Memories of a Vivid Life.* New York: Harper & Brothers, 1932.
Frankfurter, Felix. *Felix Frankfurter Reminisces.* Recorded in talks with Harlan B. Phillips. New York: Reynal & Co., 1960.
Freidel, Frank. *The Splendid Little War.* Boston: Little, Brown & Co., 1958
Funeral notice, Henry Glass. *San Francisco Chronicle,* 4 September 1908, 9.
Garraty, John A., and Mark C. Carnes, eds. *American National Biography.* Vols. 4, 15, 18. New York: Oxford University Press, 1999.
"Gen. M'Intyre, 78, in Army 43 Years." *New York Times,* 17 February 1944, 19.
Gilson, R. P. *Samoa 1830–1900: The Politics of a Multi-Cultural Community.* Melbourne: Oxford University Press, 1970.
Glass, Henry. "Operations at Guam Island." *Annual Reports of the Navy Department: 1898.* Appendix to the Report of the Chief of the Bureau of Navigation. Washington, D.C.: U.S. Government Printing Office, 1898.
_____, comp. *Marine International Law.* Annapolis, Md.: United States Naval Institute, 1885 (proceedings of the United States Naval Institute, vol. 11, no. 3).
Godfrey, Barbara Pearson Lange. *Man of Chautauqua and His Caravans of Culture: The Life of Paul M. Pearson.* N.p., 2001.
Goode, James M. *Capital Losses: A Cultural History of Washington's Destroyed Buildings.* Washington, D.C.: Smithsonian Institution Press, 1979.
Gordon-Cumming, Constance F. *At Home in Fiji.* Edinburgh: William Blackwood & Sons, 1882.
Grant, Ulysses S. *The Papers of Ulysses S. Grant.* Vols. 10, 17, 23. Edited by John Y. Simon. Carbondale: Southern Illinois University Press, 1982, 1991, 2000.
Gray, J. A. C. *Amerika Samoa: A History of American Samoa and Its United States Naval Administration.* Annapolis, Md.: United States Naval Institute, 1960.
Hahn, Emily. *The Islands: America's Imperial Adventure in the Philippines.* New York: Coward, McCann & Geohegan, 1981.
Halberstam, David. *The Best and the Brightest.* New York: Random House, 1969.
Harvard University. *Directory of University Officers and Students.* Cambridge, Mass.: Harvard University, 1962.
Harvard University Art Museums. "Harvard's Arthur M. Sackler Museum Presents the Largest and Finest Private Collection of Cold-Painted Chinese Tomb Sculptures in the West." Press release, 25 July 2002.
Hayes, Peter, Lyuba Zarsky, and Walden Bello. *American Lake: Nuclear Peril in the Pacific.* New York: Viking Penguin, 1986.
Henderson, Daniel. *The Hidden Coasts: A Biography of Charles Wilkes.* New York: William Sloane Associates, 1953.
Jeffers, H. Paul. *Theodore Roosevelt, Jr.: The Life of a War Hero.* Novato, Calif.: Presidio Press, 2002.
Johnson, Allen, and Dumas Malone, eds. *Dictionary of American Biography.* Vol. 3, pt. 2. New York: Charles Scribner's Sons, 1931.

Johnson, Virginia Weisel. *The Unregimented General: A Biography of Nelson A. Miles.* Boston: Houghton Mifflin Co., 1962.
"Joseph B. Foraker, Ex-Senator, Dead." *New York Times,* 11 May 1917, 11.
Karnow, Stanley. *In Our Image: America's Empire in the Philippines.* New York: Random House, 1989.
Keesing, Felix M. *Modern Samoa: Its Government and Changing Life.* London: George Allen & Unwin, 1934.
Kennedy, John F. *Public Papers of the Presidents of the United States.* 4 vols. Washington, D.C.: U.S. Government Printing Office, 1962–64.
Kennedy, Paul M. *The Samoan Tangle: A Study in Anglo-German-American Relations, 1878–1900.* Dublin: Irish University Press, 1974.
Kluge, P. F. *The Edge of Paradise: America in Micronesia.* Honolulu: University of Hawaii Press, 1991.
Knightley, Phillip. *The First Casualty: From the Crimea to Vietnam, the War Correspondent as Hero, Propagandist, and Myth Maker.* New York: Harcourt Brace Jovanovich, 1975.
Kunitz, Stanley J., ed. *Twentieth Century American Authors: A Biographical Dictionary of Modern Literature.* 1st supp. New York: H.W. Wilson Co., 1955.
Leary, Richard P. "Proclamation to the Inhabitants of Guam and to Whom It May Concern." Navy Department Library Naval Historical Center, Washington, D.C., 1899.
Leech, Margaret. *In the Days of McKinley.* New York: Harper & Brothers, 1959.
Lewis, Gordon K. *Puerto Rico: Freedom and Power in the Caribbean.* New York: Monthly Review Press, 1963.
_____. *The Virgin Islands: A Caribbean Lilliput.* Evanston, Ill.: Northwestern University Press, 1972.
Lincoln, Abraham. *The Collected Works of Abraham Lincoln.* Edited by Roy P. Basler. Vol. 8. New Brunswick, N.J.: Rutgers University Press, 1953.
Loosbrock, Richard J. "Worthy Son of a Worthy Sire — The Early Years of Theodore Roosevelt, Jr." In *Theodore Roosevelt: Many-Sided American,* edited by Natalie A. Naylor, Douglas Brinkley, and John Allen Gable. Interlaken, N.Y.: Heart of the Lakes Publishing, 1992.
Maga, Timothy P. *John F. Kennedy and the New Pacific Community, 1961–1963.* New York: St. Martin's Press, 1990.
"Marriage in the Hill City." *Northern Neck (Va.) News,* 1 February 1889.
Maugham, W. Somerset. *The Complete Short Stories of W. Somerset Maugham.* Vol. 1, *East and West.* Garden City, N.Y.: Doubleday & Co., 1953.
_____. *A Writer's Notebook.* New York: Hearst Magazines, 1949.
McHenry, Donald F. *Micronesia: Trust Betrayed.* New York: Carnegie Endowment for International Peace, 1975.
McIntyre, Frank. "American Territorial Administration." *Foreign Affairs* 10 (January 1932): 293–303.
Meade, Richard W., Jr. Letters. Navy Department Library. Naval Historical Center, Washington, D.C.
Meade, Richard W., III. "A Winter Voyage through the Straits of Magellan." *National Geographic,* May 1897, 129–142.
Melville, Herman. *Mardi and a Voyage Thither.* 1849. Reprint, Boston: St. Botolph Society, 1923.
Michener, James A. *The Bridges at Toko-ri.* New York: Random House, 1953.
Miles, Nelson A. *Personal Recollections and Observations of General Nelson A. Miles, Embracing a Brief View of the Civil War: or, From New England to the Golden Gate, and the Story of His Indian Campaigns, with Comments on the Exploration, Development, and Progress of Our Great Western Empire.* 1896. Reprint (2 vols.), Lincoln: University of Nebraska Press, 1992.
_____. *Serving the Republic: Memoirs of the Civil and Military Life of Nelson A. Miles, Lieutenant-General, United States Army.* New York: Harper & Brothers, 1911.
Moorehead, Alan. *The Fatal Impact: An Account of the Invasion of the South Pacific, 1767–1840.* New York: Harper & Row, 1966.
Morales Carrión, Arturo. *Puerto Rico: A Political and Cultural History.* New York: W. W. Norton & Co., 1983.
Morris, Edmund. *Theodore Rex.* New York: Random House, 2001.
Morris, James. *Heaven's Command: An Imperial Progress.* New York: Harcourt Brace Jovanovich, 1974.

———. *Pax Britannica: The Climax of an Empire.* New York: Harcourt, Brace & World, 1968.
Murray, Robert K. *The Harding Era: Warren G. Harding and His Administration.* Minneapolis: University of Minnesota Press, 1969.
Musicant, Ivan. *Empire by Default: The Spanish-American War and the Dawn of the American Century.* New York: Henry Holt & Co., 1998.
Nagel, Paul C. *John Quincy Adams: A Public Life, a Private Life.* New York: Alfred A. Knopf, 1998.
The National Cyclopaedia of American Biography 63 vols. New York: James T. White & Co., 1892–1984.
National Security Files, boxes 341 and 342. John F. Kennedy Library, Boston.
National Security Council Files, box 299. Nixon Presidential Materials. National Archives, Washington, D.C.
Nevin, David. *The American Touch in Micronesia.* New York: W. W. Norton & Co., 1977.
New York Journal. December 1898.
Obituary, Henry Glass. *Army and Navy Journal,* 5 September 1908, 8.
Obituary, Frank McIntyre. *Army and Navy Journal,* 19 February 1944, 740.
Obituary, Richard W. Meade, Jr. *Army and Navy Journal,* 23 April 1870, 566–567.
Obituary, Richard W. Meade III. *Army and Navy Journal,* 8 May 1897, 658.
Obituary, B.F. Tilley. *Army and Navy Journal,* 23 March 1907, 812.
Olsen, Frederick H. "The Navy and the White Man's Burden: Naval Administration of Samoa." Ph.D. diss., Washington University, 1976.
O'Neill, Edward A. *Rape of the American Virgins.* New York: Praeger Publishers, 1972.
O'Toole, Patricia. *The Five of Hearts: An Intimate Portrait of Henry Adams and His Friends, 1880–1918.* New York: Clarkson N. Potter, 1990.
Pakenham, Valerie. *Out in the Noonday Sun: Edwardians in the Tropics.* New York: Random House, 1985.
Paullin, Charles O. *Diplomatic Negotiations of American Naval Officers, 1778–1883.* 1912. Reprint, Gloucester, Mass.: Peter Smith, 1967.
Pearlman, Michael. *To Make Democracy Safe for America: Patricians and Preparedness in the Progressive Era.* Urbana: University of Illinois Press, 1984.
Pearson, Drew. "Virgin Islands Rebound from 'Poorhouse' Status." *Philadelphia Evening Bulletin,* 5 March 1952.
Pearson, Paul M. Papers. Friends Historical Library, Swarthmore College, Swarthmore, Pa.
Perkins, Whitney T. *Denial of Empire: The United States and Its Dependencies.* Leyden, Netherlands: A. W. Sythoff, 1962.
Perret, Geoffrey. *Jack: A Life Like No Other.* New York: Random House, 2001.
Pomeroy, Earl S. "The American Colonial Office." *Mississippi Valley Historical Review* 30 (March 1944): 521–532.
———. *Pacific Outpost: American Strategy in Guam and Micronesia.* Stanford, Calif.: Stanford University Press, 1951.
Pratt, Julius W. *America's Colonial Experiment: How the United States Gained, Governed, and in Part Gave Away a Colonial Empire.* New York: Prentice-Hall, Inc., 1950.
———. *Expansionists of 1898: The Acquisition of Hawaii and the Spanish Islands.* Baltimore: Johns Hopkins Press, 1936.
"Rear-Admiral Glass." *San Francisco Chronicle,* 3 September 1908, 6.
Remington, Frederic. *Frederic Remington: Selected Writings.* Compiled by Frank Oppel. Secaucus, N.J.: Castle, 1981.
Renehan, Edward J., Jr. *The Lion's Pride: Theodore Roosevelt and His Family in Peace and War.* New York: Oxford University Press, 1998.
A Report by the U.S. Government Survey Mission to the Trust Territory of the Pacific Islands. 9 October 1963. National Security Files, box 341. John F. Kennedy Library, Boston.
Richardson, James D. *A Compilation of the Messages and Papers of the Presidents, 1789–1897.* Vols. 2 and 7. Washington, D.C.: U.S. Government Printing Office, 1897.
Rieman, George B. *Papalangee, or Uncle Sam in Samoa: A Narrative of the Cruise of the U.S. Steamer Narragansett among the Samoan or Navigator Islands, Polynesia.* Oakland, Calif.: Butler & Stillwell, 1874.

Rigby, Barry. "Private Interests and the Origin of American Involvement in Samoa, 1872–1877." *Journal of Pacific History* 8 (1973): 75–87.
Riley, James Whitcomb. *The Complete Poetical Works of James Whitcomb Riley.* New York: Grosset & Dunlap, 1937.
Robson, R. W. *Queen Emma: The Samoan-American Girl Who Founded an Empire in Nineteenth Century New Guinea.* Sydney: Pacific Publications, 1965.
Roff, Sue Rabbitt. *Overreaching in Paradise: United States Policy in Palau Since 1945.* Juneau, Alaska: Denali Press, 1991.
Rogers, Robert F. *Destiny's Landfall: A History of Guam.* Honolulu: University of Hawaii Press, 1995.
Roosevelt, Eleanor. *The Autobiography of Eleanor Roosevelt.* 1961. Reprint, New York: Da Capo Press, 1992.
Roosevelt, Eleanor B. *Day Before Yesterday: The Reminiscences of Mrs. Theodore Roosevelt, Jr.* Garden City, N.Y.: Doubleday & Co., 1959.
Roosevelt, Franklin D. *Roosevelt and Churchill: Their Secret Wartime Correspondence.* Edited by Francis L. Loewenheim, Harold D. Langley, and Manfred Jonas. London: Barrie & Jenkins, 1975.
Roosevelt, Theodore. *The Letters of Theodore Roosevelt.* Selected and edited by Elting E. Morison. 8 vols. Cambridge, Mass.: Harvard University Press, 1951–54.
Roosevelt, Theodore, Jr. *Colonial Policies of the United States.* Garden City, N.Y.: Doubleday, Doran & Co., 1937.
———. Papers. Library of Congress, Washington, D.C.
Root, Elihu. *The Military and Colonial Policy of the United States: Addresses and Reports.* Collected and edited by Robert Bacon and James Brown Scott. Cambridge, Mass.: Harvard University Press, 1916.
Rutland, Robert A. *James Madison: The Founding Father.* New York: Macmillan Publishing Co., 1987.
Ryden, George Herbert. *The Foreign Policy of the United States in Relation to Samoa.* New Haven, Conn.: Yale University Press, 1933.
Ryland, Elizabeth Lowell. *Richmond County, Virginia: A Review Commemorating the Bicentennial.* Warsaw, Va.: Richmond County Board of Supervisors, 1976.
Sandberg, Carl. *Abraham Lincoln: The War Years.* Vol. 3. New York: Harcourt, Brace, 1939.
Shelton, Charlotte Jean. "William Atkinson Jones, 1849–1918: Independent Democracy in Gilded Age Virginia." Ph.D. diss., University of Virginia, 1980.
Silverberg, Robert. *Stormy Voyager: The Story of Charles Wilkes.* Philadelphia: Lippincott, 1968.
Snyder, Charles W. "An American Original: Theodore Roosevelt, Jr." In *Theodore Roosevelt: Many-Sided American,* edited by Natalie A. Naylor, Douglas Brinkley, and John Allen Gable. Interlaken, N.Y.: Heart of the Lakes Publishing, 1992.
Solomon, Anthony M. Interview by author. New York, N.Y., 9 April 2005.
Souhami, Diana. *Selkirk's Island: The True and Strange Adventures of the Real Robinson Crusoe.* New York: Harcourt, Inc., 2001.
Stathis, Stephen W. "Albert B. Steinberger: President Grant's Man in Samoa." *Hawaiian Journal of History* 16 (1982): 86–111.
Stevenson, Robert Louis. *The Beach of Falesá.* In *Island Nights' Entertainments.* London: Cassell & Co., 1893.
Stewart, Kenneth, and John Tebbel. *Makers of Modern Journalism.* New York: Prentice-Hall, 1952.
Strauss, W. Patrick. *Americans in Polynesia, 1783–1842.* East Lansing: Michigan State University Press, 1963.
Stuart, Peter C. *Isles of Empire: The United States and Its Overseas Possessions.* Lanham, Md.: University Press of America, 1999.
"Survey Group to Seek Ways to Spur Trust Islands." *New York Times,* 24 May 1963, 32.
Sweetman, David. *Paul Gauguin: A Life.* New York: Simon & Schuster, 1995.
Thompson, Laura. *Guam and Its People.* 1947. Reprint, New York: Greenwood Press, 1969.
Tilley, B. F. "Report of the Commandant of Naval Station, Tutuila." *Annual Reports of the Navy Department: 1901,* pt. 1. Washington, D.C.: U.S. Government Printing Office, 1901.
"To Succeed Gen. Edwards." *New York Times,* 5 July 1912, 6.
Torodash, Martin. "Steinberger of Samoa: Some Biographical Notes." *Pacific Northwest Quarterly* 68, no. 2 (1977): 49–59.
Traxel, David. *1898: The Birth of the American Century.* New York: Alfred A. Knopf, 1998.

Trumbull, Robert. *Paradise in Trust: A Report on Americans in Micronesia, 1946–1958*. New York: William Sloane Associates, 1959.
United States. Congress. House. *American Rights in Samoa*. 50th Cong., 1st sess., 1888. Executive Doc. 238. Serial 2560.
_____. _____. _____. *William Atkinson Jones (Late a Representative from Virginia): Memorial Addresses Delivered in the House of Representatives of the United States*. 65th Cong., 3rd sess., 1919. H. Doc. 1856.
_____. _____. Senate. *Biographical Directory of the United States Congress, 1774–1989*. 100th Cong., 1st sess., 1989. S. Doc. 34.
_____. Department of the Navy. *Dictionary of American Naval Fighting Ships*. 9 vols. Washington, D.C.: Naval Historical Center, 1959–91.
_____. _____. _____. Biographical summary, Henry Glass. Files of Navy Department Library, Washington, D.C., n.d.
_____. _____. _____. Biographical summary, Richard W. Meade III. Files of Navy Department Library, Washington, D.C., 1918.
_____. _____. _____. Biographical summary, B. F. Tilley. Files of Navy Department Library, Washington, D.C., n.d.
_____. _____. _____. Photographic portrait, Henry Glass. NH 000350. Files of Navy Department Library, Washington, D.C., 1898.
_____. _____. _____. Photographic portraits, B. F. Tilley. NH 43893 and NH 67313. Files of Navy Department Library, Washington, D.C., 1890s and n.d.
_____. _____. _____. Photographs, Pago Pago and Tutuila. Files of Navy Department Library, Washington, D.C., 1899–1943.
_____. _____. _____. Photographs, Benjamin F. Tilley, Jr. Files of Navy Department Library, Washington, D.C., 1892 and 1914.
_____. _____. "Seizure of the Ladrone Islands." *Annual Reports of the Navy Department: 1898*. Appendix to the Report of the Chief of the Bureau of Navigation. Washington, D.C.: U.S. Government Printing Office, 1898.
_____. General Services Administration. National Archives and Records Service. *Preliminary Inventory of the Records of the Bureau of Insular Affairs*. Compiled by Richard S. Maxwell. Washington, D.C.: U.S. Government Printing Office, 1960.
Van Buren, Martin. *The Autobiography of Martin Van Buren*. Vol. 1. Edited by John C. Fitzpatrick. 1920. Reprint, New York: Da Capo Press, 1973.
Van Cleve, Ruth G. *The Office of Territorial Affairs*. New York: Praeger Publishers, 1974.
Wagenheim, Kal, ed. *The Puerto Ricans: A Documentary History*. New York: Praeger Publishers, 1973.
Walters, Everett. *Joseph Benson Foraker: An Uncompromising Republican*. Columbus: Ohio History Press, 1948.
Washington Post, May 1898–August 1935.
Waugh, Alec. *The Sugar Islands*. London: Cassell & Co., Ltd., 1958.
Weaver, John D. *The Senator and the Sharecropper's Son: Exoneration of the Brownsville Soldiers*. College Station: Texas A & M University Press, 1997.
Webb, James H., Jr. *Micronesia and U.S. Pacific Strategy: A Blueprint for the 1980s*. New York: Praeger Publishers, 1974.
Who Was Who in America. Vols. 1 (1897–1942) and 2 (1943–50). Chicago: Marquis—Who's Who, Inc., 1966.
Wilkes, Charles. *Autobiography of Rear Admiral Charles Wilkes, United States Navy, 1798–1877*. Edited by William James Morgan et al. Washington, D.C.: Naval History Division, U.S. Department of the Navy, 1978.
_____. *Narrative of the United States Exploring Expedition*. 5 vols. Philadelphia: Lea & Blanchard, 1845.
Willens, Howard P., and Deanne C. Siemer. *National Security and Self-Determination: United States Policy in Micronesia (1961–1972)*. Westport, Conn.: Praeger Publishers, 2000.
Wilson, Major L. *The Presidency of Martin Van Buren*. Lawrence: University Press of Kansas, 1984.
Wilson, Woodrow. *The Papers of Woodrow Wilson*. Edited by Arthur S. Link. 69 vols. Princeton, N.J.: Princeton University Press, 1966–94.
Wooster, Robert. *Nelson A. Miles and the Twilight of the Frontier Army*. Lincoln: University of Nebraska Press, 1995.

Index

Adams, John 4, 7
Adams, John Quincy 8, 12, 13, 21
African-Americans 67, 84, 115, 123; discrimination against 72, 181; equality toward 112, 162, 181, 184, 192; slavery 62, 66, 67, 99, 100–101, 107, 129; *see also* Brownsville Affair
agriculture (in overseas possessions) 43, 80, 94, 107, 143, 179, 183, 194–195; plantations 33, 45, 56, 128, 130, 180
Aguinaldo, Emilio 128
Alaska 30, 52, 83
alcoholic beverages 33, 88, 96–97; banning of 16, 17, 85–86, 92; Prohibition 161, 180, 183; Prohibition party 85–86; rum industry 179, 180, 183
Alger, Russell A. 75, 80
Allen, Charles H. 109
American Legion 151
American Samoa *see* Samoa, American
Americanization (in overseas possessions) 78–79, 157–158, 196, 200
Antarctica 15, 18–19, 26
Archbold, John D. 114
Asia, central, (Turkistan) 154
Aspinall, Wayne N. 192, 198
Audubon, John James 22
Australia 18, 19, 31, 48, 192

Babcock, Orville E. 43
Bismarck, Otto von 31
Blackwell, Edward M. 95, 97
Blumenthal, W. Michael 202
Bolivia 190, 193
Bradley, Omar N. 164, 165
Braunersreuther, William 55
British Virgin Islands *see* Virgin Islands, British
Brown, Herbert D. 178
Brownsville Affair 113, 117
Bryan, William Jennings 126, 170, 176
Bundy, Hezekiah S. 102
Bundy, McGeorge 197
Bureau of Insular Affairs *see* War, U.S. Department of
Burroughs, John 147

Canada 36, 68, 173, 177
Caroline Islands 58, 190–191, 196
Carter, Jimmy 202
Central Intelligence Agency 191, 192, 201

Chautauqua movement 170–171, 176; *see also* Pearson, Paul M.
Chile 16, 91
China 112, 201, 202–203
Christmas Island 34
Churchill, Winston S. 189
citizenship, U.S. (in overseas possessions) 108, 110, 116, 129, 131
Civil War, U.S. *see* Foraker, Joseph B.; Glass, Henry; Jones, William A.; Meade, Richard W., III; Wilkes, Charles
Clark, Champ 176
Clemenceau, Georges 177
Cleveland, Grover 37, 48, 73, 102
Cody, William F. "Buffalo Bill" 85
Cold War 191
Cole, Emma 42
Cole, Jonas M. 47
Congress, U.S. 70, 103, 125; interest in oceanic exploration 8, 12, 13, 21, 22; interest in overseas expansion 43, 105, 202; investigations by 35, 40, 48, 113, 153, 183–184; territorial legislation by 106–111, 140, 179; territorial oversight by 106, 126, 128, 130, 131, 143, 192, 198, 199, 200; territorial treaty actions by 35; *see also* Foraker, Joseph B.; Jones, William A.
Cook, James 7, 13, 15, 18
Coolidge, Calvin 87, 143–144, 152
Coontz, Robert E. 57
Cooper, James Fenimore 15
Cooper, Richard N. 193
Cordova Davila, Felix 131, 132
Cox, James M. 152
Cramer, Lawrence N. 184
Cuba 24; independence of 83, 106; Spanish-American War in 74–75, 80, 91, 105, 116, 149; U.S. interim rule of 139; U.S. intervention in 112–113, 140, 192

Daniel, John W. 127
Darwin, Charles 12
Davis, Jefferson 66
Davis, Richard Harding 80
Denmark: as colonial ruler 177; sale of Virgin Islands to United States by 105, 142, 177
Depression, Great 159, 164, 176, 177, 178, 179, 180, 184, 188
Dewey, George 56, 58

249

Dominican Republic 140, 142, 143
Dooley, Mr. *see* Dunne, Finley Peter
Dunbar, Paul Laurence 181
Dunne, Finley Peter 60, 74
d'Urville, Dumont 18

economic development (in overseas possessions) 43, 128, 156–157, 183, 194, 199
education, public (in overseas possessions) 158, 191, 194; improvement of 95, 157, 161, 179, 181, 183, 192, 194, 196, 199
Edwards, Clarence R. 139–140
Eisenhower, Dwight D. 165
elocution 100, 170, 171–172, 174
emigration: from overseas possessions to U.S. mainland 183; to United States 8–9, 99, 134–135, 187
environmental protection (in overseas possessions) 94, 154, 158
Evans, Robley D. 97
Exploring Expedition, U.S.: activities of 14–20; origins of 7–8, 11; preparations for 12–14; return and reception of 20–21; *see also* Wilkes, Charles

Fall, Albert B. 153
Field, Eugene 172
Fiji 19, 38, 47
Fish, Hamilton 41, 42, 43, 45, 46, 48
Foraker, Joseph B.: autobiography of 116; and Brownsville Affair 112–113, 117; children of 103, 111–112, 115–116; Civil War service of 100; as corporate lawyer 103, 115; description of 102–103, 104; education of 100, 101, 102; as foe of racism 100–101, 107, 112, 115; forebears of 99; as framer of Puerto Rico government 106–110, 116, 127, 138; as friend of big business 103, 114; as machine politician 102, 112; as Ohio governor 102–103; as orator 100, 102–103, 104; parents and childhood of 99–100; perception of, by others 99, 104, 109, 112, 114, 115; personal qualities of 99, 100, 102, 103, 106; political ambitions of 103–104, 113; relations with McKinley 103, 104, 105, 109, 111; relations with Roosevelt 109, 110, 111, 112–113, 114, 116; relations with Taft 110, 112, 114; and Standard Oil scandal 114–115; as territorial expansionist 105; Washington lifestyle of 111–112, 115; *see also* Foraker, Julia
Foraker, Julia (Mrs. Joseph B.) 101–102, 103, 111, 116
Forbes, W. Cameron 141
Forrestal, Michael V. 193, 197, 198
Foster, Samuel S. 45, 48
France 8, 18, 24, 40, 62, 142, 177; as colonial ruler 3, 138, 162, 193; territorial expansionism of 105; *see also* World War I; World War II
Frankfurter, Felix 129, 140
Franklin, Benjamin 7, 89
Frémont, John C. 100

Garrison, Lindley M. 141
Germany 43, 46, 78; as colonial ruler 33, 42, 138; overseas communities of 31, 45–46, 92; territorial expansionism of 31, 34, 49, 58, 90, 105; *see also* World War I; World War II
Geronimo 68, 69, 70
Gilbert Islands 34, 190–191
Glass, Henry: capture of Guam by 50, 53–56; Civil War service of 51; description of 50, 54; early naval voyages of 51–52; forebears of 51; interim rule of Guam arranged by 56–57; parents and childhood of 51; personal qualities of 51, 54, 59; Philippines service of 58; postwar service of 59, 98; retirement life of 59; wife and children of 59
Gordon, Sir Arthur H. 47
Grant, Ulysses S. 35, 39–40, 65, 66, 71; *see also* Steinberger, Albert B.
Great Britain 24, 47, 48, 78, 91, 134, 162, 164, 201, 203; as colonial ruler 3, 19, 88, 106, 138, 162, 188–189, 190–191; overseas communities of 45–46; territorial expansionism of 8, 90, 105
Gruening, Ernest H. 160
Guam: description of 52, 53; historical distinction among U.S. possessions 57, 90; Japanese military conquest of 57; naval administration of 58–59, 138; revising U.S. government of 110–111; Spanish rule of 52–53, 54, 56; and trust territory 192; U.S. perception of 50, 57; U.S. relations with inhabitants of 56–57, 59; *see also* Glass, Henry

Haiti 142, 143
Hancock, Winfield Scott 122
Hanna, Marcus A. 102, 103, 104, 105
Harding, Warren G. 115, 152, 153, 154–155; and overseas possessions 141, 143–144
Harrison, Benjamin 72, 104
Harrison, Francis B. 143
Harrison, William Henry 20
Hawaii 31, 44, 50, 52, 53, 190, 192, 199, 200; U.S. acquisition of 105, 127
Hawthorne, Nathaniel 14
Hayes, Rutherford B. 86
Hayes, William Henry "Bully" 33
health, public (in overseas possessions) 95, 194, 198
Henry, Guy V. 136–137
Hoover, Herbert 154, 161; and overseas possessions 143–144, 156, 159, 161, 177–178, 179, 181
Horn, Cape 19, 30, 91
Howard, Oliver O. 63, 64, 67, 72, 73
Hudson, William L. 13, 14
hunting 61, 71–72, 74, 148, 161

Ickes, Harold L. 183, 184
imperialism: American attitude toward 3, 83, 86, 106, 138, 162, 196; decline of 191, 196; inauguration of U.S. 57, 105; movement in United States against 83, 126
indigenous people: American perception of 4, 18, 47, 108, 110, 156, 157, 162, 179, 195; Native Americans 19, 172; perception of Americans by 96, 131, 137, 143; racism toward 127, 181, 182; territorial self-government by 93, 128–129, 131, 142, 160, 181, 183, 195, 198; U.S. relations with

19, 118, 126, 142, 194; *see also* individual overseas possessions; Miles, Nelson A. (on Native Americans); Philippines
Indochina 154–155; *see also* Vietnam War
industrialization *see* economic development
Interior, U.S., Department of the 153; territorial administration by 145, 183, 197
Iran 188–189, 190
Iraq 188–189

Jackson, Andrew 12–13
Jackson, Henry M. 198
Japan 9, 19, 53, 147; as colonial ruler 138, 190–191, 194, 195; *see also* World War II
Jefferson, Thomas 4, 7
Johnson, Hiram 149
Johnson, Lyndon B. 199
Jones, Thomas ap Catesby 12
Jones, William A.: anti-imperialism of 5, 126, 128; childhood of 120; Civil War service of 120; congressional campaigns of 123–124, 132; description of 118, 122, 132; early political career of 121–122; education of 120; forebears of 119, 121; legal career of 121; locality of 120–121, 123, 124; parents of 119–120, 121; personal qualities of 119, 122; as Philippines liberalizer 128–129, 142; as political reformer 124–125; political style of 122, 123, 125–126, 126–127, 132; populism of 123–124, 127; as Puerto Rico liberalizer 118–119, 127–128, 129–132; racial views of 123, 127; regard of, in possessions 132, 133; Senate candidacy of 132; wife and children of 122
Joseph, Chief 68, 69, 70, 72

Kalakaua, King 44, 89
Kennedy, John F. 190, 191–192; and Micronesia 186–187, 193, 195, 197, 198, 199
Khrushchev, Nikita S. 191
Kissinger, Henry A. 200

LaFollette, Robert M. 176
land (in overseas possessions): alienation of 42, 45–46, 92; redistribution of 157, 161, 179, 183; *see also* agriculture
Latrobe, John H.B., Jr. 45, 46, 47
League of Nations 190–191
Lee, Robert E. 120
Lewis, Sinclair 171
Liebling, A.J. 166
Lincoln, Abraham 23, 24, 25, 51, 63, 64, 87, 100, 102
Lyceum movement 171; *see also* Pearson, Paul M.

Mabini, Apolinario 84
MacArthur, Douglas 142
Macías y Casado, Manuel 76, 80
Madison, Dolley 23
Madison, James 8, 120
Magellan, Ferdinand 52, 53
Mahan, Alfred Thayer 74
Malietoa Laupepa 44–45, 46–47
March, Peyton C. 135, 142
María Cristina, Queen 55

Mariana Islands 53, 190–191, 196; *see also* Northern Mariana Islands
Marina, Juan 54–55
Marshall, Francis C. 151
Marshall, George C. 164
Marshall Islands 190–191, 196, 198
Martin, Thomas S. 124, 125, 132
McIntyre, Frank: administrative style of 140, 141, 143; description of 137, 142; early army career of 135; education of 135; parents and childhood of 134–135, 144; personal qualities of 134, 137; and Philippines 137, 138, 140, 141–142, 142–143, 144, 145; and Puerto Rico 136–137, 140, 141, 143, 144; regard of, in possessions 136, 137, 143; relations with presidents 139, 140, 141, 142, 143–144; retirement life of 144–145; Spanish-American War service of 136; as War Department territorial administrator 134, 137–138, 139–141, 142–144; wife and children of 135, 143, 144–145; World War I service of 142
McKean, Josiah S. 57
McKinley, William 75, 80, 108; *see also* Foraker, Joseph B.
McNamara, Robert S. 200
Meade, George G. 29
Meade, Richard W., Jr. 27, 29, 31
Meade, Richard W., III: childhood of 27, 29; Civil War service of 29; conflicts of, with superiors 29, 30, 35, 36–37; description of 30, 34; early naval career of 29; family background of 27, 29; involvement in Samoan affairs by 33–34; as naval modernizer 30, 35–36; personal qualities of 29, 33, 35, 36; railway service of 36; retirement life of 37; Samoa expedition of 30–35; Samoa treaty negotiated by 31, 34, 35; wife and children of 30; as yacht racer 30
Mexico 189–190; Mexican War 22–23
Michener, James A. 175
Micronesia: description of 190, 193, 194, 204; foreign rule of 190–191, 196; independent nations of 204; Micronesians' and Americans' perceptions of each other 195, 196, 198, 200; political breakup of 201–202; profile of 190; revising government of 195, 199; stepped-up U.S. assistance to 192, 194–195, 196, 199; U.S. interest in closer ties with 191, 193, 194, 195, 201; U.S. relations with inhabitants of 193, 194, 195–196; U.S. trusteeship of 191, 194, 198, 200, 201; views of inhabitants on closer U.S. ties 194, 195–196, 197, 198, 199–200, 202; in World War II 191; *see also* Caroline Islands; Gilbert Islands; Mariana Islands; Marshall Islands; Northern Mariana Islands; Solomon, Anthony M.
Miles, Mary (Mrs. Nelson A.) 66–67, 71, 72, 74, 81, 84–85
Miles, Nelson A.: abolitionism of 62, 67, 73; ambitiousness of 63, 64, 66, 72; army beef allegations of 82–83; as author 73, 85; childhood of 60–61; children of 71, 74, 78, 81, 83, 84, 85, 86; Civil War service of 62–65; as commanding general 74–75, 82–84, 138; con-

quest of Puerto Rico by 60, 76–81, 85; description of 61, 62, 63, 65, 71, 73, 82; education of 62, 70; forebears of 61–62; as hunter 61, 71–72; in Indian wars 61, 67–71, 72; as investor 72, 84; leadership style of 63, 64, 65, 69; military skills of 60, 63–64, 68–69, 79, 81; parents of 61, 65, 71, 72; personal qualities of 60, 61, 62, 71, 73, 82, 83, 85; Philippines investigation by 83–84; as political candidate 75, 83, 85–86; public image of 60, 74; in Pullman strike 73; Reconstruction activities of 65–67; relations with Native Americans 67, 69–71, 85; relations with Theodore Roosevelt 73, 82, 83, 84, 86; Spanish-American War preparations of 74–75; views on territorial expansion 5, 81, 83, 86; and World War I 86–87; *see also* Miles, Mary
missionaries 18, 38, 41, 43, 45–46, 96, 193; schools of 44, 92, 95
Monroe, James 8, 10, 120
Muñoz Marín, Luis 143, 156
Muñoz Rivera, Luis 76, 109–110, 129, 131

Napoleon III (emperor of France) 40
native people *see* indigenous people
Navy, U.S. Department of the: territorial administration by 58–59, 90, 138, 192
Netherlands: as colonial ruler 138
New Zealand 48
news media 70, 72, 114, 171–172, 176, 178; censorship of 137, 142; pre-territorial overseas reportage by 20, 37, 43, 45, 47–48, 49; Spanish-American War coverage by 75, 80, 82–83; territorial reportage by 57, 143, 156, 160, 161, 179, 186, 199–200
Nixon, Richard M. 117, 200
Northern Mariana Islands: affiliation of, with United States 202; description of 201; relations of, with rest of Micronesia 201–202; U.S. close relationship with 191, 192, 201; U.S. military conquest of 186; *see also* Mariana Islands
nuclear weapons 191

Osmeña, Sergio 137
overseas possessions, U.S. (collectively): administrative apparatus for 129, 138–139, 141; Americans as rulers of 126, 162; constitutional status of 106, 109, 195; governmental systems of 110; national security role of 19, 57–58, 177, 191, 194, 201; plebiscites in 195; population of 3; selection of administrators of 141, 178; self-government of 130, 160; sequence of acquisition of 57, 202; *see also* imperialism

Pacific Northwest (U.S.) 8, 19, 39–40, 69, 70
Panama Canal Zone 5, 105, 143, 144
Papua New Guinea 42
Parker, Alton B. 86
Patterson, Eleanor Medill "Cissy" 178
Patton, George S. 164–165
Peace Corps 196, 199
Pearson, Drew 172–173, 176, 178, 182, 185
Pearson, Edna (Mrs. Paul M.) 168, 170, 171, 174, 180, 182, 184; adversities of 172–173, 176

Pearson, Paul M.: as author and editor 171, 174–175; as Chautauqua impresario 175–176; childhood of 167–168; children of 172–173, 176, 180, 181; choice of, as Virgin Islands governor 178; as college instructor and professor 170, 171, 174, 175, 176; departure from governorship 183–184; description of 168, 169, 176, 178–179; education of 168, 170, 173–174; as federal housing official 184–185; financial distress of 173, 175, 176; gubernatorial style of 167, 179, 180, 182; home life of 172–173, 174, 176, 180; initiatives of, as Virgin Islands governor 178–181, 182–183; marriage of 170; parents of 167–168, 169; personal qualities of 167, 173, 174, 181, 185; as platform speaker 169–170, 171, 172–173, 174; regard of, as governor 181–182, 183, 185; as young schoolteacher 168–169; *see also* Pearson, Edna
Perez, Joaquin 59
Perry, Matthew C. 9
Pershing, John J. 74, 87, 135, 139, 140, 150
Philippines 5, 19, 139, 140, 190; independence of 128–129, 142; U.S. acquisition of 57, 58, 80; U.S. relations with inhabitants of 142–143, 161; U.S. rule of 106, 108, 127, 128–129, 141; *see also* Glass, Henry; Jones, William A.; McIntyre, Frank; Miles, Nelson A.; Roosevelt, Theodore, Jr.
piracy 19, 32, 33
Pitcairn Island 38, 91
Poinsett, Joel R. 13, 21
Polk, James K. 29
Polynesia 16, 38; *see also* Hawaii; Samoa, American; Samoa, Western; Tahiti; Tuamotu archipelago
Porter, David D. 35, 43
Portugal: as colonial ruler 138
Portusach, Francisco 56–57, 58–59
possessions *see* overseas possessions, U.S.
poverty (in overseas possessions) 107, 143, 156; *see also* Depression, Great
presidents, U.S.: interest in overseas possessions 105, 108, 110, 129, 130–131, 142, 181, 184, 192; visits to overseas possessions 109, 155, 159, 179, 182, 197; *see also* individual presidents
progressivism 123–125
public works (in overseas possessions) 94, 180
Puerto Rico: description of 60, 77, 78, 80, 155–156; economic conditions in 143, 156; name of 106, 118–119; profile of 75–76; Spanish rule of 76, 107; U.S. constitutional relationship with 160; U.S. military conquest of 57, 81; U.S. relations with inhabitants of 78, 80, 81, 109–110, 131, 136, 157; U.S. retention of 83, 106, 127; *see also* Foraker, Joseph B.; Jones, William A.; McIntyre, Frank; Miles, Nelson A.; Roosevelt, Theodore, Jr.

Quezon, Manuel L. 133, 143

Ramos, Amelita Martinez 133
Reber, Samuel 78
religion 17, 27, 160, 162, 170, 181, 182; personal affiliation 16, 30–31, 61, 99–100, 116, 137, 168, 169, 174, 178; *see also* missionaries

Remington, Frederic 72, 73
Renwick, James 11
Revolution, American 9, 62, 119
Riley, James Whitcomb 169, 170
Ringling, John 87
Rizal, José 133
Roosevelt, Eleanor (Mrs. Franklin D.) 154, 182
Roosevelt, Eleanor B. (Mrs. Theodore, Jr.) 148, 149, 151, 153, 163, 166; relations with overseas possessions 154, 155, 156, 157, 158; in world wars 150, 164
Roosevelt, Franklin D. 153, 182, 183–184, 189, 190; *see also* Roosevelt, Theodore, Jr.
Roosevelt, Theodore 75, 130, 138, 140; *see also* Foraker, Joseph B.; Miles, Nelson A.; Roosevelt, Theodore, Jr.
Roosevelt, Theodore, Jr.: as author and bibliophile 152–153, 154, 158, 161–162, 163; childhood of 146–148, 154, 160; children of 149, 152, 158, 164, 165; choice of, as Puerto Rico governor 154–155; description of 146, 147, 148–149, 152, 165; early employment of 148, 149; education of 147, 148; as elective politician 151–152, 153–154; gubernatorial style of 155, 156, 158, 161; home life of 152, 162–163; initiatives of, as Puerto Rico governor 146, 155–160; marriage of 148; military leadership style of 150, 164, 165; as navy official 153, 162; as outdoorsman 147, 148, 154–155; personal qualities of 147, 148, 152, 162; as Philippines governor 155, 161; political apprenticeship of 149; regard of, in overseas possessions 156, 159, 160, 161; relationship with father 146–148, 149, 150, 151, 152, 158, 162, 163–164, 165–166; rivalry with Franklin D. Roosevelt 152, 161, 162, 164; siblings of 147, 148, 150, 151, 153, 154, 163; and Teapot Dome scandal 153, 154; views on U.S. territorial rule 160, 162; World War I service of 149–151, 153, 154; World War II service of 164–166; *see also* Roosevelt, Eleanor B.
Root, Elihu 83, 84, 106, 139
Russia 20, 87, 105, 187; *see also* Soviet Union

Samoa, American (as now named): American interaction with inhabitants of 17, 33–34, 41–42, 45, 49, 95; amity toward United States by 34, 91; cession of, to United States 35, 49, 91–92; description of 32, 41, 88; description of inhabitants of 17, 32, 41, 91, 94; foreign influence in 30, 31, 32–33, 33–34, 40, 41, 49, 89–90; name of 91; nautical charting of 17, 33; naval administration of 90, 138; opening of U.S. relations with 17, 33–34, 35; partition of 89–90; preserving culture of 93, 96; profile of 17–18, 91; revising U.S. governance of 110–111; U.S. treaty with 34, 35; *see also* Meade, Richard W., III; Steinberger, Albert B.; Tilley, B.F.; Wilkes, Charles
Samoa, Western (as now named) 33, 34, 90, 94, 95
Schurman, Jacob G. 115
Schurz, Carl 71
Scott, Winfield 74
Seward, William H. 23, 24

Shafroth, John F. 130
Shafter, William R. 75
Sheridan, Philip H. 66, 74
Sherman, Charles T. 66
Sherman, John 66, 72, 103–104
Sherman, William Tecumseh 66, 69, 70, 72, 74, 87, 100
shipping 41, 53, 94, 180; promotion and protection of 31, 33, 40, 59; *see also* piracy
Short Bull 70
Sicily 164, 165
Sinclair, Upton 83
Singapore 19
Sitting Bull 68, 70
Smith, Alfred E. "Al" 153, 154
Smithsonian Institution 21
Solomon, Anthony M.: artistic interests of 201, 203–204; as businessman 190; childhood of 188; children of 190, 201, 203; as college lecturer 190; description of 189, 203; education of 188, 189; as federal official in international affairs and trade 199, 200–201; as Federal Reserve bank president 203; as financial adviser in Iran 188–189; as government economist 188; and implementation of Micronesia report 196–199; as leader of Micronesia task force 186, 193–196; marriage of 189; on Northern Marianas affiliation with United States 202, 204; parents of 187–188; personal qualities of 187, 188, 194, 203; relations with presidents 189, 190, 193, 197, 200, 202; retirement life of 203–204; *see also* Solomon, Constance
Solomon, Constance (Mrs. Anthony M.) 189, 203
Solomon Islands 191–192
Southard, Samuel L. 11–12
Soviet Union 189, 191; *see also* Cold War
Spain 8, 58; as colonial ruler 52–53, 54, 56, 76, 107, 159; *see also* Spanish-American War
Spanish-American War 36, 74, 80, 89, 133; *see also* Cuba; Glass, Henry; McIntyre, Frank; Miles, Nelson A.; news media; Tilley, B.F.
State, U.S. Department of 198, 199, 200, 202
Steinberger, Albert B.: debate over role in Samoa 45, 47–48; description of 40, 41; French munitions contract of 40; parents and childhood of 38–39; personal qualities of 39, 40, 48; as political adviser to Samoa 42, 44; post–Samoa activities of 47–49; as premier of Samoa 44–47, 49; regard of, in Samoa 43, 48, 49; relations with Grant 40, 42, 43, 44, 45, 48; remarriage of 48; removal from Samoa 46–47; as U.S. agent to Samoa 40–44, 49; U.S. public image of 38, 47–48, 49; wife of 40; youth of, in Colorado 39
Steinberger, Justus 39–40, 41
Stevens, Charles E. 46–47, 48
Stimson, Henry L. 141, 143
Stowe, Harriet Beecher 100
Supreme Court, U.S. 109, 129, 140

Taft, William Howard 128, 129, 139, 176; *see also* Foraker, Joseph B.
Tahiti 17, 38, 91

254 Index

Taylor, Zachary 23
Theocritus 152
Thomas, Lowell 163
Tilley, B.F.: court-martial of 96–98; description of 88, 90; early naval career of 89; gubernatorial style of 92, 93, 95; initiatives of, as governor in Samoa 90, 92, 94–95; on naval academy faculty 89; parents and childhood of 89; post–Samoa service of 98; regard of, in Samoa 95–96, 98; Samoa cession secured by 91–92; Samoa territorial government devised by 93–94; Spanish-American War service of 89; wife and children of 89, 97, 98
tourism (in overseas possessions) 156, 180, 183
Towner, Horace Mann 143
trade (in overseas possessions) 94–95, 107–108, 110, 157
traders 41, 46, 94, 96, 198
Treasury, U.S. Department of the 199, 202
Trent Affair 24
Trust Territory of the Pacific Islands *see* Micronesia
Tuamotu archipelago 16
Tunisia 164
Tydings, Millard E. 183
Tyler, John 20–21, 22

Udall, Stewart L. 197, 198
United Nations 191, 196
U.S. Exploring Expedition *see* Exploring Expedition, U.S.
U.S. Virgin Islands *see* Virgin Islands, U.S.
Upshur, Abel P. 21

Van Buren, Martin 13–14, 20
Vernon, Mabel 175
Victoria, Queen 159
Vietnam War 199
Virgin Islands, British 107
Virgin Islands, U.S. 193; Danish rule of 177, 180; description of 177, 178, 179, 180; economic conditions in 178, 179, 183; U.S. naval rule of 142, 177, 180, 181; U.S. purchase of 105, 177; U.S. relations with inhabitants of 179, 181, 183; *see also* Pearson, Paul M.

Wake Island 19
Wakeman, Edgar 31
War, U.S. Department of: territorial administration by 129, 138–139, 141, 142, 144, 145, 156, 159
Washington, Booker T. 112
Washington, George 7, 62, 120
Webb, William H. 31, 40
Welles, Gideon 23, 24–25
Western Samoa *see* Samoa, Western
whaling 15, 17, 53
Wilbur, Ray Lyman 181, 182
Wilder, Thornton 163
Wilkes, C. Denby 26
Wilkes, Charles: Antarctic explorations of 15–16, 18–19, 26; autobiography of 25; childhood of 8–9; children of 14, 20, 22, 23, 25; Civil War service of 24–25; as commander of U.S. Exploring Expedition 13–20, 89; courts-martial of 21–22, 24; description of 10, 17; early nautical career of 10–11; expedition narrative of 14, 21, 22, 25; forebears and parents of 8–9; information on Samoa compiled by 17–18; as nautical surveyor, 13, 16–17, 19, 20, 26; personal qualities of 7, 11, 12, 14, 15–16, 17, 21, 23, 25; remarriage of 23, 25; scientific interests of 11–12, 15, 19, 20, 22, 25; and *Trent* Affair 24; U.S. relations with Samoa opened by 17; *see also* Wilkes, Jane
Wilkes, Jane (Mrs. Charles) 11, 14, 20, 22, 23
Willis, Dorsie W. 117
Wilson, James H. 78
Wilson, Woodrow 149; and overseas possessions 116, 129, 130–131, 141, 142
women's rights 74, 175, 182
Wood, Leonard 149
Woollcott, Alexander 163
World War I 86–87, 142, 149–151, 152, 153, 164, 177; and overseas possessions 57–58, 130, 196
World War II 26, 94, 164–166, 188–189, 191–192; *see also* Guam; Northern Mariana Islands

Yager, Arthur 131
Yugoslavia 200

www.ingramcontent.com/pod-product-compliance
Lightning Source LLC
Chambersburg PA
CBHW051216300426
44116CB00006B/593